THE CENTENARY BURNS

After JOHN FAED

WHEN WILD WAR'S DEADLY BLAST

"Sae wistfully she gaz'd on me,
   And lovelier was than ever.
Quo' she: 'A sodger ance I lo'ed,
   Forget him shall I never.'"
—*Verse v.*

THE POETRY OF
ROBERT BURNS

Edited by

W. E. HENLEY AND T. F. HENDERSON

With Numerous Illustrations

VOLUME III

AMS PRESS
NEW YORK

Reprinted from the edition of 1896-97, Edinburgh
and London
First AMS EDITION published 1970
Manufactured in the United States of America

International Standard Book Number:
Complete set: 0-404-01250-7
Volume 3: 0-404-01253-1

Library of Congress Card Catalog Number: 78-113567

AMS PRESS, INC.
NEW YORK, N.Y. 10003

CONTENTS

	PAGE
YOUNG PEGGY	1
BONIE DUNDEE	2
TO THE WEAVER'S GIN YE GO	3
WHISTLE AN' I'LL COME TO YOU, MY LAD	5
I'M O'ER YOUNG TO MARRY YET	6
THE BIRKS OF ABERFELDIE	7
M'PHERSON'S FAREWELL	9
MY HIGHLAND LASSIE, O	10
THO' CRUEL FATE	12
STAY MY CHARMER	12
STRATHALLAN'S LAMENT	13
MY HOGGIE	14
JUMPIN JOHN	14
UP IN THE MORNING EARLY	15
THE YOUNG HIGHLAND ROVER	16
THE DUSTY MILLER	17
I DREAM'D I LAY	18
DUNCAN DAVISON	19
THENIEL MENZIES' BONIE MARY	20
LADY ONLIE, HONEST LUCKY	21
THE BANKS OF THE DEVON	22
DUNCAN GRAY (FIRST SET)	23

CONTENTS

	PAGE
THE PLOUGHMAN	24
LANDLADY, COUNT THE LAWIN	25
RAVING WINDS AROUND HER BLOWING	26
HOW LANG AND DREARY IS THE NIGHT	27
MUSING ON THE ROARING OCEAN	28
BLYTHE WAS SHE	29
TO DAUNTON ME	30
O'ER THE WATER TO CHARLIE	32
A ROSE-BUD, BY MY EARLY WALK	33
AND I'LL KISS THEE YET	34
RATTLIN, ROARIN WILLIE	35
WHERE, BRAVING ANGRY WINTER'S STORMS	36
O TIBBIE, I HAE SEEN THE DAY	37
CLARINDA, MISTRESS OF MY SOUL	39
THE WINTER IT IS PAST	40
I LOVE MY LOVE IN SECRET	41
SWEET TIBBIE DUNBAR	42
HIGHLAND HARRY	42
THE TAILOR FELL THRO' THE BED	44
AY WAUKIN O	45
BEWARE O' BONIE ANN	46
LADDIE, LIE NEAR ME	47
THE GARD'NER WI' HIS PAIDLE	48
ON A BANK OF FLOWERS	49
THE DAY RETURNS	50
MY LOVE, SHE'S BUT A LASSIE YET	51
JAMIE, COME TRY ME	52
THE SILVER TASSIE	53
THE LAZY MIST	54

CONTENTS

	PAGE
THE CAPTAIN'S LADY	55
OF A' THE AIRTS	56
CARL, AN THE KING COME	57
WHISTLE O'ER THE LAVE O'T	58
O, WERE I ON PARNASSUS HILL	59
THE CAPTIVE RIBBAND	60
THERE'S A YOUTH IN THIS CITY	61
MY HEART'S IN THE HIGHLANDS	62
JOHN ANDERSON MY JO	63
AWA, WHIGS, AWA	64
CA' THE YOWES TO THE KNOWES (FIRST SET)	65
O, MERRY HAE I BEEN	66
A MOTHER'S LAMENT	67
THE WHITE COCKADE	68
THE BRAES O' BALLOCHMYLE	69
THE RANTIN DOG, THE DADDIE O'T	70
THOU LING'RING STAR	71
EPPIE ADAIR	72
THE BATTLE OF SHERRAMUIR	73
YOUNG JOCKIE WAS THE BLYTHEST LAD	76
A WAUKRIFE MINNIE	77
THO' WOMEN'S MINDS	78
WILLIE BREW'D A PECK O' MAUT	80
KILLIECRANKIE	81
THE BLUE-EYED LASSIE	82
THE BANKS OF NITH	83
TAM GLEN	84
CRAIGIEBURN WOOD	86
FRAE THE FRIENDS AND LAND I LOVE	88

CONTENTS

	PAGE
O JOHN, COME KISS ME NOW	88
COCK UP YOUR BEAVER	89
MY TOCHER'S THE JEWEL	90
GUIDWIFE, COUNT THE LAWIN	91
THERE'LL NEVER BE PEACE TILL JAMIE COMES HAME	92
WHAT CAN A YOUNG LASSIE	93
THE BONIE LAD THAT'S FAR AWA	94
I DO CONFESS THOU ART SAE FAIR	96
SENSIBILITY HOW CHARMING	96
YON WILD MOSSY MOUNTAINS	97
I HAE BEEN AT CROOKIEDEN	99
IT IS NA, JEAN, THY BONIE FACE	100
MY EPPIE MACNAB	101
WHA IS THAT AT MY BOWER DOOR	102
BONIE WEE THING	103
THE TITHER MORN	104
AE FOND KISS	105
LOVELY DAVIES	106
THE WEARY PUND O' TOW	108
I HAE A WIFE O' MY AIN	109
WHEN SHE CAM BEN, SHE BOBBED	110
O, FOR ANE-AND-TWENTY, TAM	111
O, KENMURE'S ON AND AWA, WILLIE	112
O, LEEZE ME ON MY SPINNIN-WHEEL	114
MY COLLIER LADDIE	115
NITHSDALE'S WELCOME HAME	117
IN SIMMER WHEN THE HAY WAS MAWN	117
FAIR ELIZA	119

CONTENTS

	PAGE
YE JACOBITES BY NAME	120
THE POSIE	122
THE BANKS O' DOON	124
WILLIE WASTLE	125
LADY MARY ANN	126
SUCH A PARCEL OF ROGUES IN A NATION	127
KELLYBURN BRAES	129
THE SLAVE'S LAMENT	132
THE SONG OF DEATH	133
SWEET AFTON	134
BONIE BELL	135
THE GALLANT WEAVER	136
HEY, CA' THRO'	137
O, CAN YE LABOUR LEA	138
THE DEUK'S DANG O'ER MY DADDIE	139
SHE'S FAIR AND FAUSE	140
THE DEIL'S AWA WI' TH' EXCISEMAN	141
THE LOVELY LASS OF INVERNESS	142
A RED, RED ROSE	143
AS I STOOD BY YON ROOFLESS TOWER	144
O, AN YE WERE DEAD, GUIDMAN	146
AULD LANG SYNE	147
LOUIS, WHAT RECK I BY THEE	149
HAD I THE WYTE?	149
COMIN THRO' THE RYE	151
YOUNG JAMIE	152
OUT OVER THE FORTH	153
WANTONNESS FOR EVERMAIR	154
CHARLIE HE'S MY DARLING	154

CONTENTS

	PAGE
THE LASS O' ECCLEFECHAN	156
THE COOPER O' CUDDY	157
FOR THE SAKE O' SOMEBODY	158
THE CARDIN O'T	159
THERE'S THREE TRUE GUID FELLOWS	160
SAE FLAXEN WERE HER RINGLETS	160
THE LASS THAT MADE THE BED	162
SAE FAR AWA	165
THE REEL O' STUMPIE	166
I'LL AY CA' IN BY YON TOWN	166
O, WAT YE WHA'S IN YON TOWN	167
WHEREFORE SIGHING ART THOU, PHYLLIS?	169
O MAY, THY MORN	170
AS I CAME O'ER THE CAIRNEY MOUNT	171
HIGHLAND LADDIE	172
WILT THOU BE MY DEARIE	173
LOVELY POLLY STEWART	174
THE HIGHLAND BALOU	175
BANNOCKS O' BEAR MEAL	175
WAE IS MY HEART	176
HERE'S HIS HEALTH IN WATER	177
THE WINTER OF LIFE	178
THE TAILOR	179
THERE GROWS A BONIE BRIER-BUSH	180
HERE'S TO THY HEALTH	181
IT WAS A' FOR OUR RIGHTFU' KING	182
THE HIGHLAND WIDOW'S LAMENT	184
THOU GLOOMY DECEMBER	185
MY PEGGY'S FACE, MY PEGGY'S FORM	186

CONTENTS

	PAGE
O, STEER HER UP, AN' HAUD HER GAUN	187
WEE WILLIE GRAY	188
WE'RE A' NODDIN	189
O, AY MY WIFE SHE DANG ME	191
SCROGGAM	192
O, GUID ALE COMES	193
ROBIN SHURE IN HAIRST	194
DOES HAUGHTY GAUL INVASION THREAT?	195
O, ONCE I LOV'D A BONIE LASS	197
MY LORD A-HUNTING	198
SWEETEST MAY	200
MEG O' THE MILL	200
JOCKIE'S TA'EN THE PARTING KISS	201
O, LAY THY LOOF IN MINE, LASS	202
CAULD IS THE E'ENIN BLAST	203
THERE WAS A BONIE LASS	204
THERE'S NEWS, LASSES, NEWS	205
O, THAT I HAD NE'ER BEEN MARRIED	206
MALLY'S MEEK, MALLY'S SWEET	207
WANDERING WILLIE	208
BRAW LADS O' GALLA WATER	209
AULD ROB MORRIS	210
OPEN THE DOOR TO ME, O	211
WHEN WILD WAR'S DEADLY BLAST	212
DUNCAN GRAY (SECOND SET)	215
DELUDED SWAIN, THE PLEASURE	217
HERE IS THE GLEN	218
LET NOT WOMEN E'ER COMPLAIN	219
LORD GREGORY	220

CONTENTS

	PAGE
O POORTITH CAULD	221
O, STAY, SWEET WARBLING WOOD-LARK	223
SAW YE BONIE LESLEY	224
SWEET FA'S THE EVE	225
YOUNG JESSIE	226
ADOWN WINDING NITH	227
A LASS WI' A TOCHER	229
BLYTHE HAE I BEEN ON YON HILL	230
BY ALLAN STREAM	231
CANST THOU LEAVE ME	232
COME, LET ME TAKE THEE	233
CONTENTED WI' LITTLE	234
FAREWELL, THOU STREAM	235
HAD I A CAVE	236
HERE'S A HEALTH	237
HOW CRUEL ARE THE PARENTS	238
HUSBAND, HUSBAND, CEASE YOUR STRIFE	239
IT WAS THE CHARMING MONTH	240
LAST MAY A BRAW WOOER	242
MY NANIE'S AWA	244
NOW ROSY MAY	245
NOW SPRING HAS CLAD	246
O, THIS IS NO MY AIN LASSIE	248
O, WAT YE WHA THAT LO'ES ME	249
SCOTS, WHA HAE	251
THEIR GROVES O' SWEET MYRTLE	252
THINE AM I	253
THOU HAST LEFT ME EVER, JAMIE	254
HIGHLAND MARY	255

CONTENTS

	PAGE
MY CHLORIS, MARK	256
FAIREST MAID ON DEVON BANKS	258
LASSIE WI' THE LINT-WHITE LOCKS	259
LONG, LONG THE NIGHT	260
LOGAN WATER	262
YON ROSY BRIER	263
WHERE ARE THE JOYS	264
BEHOLD THE HOUR	265
FORLORN MY LOVE	266
CA' THE YOWES TO THE KNOWES (SECOND SET)	268
HOW CAN MY POOR HEART	269
IS THERE FOR HONEST POVERTY	271
MARK YONDER POMP	273
O, LET ME IN THIS AE NIGHT	274
O PHILLY, HAPPY BE THAT DAY	277
O, WERE MY LOVE	279
SLEEP'ST THOU	280
THERE WAS A LASS	281
THE LEA-RIG	284
MY WIFE'S A WINSOME WEE THING	285
MARY MORISON	286
BIBLIOGRAPHICAL	291

NOTES :—

YOUNG PEGGY	299
BONIE DUNDEE	301
TO THE WEAVER'S GIN YE GO	303
WHISTLE AN' I'LL COME TO YOU, MY LAD	304

CONTENTS

NOTES :—*Continued.*

	PAGE
I'M O'ER YOUNG TO MARRY YET	305
THE BIRKS OF ABERFELDIE	306
M'PHERSON'S FAREWELL	307
MY HIGHLAND LASSIE, O	308
THO' CRUEL FATE	312
STAY MY CHARMER	312
STRATHALLAN'S LAMENT	312
MY HOGGIE	313
JUMPIN JOHN	315
UP IN THE MORNING EARLY	315
THE YOUNG HIGHLAND ROVER	318
THE DUSTY MILLER	318
I DREAM'D I LAY	318
DUNCAN DAVISON	319
THENIEL MENZIES' BONIE MARY	320
LADY ONLIE, HONEST LUCKY	320
THE BANKS OF THE DEVON	320
DUNCAN GRAY (FIRST SET)	321
THE PLOUGHMAN	322
LANDLADY, COUNT THE LAWIN	323
RAVING WINDS AROUND HER BLOWING	323
HOW LANG AND DREARY IS THE NIGHT	324
MUSING ON THE ROARING OCEAN	325
BLYTHE WAS SHE	326
TO DAUNTON ME	327
O'ER THE WATER TO CHARLIE	328
A ROSE-BUD, BY MY EARLY WALK	329
AND I'LL KISS THEE YET	330

CONTENTS

NOTES:—*Continued.*

	PAGE
RATTLIN, ROARIN WILLIE	330
WHERE, BRAVING ANGRY WINTER'S STORMS	332
O TIBBIE, I HAE SEEN THE DAY	333
CLARINDA, MISTRESS OF MY SOUL	334
THE WINTER IT IS PAST	334
I LOVE MY LOVE IN SECRET	335
SWEET TIBBIE DUNBAR	335
HIGHLAND HARRY	335
THE TAILOR FELL THRO' THE BED	336
AY WAUKIN O	337
BEWARE O' BONIE ANN	338
LADDIE, LIE NEAR ME	338
THE GARD'NER WI' HIS PAIDLE	339
ON A BANK OF FLOWERS	339
THE DAY RETURNS	340
MY LOVE, SHE'S BUT A LASSIE YET	341
JAMIE, COME TRY ME	342
THE SILVER TASSIE	343
THE LAZY MIST	344
THE CAPTAIN'S LADY	344
OF A' THE AIRTS	345
CARL, AN THE KING COME	346
WHISTLE O'ER THE LAVE O'T	346
O, WERE I ON PARNASSUS HILL	346
THE CAPTIVE RIBBAND	348
THERE'S A YOUTH IN THIS CITY	348
MY HEART'S IN THE HIGHLANDS	348
JOHN ANDERSON MY JO	349

CONTENTS

NOTES:—*Continued.*

	PAGE
AWA, WHIGS, AWA	350
CA' THE YOWES TO THE KNOWES (FIRST SET)	350
O, MERRY HAE I BEEN	351
A MOTHER'S LAMENT	352
THE WHITE COCKADE	353
THE BRAES O' BALLOCHMYLE	353
THE RANTIN DOG, THE DADDIE O'T	354
THOU LING'RING STAR	355
EPPIE ADAIR	356
THE BATTLE OF SHERRAMUIR	356
YOUNG JOCKIE WAS THE BLYTHEST LAD	358
A WAUKRIFE MINNIE	358
THO' WOMEN'S MINDS	359
WILLIE BREW'D A PECK O' MAUT	359
KILLIECRANKIE	361
THE BLUE-EYED LASSIE	362
THE BANKS OF NITH	362
TAM GLEN	363
CRAIGIEBURN WOOD	363
FRAE THE FRIENDS AND LAND I LOVE	364
O JOHN, COME KISS ME NOW	365
COCK UP YOUR BEAVER	366
MY TOCHER'S THE JEWEL	366
GUIDWIFE, COUNT THE LAWIN	366
THERE'LL NEVER BE PEACE TILL JAMIE COMES HAME	367
WHAT CAN A YOUNG LASSIE	368
THE BONIE LAD THAT'S FAR AWA	369

CONTENTS

NOTES:—*Continued.*

	PAGE
I DO CONFESS THOU ART SAE FAIR	371
SENSIBILITY HOW CHARMING	372
YON WILD MOSSY MOUNTAINS	373
I HAE BEEN AT CROOKIEDEN	374
IT IS NA, JEAN, THY BONIE FACE	374
MY EPPIE MACNAB	375
WHA IS THAT AT MY BOWER DOOR	375
BONIE WEE THING	378
THE TITHER MORN	379
AE FOND KISS	379
LOVELY DAVIES	380
THE WEARY PUND O' TOW	380
I HAE A WIFE O' MY AIN	381
O WHEN SHE CAM BEN, SHE BOBBED	381
O, FOR ANE-AND-TWENTY, TAM	382
O, KENMURE'S ON AND AWA, WILLIE	382
O, LEEZE ME ON MY SPINNIN-WHEEL	383
MY COLLIER LADDIE	383
NITHSDALE'S WELCOME HAME	384
IN SIMMER WHEN THE HAY WAS MAWN	384
FAIR ELIZA	385
YE JACOBITES BY NAME	386
THE POSIE	386
THE BANKS O' DOON	388
WILLIE WASTLE	388
LADY MARY ANN	389
SUCH A PARCEL OF ROGUES IN A NATION	391
KELLYBURN BRAES	391

VOL. III.   *b*

CONTENTS

NOTES :—*Continued.*

	PAGE
THE SLAVE'S LAMENT	392
THE SONG OF DEATH	394
SWEET AFTON	394
BONIE BELL	396
THE GALLANT WEAVER	396
HEY, CA' THRO'	397
O, CAN YE LABOUR LEA	397
THE DEUK'S DANG O'ER MY DADDIE	398
SHE'S FAIR AND FAUSE	399
THE DEIL'S AWA WI' TH' EXCISEMAN	399
THE LOVELY LASS OF INVERNESS	401
A RED, RED ROSE	402
AS I STOOD BY YON ROOFLESS TOWER	406
O, AN YE WERE DEAD, GUIDMAN	407
AULD LANG SYNE	407
LOUIS, WHAT RECK I BY THEE	410
HAD I THE WYTE?	410
COMIN THRO' THE RYE	411
YOUNG JAMIE	413
OUT OVER THE FORTH	413
WANTONNESS FOR EVERMAIR	414
CHARLIE, HE'S MY DARLING	414
THE LASS O' ECCLEFECHAN	415
THE COOPER O' CUDDY	416
FOR THE SAKE O' SOMEBODY	416
THE CARDIN O'T	417
THERE'S THREE TRUE GUID FELLOWS	418
SAE FLAXEN WERE HER RINGLETS	418

CONTENTS

NOTES :—*Continued.*

	PAGE
THE LASS THAT MADE THE BED	419
SAE FAR AWA	422
THE REEL O' STUMPIE	422
I'LL AY CA' IN BY YON TOWN	423
O, WAT YE WHA'S IN YON TOWN	424
WHEREFORE SIGHING ART THOU, PHYLLIS	426
O MAY, THY MORN	427
AS I CAME O'ER THE CAIRNEY MOUNT	427
HIGHLAND LADDIE	428
WILT THOU BE MY DEARIE	428
LOVELY POLLY STEWART	429
THE HIGHLAND BALOU	429
BANNOCKS O' BEAR MEAL	430
WAE IS MY HEART	430
HERE'S HIS HEALTH IN WATER	431
THE WINTER OF LIFE	431
THE TAILOR	432
THERE GROWS A BONIE BRIER-BUSH	432
HERE'S TO THY HEALTH	433
IT WAS A' FOR OUR RIGHTFU' KING	433
THE HIGHLAND WIDOW'S LAMENT	436
THOU GLOOMY DECEMBER	437
MY PEGGY'S FACE, MY PEGGY'S FORM	437
O, STEER HER UP, AN' HAUD HER GAUN	438
WEE WILLIE GRAY	438
WE'RE A' NODDIN	438
O, AY MY WIFE SHE DANG ME	439
SCROGGAM	440

CONTENTS

NOTES :—*Continued.*

	PAGE
O, GUID ALE COMES	440
ROBIN SHURE IN HAIRST	440
DOES HAUGHTY GAUL INVASION THREAT ?	441
O, ONCE I LOV'D A BONIE LASS	442
MY LORD A-HUNTING	443
SWEETEST MAY	444
MEG O' THE MILL	444
JOCKIE'S TA'EN THE PARTING KISS	444
O, LAY THY LOOF IN MINE, LASS	444
CAULD IS THE E'ENIN BLAST	444
THERE WAS A BONIE LASS	445
THERE'S NEWS, LASSES, NEWS	445
O, THAT I HAD NE'ER BEEN MARRIED	446
MALLY'S MEEK, MALLY'S SWEET	446
WANDERING WILLIE	446
BRAW LADS O' GALLA WATER	448
AULD ROB MORRIS	449
OPEN THE DOOR TO ME, O	450
WHEN WILD WAR'S DEADLY BLAST	451
DUNCAN GRAY (SECOND SET)	452
DELUDED SWAIN, THE PLEASURE	454
HERE IS THE GLEN	454
LET NOT WOMEN E'ER COMPLAIN	455
LORD GREGORY	455
O POORTITH CAULD	456
O, STAY, SWEET WARBLING WOOD-LARK	457
SAW YE BONIE LESLEY	458
SWEET FA'S THE EVE	459

CONTENTS

NOTES :—*Continued.*

	PAGE
YOUNG JESSIE	459
ADOWN WINDING NITH	460
A LASS WI' A TOCHER	461
BLYTHE HAE I BEEN ON YON HILL	461
BY ALLAN STREAM	462
CANST THOU LEAVE ME THUS, MY KATIE	463
COME, LET ME TAKE THEE TO MY BREAST	463
CONTENTED WI' LITTLE	464
FAREWELL, THOU STREAM	465
HAD I A CAVE	467
HERE'S A HEALTH	467
HOW CRUEL ARE THE PARENTS	468
HUSBAND, HUSBAND, CEASE YOUR STRIFE	469
IT WAS THE CHARMING MONTH OF MAY	469
LAST MAY A BRAW WOOER	470
MY NANIE'S AWA	472
NOW ROSY MAY	473
NOW SPRING HAS CLAD	473
O, THIS IS NO MY AIN LASSIE	473
O, WAT YE WHA THAT LO'ES ME	474
SCOTS, WHA HAE	474
THEIR GROVES O' SWEET MYRTLE	478
THINE AM I	479
THOU HAST LEFT ME EVER, JAMIE	480
HIGHLAND MARY	480
MY CHLORIS, MARK	481
FAIREST MAID ON DEVON BANKS	481
LASSIE WI' THE LINT-WHITE LOCKS	482

CONTENTS

NOTES:—*Continued.*

	PAGE
LONG, LONG THE NIGHT	484
LOGAN WATER	484
YON ROSY BRIER	486
WHERE ARE THE JOY	486
BEHOLD THE HOUR	487
FORLORN MY LOVE	487
CA' THE YOWES TO THE KNOWES (SECOND SET)	488
HOW CAN MY POOR HEART	488
IS THERE FOR HONEST POVERTY	489
MARK YONDER POMP	492
O, LET ME IN THIS AE NIGHT	492
O PHILLY, HAPPY BE THAT DAY	493
O, WERE MY LOVE	493
SLEEP'ST THOU	494
THERE WAS A LASS	495
THE LEA-RIG	497
MY WIFE'S A WINSOME WEE THING	498
MARY MORISON	499

INDEX OF TITLES . . . 501

LIST OF ILLUSTRATIONS

WHEN WILD WAR'S DEADLY BLAST
                             (*coloured*) *Frontispiece*
'Sae wistfully she gaz'd on me.'

	AT PAGE
JOHN ANDERSON, MY JO	62
CA' THE YOWES TO THE KNOWES	64
WHAT CAN A YOUNG LASSIE (*coloured*)	94
I HAE A WIFE O' MY AIN	110
O, LEEZE ME ON MY SPINNIN'-WHEEL (*coloured*)	114
WILLIE WASTLE	124
THE DEIL'S AWA WI' TH' EXCISEMAN	140
AULD LANG SYNE	148
WHEN WILD WAR'S DEADLY BLAST (*coloured*)	212
'Wi' mony a sweet babe fatherless.'	
DUNCAN GRAY	214
LAST MAY A BRAW WOOER . (*coloured*)	242
HIGHLAND MARY	256
LOGAN WATER	262
IS THERE FOR HONEST POVERTY	272

YOUNG PEGGY

I

Young Peggy blooms our boniest lass:
    Her blush is like the morning,
The rosy dawn the springing grass
    With early gems adorning;
Her eyes outshine the radiant beams
    That gild the passing shower,
And glitter o'er the crystal streams,
    And cheer each fresh'ning flower.

II

Her lips, more than the cherries bright—
    A richer dye has graced them—
They charm the admiring gazer's sight,
    And sweetly tempt to taste them.
Her smile is as the evening mild,
    When feather'd pairs are courting,
And little lambkins wanton wild,
    In playful bands disporting.

III

Were Fortune lovely Peggy's foe,
    Such sweetness would relent her:
As blooming Spring unbends the brow
    Of surly, savage Winter.
Detraction's eye no aim can gain
    Her winning powers to lessen,
And fretful Envy grins in vain
    The poison'd tooth to fasten.

IV

Ye Pow'rs of Honour, Love, and Truth,
    From ev'ry ill defend her!
Inspire the highly-favour'd youth
    The destinies intend her!
Still fan the sweet connubial flame
    Responsive in each bosom,
And bless the dear parental name
    With many a filial blossom!

BONIE DUNDEE

I

[Notes]   'O, whar gat ye that hauver-meal bannock?'
do not   'O silly blind body, O, dinna ye see?
    I gat it frae a young, brisk sodger laddie
Perth   Between Saint Johnston and bonie Dundee.

TO THE WEAVER'S GIN YE GO

O, gin I saw the laddie that gae me 't!   *would that*
  Aft has he doudl'd me up on his knee: *dandled*
May Heaven protect my bonie Scots laddie,
  And send him hame to his babie and me!

II

'My blessin's upon thy sweet, wee lippie!
  My blessin's upon thy bonie e'e brie!   *eyebrow*
Thy smiles are sae like my blythe sodger laddie,
  Thou's ay the dearer and dearer to me!   *Thou art*
But I'll big a bow'r on yon bonie banks,   *build*
  Whare Tay rins wimplin by sae clear;   *meandering*
And I'll cleed thee in the tartan sae fine,   *clothe*
  And mak thee a man like thy daddie dear.'

TO THE WEAVER'S GIN YE GO   *should*

Chorus

To the weaver's gin ye go, fair maids,
  To the weaver's gin ye go,
I rede you right, gang ne'er at night,   *warn you*
  To the weaver's gin ye go.   *true; go*

I

My heart was ance as blythe and free   *once*
  As simmer days were lang;
But a bonie, westlin weaver lad   *western*
  Has gart me change my sang.   *made*

4 TO THE WEAVER'S GIN YE GO

II

My mither sent me to the town,
    To warp a plaiden wab;
But the weary, weary warpin o't
    Has gart me sigh and sab.

[Notes] *sob*

III

A bonie, westlin weaver lad
    Sat working at his loom;
He took my heart, as wi' a net,
    In every knot and thrum.

IV

I sat beside my warpin-wheel,
    And ay I ca'd it roun';
And every shot and every knock,
    My heart it gae a stoun.

drove

ache

V

The moon was sinking in the west
    Wi' visage pale and wan,
As my bonie, westlin weaver lad
    Convoy'd me thro' the glen.

VI

But what was said, or what was done,
    Shame fa' me gin I tell;
But O! I fear the kintra soon
    Will ken as weel's mysel!

Befall; if

country

O, WHISTLE AN' I'LL COME TO YE

Chorus

To the weaver's gin ye go, fair maids,
  To the weaver's gin ye go,
I rede you right, gang ne'er at night,
  To the weaver's gin ye go.

O, WHISTLE AN' I'LL COME TO YE, MY LAD

Chorus

O, whistle an' I'll come to ye, my lad!
O, whistle an' I'll come to ye, my lad!
Tho' father an' mother an' a' should gae mad,   go
O, whistle an' I'll come to ye, my lad!

I

But warily tent when ye come to court me,   spy
And come nae unless the back-yett be a-jee;   not; -gate; ajar
Syne up the back-style, and let naebody see,   Then
And come as ye were na comin to me,   not
And come as ye were na comin to me!

II

At kirk, or at market, whene'er ye meet me,
Gang by me as tho' that ye car'd na a flie;   Go; fly
But steal me a blink o' your bonie black e'e,   glance
Yet look as ye were na lookin to me,
Yet look as ye were na lookin to me!

6 I'M O'ER YOUNG TO MARRY YET

III

<small>sometimes;
disparage;
little</small>

<small>entice</small>

Ay vow and protest that ye care na for me,
And whyles ye may lightly my beauty a wee;
But court na anither tho' jokin ye be,
For fear that she wyle your fancy frae me,
For fear that she wyle your fancy frae me!

Chorus

O, whistle an' I'll come to ye, my lad!
O, whistle an' I'll come to ye, my lad!
Tho' father an' mother an' a' should gae mad,
O, whistle an' I'll come to ye, my lad!

I'M O'ER YOUNG TO MARRY YET

Chorus

I'm o'er young, I'm o'er young,
I'm o'er young to marry yet!
I'm o'er young, 'twad be a sin
To tak me frae my mammie yet.

I

<small>only child</small>

<small>strange</small>

<small>I fear;
[Notes]</small>

I AM my mammie's ae bairn,
Wi' unco folk I weary, Sir,
And lying in a man's bed,
I'm fley'd it make me eerie, Sir.

THE BIRKS OF ABERFELDIE

II

Hallowmass is come and gane,
   The nights are lang in winter, Sir,
And you an' I in ae bed— *one*
   In trowth, I dare na venture, Sir!

III

Fu' loud and shrill the frosty wind
   Blaws thro' the leafless timmer, Sir, *woods*
But if ye come this gate again, *way*
   I'll aulder be gin simmer, Sir. *older be by*

Chorus

I'm o'er young, I'm o'er young,
   I'm o'er young to marry yet!
I'm o'er young, 'twad be a sin
   To tak me frae my mammie yet.

THE BIRKS OF ABERFELDIE *birches*

Chorus

Bonie lassie, will ye go,
Will ye go, will ye go?
Bonie lassie, will ye go
   To the birks of Aberfeldie?

8 THE BIRKS OF ABERFELDIE

I

<small>shines;
slopes</small>

Now simmer blinks on flow'ry braes,
And o'er the crystal streamlets plays,
Come, let us spend the lightsome days
    In the birks of Aberfeldie!

II

<small>hang</small>

The little birdies blythely sing,
While o'er their heads the hazels hing,
Or lightly flit on wanton wing
    In the birks of Aberfeldie.

III

<small>woods</small>

The braes ascend like lofty wa's,
The foaming stream, deep-roaring, fa's
O'er hung with fragrant-spreading shaws,
    The birks of Aberfeldie.

IV

<small>falls;
brooklet
wets</small>

The hoary cliffs are crown'd wi' flowers,
White o'er the linns the burnie pours,
And, rising, weets wi' misty showers
    The birks of Aberfeldie.

V

Let Fortune's gifts at random flee,
They ne'er shall draw a wish frae me,
Supremely blest wi' love and thee
    In the birks of Aberfeldie.

Chorus
Bonie lassie, will ye go,
Will ye go, will ye go?
Bonie lassie, will ye go
　　To the birks of Aberfeldie?

M'PHERSON'S FAREWELL

Chorus
Sae rantingly, sae wantonly,　　jovially
　Sae dauntingly gaed he,　　went
He play'd a spring, and danc'd it round
　Below the gallows-tree.

I

Farewell, ye dungeons dark and strong,
　The wretch's destinie!
M'Pherson's time will not be long
　On yonder gallows-tree.

II

O, what is death but parting breath?
　On many a bloody plain
I 've dar'd his face, and in this place
　I scorn him yet again!

III

Untie these bands from off my hands,
　And bring to me my sword,
And there 's no a man in all Scotland
　But I 'll brave him at a word.

10 MY HIGHLAND LASSIE, O

IV

trouble

I 've liv'd a life of sturt and strife;
   I die by treacherie:
It burns my heart I must depart,
   And not avengèd be.

V

Now farewell light, thou sunshine bright,
   And all beneath the sky!
May coward shame distain his name,
   The wretch that dare not die!

Chorus

Sae rantingly, sae wantonly,
   Sae dauntingly gaed he,
He play'd a spring, and danc'd it round
   Below the gallows-tree.

MY HIGHLAND LASSIE, O

Chorus

Above; rushy

Within the glen sae bushy, O,
Aboon the plain sae rashy, O,
I set me down wi' right guid will
To sing my Highland lassie, O!

I

No highborn

Nae gentle dames, tho' ne'er sae fair,
Shall ever be my Muse's care:
Their titles a' are empty show—

Give

Gie me my Highland lassie, O!

II

O, were yon hills and vallies mine,
Yon palace and yon gardens fine,
The world then the love should know
I bear my Highland lassie, O!

III

But fickle Fortune frowns on me,
And I maun cross the raging sea;   must
But while my crimson currents flow
I'll love my Highland lassie, O.

IV

Altho' thro' foreign climes I range,
I know her heart will never change;
For her bosom burns with honour's glow,
My faithful Highland lassie, O.

V

For her I'll dare the billows' roar,
For her I'll trace a distant shore,
That Indian wealth may lustre throw
Around my Highland lassie, O.

VI

She has my heart, she has my hand,
My secret troth and honour's band!
'Till the mortal stroke shall lay me low,
I'm thine, my Highland lassie, O!

Chorus

Farewell the glen sae bushy, O!
Farewell the plain sae rashy, O!
To other lands I now must go
To sing my Highland lassie, O.

THO' CRUEL FATE

Tho' cruel fate should bid us part
    Far as the pole and line,
Her dear idea round my heart
    Should tenderly entwine.
Tho' mountains rise, and deserts howl,
    And oceans roar between,
Yet dearer than my deathless soul
    I still would love my Jean.

STAY, MY CHARMER

I

Stay, my charmer, can you leave me?
Cruel, cruel to deceive me!
Well you know how much you grieve me:
    Cruel charmer, can you go?
    Cruel charmer, can you go?

II

By my love so ill-requited,
By the faith you fondly plighted,
By the pangs of lovers slighted,
　Do not, do not leave me so!
　Do not, do not leave me so!

STRATHALLAN'S LAMENT

I

Thickest night, surround my dwelling!
　Howling tempests, o'er me rave!
Turbid torrents wintry-swelling,
　Roaring by my lonely cave!
Crystal streamlets gently flowing,
　Busy haunts of base mankind,
Western breezes softly blowing,
　Suit not my distracted mind.

II

In the cause of Right engagèd,
　Wrongs injurious to redress,
Honour's war we strongly wagèd,
　But the heavens deny'd success.
Ruin's wheel has driven o'er us:
　Not a hope that dare attend,
The wide world is all before us,
　But a world without a friend.

MY HOGGIE

I

What will I do gin my hoggie die?
   My joy, my pride, my hoggie!
My only beast, I had nae mae,
   And vow but I was vogie!
The lee-lang night we watched the fauld,
   Me and my faithfu' doggie;
We heard nocht but the roaring linn
   Amang the braes sae scroggie.

II

But the houlet cry'd frae the castle wa',
   The blitter frae the boggie,
The tod reply'd upon the hill:
   I trembled for my hoggie.
When day did daw, and cocks did craw,
   The morning it was foggie,
An unco tyke lap o'er the dyke,
   And maist has kill'd my hoggie!

JUMPIN JOHN

Chorus

The lang lad they ca' Jumpin John
   Beguil'd the bonie lassie!
The lang lad they ca' Jumpin John
   Beguil'd the bonie lassie!

Margin glosses:
lamb
should
no more
vain
live-long; fold
waterfall
hill-sides; scrubby
owl
snipe
fox
dawn
strange dog; leaped; stone fence
almost

UP IN THE MORNING EARLY

I

Her daddie forbad, her minnie forbad;
  Forbidden she wadna be: *would not*
She wadna trow't, the browst she brew'd *believe it; liquor*
  Wad taste sae bitterlie!

II

A cow and a cauf, a yowe and a hauf, *ewe; half*
  And thretty guid shillins and three: *thirty*
A vera guid tocher! a cotter-man's dochter, *dowry; daughter*
  The lass with the bonie black e'e!

Chorus

  The lang lad they ca' Jumpin John
    Beguil'd the bonie lassie!
  The lang lad they ca' Jumpin John
    Beguil'd the bonie lassie!

UP IN THE MORNING EARLY

Chorus

Up in the morning's no for me,
  Up in the morning early!
When a' the hills are covered wi' snaw
  I'm sure it's winter fairly!

THE YOUNG HIGHLAND ROVER

I

Cauld blaws the wind frae east to west,
    The drift is driving sairly,
Sae loud and shrill's I hear the blast—
    I'm sure it's winter fairly!

sorely

II

The birds sit chittering in the thorn,
    A' day they fare but sparely;
And lang's the night frae e'en to morn—
    I'm sure it's winter fairly.

All

Chorus

Up in the morning's no for me,
    Up in the morning early!
When a' the hills are cover'd wi' snaw,
    I'm sure it's winter fairly!

THE YOUNG HIGHLAND ROVER

I

Loud blaw the frosty breezes,
    The snaws the mountains cover.
Like winter on me seizes,
    Since my young Highland rover
    Far wanders nations over.

THE DUSTY MILLER

Where'er he go, where'er he stray,
    May Heaven be his warden!
Return him safe to fair Strathspey
And bonie Castle Gordon!

II

The trees, now naked groaning,
    Shall soon wi' leaves be hinging,   *hanging*
The birdies, dowie moaning,   *droopingly*
    Shall a' be blythely singing,
And every flower be springing:
Sae I'll rejoice the lee-lang day,   *live-long*
    When (by his mighty Warden)
My youth's return'd to fair Strathspey
And bonie Castle Gordon.

THE DUSTY MILLER

I

Hey the dusty miller
    And his dusty coat!
He will spend a shilling
    Or he win a groat.   *Ere*
Dusty was the coat,
    Dusty was the colour,
Dusty was the kiss
    That I gat frae the miller!

18 I DREAM'D I LAY

II

  Hey the dusty miller
  And his dusty sack!
  Leeze me on the calling
   Fills the dusty peck!
  Fills the dusty peck,
   Brings the dusty siller!
  I wad gie my coatie
   For the dusty miller!

I DREAM'D I LAY

I

I DREAM'D I lay where flowers were springing
 Gaily in the sunny beam,
List'ning to the wild birds singing,
 By a falling crystal stream;
Straight the sky grew black and daring,
 Thro' the woods the whirlwinds rave,
Trees with agèd arms were warring
turbid O'er the swelling, drumlie wave.

II

Such was my life's deceitful morning,
 Such the pleasures I enjoy'd!
ere But lang or noon loud tempests, storming,
All A' my flowery bliss destroy'd.

Tho' fickle Fortune has deceiv'd me
    (She promis'd fair, and perform'd but ill),
Of monie a joy and hope bereav'd me,
    I bear a heart shall support me still.

DUNCAN DAVISON

I

There was a lass, they ca'd her Meg,
    And she held o'er the moors to spin;
There was a lad that follow'd her,
    They ca'd him Duncan Davison.
The moor was dreigh, and Meg was skeigh,   *dull; skittish*
    Her favour Duncan could na win;
For wi' the rock she wad him knock,   *distaff*
    And ay she shook the temper-pin.   *[Notes]*

II

As o'er the moor they lightly foor,   *fared*
    A burn was clear, a glen was green;
Upon the banks they eas'd their shanks,
    And ay she set the wheel between:
But Duncan swoor a haly aith,   *holy oath*
    That Meg should be a bride the morn;   *to-morrow*
Then Meg took up her spinnin-graith,   *-instruments*
    And flang them a' out o'er the burn.   *across the brook*

20 THENIEL MENZIES' BONIE MARY

III

<small>build</small>

  We will big a wee, wee house,
   And we will live like king and queen,
  Sae blythe and merry 's we will be,

<small>aside</small>

   When ye set by the wheel at e'en!
  A man may drink, and no be drunk;
   A man may fight, and no be slain;
  A man may kiss a bonie lass,
   And ay be welcome back again!

THENIEL MENZIES' BONIE MARY

Chorus

  Theniel Menzies' bonie Mary,
  Theniel Menzies' bonie Mary,

<small>lost</small>

  Charlie Grigor tint his plaidie,
  Kissin Theniel's bonie Mary!

I

  In comin by the brig o' Dye,

<small>while</small>

   At Darlet we a blink did tarry;

<small>dawning</small>

  As day was dawin in the sky,
   We drank a health to bonie Mary.

II

<small>eyes</small>

  Her een sae bright, her brow sae white,

<small>side</small>

   Her haffet locks as brown 's a berry,
  And ay they dimpl't wi' a smile,
   The rosy cheeks o' bonie Mary.

LADY ONLIE, HONEST LUCKY

III

We lap an' danc'd the lee-lang day,   *leaped; livelong*
  Till piper-lads were wae and weary;   *sad*
But Charlie gat the spring to pay,   *tune*
  For kissin Theniel's bonie Mary.

Chorus

Theniel Menzies' bonie Mary,
Theniel Menzies' bonie Mary,
Charlie Grigor tint his plaidie,
Kissin Theniel's bonie Mary!

LADY ONLIE, HONEST LUCKY

Chorus

Lady Onlie, honest lucky,   [Notes]
  Brews guid ale at shore o' Bucky: *Buchan*
I wish her sale for her guid ale,
  The best on a' the shore o' Bucky!

I

A' THE lads o' Thorniebank,
  When they gae to the shore o' Bucky,   *go*
They'll step in an' tak a pint
  Wi' Lady Onlie, honest lucky.

II

<small>snug;
kerchief
old dear
glances;
-blaze</small>

Her house sae bien, her curch sae clean—
  I wat she is a dainty chuckie,
And cheery blinks the ingle-gleede
  O' Lady Onlie, honest lucky!

Chorus

Lady Onlie, honest lucky,
  Brews guid ale at shore o' Bucky:
I wish her sale for her guid ale,
  The best on a' the shore o' Bucky!

THE BANKS OF THE DEVON

I

How pleasant the banks of the clear winding Devon,
  With green spreading bushes and flow'rs blooming fair!
But the boniest flow'r on the banks of the Devon

<small>slopes</small>   Was once a sweet bud on the braes of the Ayr.
Mild be the sun on this sweet blushing flower,
  In the gay rosy morn, as it bathes in the dew!
And gentle the fall of the soft vernal shower,
  That steals on the evening each leaf to renew!

II

O, spare the dear blossom, ye orient breezes,
  With chill, hoary wing as ye usher the dawn!
And far be thou distant, thou reptile that seizes
  The verdure and pride of the garden or lawn!

Let Bourbon exult in his gay gilded lilies,
  And England triumphant display her proud rose!
A fairer than either adorns the green vallies,
  Where Devon, sweet Devon, meandering flows.

DUNCAN GRAY

I

Weary fa' you, Duncan Gray!   Woe befall
  (Ha, ha, the girdin o't!)   girthing
Wae gae by you, Duncan Gray!   Woe go with
  (Ha, ha, the girdin o't!)
When a' the lave gae to their play,   rest
Then I maun sit the lee-lang day, must; live-long
And jeeg the cradle wi' my tae,   jog; toe
  And a' for the girdin o't!

II

Bonie was the Lammas moon
  (Ha, ha, the girdin o't!),
Glowrin a' the hills aboon   above
  (Ha, ha, the girdin o't!).
The girdin brak, the beast cam down,
I tint my curch and baith my shoon,   kerchief; shoes
And, Duncan, ye're an unco loun—   terrible rogue
  Wae on the bad girdin o't!

THE PLOUGHMAN

III

<small>if ; oath</small>

<small>I ll</small>

<small>damage</small>
<small>patch</small>

But Duncan, gin ye 'll keep your aith
　(Ha, ha, the girdin o't!),
I 'se bless you wi' my hindmost breath
　(Ha, ha, the girdin o't!).
Duncan, gin ye 'll keep your aith,
　The beast again can bear us baith,
And auld Mess John will mend the skaith
　And clout the bad girdin o't.

THE PLOUGHMAN

Chorus

Then up wi't a', my ploughman lad,
　And hey, my merry ploughman!
Of a' the trades that I do ken,
　Commend me to the ploughman!

I

The ploughman, he 's a bonie lad,
　His mind is ever true, jo!
His garters knit below his knee,
　His bonnet it is blue, jo.

II

<small>Pertn</small>

I hae been east, I hae been west,
　I hae been at St. Johnston;
The boniest sight that e'er I saw
　Was the ploughman laddie dancin.

III

Snaw-white stockings on his legs
   And siller buckles glancin,   *silver*
A guid blue bonnet on his head,
   And O, but he was handsome!

IV

Commend me to the barn-yard   *stack-*
   And the corn mou, man!   *heap*
I never got my coggie fou   *little dish full*
   Till I met wi' the ploughman.

Chorus

Then up wi't a', my ploughman lad,
   And hey, my merry ploughman!
Of a' the trades that I do ken,
   Commend me to the ploughman!

LANDLADY, COUNT THE LAWIN   *reckoning*

Chorus

Hey tutti, taiti,
How tutti, taiti,
Hey tutti, taiti,
Wha's fou now?   *drunk*

I

Landlady, count the lawin,
The day is near the dawin;   *dawning*
Ye're a' blind drunk, boys,
   And I'm but jolly fou.

26 RAVING WINDS AROUND HER BLOWING

II

Stoup; full

Cog, an ye were ay fou,
Cog, an ye were ay fou,
I wad sit and sing to you,
    If ye were ay fou !

III

all

Weel may ye a' be !
Ill may ye never see !
God bless the king
    And the companie !

Chorus

Hey tutti, taiti,
How tutti, taiti,
Hey tutti, taiti,
Wha's fou now ?

RAVING WINDS AROUND HER BLOWING

I

Raving winds around her blowing,
Yellow leaves the woodlands strowing,
By a river hoarsely roaring,
Isabella stray'd deploring :—
' Farewell hours that late did measure
Sunshine days of joy and pleasure !
Hail, thou gloomy night of sorrow—
Cheerless night that knows no morrow !

II

'O'er the Past too fondly wandering,
On the hopeless Future pondering,
Chilly Grief my life-blood freezes,
Fell Despair my fancy seizes.
Life, thou soul of every blessing,
Load to Misery most distressing,
Gladly how would I resign thee,
And to dark Oblivion join thee!'

HOW LANG AND DREARY IS THE NIGHT

Chorus

For O, her lanely nights are lang,
   And O, her dreams are eerie,   full of fear
And O, her widow'd heart is sair,
   That's absent frae her dearie!

I

How lang and dreary is the night,
   When I am frae my dearie!
I restless lie frae e'en to morn,
   Tho' I were ne'er sae weary.

II

When I think on the lightsome days
   I spent wi' thee, my dearie,
And now what seas between us roar,
   How can I be but eerie?

III

  How slow ye move, ye heavy hours!
   The joyless day how dreary!
sparkled It was na sae ye glinted by,
   When I was wi' my dearie!

Chorus

  For O, her lanely nights are lang,
   And O, her dreams are eerie,
  And O, her widow'd heart is sair,
   That's absent frae her dearie!

MUSING ON THE ROARING OCEAN

I

  Musing on the roaring ocean,
   Which divides my love and me,
  Wearying heav'n in warm devotion
welfare   For his weal where'er he be:

II

  Hope and Fear's alternate billow
   Yielding late to Nature's law,
  Whispering spirits round my pillow,
[Notes]   Talk of him that's far awa.

III

  Ye whom sorrow never wounded,
   Ye who never shed a tear,

BLYTHE WAS SHE   29

Care-untroubled, joy-surrounded,
  Gaudy day to you is dear!

IV

Gentle night, do thou befriend me!
Downy sleep, the curtain draw!
Spirits kind, again attend me,
  Talk of him that's far awa!

BLYTHE WAS SHE

Chorus

Blythe, blythe and merry was she,
  Blythe was she butt and ben,   *in kitchen and parlour, [Notes]*
Blythe by the banks of Earn,
  And blythe in Glenturit glen!

I

By Oughtertyre grows the aik,   *oak*
  On Yarrow banks the birken shaw;   *birch wood*
But Phemie was a bonier lass
  Than braes o' Yarrow ever saw.   *heights*

II

Her looks were like a flow'r in May,
  Her smile was like a simmer morn.
She trippèd by the banks o' Earn
  As light's a bird upon a thorn.   *light as*

III

Her bonie face it was as meek
    As onie lamb upon a lea.
The evening sun was ne'er sae sweet
    As was the blink o' Phemie's e'e.

<small>glance</small>

IV

The Highland hills I 've wander'd wide,
    As o'er the Lawlands I hae been,
But Phemie was the blythest lass
    That ever trod the dewy green.

Chorus

Blythe, blythe and merry was she,
    Blythe was she butt and ben,
Blythe by the banks of Earn,
    And blythe in Glenturit Glen!

TO DAUNTON ME

<small>conquer</small>

Chorus

To daunton me, to daunton me,
An auld man shall never daunton me!

I

The blude-red rose at Yule may blaw,
The simmer lilies bloom in snaw,
The frost may freeze the deepest sea,
But an auld man shall never daunton me.

TO DAUNTON ME

II

To daunton me, and me sae young,
Wi' his fause heart and flatt'ring tongue
That is the thing you ne'er shall see,
For an auld man shall never daunton me.

III

For a' his meal and a' his maut, — malt
For a' his fresh beef and his saut,
For a' his gold and white monie,
An auld man shall never daunton me.

IV

His gear may buy him kye and yowes, — money; kine; sheep
His gear may buy him glens and knowes; — knolls
But me he shall not buy nor fee, — hire
For an auld man shall never daunton me.

V

He hirples twa-fauld as he dow, — hobbles twofold; can
Wi' his teethless gab and his auld beld pow, — mouth; bald pate
And the rain rains down frae his red blear'd
   e'e—
That auld man shall never daunton me!

Chorus

To daunton me, to daunton me,
An auld man shall never daunton me!

O'ER THE WATER TO CHARLIE

Chorus

We'll o'er the water, we'll o'er the sea,
We'll o'er the water to Charlie!
Come weal, come woe, we'll gather and go,
And live and die wi' Charlie!

I

Come boat me o'er, come row me o'er,
Come boat me o'er to Charlie!
I'll gie John Ross another bawbee
To boat me o'er to Charlie.

II

I lo'e weel my Charlie's name,
Tho' some there be abhor him;
But O, to see Auld Nick gaun hame,
And Charlie's faes before him!

III

I swear and vow by moon and stars
And sun that shines so early,
If I had twenty thousand lives,
I'd die as aft for Charlie!

A ROSE-BUD, BY MY EARLY WALK

Chorus

We'll o'er the water, we'll o'er the sea,
    We'll o'er the water to Charlie!
Come weal, come woe, we'll gather and go,
    And live and die wi' Charlie!

A ROSE-BUD, BY MY EARLY WALK

I

A ROSE-BUD, by my early walk
Adown a corn-inclosèd bawk,   field-path
Sae gently bent its thorny stalk,
    All on a dewy morning.
Ere twice the shades o' dawn are fled,
In a' its crimson glory spread
And drooping rich the dewy head,
    It scents the early morning.

II

Within the bush her covert nest
A little linnet fondly prest,
The dew sat chilly on her breast,
    Sae early in the morning.
She soon shall see her tender brood,
The pride, the pleasure o' the wood,
Amang the fresh green leaves bedew'd,
    Awake the early morning.

AND I'LL KISS THEE YET

III

So thou, dear bird, young Jeany fair,
On trembling string or vocal air
Shall sweetly pay the tender care
 That tents[guards] thy early morning!
So thou, sweet rose-bud, young and gay,
Shalt beauteous blaze upon the day,
And bless the parent's evening ray
 That watch'd thy early morning!

AND I'LL KISS THEE YET

Chorus

And I'll kiss thee yet, yet,
And I'll kiss thee o'er again,
And I'll kiss thee yet, yet,
My bonie Peggy Alison.

I

WHEN in my arms, wi' a' thy charms,
I clasp my countless treasure, O,
I seek nae mair o' Heav'n to share
 Than sic[such] a moment's pleasure, O!

II

And by thy een[eyes] sae bonie blue
I swear I'm thine for ever, O!
And on thy lips I seal my vow,
And break it shall I never, O!

RATTLIN, ROARIN WILLIE

Chorus

And I'll kiss thee yet, yet,
  And I'll kiss thee o'er again.
And I'll kiss thee yet, yet,
  My bonie Peggy Alison.

RATTLIN, ROARIN WILLIE

I

O, RATTLIN, roarin Willie,
  O, he held to the fair,
An' for to sell his fiddle
  And buy some other ware;
But parting wi' his fiddle,
  The saut tear blin't his e'e—
And, rattlin, roarin Willie,
  Ye 're welcome hame to me

II

O Willie, come sell your fiddle,
  O, sell your fiddle sae fine!
O Willie come sell your fiddle
  And buy a pint o' wine!'
'If I should sell my fiddle,
  The warld would think I was mad;
For monie a rantin day   *merry*
  My fiddle and I hae had.'

III

<small>quietly looked in</small>

As I cam by Crochallan,
   I cannily keekit ben,
Rattlin, roarin Willie
   Was sitting at yon boord-en':
Sitting at yon boord-en',
   And amang guid companie!
Rattlin, roarin Willie,
   Ye're welcome hame to me.

WHERE, BRAVING ANGRY WINTER'S STORMS

I

Where, braving angry winter's storms,
   The lofty Ochils rise,
Far in their shade my Peggy's charms
   First blest my wondering eyes:
As one who by some savage stream
   A lonely gem surveys,
Astonish'd doubly, marks it beam
   With art's most polish'd blaze.

II

Blest be the wild, sequester'd glade,
   And blest the day and hour,
Where Peggy's charms I first survey'd,
   When first I felt their pow'r!

The tyrant Death with grim control
  May seize my fleeting breath,
But tearing Peggy from my soul
  Must be a stronger death.

O TIBBIE, I HAE SEEN THE DAY

Chorus

O Tibbie, I hae seen the day,
  Ye wadna been sae shy!   *would not have*
For laik o' gear ye lightly me,   *lack of wealth; scorn*
  But, trowth, I care na by.   *I care not although you do*

I

Yestreen I met you on the moor,   *Last night*
Ye spak na, but gaed by like stoure!   *spoke not; went; blowing dust*
Ye geck at me because I'm poor—   *toss your head*
  But fient a hair care I!   *fiend*

II

When comin hame on Sunday last,
Upon the road as I cam past,
Ye snufft an' gae your head a cast—   *gave*
  But, trowth, I care't na by!   *cared*

III

I doubt na, lass, but ye may think,
Because ye hae the name o' clink,   *wealth*
That ye can please me at a wink,
  Whene'er ye like to try.

38 O TIBBIE, I HAE SEEN THE DAY

IV

But sorrow tak him that's sae mean,
Altho' his pouch o' coin were clean,
Wha follows onie saucy quean,
 That looks sae proud and high!

V

Altho' a lad were e'er sae smart,
If that he want the yellow dirt,
<small>direction</small> Ye'll cast your head anither airt,
 And answer him fu' dry.

VI

But if he hae the name o' gear,
Ye'll fasten to him like a brier,
<small>learning</small> Tho' hardly he for sense or lear
<small>kine</small> Be better than the kye.

VII

But, Tibbie, lass, tak my advice:
Your daddie's gear maks you sae nice,
<small>ask</small> The Deil a ane wad spier your price,
 Were ye as poor as I.

VIII

There lives a lass beside yon park,
<small>shift</small> I'd rather hae her in her sark
Than you wi' a' your thousand mark,
<small>makes</small> That gars you look sae high.

Chorus

O Tibbie, I hae seen the day,
    Ye wadna been sae shy!
For laik o' gear ye lightly me,
    But, trowth, I care na by.

CLARINDA, MISTRESS OF MY SOUL

I

CLARINDA, mistress of my soul,
    The measur'd time is run!
The wretch beneath the dreary pole
    So marks his latest sun.

II

To what dark cave of frozen night
    Shall poor Sylvander hie,
Depriv'd of thee, his life and light,
    The sun of all his joy?

III

We part—but, by these precious drops
    That fill thy lovely eyes,
No other light shall guide my steps
    Till thy bright beams arise!

IV

She, the fair sun of all her sex,
    Has blest my glorious day;
And shall a glimmering planet fix
    My worship to its ray?

THE WINTER IT IS PAST

I

The winter it is past, and the simmer comes at last,
    And the small birds sing on ev'ry tree:
The hearts of these are glad, but mine is very sad,
    For my love is parted from me.

II

The rose upon the brier by the waters running clear
    May have charms for the linnet or the bee:
Their little loves are blest, and their little hearts at rest,
    But my lover is parted from me.

III

My love is like the sun in the firmament does run—
    Forever is constant and true;
But his is like the moon, that wanders up and down,
    And every month it is new.

I LOVE MY LOVE IN SECRET

IV

All you that are in love, and cannot it remove,
  I pity the pains you endure,
For experience makes me know that your hearts are
    full of woe,
  A woe that no mortal can cure.

I LOVE MY LOVE IN SECRET

Chorus

  My Sandy O, my Sandy O,
  My bonie, bonie Sandy O!
  Tho' the love that I owe
  To thee I dare na show,
  Yet I love my love in secret,
    My Sandy O!

I

My Sandy gied to me a ring   *gave*
Was a' beset wi' diamonds fine;
But I gied him a far better thing,
I gied my heart in pledge o' his ring.

II

My Sandy brak a piece o' gowd,   *gold*
While down his cheeks the saut tears row'd,   *salt; rolled*
He took a hauf, and gied it to me,   *half*
And I'll keep it till the hour I die.

SWEET TIBBIE DUNBAR

Chorus

My Sandy O, my Sandy O,
My bonie, bonie Sandy O !
Tho' the love that I owe
To thee I dare na show,
Yet I love my love in secret,
My Sandy O !

SWEET TIBBIE DUNBAR

I

O, WILT thou go wi' me, sweet Tibbie Dunbar?
O, wilt thou go wi' me, sweet Tibbie Dunbar?
Wilt thou ride on a horse, or be drawn in a car,
Or walk by my side, O sweet Tibbie Dunbar?

II

I care na thy daddie, his lands and his money;
I care na thy kin, sae high and sae lordly;
But say that thou 'lt hae me for better or waur, *worse*
And come in thy coatie, sweet Tibbie Dunbar. *short petticoat*

HIGHLAND HARRY

Chorus

O, for him back again !
O, for him back again !
I wad gie a' Knockhaspie's land
For Highland Harry back again.

HIGHLAND HARRY

I

My Harry was a gallant gay,
   Fu' stately strade he on the plain,   *strode*
But now he's banish'd far away:
   I'll never see him back again.

II

When a' the lave gae to their bed,   *rest; go*
   I wander dowie up the glen,   *drooping*
I set mè down, and greet my fill,   *weep*
   And ay I wish him back again.

III

O, were some villains hangit high,
   And ilka body had their ain,   *every; own*
Then I might see the joyfu' sight,
   My Highland Harry back again!

Chorus

   O, for him back again!
   O, for him back again!
I wad gie a' Knockhaspie's land,
For Highland Harry back again.

THE TAILOR FELL THRO' THE BED

I

The tailor fell thro' the bed, thimble an' a',
The tailor fell thro' the bed, thimble an' a';
The blankets were thin, and the sheets they were sma'—
The tailor fell thro' the bed, thimble an' a'!

II

<small>small</small>

The sleepy bit lassie, she dreaded nae ill,
The sleepy bit lassie, she dreaded nae ill;
The weather was cauld, and the lassie lay still:
She thought that a tailor could do her nae ill!

III

<small>gentle</small>

Gie me the groat again, cannie young man!
Gie me the groat again, cannie young man!
The day it is short, and the night it is lang—

<small>[Notes]</small>

The dearest siller that ever I wan!

IV

<small>alone</small>

There's somebody weary wi' lying her lane,
There's somebody weary wi' lying her lane!

<small>drooping;
glad</small>

There's some that are dowie, I trow wad be fain
To see the bit tailor come skippin again.

AY WAUKIN, O   *awake*

Chorus
Ay waukin, O,
  Waukin still and weary:
Sleep I can get nane
  For thinking on my dearie.

I

SIMMER's a pleasant time:
Flowers of every colour,
The water rins owre the heugh,   *crag*
And I long for my true lover.

II

When I sleep I dream,
  When I wauk I'm eerie,   *apprehensive*
Sleep I can get nane
  For thinkin on my dearie.

III

Lanely night comes on,
  A' the lave are sleepin,   *rest*
I think on my bonie lad,
  And I bleer my een wi' greetin.   *eyes; weeping*

Chorus
Ay waukin, O,
  Waukin still and weary:
Sleep I can get nane
  For thinking on my dearie.

BEWARE O' BONIE ANN

I

<small>warn you</small>
<small>true</small>
Ye gallants bright, I rede you right,
    Beware o' bonie Ann!
Her comely face sae fu' o' grace,
    Your heart she will trepan.

II

<small>eyes</small>
Her een sae bright like stars by night,
    Her skin is like the swan.
<small>trim</small>
Sae jimply lac'd her genty waist
    That sweetly ye might span.

III

Youth, Grace, and Love attendant move,
    And Pleasure leads the van:
In a' their charms, and conquering arms,
    They wait on bonie Ann.

IV

The captive bands may chain the hands,
    But Love enslaves the man:
<small>fine</small>
Ye gallants braw, I rede you a',
    Beware o' bonie Ann!

LADDIE, LIE NEAR ME

Chorus

Near me, near me,
Laddie, lie near me!
Lang hae I lain my lane—   alone
Laddie, lie near me!

I

Lang hae we parted been,
Laddie, my dearie;
Now we are met again—
Laddie, lie near me!

II

A' that I hae endur'd,
Laddie, my dearie,
Here in thy arms is cur'd—
Laddie, lie near me!

Chorus

Near me, near me,
Laddie, lie near me!
Lang hae I lain my lane—
Laddie, lie near me!

THE GARD'NER WI' HIS PAIDLE

spade

I

When rosy May comes in wi' flowers
To deck her gay, green-spreading bowers,
Then busy, busy are his hours,
    The gard'ner wi' his paidle.

II

The crystal waters gently fa',
The merry birds are lovers a',
The scented breezes round him blaw—
    The gard'ner wi' his paidle.

III

When purple morning starts the hare
To steal upon her early fare,
must   Then thro' the dew he maun repair—
    The gard'ner wi' his paidle.

IV

When Day, expiring in the west,
The curtain draws o' Nature's rest,
He flies to her arms he lo'es best,
    The gard'ner wi' his paidle.

ON A BANK OF FLOWERS

I

On a bank of flowers in a summer day,
　For summer lightly drest,
The youthful, blooming Nelly lay
　With love and sleep opprest;
When Willie, wand'ring thro' the wood,
Who for her favour oft had sued—
　　He gaz'd, he wish'd,
　　He fear'd, he blush'd,
And trembled where he stood.

II

Her closèd eyes, like weapons sheath'd,
　Were seal'd in soft repose;
Her lips, still as she fragrant breath'd,
　It richer dyed the rose;
The springing lilies, sweetly prest,
Wild-wanton kiss'd her rival breast:
　　He gaz'd, he wish'd,
　　He fear'd, he blush'd,
His bosom ill at rest.

III

Her robes, light-waving in the breeze,
    Her tender limbs embrace;
Her lovely form, her native ease,
    All harmony and grace.
Tumultuous tides his pulses roll,
A faltering, ardent kiss he stole ·
    He gaz'd, he wish'd,
    He fear'd, he blush'd,
And sigh'd his very soul.

IV

As flies the partridge from the brake
    On fear-inspired wings,
So Nelly starting, half-awake,
    Away affrighted springs.
But Willie follow'd—as he should;
He overtook her in the wood;
    He vow'd, he pray'd,
    He found the maid
Forgiving all, and good.

THE DAY RETURNS

I

THE day returns, my bosom burns,
    The blissful day we twa did meet!
Tho' winter wild in tempest toil'd,
    Ne'er summer sun was half sae sweet.

Than a' the pride that loads the tide,
    And crosses o'er the sultry line,
Than kingly robes, than crowns and globes,
    Heav'n gave me more—it made thee mine.

II

While day and night can bring delight,
    Or Nature aught of pleasure give,
While joys above my mind can move,
    For thee, and thee alone, I live!
When that grim foe of Life below
    Comes in between to make us part,
The iron hand that breaks our band,
    It breaks my bliss, it breaks my heart!

MY LOVE, SHE'S BUT A LASSIE YET

Chorus

My love, she's but a lassie yet,
My love, she's but a lassie yet!
We'll let her stand a year or twa,
    She'll no be half sae saucy yet!

I

I RUE the day I sought her, O!
I rue the day I sought her, O!
Wha gets her need na say he's woo'd,
    But he may say he has bought her, O.

JAMIE, COME TRY ME

II

Come draw a drap o' the best o't yet,
Come draw a drap o' the best o't yet!
Gae seek for pleasure whare ye will,
But here I never missed it yet.

III

We're a' dry wi' drinkin o't,
We're a' dry wi' drinkin o't!
The minister kiss't the fiddler's wife—
He could na preach for thinkin o't!

Chorus

My love, she's but a lassie yet,
My love, she's but a lassie yet!
We'll let her stand a year or twa,
She'll no be half sae saucy yet!

JAMIE, COME TRY ME

Chorus

Jamie, come try me,
Jamie, come try me!
If thou would win my love,
Jamie, come try me!

THE SILVER TASSIE

I

If thou should ask my love,
  Could I deny thee?
If thou would win my love,
  Jamie, come try me!

II

If thou should kiss me, love,
  Wha could espy thee?
If thou wad be my love,
  Jamie, come try me!

Chorus

Jamie, come try me,
Jamie, come try me!
If thou would win my love,
Jamie, come try me!

THE SILVER TASSIE

I

Go, fetch to me a pint o' wine,
  And fill it in a silver tassie,
That I may drink before I go
  A service to my bonie lassie!
The boat rocks at the pier o' Leith,
  Fu' loud the wind blaws frae the Ferry,
The ship rides by the Berwick-Law,   [Notes]
  And I maun leave my bonie Mary.   must

II

The trumpets sound, the banners fly,
    The glittering spears are rankèd ready,
The shouts o' war are heard afar,
    The battle closes deep and bloody.
It's not the roar o' sea or shore
    Wad mak me langer wish to tarry,
Nor shouts o' war that's heard afar:
    It's leaving thee, my bonie Mary!

THE LAZY MIST

I

The lazy mist hangs from the brow of the hill,
Concealing the course of the dark winding rill.
How languid the scenes, late so sprightly, appear,
As Autumn to Winter resigns the pale year!

II

The forests are leafless, the meadows are brown,
And all the gay foppery of summer is flown.
Apart let me wander, apart let me muse,
How quick Time is flying, how keen Fate pursues!

III

How long I have liv'd, but how much liv'd in vain!
How little of life's scanty span may remain!
What aspects old Time in his progress has worn!
What ties cruel Fate in my bosom has torn!

THE CAPTAIN'S LADY

IV

How foolish, or worse, till our summit is gain'd!
And downward, how weaken'd, how darken'd, how pain'd!
Life is not worth having with all it can give:
For something beyond it poor man, sure, must live.

THE CAPTAIN'S LADY

Chorus

O, mount and go,
   Mount and make you ready!
O, mount and go,
   And be the Captain's Lady!

I

WHEN the drums do beat,
   And the cannons rattle,
Thou shalt sit in state,
   And see thy love in battle:

II

When the vanquish'd foe
   Sues for peace and quiet,
To the shades we'll go,
   And in love enjoy it.

OF A' THE AIRTS

Chorus

O, mount and go,
    Mount and make you **ready**!
O, mount and go,
    And be the Captain's La**d**y!

OF A' THE AIRTS

I

Of a' the airts the wind can blaw
    I dearly like the west,
For there the bonie lassie lives,
    The lassie I lo'e best.
There wild woods grow, and rivers row,
    And monie a hill between,
But day and night my fancy's flight
    Is ever wi' my Jean.

II

I see her in the dewy flowers—
    I see her sweet and fair.
I hear her in the tunefu' birds—
    I hear her charm the air.
There's not a bonie flower that springs
    By fountain, shaw, or green,
There's not a bonie bird that sings,
    But minds me o' my Jean.

Glosses: directions; roll; wood; reminds

CARL, AN THE KING COME   _{if}

Chorus

    Carl, an the King come,
    Carl, an the King come,
    Thou shalt dance, and I will sing,
        Carl, an the King come!

I

An somebodie were come again,
Then somebodie maun cross the main,   must
And every man shall hae his ain,   own
    Carl, an the King come!

II

I trow we swappèd for the worse: swopped
We gae the boot and better horse,   gave
And that we'll tell them at the Cross,
    Carl, an the King come!

III

Coggie, an the King come,   Stoup
Coggie, an the King come,
I'll be fou, and thou 'se be toom,   I'll be full; (*i.e.* drunk); thou 'lt; empty
    Coggie, an the King come!

58 WHISTLE O'ER THE LAVE O'T

Chorus

Carl, an the King come,
Carl, an the King come,
Thou shalt dance, and I will sing,
Carl, an the King come!

WHISTLE O'ER THE LAVE O'T

rest of it

I

FIRST when Maggie was my care,
Heav'n, I thought, was in her air;
Now we're married, spier nae mair,
 But—whistle o'er the lave o't!
Meg was meek, and Meg was mild,
Sweet and harmless as a child:
Wiser men than me's beguiled—
 Whistle o'er the lave o't!

ask no more

II

How we live, my Meg and me,
How we love, and how we gree,
I care na by how few may see—
 Whistle o'er the lave o't!
Wha I wish were maggots' meat,
Dish'd up in her winding-sheet,
I could write (but Meg wad see't)—
 Whistle o'er the lave o't!

care nothing

O, WERE I ON PARNASSUS HILL

O, were I on Parnassus hill,
Or had o' Helicon my fill,
That I might catch poetic skill
    To sing how dear I love thee!
But Nith maun be my Muses' well,   *must*
My Muse maun be thy bonie sel',
On Corsincon I'll glowr and spell,   *gaze;* [Notes]
    And write how dear I love thee.

II

Then come, sweet Muse, inspire my lay!
For a' the lee-lang simmer's day   *live-long*
I couldna sing, I couldna say
    How much, how dear I love thee.
I see thee dancing o'er the green,
Thy waist sae jimp, thy limbs sae clean,
Thy tempting lips, thy roguish een—   *eyes*
    By Heaven and Earth I love thee!

III

By night, by day, a-field, at hame,
The thoughts o' thee my breast inflame,
And ay I muse and sing thy name—
    I only live to love thee.

Tho' I were doom'd to wander on,
Beyond the sea, beyond the sun,
Till my last weary sand was run,
    Till then—and then—I'd love thee!

THE CAPTIVE RIBBAND

I

Myra, the captive ribband's mine!
    'Twas all my faithful love could gain,
And would you ask me to resign
    The sole reward that crowns my pain?

II

Go, bid the hero, who has run
    Thro' fields of death to gather fame—
Go, bid him lay his laurels down,
    And all his well-earn'd praise disclaim!

III

The ribband shall its freedom lose—
    Lose all the bliss it had with you!—
And share the fate I would impose
    On thee, wert thou my captive too.

IV

It shall upon my bosom live,
   Or clasp me in a close embrace;
And at its fortune if you grieve,
   Retrieve its doom, and take its place.

THERE'S A YOUTH IN THIS CITY

I

There's a youth in this city, it were a great pity
   That he from our lasses should wander awa';
For he's bonie and braw, weel-favor'd witha',   *smart*
   An' his hair has a natural buckle an' a'.   *curl*

II

His coat is the hue o' his bonnet sae blue,
   His fecket is white as the new-driven snaw,   *waistcoat*
His hose they are blae, and his shoon like the slae,   *blue; sloe*
   And his clear siller buckles, they dazzle us a'.

III

For beauty and fortune the laddie's been courtin:
   Weel-featur'd, weel-tocher'd, weel-mounted, an' braw,   *-dowered*
But chiefly the siller that gars him gang till her—   *money; makes; go to*
   The penny's the jewel that beautifies a'!

IV

<small>farm; gladly would have had</small>　There's Meg wi' the mailen, that fain wad a haen him,
　And Susie, wha's daddie was laird of the Ha',
<small>almost</small>　There's lang-tocher'd Nancy maist fetters his fancy;
<small>self</small>　But the laddie's dear sel he loes dearest of a.

MY HEART'S IN THE HIGHLANDS

Chorus

My heart's in the Highlands, my heart is not here,
My heart's in the Highlands a-chasing the deer,
A-chasing the wild deer and following the roe—
My heart's in the Highlands, wherever I go!

I

FAREWELL to the Highlands, farewell to the North,
The birthplace of valour, the country of worth!
Wherever I wander, wherever I rove,
The hills of the Highlands for ever I love.

II

Farewell to the mountains high cover'd with snow,
Farewell to the straths and green valleys below,
Farewell to the forests and wild-hanging woods,
Farewell to the torrents and loud-pouring floods!

J. M. WRIGHT

JOHN ANDERSON MY JO

"John Anderson my jo, John,
　We clamb the hill thegither,
And monie a cantie day, John,
　We've had wi' ane anither;

Now we maun totter down, John,
　And hand in hand we'll go,
And sleep thegither at the foot,
　John Anderson my jo!"

JOHN ANDERSON MY JO

Chorus

My heart's in the Highlands, my heart is not here,
My heart's in the Highlands a-chasing the deer,
A-chasing the wild deer and following the roe—
My heart's in the Highlands, wherever I go!

JOHN ANDERSON MY JO

I

John Anderson my jo, John,
    When we were first acquent,   *acquainted*
Your locks were like the raven,
    Your bonie brow was brent;   *straight*
But now your brow is beld, John,   *bald*
    Your locks are like the snaw,
But blessings on your frosty pow,   *pate*
    John Anderson my jo!

II

John Anderson my jo, John,
    We clamb the hill thegither,   *climbed; together*
And monie a cantie day, John,   *jolly*
    We've had wi' ane anither;
Now we maun totter down, John,   *must*
    And hand in hand we'll go,
And sleep thegither at the foot,
    John Anderson my jo!

AWA', WHIGS, AWA'

Chorus

Awa', Whigs, awa'!
Awa', Whigs, awa'!
Ye 're but a pack o' traitor louns,
Ye 'll do nae guid at a'.

I

<small>thistles</small>

Our thrissles flourish'd fresh and fair,
And bonie bloom'd our roses;
But Whigs cam like a frost in June,
An' wither'd a' our posies.

II

<small>dust-whirl</small>
<small>book</small>

Our ancient crown 's fa'n in the dust—
Deil blin' them wi' the stoure o't,
An' write their names in his black beuk,
Wha gae the Whigs the power o't!

III

<small>describing</small>

Our sad decay in church and state
Surpasses my descriving.
The Whigs cam o'er us for a curse,
And we hae done wi' thriving.

IV

<small>awake</small>
<small>hare</small>

Grim Vengeance lang has taen a nap,
But we may see him waukin—
Gude help the day when Royal heads
Are hunted like a maukin!

Sir GEORGE HARVEY

CA' THE YOWES TO THE KNOWES

"Ca' the yowes to the knowes,
Ca' them where the heather grows,
Ca' them where the burnie rowes,
My bonie dearie."—*Chorus.*

CA' THE YOWES TO THE KNOWES

Chorus

Awa', Whigs, awa'!
Awa', Whigs, awa'!
Ye 're but a pack o' traitor louns,
Ye 'll do nae guid at a'.

CA' THE YOWES TO THE KNOWES   Drive; ewes; knolls

Chorus
Ca' the yowes to the knowes,
Ca' them where the heather grows,
Ca' them where the burnie rowes,   brooklet; rolls
My bonie dearie!

I

As I gaed down the water-side,   went
There I met my shepherd lad:
He row'd me sweetly in his plaid,   wrapped
And he ca'd me his dearie.   called

II

'Will ye gang down the water-side,   go
And see the waves sae sweetly glide
Beneath the hazels spreading wide?
The moon it shines fu' clearly.'

III

'I was bred up in nae sic school,   such
My shepherd lad, to play the fool,
An' a' the day to sit in dool,   sorrow
An' naebody to see me.'

O, MERRY HAE I BEEN

IV

'Ye sall get gowns and ribbons meet,
> Calf. Cauf-leather shoon upon your feet,
And in my arms thou 'lt lie and sleep,
An' ye sall be my dearie.'

V

'If ye 'll but stand to what ye 've said,
> I'll go I 'se gang wi' you, my shepherd lad,
And ye may row me in your plaid,
And I sall be your dearie.'

VI

'While waters wimple to the sea,
> wind
> shines;
> welkin; high
While day blinks in the lift sae hie,
Till clay-cauld death sall blin' my e'e,
Ye sall be my dearie.'

Chorus

Ca' the yowes to the knowes,
Ca' them where the heather grows,
Ca' them where the burnie rowes,
My bonie dearie!

O, MERRY HAE I BEEN

I

> huckling-
> comb
O, MERRY hae I been teethin a heckle,
An' merry hae I been shapin a spoon!
> patching
O, merry hae I been cloutin a kettle,
An' kissin my Katie when a' was done!

A MOTHER'S LAMENT

O, a' the lang day I ca' at my hammer, — knock
    An' a' the lang day I whistle an' sing !
O, a' the lang night I cuddle my kimmer, — mistress
    An' a' the lang night as happy 's a king !

II

Bitter in dool, I lickit my winnins — sorrow; supped; earnings
    O' marrying Bess, to gie her a slave.
Blest be the hour she cool'd in her linens, — winding-sheet
    And blythe be the bird that sings on her grave!
Come to my arms, my Katie, my Katie,
    An' come to my arms, and kiss me again !
Drucken or sober, here 's to thee, Katie,
    And blest be the day I did it again !

A MOTHER'S LAMENT

I

FATE gave the word—the arrow sped,
    And pierc'd my darling's heart,
And with him all the joys are fled
    Life can to me impart.
By cruel hands the sapling drops,
    In dust dishonor'd laid :
So fell the pride of all my hopes,
    My age's future shade.

II

The mother linnet in the brake
  Bewails her ravish'd young:
So I for my lost darling's sake
  Lament the live-day long.
Death, oft I've fear'd thy fatal blow!
  Now fond I bare my breast!
O, do thou kindly lay me low,
  With him I love at rest!

THE WHITE COCKADE

Chorus

<small>rollicking</small> O, he's a ranting, roving lad!
He is a brisk an' a bonie lad!
Betide what may, I will be wed,
And follow the boy wi' the White Cockade:

I

My love was born in Aberdeen,
The boniest lad that e'er was seen;
But now he makes our hearts fu' sad—
He takes the field wi' his White Cockade.

II

<small>distaff; flax</small> I'll sell my rock, my reel, my tow,
<small>white-faced</small> My guid gray mare and hawkit cow,
To buy mysel a tartan plaid,
To follow the boy wi' the White Cockade.

THE BRAES O' BALLOCHMYLE

Chorus

O, he's a ranting, roving lad!
He is a brisk an' a bonie lad!
Betide what may, I will be wed,
And follow the boy wi' the White Cockade!

THE BRAES O' BALLOCHMYLE   hills

I

THE Catrine woods were yellow seen,
   The flowers decay'd on Catrine lea;
Nae lav'rock sang on hillock green,   lark
   But nature sicken'd on the e'e;   eye
Thro' faded groves Maria sang,
   Hersel in beauty's bloom the while,
And aye the wild-wood echoes rang :—
   'Fareweel the braes o' Ballochmyle!

II

'Low in your wintry beds, ye flowers,
   Again ye'll flourish fresh and fair;
Ye birdies, dumb in with'ring bowers,
   Again ye'll charm the vocal air;
But here, alas! for me nae mair
Shall birdie charm, or floweret smile:
   Fareweel the bonie banks of Ayr!
Fareweel! fareweel sweet Ballochmyle!'

THE RANTIN DOG, THE DADDIE O'T

I

-clothes   O, WHA my babie-clouts will buy?
attend to   O, wha will tent me when I cry?
             Wha will kiss me where I lie?—
               The rantin dog, the daddie o't!

II

fault   O, wha will own he did the faut?
[Notes]   O, wha will buy the groanin maut?
name it   O, wha will tell me how to ca't?—
               The rantin dog, the daddie o't!

III

[Notes]   When I mount the creepie-chair,
             Wha will sit beside me there?
             Gie me Rob, I'll seek nae mair—
               The rantin dog, the daddie o't!

IV

talk; alone   Wha will crack to me my lane?
[Notes]   Wha will mak me fidgin fain?
             Wha will kiss me o'er again?—
               The rantin dog, the daddie o't!

THOU LINGERING STAR

I

Thou ling'ring star with less'ning ray,
   That lov'st to greet the early morn,
Again thou usher'st in the day
   My Mary from my soul was torn.
O Mary, dear departed shade!
   Where is thy place of blissful rest?
See'st thou thy lover lowly laid?
   Hear'st thou the groans that rend his breast?

II

That sacred hour can I forget,
   Can I forget the hallow'd grove,
Where, by the winding Ayr, we met
   To live one day of parting love?
Eternity cannot efface
   Those records dear of transports past,
Thy image at our last embrace—
   Ah! little thought we 'twas our last!

III

Ayr, gurgling, kiss'd his pebbled shore,
   O'erhung with wild woods thickening green;
The fragrant birch and hawthorn hoar
   'Twin'd amorous round the raptur'd scene;

EPPIE ADAIR

 The flowers sprang wanton to be prest,
  The birds sang love on every spray,
 Till too, too soon, the glowing west
  Proclaim'd the speed of wingèd day.

IV

 Still o'er these scenes my mem'ry wakes,
  And fondly broods with miser-care.
 Time but th' impression stronger makes,
  As streams their channels deeper wear.
 O Mary, dear departed shade!
  Where is thy place of blissful rest?
 See'st thou thy lover lowly laid?
  Hear'st thou the groans that rend his breast?

EPPIE ADAIR

Chorus

 An' O my Eppie,
 My jewel, my Eppie!
 Wha wadna be happy *[wouldn't]*
 Wi' Eppie Adair?

I

 By love and by beauty,
 By law and by duty,
 I swear to be true to
 My Eppie Adair!

II

A' pleasure exile me,   All
Dishonour defile me,
If e'er I beguile thee,
My Eppie Adair!

Chorus

An' O my Eppie,
My jewel, my Eppie!
Wha wadna be happy
Wi' Eppie Adair?

THE BATTLE OF SHERRAMUIR

I

' O, CAM ye here the fight to shun,
   Or herd the sheep wi' me, man?
Or were ye at the Sherra-moor,
   Or did the battle see, man?'
' I saw the battle, sair and teugh,   sore and tough
And reekin-red ran monie a sheugh;   furrow
My heart for fear gae sough for sough,   gave; sigh
To hear the thuds, and see the cluds   clouds
O' clans frae woods in tartan duds,   clothes
   Wha glaum'd at kingdoms three, man.   grasped

74 THE BATTLE OF SHERRAMUIR

II

	' The red-coat lads wi' black cockauds
not slow	To meet them were na slaw, man:
	They rush'd and push'd and bluid outgush'd,
trunk	And monie a bouk did fa', man!
	The great Argyle led on his files,
wot; shone	I wat they glanc'd for twenty miles;
hocked; skittles	They hough'd the clans like nine-pin kyles,
	They hack'd and hash'd, while braid-swords clash'd,
	And thro' they dash'd, and hew'd and smash'd,
fated	Till fey men died awa, man.

III

kilts	' But had ye seen the philibegs
flaring; trousers	And skyrin tartan trews, man,
dared	When in the teeth they daur'd our Whigs
	And Covenant trueblues, man!
	In lines extended lang and large,
bayonets	When baig'nets o'erpower'd the targe,
	And thousands hasten'd to the charge,
	Wi' Highland wrath they frae the sheath
	Drew blades o' death, till out o' breath
pigeons	They fled like frighted dows, man!'

IV

how the Devil	' O, how Deil! Tam, can that be true?
went	The chase gaed frae the north, man!
	I saw mysel, they did pursue
	The horseman back to Forth, man;

THE BATTLE OF SHERRAMUIR

And at Dunblane, in my ain sight,
They took the brig wi' a' their might,   *bridge*
And straught to Stirling wing'd their flight;
But, cursed lot! the gates were shut,
And monie a huntit poor red-coat,
  For fear amaist did swarf, man!'   *almost; swoon*

V

'My sister Kate cam up the gate   *road*
  Wi' crowdie unto me, man: *meal and water*
She swoor she saw some rebels run
  To Perth and to Dundee, man!
Their left-hand general had nae skill;
The Angus lads had nae good will
That day their neebors' bluid to spill;
For fear by foes that they should lose
Their cogs o' brose, they scar'd at blows,   *mugs of porridge*
  And hameward fast did flee, man.

VI

'They've lost some gallant gentlemen,
  Amang the Highland clans, man!
I fear my Lord Panmure is slain,
  Or in his en'mies' hands, man.
Now wad ye sing this double flight,
Some fell for wrang, and some for right,
But monie bade the world guid-night:
Say, pell and mell, wi' muskets' knell
How Tories fell, and Whigs to Hell
  Flew off in frighted bands, man!'

YOUNG JOCKIE WAS THE BLYTHEST LAD

I

<small>round about
goad; [Notes]</small>

Young Jockie was the blythest lad,
　　In a' our town or here awa :
Fu' blythe he whistled at the gaud,
　　Fu' lightly danc'd he in the ha'.

II

<small>praised ; eyes
trimly
mouth</small>

He roos'd my een sae bonie blue,
　　He roos'd my waist sae genty sma' ;
An' ay my heart cam to my mou',
　　When ne'er a body heard or saw.

III

<small>longingly
oxen ; drive</small>

My Jockie toils upon the plain
　　Thro' wind and weet, thro' frost and snaw ;
And o'er the lea I leuk fu' fain,
　　When Jockie's owsen hameward ca'.

IV

An' ay the night comes round again,
　　When in his arms he taks me a',
An' ay he vows he'll be my ain
　　As lang's he has a breath to draw.

A WAUKRIFE MINNIE

wakeful mother

I

'Whare are you gaun, my bonie lass? *going*
    Whare are you gaun, my hinnie?' *honey*
She answer'd me right saucilie:—
    'An errand for my minnie!'

II

'O, whare live ye, my bonie lass?
    O, whare live ye, my hinnie?'
'By yon burnside, gin ye maun ken, *brookside; if; must*
    In a wee house wi' my minnie!'

III

But I foor up the glen at e'en *went*
    To see my bonie lassie,
And lang before the grey morn cam
    She was na hauf sae saucy. *half*

IV

O, weary fa' the waukrife cock, *woe befall;*
    And the foumart lay his crawin! *polecat; stop; crowing*
He wauken'd the auld wife frae her sleep *woman*
    A wee blink or the dawin. *bit ere the dawn*

78 THO' WOMEN'S MINDS

V

<small>wot; rose</small>
<small>big; -cudgel</small>
<small>well-thrashed</small>

An angry wife I wat she raise,
And o'er the bed she brought her,
And wi' a meikle hazel-rung
She made her a weel-pay'd dochter.

VI

O, fare-thee-weel, my bonie lass!
O, fare-thee-weel, my hinnie!
Thou art a gay and a bonie lass,
But thou has a waukrife minnie!'

THO' WOMEN'S MINDS

Chorus

<small>much as</small>

For a' that, an' a' that,
And twice as meikle 's a' that,
The bonie lass that I loe best,
She'll be my ain for a' that!

I

<small>most</small>

Tho' women's minds like winter winds
May shift, and turn, an' a' that,
The noblest breast adores them maist—
A consequence, I draw that.

II

Great love I bear to a' the fair,
   Their humble slave, an' a' that;
But lordly will, I hold it still
   A mortal sin to thraw that.   *contradict*

III

In rapture sweet this hour we meet,
   Wi' mutual love an' a' that,
But for how lang the flie may stang,   *fly; sting*
   Let inclination law that!

IV

Their tricks an' craft hae put me daft,
   They 've taen me in an' a' that,
But clear your decks, and here 's:—'The Sex!'
   I like the jads for a' that!   *jades*

Chorus

For a' that, an' a' that,
   And twice as meikle 's a' that,
The bonie lass that I loe best,
   She 'll be my ain for a' that!

WILLIE BREW'D A PECK O' MAUT

malt

Chorus

full (*i.e.* drunk)
droplet
crow; dawn
-brew

We are na fou, we're nae that fou,
But just a drappie in our e'e!
The cock may craw, the day may daw,
And ay we'll taste the barley-bree!

I

O, WILLIE brewed a peck o' maut,
And Rob and Allan cam to see.

live-long
would not have;
Christendom

Three blyther hearts that lee-lang night
Ye wad na found in Christendie.

II

[Notes]

Here are we met three merry boys,
Three merry boys I trow are we;
And monie a night we've merry been,

more

And monie mae we hope to be!

III

It is the moon, I ken her horn,

shining;
sky; high
entice

That's blinkin in the lift sae hie:
She shines sae bright to wyle us hame,
But, by my sooth, she'll wait a wee!

KILLIECRANKIE

IV

Wha first shall rise to gang awa, — *go*
A cuckold, coward loun is he! — *rogue*
Wha first beside his chair shall fa',
He is the King amang us three!

Chorus

We are na fou, we're nae that fou,
But just a drappie in our e'e!
The cock may craw, the day may daw,
And ay we'll taste the barley-bree!

KILLIECRANKIE

Chorus

An ye had been whare I hae been, — *If*
Ye wad na been sae cantie, O! — *would not have; jolly*
An ye had seen what I hae seen
On the braes o' Killiecrankie, O! — *heights*

I

'Whare hae ye been sae braw, lad? — *fine*
Whare hae ye been sae brankie, O? — *spruce*
Whare hae ye been sae braw, lad?
Cam ye by Killiecrankie, O?'

82 THE BLUE-EYED LASSIE

II

'I faught at land, I faught at sea,
   At hame I faught my auntie, O;
But I met the Devil and Dundee
   On the braes o' Killiecrankie, O.

III

<small>furrow</small>
<small>knock</small>
<small>Else; hawk</small>

'The bauld Pitcur fell in a furr,
   An' Clavers gat a clankie, O,
Or I had fed an Athole gled
   On the braes o' Killiecrankie, O!'

Chorus

An ye had been whare I hae been,
   Ye wad na been sae cantie, O!
An ye had seen what I hae seen
   On the braes o' Killiecrankie, O!

THE BLUE-EYED LASSIE

I

<small>I went a
woful way
last night</small>

<small>eyes</small>

I GAED a waefu' gate yestreen,
   A gate I fear I'll dearly rue:
I gat my death frae twa sweet een,
   Twa lovely een o' bonie blue!

'Twas not her golden ringlets bright,
   Her lips like roses wat wi' dew,   *wet*
Her heaving bosom lily-white :
   It was her een sae bonie blue.

II

She talk'd, she smil'd, my heart she wyl'd,   *snared*
   She charm'd my soul I wist na how ;
And ay the stound, the deadly wound,   *ache*
   Cam frae her een sae bonie blue.
But 'spare to speak, and spare to speed '—   [Notes]
   She 'll aiblins listen to my vow :   *may be*
Should she refuse, I 'll lay my dead   *death*
   To her twa een sae bonie blue.

THE BANKS OF NITH

I

THE Thames flows proudly to the sea,
   Where royal cities stately stand ;
But sweeter flows the Nith to me,
   Where Cummins ance had high command.   [Notes]
   When shall I see that honor'd land,
That winding stream I love so dear ?
   Must wayward Fortune's adverse hand
For ever—ever keep me here ?

II

How lovely, Nith, thy fruitful vales,
    Where bounding hawthorns gaily bloom,
And sweetly spread thy sloping dales,
    Where lambkins wanton thro' the broom!
Tho' wandering now must be my doom
Far from thy bonie banks and braes,
    May there my latest hours consume
Amang my friends of early days!

TAM GLEN

I

sister   My heart is a-breaking, dear tittie,
    Some counsel unto me come len'
To anger them a' is a pity,
    But what will I do wi' Tam Glen?

II

such; fine   I'm thinking, wi' sic a braw fellow
poverty;
shift   In poortith I might mak a fen'.
What care I in riches to wallow,
must not   If I mauna marry Tam Glen?

III

There's Lowrie the laird o' Dumeller;
in   'Guid day to you,' brute! he comes ben.
money   He brags and he blaws o' his siller,
    But when will he dance like Tam Glen?

TAM GLEN

IV

My minnie does constantly deave me, mother
deafen
   And bids me beware o' young men.
They flatter, she says, to deceive me—
   But wha can think sae o' Tam Glen?

V

My daddie says, gin I'll forsake him, if
   He'd gie me guid hunder marks ten.
But if it's ordain'd I maun take him,
   O, wha will I get but Tam Glen?

VI

Yestreen at the valentines' dealing, Last night
   My heart to my mou gied a sten, mouth;
spring
For thrice I drew ane without failing,
   And thrice it was written 'Tam Glen'!

VII

The last Halloween I was waukin [Notes]
   My droukit sark-sleeve, as ye ken— wetted shift
His likeness came up the house staukin, stalking
   And the very grey breeks o' Tam Glen! breeches

VIII

Come, counsel, dear tittie, don't tarry!
   I'll gie ye my bonie black hen,
Gif ye will advise me to marry If
   The lad I lo'e dearly, Tam Glen.

CRAIGIEBURN WOOD

Chorus

Beyond thee, dearie, beyond thee, dearie,
And O, to be lying beyond thee!
O, sweetly, soundly, weel may he sleep
That's laid in the bed beyond thee!

I

Sweet closes the ev'ning on Craigieburn Wood
And blythely awaukens the morrow;
But the pride o' the spring on the Craigieburn
Wood
Can yield me naught but sorrow.

II

I see the spreading leaves and flowers,
I hear the wild birds singing;
But pleasure they hae nane for me,
While care my heart is wringing.

III

I can na tell, I maun na tell,
I daur na for your anger;
But secret love will break my heart,
If I conceal it langer.

IV

I see thee gracefu', straight, and tall,
   I see thee sweet and bonie;
But O, what will my torment be,
   If thou refuse thy Johnie!

V

To see thee in another's arms
   In love to lie and languish,
'Twad be my dead, that will be seen—   *death*
   My heart wad burst wi' anguish!

VI

But, Jeanie, say thou wilt be mine,
   Say thou lo'es nane before me,
And a' my days o' life to come
   I'll gratefully adore thee.

Chorus

Beyond thee, dearie, beyond thee, dearie,
   And O, to be lying beyond thee!
O, sweetly, soundly, weel may he sleep
   That's laid in the bed beyond thee!

88 O JOHN, COME KISS ME NOW

FRAE THE FRIENDS AND LAND I LOVE

I

Frae the friends and land I love
    Driv'n by Fortune's felly spite,   *relentless*
Frae my best belov'd I rove,
    Never mair to taste delight!
Never mair maun hope to find   *must*
    Ease frae toil, relief frae care.
When remembrance wracks the mind,
    Pleasures but unveil despair.

II

Brightest climes shall mirk appear,   *gloomy*
    Desert ilka blooming shore,   *every*
Till the Fates, nae mair severe,
    Friendship, love, and peace restore;
Till Revenge wi' laurell'd head
    Bring our banish'd hame again,
And ilk loyal, bonie lad   *each*
    Cross the seas, and win his ain!

O JOHN, COME KISS ME NOW

Chorus

O John, come kiss me now, now, now!
O John, my love, come kiss me now!
  O John, come kiss me by and by,
For weel ye ken the way to woo!

COCK UP YOUR BEAVER

I

O, some will court and compliment,
    And ither some will kiss and daut; *others; pet*
But I will mak o' my guidman, *husband*
    My ain guidman—it is nae faut! *fault*

II

O, some will court and compliment,
    And ither some will prie their mou', *taste*
And some will hause in ither's arms, *cuddle*
    And that's the way I like to do!

Chorus

O John, come kiss me now, now, now!
O John, my love, come kiss me now!
O John, come kiss me by and by,
For weel ye ken the way to woo!

COCK UP YOUR BEAVER

I

When first my brave Johnie lad came to this town,
He had a blue bonnet that wanted the crown,
But now he has gotten a hat and a feather—
Hey, brave Johnie lad, cock up your beaver!

90 MY TOCHER'S THE JEWEL

II

<small>spruce</small> Cock up your beaver, and cock it fu' sprush!
We'll over the border and gie them a brush:
There's somebody there we'll teach better behaviour—
Hey, brave Johnie lad, cock up your beaver!

<small>dowry's</small> ## MY TOCHER'S THE JEWEL

I

<small>much</small> O, MEIKLE thinks my luve o' my beauty,
And meikle thinks my luve o' my kin;
<small>finely</small> But little thinks my luve I ken brawlie
My tocher's the jewel has charms for him.
It's a' for the apple he'll nourish the tree,
<small>honey</small> It's a' for the hiney he'll cherish the bee!
<small>much; money</small> My laddie's sae meikle in luve wi' the siller,
He canna hae luve to spare for me!

II

<small>hansel-</small> Your proffer o' luve 's an airle-penny,
My tocher's the bargain ye wad buy;
<small>if</small> But an ye be crafty, I am cunnin,
Sae ye wi' anither your fortune may try.
<small>timber</small> Ye're like to the timmer o' yon rotten wood,
Ye're like to the bark o' yon rotten tree:
Ye'll slip frae me like a knotless thread,
An' ye'll crack ye're credit wi' mair nor me!

GUIDWIFE, COUNT THE LAWIN   Hostess; reckoning

Chorus

Then, guidwife, count the lawin,
    The lawin, the lawin!
Then, guidwife, count the lawin,
    And bring a coggie mair!   [Notes]

I

GANE is the day, and mirk 's the night,   Gone; dark's
But we 'll ne'er stray for faut o' light,   want
For ale and brandy 's stars and moon,
And blude-red wine 's the risin sun.

II

There 's wealth and ease for gentlemen,   simple; fight and defend (*i.e.* shift for themselves)
And semple folk maun fecht and fen';
But here we 're a' in ae accord,   one
For ilka man that 's drunk 's a lord.   every

III

My coggie is a haly pool,   stoup; holy
That heals the wounds o' care and dool,   sorrow
And Pleasure is a wanton trout:
An ye drink it a', ye 'll find him out!   If

Chorus

 Then, guidwife, count the lawin,
  The lawin, the lawin!
 Then, guidwife, count the lawin,
  And bring a coggie mair!

THERE'LL NEVER BE PEACE TILL JAMIE COMES HAME

I

By yon castle wa' at the close of the day,
I heard a man sing, tho' his head it was grey,
And as he was singing, the tears doon came :—
'There'll never be peace till Jamie comes hame!

II

'The Church is in ruins, the State is in jars,
Delusions, oppressions, and murderous wars,
We dare na weel say 't, but we ken wha's to blame—
There'll never be peace till Jamie comes hame!

III

<small>fine</small> 'My seven braw sons for Jamie drew sword,
<small>weep; earth</small> But now I greet round their green beds in the yerd;
It brak the sweet heart o' my faithfu' auld dame—
There'll never be peace till Jamie comes hame˙

IV

'Now life is a burden that bows me down,
Sin I tint my bairns, and he tint his crown;   *since; lost; children*
But till my last moments my words are the same—
There'll never be peace till Jamie comes hame!'

WHAT CAN A YOUNG LASSIE

I

What can a young lassie,
What shall a young lassie,
What can a young lassie
   Do wi' an auld man?
Bad luck on the penny
That tempted my minnie   *mother*
To sell her puir Jenny
   For siller an' lan'!   *money*

II

He's always compleenin
Frae mornin to eenin;
He hoasts and he hirples   *coughs; hobbles*
   The weary day lang;
He's doylt and he's dozin;   *stupid; torpid*
His blude it is frozen—
O, dreary's the night
   Wi' a crazy auld man!

III

He hums and he hankers,
He frets and he cankers,
I never can please him
    Do a' that I can.
He's peevish an' jealous
Of a' the young fellows—
    O, dool on the day
I met wi' an auld man!

IV

My auld auntie Katie
Upon me taks pity,
I'll do my endeavour
    To follow her plan:
I'll cross him an' wrack him
Until I heartbreak him,
And then his auld brass
    Will buy me a new pan.

THE BONIE LAD THAT'S FAR AWA

I

O, how can I be blythe and glad,
    Or how can I gang brisk and braw,
When the bonie lad that I lo'e best
    Is o'er the hills and far awa?

After J. M. WRIGHT

WHAT CAN A YOUNG LASSIE

" He hums and he hankers, Do a' that I can; O, dool on the day
He frets and he cankers, He's peevish an' jealous I met wi' an auld man!"
I never can please him Of a' the young fellows— —*Stanza iii.*

II

It's no the frosty winter wind,
  It's no the driving drift and snaw;
But ay the tear comes in my e'e
  To think on him that's far awa.

III

My father pat me frae his door, *put*
  My friends they hae disown'd me a';
But I hae ane will tak my part—
  The bonie lad that's far awa.

IV

A pair o' glooves he bought to me,
  And silken snoods he gae me twa, *fillets; gave*
And I will wear them for his sake,
  The bonie lad that's far awa.

V

O, weary Winter soon will pass,
  And Spring will cleed the birken shaw, *clothe; birch-woods*
And my sweet babie will be born,
  And he'll be hame that's far awa!

I DO CONFESS THOU ART SAE FAIR

I

<small>would have; ears</small>
<small>not</small>

I do confess thou art sae fair,
    I wad been o'er the lugs in luve,
Had I na found the slightest prayer
    That lips could speak thy heart could muve.
I do confess thee sweet, but find
    Thou art so thriftless o' thy sweets,
Thy favours are the silly wind

<small>every</small>

    That kisses ilka thing it meets.

II

See yonder rosebud rich in dew,
    Amang its native briers sae coy,

<small>soon; loses</small>
<small>pulled</small>
<small>Such</small>

How sune it tines its scent and hue,
    When pu'd and worn a common toy!
Sic fate ere lang shall thee betide,
    Tho' thou may gaily bloom awhile,
And sune thou shalt be thrown aside,
    Like onie common weed, an' vile.

SENSIBILITY HOW CHARMING

I

SENSIBILITY how charming,
    Thou, my friend, can'st truly tell!
But Distress with horrors arming
    Thou alas! hast known too well!

II

Fairest flower, behold the lily
    Blooming in the sunny ray :
Let the blast sweep o'er the valley,
    See it prostrate in the clay.

III

Hear the woodlark charm the forest,
    Telling o'er his little joys;
But alas! a prey the surest
    To each pirate of the skies!

IV

Dearly bought the hidden treasure
    Finer feelings can bestow :
Chords that vibrate sweetest pleasure
    Thrill the deepest notes of woe.

YON WILD MOSSY MOUNTAINS

I

Yon wild mossy mountains sae lofty and wide,
That nurse in their bosom the youth o' the Clyde,
Where the grouse lead their coveys thro' the heather to feed,
And the shepherd tents his flock as he pipes on his reed.   *tends*

98 YON WILD MOSSY MOUNTAINS

II

Not Gowrie's rich valley nor Forth's sunny shores
To me hae the charms o' yon wild, mossy moors;
For there, by a lanely, sequesterèd stream,
Resides a sweet lassie, my thought and my dream.

III

<small>those</small>   Amang thae wild mountains shall still be my path,
<small>Each</small>   Ilk stream foaming down its ain green, narrow strath;
For there wi' my lassie the lang day I rove,
While o'er us unheeded flie the swift hours o' love.

IV

She is not the fairest, altho' she is fair;
O' nice education but sma' is her share;
Her parentage humble as humble can be;
But I lo'e the dear lassie because she lo'es me.

V

<small>must</small>   To Beauty what man but maun yield him a prize,
In her armour of glances, and blushes, and sighs?
And when Wit and Refinement hae polish'd her darts,
<small>eyes</small>   They dazzle our een, as they flie to our hearts.

VI

But kindness, sweet kindness, in the fond-sparkling
    e'e
Has lustre outshining the diamond to me,
And the heart beating love as I'm clasp'd in her
    arms,
O, these are my lassie's all-conquering charms !

I HAE BEEN AT CROOKIEDEN   *Hell*

I

I HAE been at Crookieden—
    My bonie laddie, Highland laddie !
Viewing Willie and his men—   *William of Cumberland*
    My bonie laddie, Highland laddie !
There our foes that burnt and slew—
    My bonie laddie, Highland laddie !
There at last they gat their due—
    My bonie laddie, Highland laddie !

II

Satan sits in his black neuk—   *corner*
    My bonie laddie, Highland laddie !
Breaking sticks to roast the Duke—
    My bonie laddie, Highland laddie !

The bloody monster gae a yell—
My bonie laddie, Highland laddie!
And loud the laugh gaed round a' Hell—
My bonie laddie, Highland laddie!

IT IS NA, JEAN, THY BONIE FACE

I

<small>not</small>

It is na, Jean, thy bonie face
    Nor shape that I admire,
Altho' thy beauty and thy grace
    Might weel awauk desire.

<small>every</small>

Something in ilka part o' thee
    To praise, to love, I find;
But, dear as is thy form to me,
    Still dearer is thy mind.

II

Nae mair ungen'rous wish I hae,
    Nor stronger in my breast,
Than, if I canna mak thee sae,
    At least to see thee blest:

<small>so</small>

Content am I, if Heaven shall give
    But happiness to thee,
And, as wi' thee I wish to live,
    For thee I 'd bear to dee.

MY EPPIE MACNAB

I

O, saw ye my dearie, my Eppie Macnab?
O, saw ye my dearie, my Eppie Macnab?
　'She's down in the yard, she's kissin the laird.
She winna come hame to her ain Jock Rab!'　　*will not*

II

O, come thy ways to me, my Eppie Macnab!
O, come thy ways to me, my Eppie Macnab!
　Whate'er thou has done, be it late, be it soon,
Thou's welcome again to thy ain Jock Rab.　　*art*

III

What says she, my dearie, my Eppie Macnab?
What says she, my dearie, my Eppie Macnab?
　'She lets thee to wit that she has thee forgot,　*know*
And for ever disowns thee, her ain Jock Rab.'

IV

O, had I ne'er seen thee, my Eppie Macnab!
O, had I ne'er seen thee, my Eppie Macnab!
　As light as the air and as fause as thou's fair,
Thou's broken the heart o' thy ain Jock Rab!

WHA IS THAT AT MY BOWER DOOR

I

'WHA is that at my bower door?'
   'O, wha is it but Findlay!'
'Then gae your gate, ye'se nae be here.' [go your way, ye shall not]
   'Indeed maun I!' quo' Findlay. [must]
'What mak ye, sae like a thief?' [do]
   'O, come and see!' quo' Findlay.
'Before the morn ye'll work mischief?'
   'Indeed will I!' quo' Findlay.

II

'Gif I rise and let you in'— [It]
   'Let me in!' quo' Findlay—
'Ye'll keep me wauken wi' your din?' [awake]
   'Indeed will I!' quo' Findlay.
'In my bower if ye should stay'—
   'Let me stay!' quo' Findlay—
'I fear ye'll bide till break o' day?'
   'Indeed will I!' quo' Findlay.

III

'Here this night if ye remain'—
   'I'll remain!' quo' Findlay—
'I dread ye'll learn the gate again?'
   'Indeed will I!' quo' Findlay.

'What may pass within this bower'
  ('Let it pass!' quo' Findlay!)
'Ye maun conceal till your last hour'—
  'Indeed will I!' quo' Findlay.

BONIE WEE THING

Chorus

Bonie wee thing, cannie wee thing,   *gentle*
  Lovely wee thing, wert thou mine,
I wad wear thee in my bosom
  Lest my jewel it should tine.   *lose*

I

Wishfully I look and languish
  In that bonie face o' thine,
And my heart it stounds wi' anguish,   *aches*
  Lest my wee thing be na mine.

II

Wit and Grace and Love and Beauty
  In ae constellation shine!   *one*
To adore thee is my duty,
  Goddess o' this soul o' mine!

THE TITHER MORN

Chorus

Bonie wee thing, cannie wee thing,
    Lovely wee thing, wert thou mine,
I wad wear thee in my bosom
    Lest my jewel it should tine.

THE TITHER MORN

I

<small>other</small>

<small>oak</small>
<small>sweetheart</small>
<small>by the darkening</small>
<small>trim; leapt: ridge</small>
<small>pettingly</small>
<small>nevertheless</small>

THE tither morn, when I forlorn
    Aneath an aik sat moaning,
I did na trow I'd see my jo
    Beside me gin the gloaming.
But he sae trig lap o'er the rig,
    And dawtingly did cheer me,
When I, what reck, did least expeck
    To see my lad sae near me '

II

<small>aside</small>
<small>spruce</small>
<small>wot; fondness wept</small>

<small>early</small>

<small>a little ago</small>

His bonnet he a thought ajee
    Cock'd spunk when first he clasp'd me;
And I, I wat, wi' fainness grat,
    While in his grips he press'd me.
'Deil tak the war!' I late and air
    Hae wish'd since Jock departed;
But now as glad I'm wi' my lad
    As short syne broken-hearted.

AE FOND KISS

III

Fu' aft at e'en, wi' dancing keen, — Full oft
　When a' were blythe and merry,
I car'd na by, sae sad was I — cared not a jot
　In absence o' my deary.
But praise be blest! my mind's at rest,
　I'm happy wi' my Johnie!
At kirk and fair, I'se ay be there, — I'll
　And be as canty 's onie. — jolly as any

AE FOND KISS — One

I

Ae fond kiss, and then we sever!
Ae farewell, and then forever!
Deep in heart-wrung tears I'll pledge thee,
Warring sighs and groans I'll wage thee.
Who shall say that Fortune grieves him,
While the star of hope she leaves him?
Me, nae cheerfu' twinkle lights me,
Dark despair around benights me.

II

I'll ne'er blame my partial fancy:
Naething could resist my Nancy!
But to see her was to love her,
Love but her, and love for ever.

Had we never lov'd sae kindly,
Had we never lov'd sae blindly,
Never met—or never parted—
We had ne'er been broken-hearted.

III

Fare-thee-weel, thou first and fairest!
Fare-thee-weel, thou best and dearest!
Thine be ilka joy and treasure, *every*
Peace, Enjoyment, Love and Pleasure!
Ae fond kiss, and then we sever!
Ae farewell, alas, for ever!
Deep in heart-wrung tears I'll pledge thee,
Warring sighs and groans I'll wage thee.

LOVELY DAVIES

I

O, how shall I, unskilfu', try
   The Poet's occupation?
The tunefu' Powers, in happy hours
   That whisper inspiration,
Even they maun dare an effort mair *must*
   Than aught they ever gave us,
Ere they rehearse in equal verse
   The charms o' lovely Davies.

LOVELY DAVIES

II

Each eye, it cheers, when she appears,
    Like Phœbus in the morning,
When past the shower, and every flower
    The garden is adorning!
As the wretch looks o'er Siberia's shore,
    When winter-bound the wave is,
Sae droops our heart, when we maun part
    Frae charming, lovely Davies.

III

Her smile's a gift frae 'boon the lift,   *above; sky*
    That maks us mair than princes.
A sceptred hand, a king's command,
    Is in her darting glances.
The man in arms 'gainst female charms,
    Even he her willing slave is:
He hugs his chain, and owns the reign
    Of conquering lovely Davies.

IV

My Muse to dream of such a theme
    Her feeble powers surrenders;
The eagle's gaze alone surveys
    The sun's meridian splendours.
I wad in vain essay the strain—
    The deed too daring brave is!
I'll drap the lyre, and, mute, admire   *drop*
    The charms o' lovely Davies.

THE WEARY PUND O' TOW

pound; yarn

Chorus

The weary pund, the weary pund,
    The weary pund o' tow!
I think my wife will end her life
    Before she spin her tow.

I

stone; flax
I BOUGHT my wife a stane o' lint
    As guid as e'er did grow,
And a' that she has made o' that
one poor
    Is ae puir pund o' tow.

II

hole in the wall
There sat a bottle in a bole
At the back of the fire-place
    Beyont the ingle low;
other suck
And ay she took the tither souk
wet the dusty
    To drouk the stourie tow.

III

Quoth I :—' For shame, ye dirty dame,
bunch
    Gae spin your tap o' tow!'
distaff
She took the rock, and wi' a knock
pate
    She brake it o'er my pow.

IV

At last her feet—I sang to see't!— *went; hill*
Gaed foremost o'er the knowe,
And or I wad anither jad, *wed*
I'll wallop in a tow. *kick heels; rope*

Chorus

The weary pund, the weary pund,
The weary pund o' tow!
I think my wife will end her life
Before she spin her tow.

I HAE A WIFE O' MY AIN *have*

I

I HAE a wife o' my ain,
I'll partake wi' naebody:
I'll take cuckold frae nane,
I'll gie cuckold to naebody.

II

I hae a penny to spend,
There—thanks to naebody!
I hae naething to lend,
I'll borrow frae naebody.

III

I am naebody's lord,
  I'll be slave to naebody.
I hae a guid braid sword,
  I'll tak dunts frae naebody.

blows

IV

I'll be merry and free,
  I'll be sad for naebody.
Naebody cares for me,
  I care for naebody.

[Notes]

WHEN SHE CAM BEN, SHE BOBBED

into the parlour; curtseyed

I

O, when she cam ben, she bobbéd fu' law!
O, when she cam ben, she bobbéd fu' law!
And when she cam' ben, she kiss'd Cockpen,
And syne she deny'd she did it at a'!

then; at all

II

And was na Cockpen right saucy witha'?
And was na Cockpen right saucy witha',
In leaving the dochter o' a lord,
And kissin a collier lassie an' a'?

J. M. WRIGHT

I HAE A WIFE O' MY AIN

"I hae a wife o' my ain,   I'll take cuckold frae nane,
I'll partake wi' naebody ;   I'll gie cuckold to naebody."

III

O, never look down, my lassie, at a'!
O, never look down, my lassie, at a'!
Thy lips are as sweet, and thy figure complete,
  As the finest dame in castle or ha'.

IV

'Tho' thou hast nae silk, and holland sae sma',   *fine*
Tho' thou hast nae silk, and holland sae sma',
Thy coat and thy sark are thy ain handywark,   *shift*
  And Lady Jean was never sae braw.'

O, FOR ANE-AND-TWENTY, TAM   *One-*

Chorus

An' O, for ane-and-twenty, Tam!
  And hey, sweet ane-and-twenty, Tam!
I 'll learn my kin a rattlin sang
  An I saw ane-and-twenty, Tam.   *If*

I

They snool me sair, and haud me down,   *snub; sore; keep*
  And gar me look like bluntie, Tam;   *make; a stupid*
But three short years will soon wheel roun'—
  And then comes ane-and-twenty, Tam!

112 O. KENMURE'S ON AND AWA, WILLIE

II

<small>[Notes];
handful of money</small>

<small>Of; ask</small>

A gleib o' lan', a claut o' gear
  Was left me by my auntie, Tam.
At kith or kin I needna spier,
  An I saw ane-and-twenty, Tam.

III

<small>dolt</small>

<small>pain</small>

They 'll hae me wed a wealthy coof,
  Tho' I mysel hae plenty, Tam ;
But hear'st thou, laddie—there's my loof:
  I'm thine at ane-and-twenty, Tam !

Chorus

An' O, for ane-and-twenty, Tam .
  And hey, sweet ane-and-twenty, Tam !
I 'll learn my kin a rattlin sang
  An I saw ane-and-twenty, Tam.

O, KENMURE'S ON AND AWA, WILLIE

I

O, KENMURE's on and awa, Willie,
  O, Kenmure's on and awa !
An' Kenmure's lord's the bravest lord
  That ever Galloway saw !

II

Success to Kenmure's band, Willie,
    Success to Kenmure's band!
There's no a heart that fears a Whig
    That rides by Kenmure's hand.

III

Here's Kenmure's health in wine, Willie,
    Here's Kenmure's health in wine!
There ne'er was a coward o' Kenmure's blude,
    Nor yet o' Gordon's line.

IV

O, Kenmure's lads are men, Willie,
    O, Kenmure's lads are men!
Their hearts and swords are metal true,
    And that their faes shall ken.

V

They'll live or die wi' fame, Willie,
    They'll live or die wi' fame!
But soon wi' sounding Victorie
    May Kenmure's lord come hame!

VI

Here's him that's far awa, Willie,
    Here's him that's far awa!
And here's the flower that I lo'e best—
    The rose that's like the snaw!

O, LEEZE ME ON MY SPINNIN-WHEEL

blessings

I

O, leeze me on my spinnin-wheel!
And leeze me on my rock and reel,
Frae tap to tae that cleeds me bien,
And haps me fiel and warm at e'en!
I'll set me down, and sing and spin,
While laigh descends the summer sun,
Blest wi' content, and milk and meal—
O, leeze me on my spinnin-wheel!

distaff
top to toe;
clothes;
comfortably
wraps; well
place
low

II

On ilka hand the burnies trot,
And meet below my theekit cot.
The scented birk and hawthorn white
Across the pool their arms unite,
Alike to screen the birdie's nest
And little fishes' caller rest.
The sun blinks kindly in the biel,
Where blythe I turn my spinnin-wheel.

either;
brooklets
thatched
birch

cool
glances;
shelter

III

On lofty aiks the cushats wail,
And Echo cons the doolfu' tale.
The lintwhites in the hazel braes,
Delighted, rival ither's lays.

oaks
doleful
linnets;
slopes
each other's

O, LEEZE ME ON MY SPINNIN'-WHEEL

"Wi' sma to sell, and less to buy,
 Aboon distress, below envy,
O, wha wad leave this humble state
 For a' the pride of a' the great?

Amid their flaring, idle toys,
Amid their cumbrous, dinsome joys,
Can they the peace and pleasure feel
Of Bessie at her spinnin'-wheel?"—*Verse iv.*

The craik amang the claver hay, corncraik; clover
The paitrick whirrin o'er the ley, partridge; meadow
The swallow jinkin round my shiel, darting; cottage
Amuse me at my spinnin-wheel.

IV

Wi' sma to sell and less to buy, little
Aboon distress, below envy, Above
O, wha wad leave this humble state
For a' the pride of a' the great?
Amid their flaring, idle toys,
Amid their cumbrous, dinsome joys, noisy
Can they the peace and pleasure feel,
Of Bessy at her spinnin-wheel?

MY COLLIER LADDIE

I

'O, WHARE live ye, my bonie lass,
  And tell me how they ca' ye?' call
'My name,' she says, 'is Mistress Jean,
  And I follow the collier laddie.'

II

'O, see you not yon hills and dales
  The sun shines on sae brawlie? finely
They a' are mine, and they shall be thine,
  Gin ye'll leave your collier laddie! If

III

'An' ye shall gang in gay attire, _{go}
　　Weel buskit up sae gaudy, _{adorned}
And ane to wait on every hand,
　　Gin ye 'll leave your collier laddie!'

IV

'Tho' ye had a' the sun shines on,
　　And the earth conceals sae lowly,
I wad turn my back on you and it a',
　　And embrace my collier laddie.

V

'I can win my five pennies in a day,
　　An' spend it at night fu' brawlie,
And make my bed in the collier's neuk _{corner}
And lie down wi' my collier laddie.

VI

'Loove for loove is the bargain for me,
　　Tho' the wee cot-house should haud me, _{hold}
And the warld before me to win my bread—
　　And fair fa' my collier laddie!' _{good befall}

NITHSDALE'S WELCOME HAME

I

The noble Maxwells and their powers
    Are coming o'er the border;
And they'll gae big Terreagles' towers,   *go build*
    And set them a' in order;
And they declare Terreagles fair,
    For their abode they choose it:
There's no a heart in a' the land
    But's lighter at the news o't!

II

Tho' stars in skies may disappear,
    And angry tempests gather,
The happy hour may soon be near
    That brings us pleasant weather;
The weary night o' care and grief
    May hae a joyfu' morrow;
So dawning day has brought relief—
    Fareweel our night o' sorrow!

IN SIMMER, WHEN THE HAY WAS MAWN

I

In simmer, when the hay was mawn
    And corn wav'd green in ilka field,   *every*
While claver blooms white o'er the ley,   *clover; pasture*
    And roses blaw in ilka bield,   *sheltered spot*

118 IN SIMMER, WHEN THE HAY

<small>shed</small>   Blythe Bessie in the milking shiel
           Says:—'I'll be wed, come o't what will!'
<small>eld</small>   Out spake a dame in wrinkled eild:—
           'O' guid advisement comes nae ill.

II

<small>many a one</small>   'It's ye hae wooers monie ane,
                     And lassie, ye're but young, ye ken!
<small>sensibly
choose</small>   Then wait a wee, and cannie wale
<small>well-stocked
kitchen;
parlour</small>   A routhie butt, a routhie ben.
                 There Johnie o' the Buskie-Glen,
<small>Full; cow-
shed</small>   Fu' is his barn, fu' is his byre.
                 Tak this frae me, my bonie hen:
<small>fans</small>   It's plenty beets the luver's fire!'

III

                 'For Johnie o' the Buskie-Glen
<small>fly</small>   I dinna care a single flie:
<small>crops; kine</small>   He lo'es sae weel his craps and kye,
                 He has nae love to spare for me.
<small>glance; eye</small>   But blythe's the blink o' Robie's e'e,
<small>wot</small>   And weel I wat he lo'es me dear:
<small>One; give</small>   Ae blink o' him I wad na gie
<small>wealth</small>   For Buskie-Glen and a' his gear.'

IV

<small>fight</small>   'O thoughtless lassie, life's a faught!
<small>quietest way</small>   The canniest gate, the strife is sair.
<small>full-handed;
fighting</small>   But ay fu'-han't is fechtin best:
<small>terrible</small>   A hungry care's an unco care.

But some will spend, and some will spare,
An' wilfu' folk maun hae their will.   *must*
  Syne as ye brew, my maiden fair,   *Then*
Keep mind that ye maun drink the yill!'   *ale*

V

'O, gear will buy me rigs o' land,   *ridges*
  And gear will buy me sheep and kye!
But the tender heart o' leesome loove   *lawful*
  The gowd and siller canna buy!   *gold and silver*
  We may be poor, Robie and I;
Light is the burden luve lays on;
  Content and loove brings peace and joy:
What mair hae Queens upon a throne?'

FAIR ELIZA

I

Turn again, thou fair Eliza!
  Ae kind blink before we part!   *One; glance*
Rew on thy despairing lover—   *Take pity*
  Canst thou break his faithfu' heart?
Turn again, thou fair Eliza!
  If to love thy heart denies,
For pity hide the cruel sentence
  Under friendship's kind disguise!

II

Thee, dear maid, hae I offended?
  'The offence is loving thee.
Canst thou wreck his peace for ever,
  Wha for thine wad gladly die?
While the life beats in my bosom,
  Thou shalt mix in ilka throe. *every*
Turn again, thou lovely maiden,
  Ae sweet smile on me bestow! *One*

III

Not the bee upon the blossom
  In the pride o' sinny noon, *sunny*
Not the little sporting fairy
  All beneath the simmer moon,
Not the Poet in the moment
  Fancy lightens in his e'e,
Kens the pleasure, feels the rapture,
  That thy presence gies to me.

YE JACOBITES BY NAME

I

Ye Jacobites by name,
  Give an ear, give an ear!
Ye Jacobites by name,
  Give an ear!

YE JACOBITES BY NAME

Ye Jacobites by name,
Your fautes I will proclaim,   faults
Your doctrines I maun blame—   must
    You shall hear!

II

What is Right, and what is Wrang,
    By the law, by the law?
What is Right, and what is Wrang,
    By the law?
What is Right, and what is Wrang?
A short sword and a lang,
A weak arm and a strang
    For to draw!

III

What makes heroic strife
    Famed afar, famed afar?
What makes heroic strife
    Famed afar?
What makes heroic strife?
To whet th' assassin's knife,
Or hunt a Parent's life
    Wi' bluidy war!

IV

Then let your schemes alone,
    In the State, in the State!
Then let your schemes alone,
    In the State!

> Then let your schemes alone,
> Adore the rising sun,
> And leave a man undone
> To his fate!

THE POSIE

I

O, LUVE will venture in where it daur na weel be seen!
O, luve will venture in, where wisdom ance hath been!
But I will doun yon river rove amang the wood sae green,
    And a' to pu' a posie to my ain dear May!

<small>pluck</small>

II

The primrose I will pu', the firstling o' the year,
And I will pu' the pink, the emblem o' my dear,
For she's the pink o' womankind, and blooms without a peer—
    And a' to be a posie to my ain dear May!

III

I 'll pu' the budding rose when Phœbus peeps in view,
For it 's like a baumy kiss o' her sweet, bonie mou.
The hyacinth's for constancy wi' its unchanging blue—
    And a' to be a posie to my ain dear May!

<small>balmy</small>

THE POSIE

IV

The lily it is pure, and the lily it is fair,
And in her lovely bosom I 'll place the lily there.
The daisy's for simplicity and unaffected air—
   And a' to be a posie to my ain dear May!

V

The hawthorn I will pu', wi' its locks o' siller gray,
Where, like an agèd man, it stands at break o' day;
But the songster's nest within the bush I winna tak   *will not*
   away—
   And a' to be a posie to my ain dear May!

VI

The woodbine I will pu' when the e'ening star is
   near,
And the diamond draps o' dew shall be her een sae   *eyes*
   clear!
The violet's for modesty, which weel she fa's to   *claims*
   wear—
   And a' to be a posie to my ain dear May!

VII

I 'll tie the posie round wi' the silken band o' luve,
And I 'll place it in her breast, and I 'll swear by a'
   above,
That to my latest draught o' life the band shall
   ne'er remove,
   And this will be a posie to my ain dear May!

THE BANKS O' DOON

I

<small>slopes</small>   Ye banks and braes o' bonie Doon,
      How can ye bloom sae fresh and fair?
  How can ye chant, ye little birds,
      And I sae weary fu' o' care!
  Thou 'll break my heart, thou warbling bird,
      That wantons thro' the flowering thorn!
  Thou minds me o' departed joys,
      Departed never to return.

II

  Aft hae I rov'd by bonie Doon
      To see the rose and woodbine twine,
<small>every</small>   And ilka bird sang o' its luve,
      And fondly sae did I o' mine.
<small>plucked</small>   Wi' lightsome heart I pu'd a rose,
      Fu' sweet upon its thorny tree!
<small>stole</small>   And my fause luver staw my rose—
      But ah! he left the thorn wi' me.

WILLIE WASTLE

"She has a hump upon her breast,
　　Sic a wife as Willie had,
The twin o' that upon her shouther:
　　I wad'na g'e a button for her."

WILLIE WASTLE

I

Willie Wastle dwalt on Tweed,
  The spot they ca'd it Linkumdoddie.
Willie was a wabster guid   *weaver*
  Could stown a clue wi' onie bodie.   *have stolen*
He had a wife was dour and din,   *stubborn; dun*
  O, Tinkler Maidgie was her mither!   *Tinker*
Sic a wife as Willie had,   *Such*
  I wad na gie a button for her.

II

She has an e'e (she has but ane),
  The cat has twa the very colour,
Five rusty teeth, forbye a stump,   *besides*
  A clapper-tongue wad deave a miller;   *deafen*
A whiskin beard about her mou,
  Her nose and chin they threaten ither: *each other*
Sic a wife as Willie had,
  I wad na gie a button for her.

III

She's bow-hough'd, she's hem-shin'd,   *bandy; [Notes]*
  Ae limpin leg a hand-breed shorter;   *one; -breadth*
She's twisted right, she's twisted left,
  To balance fair in ilka quarter;   *either*

LADY MARY ANN

  She has a hump upon her breast,
   The twin o' that upon her shouther: *shouther: shoulder*
  Sic a wife as Willie had,
   I wad na gie a button for her.

IV

  Auld baudrans by the ingle sits, *Auld baudrans: Old pussie*
   An' wi' her loof her face a-washin; *loof: palm*
  But Willie's wife is nae sae trig, *trig: trim*
   She dights her grunzie wi' a hushion; *dights: wipes; grunzie: snout; [Notes]*
  Her walie nieves like midden-creels, *walie nieves: ample fists; [Notes]*
   Her face wad fyle the Logan Water: *fyle: foul*
  Sic a wife as Willie had,
   I wad na gie a button for her.

LADY MARY ANN

I

O, LADY Mary Ann looks o'er the Castle wa',
She saw three bonie boys playing at the ba',
The youngest he was the flower amang them a'—
  My bonie laddie's young, but he's growin yet!

II

'O father, O father, an ye think it fit,
We'll send him a year to the college yet;
We'll sew a green ribbon round about his hat,
  And that will let them ken he's to marry yet!'

III

Lady Mary Ann was a flower in the dew,
Sweet was its smell and bonie was its hue,
And the longer it blossom'd the sweeter it grew,
    For the lily in the bud will be bonier yet.

IV

Young Charlie Cochran was the sprout of an aik,   _{oak}
Bonie and bloomin and straucht was its make;
The sun took delight to shine for its sake,
    And it will be the brag o' the forest yet.

V

The simmer is gane when the leaves they were green.
And the days are awa that we hae seen;
But far better days I trust will come again,
    For my bonie laddie's young, but he's growin yet

SUCH A PARCEL OF ROGUES IN A NATION

I

    Fareweel to a' our Scottish fame,
      Fareweel our ancient glory!
    Fareweel ev'n to the Scottish name.
      Sae famed in martial story!

Now Sark rins over Solway sands,
   An' Tweed rins to the ocean,
To mark where England's province stands—
   Such a parcel of rogues in a nation!

II

What force or guile could not subdue
   Thro' many warlike ages
Is wrought now by a coward few
   For hireling traitor's wages.
The English steel we could disdain,
   Secure in valour's station;
But English gold has been our bane—
   Such a parcel of rogues in a nation!

III

O, would, or I had seen the day
   That Treason thus could sell us,
My auld grey head had lien in clay
   Wi' Bruce and loyal Wallace!
But pith and power, till my last hour
   I'll mak this declaration:—
'We're bought and sold for English gold'—
   Such a parcel of rogues in a nation!

Even when without

KELLYBURN BRAES

I

THERE lived a carl in Kellyburn Braes   *old man*
  (Hey and the rue grows bonie wi' thyme !),
And he had a wife was the plague o' his days
  (And the thyme it is wither'd, and rue is in
    prime !).

II

Ae day as the carl gaed up the lang glen   *One*
  (Hey and the rue grows bonie wi' thyme !),
He met wi' the Devil, says :—' How do you fen ? '   *are you getting on*
  (And the thyme it is wither'd, and rue is in
    prime !).

III

' I 've got a bad wife, sir, that's a' my complaint
  (Hey and the rue grows bonie wi' thyme !),
For, saving your presence, to her ye 're a saint '
  (And the thyme it is wither'd, and rue is in
    prime !).

IV

' It's neither your stot nor your staig I shall crave   *steer; young horse*
  (Hey and the rue grows bonie wi' thyme !),
' But gie me your wife, man, for her I must have'
  (And the thyme it is wither'd, and rue is in
    prime !).

V

'O welcome most kindly!' the blythe carl said
  (Hey and the rue grows bonie wi' thyme !),
worse   'But if ye can match her ye're waur than ye're ca'd'
  (And the thyme it is wither'd, and rue is in prime !).

VI

The Devil has got the auld wife on his back
  (Hey and the rue grows bonie wi' thyme !),
And like a poor pedlar he's carried his pack
  (And the thyme it is wither'd, and rue is in prime !).

VII

porch-   He's carried her hame to his ain hallan-door
  (Hey and the rue grows bonie wi' thyme !),
Then; go Syne bade her gae in for a bitch and a whore
  (And the thyme it is wither'd, and rue is in prime !).

VIII

Then straight he makes fifty, the pick o' his band
  (Hey and the rue grows bonie wi' thyme !),
Turn out on her guard in the clap o' a hand
  (And the thyme it is wither'd, and rue is in prime !).

KELLYBURN BRAES

IX

The carlin gaed thro' them like onie wud bear   *beldam ; mad*
  (Hey and the rue grows bonie wi' thyme !) :
Whae'er she gat hands on cam ne'er her nae mair
  (And the thyme it is wither'd, and rue is in prime !).

X

A reekit wee deevil looks over the wa   *smoky small*
  (Hey and the rue grows bonie wi' thyme !) :—
'O help, maister, help, or she'll ruin us a' !'
  (And the thyme it is wither'd, and rue is in prime !).

XI

The Devil he swore by the edge o' his knife
  (Hey and the rue grows bonie wi' thyme !),
He pitied the man that was tied to a wife
  (And the thyme it is wither'd, and rue is in prime !).

XII

The Devil he swore by the kirk and the bell
  (Hey and the rue grows bonie wi' thyme !),
He was not in wedlock, thank Heav'n, but in Hell
  (And the thyme it is wither'd, and rue is in prime !).

XIII

Then Satan has travell'd again wi' his pack
   (Hey and the rue grows bonie wi' thyme!),
And to her auld husband he's carried her back
   (And the thyme it is wither'd, and rue is in prime!).

XIV

_{most} 'I hae been a Devil the feck o' my life
   (Hey and the rue grows bonie wi' thyme!),
But ne'er was in Hell till I met wi' a wife'
   (And the thyme it is wither'd, and rue is in prime!).

THE SLAVE'S LAMENT

I

It was in sweet Senegal
That my foes did me enthral
   For the lands of Virginia, -ginia, O!
Torn from that lovely shore,
And must never see it more,
   And alas! I am weary, weary, O!

II

All on that charming coast
Is no bitter snow and frost,
   Like the lands of Virginia, -ginia, O!

There streams for ever flow,
And the flowers for ever blow,
   And alas! I am weary, weary, O!

III

The burden I must bear,
While the cruel scourge I fear,
   In the lands of Virginia, -ginia, O!
And I think on friends most dear
With the bitter, bitter tear,
   And alas! I am weary, weary, O!

THE SONG OF DEATH

I

Farewell, thou fair day, thou green earth, and ye skies,
   Now gay with the broad setting sun!
Farewell, loves and friendships, ye dear tender ties—
   Our race of existence is run!
Thou grim King of Terrors! thou Life's gloomy foe,
   Go, frighten the coward and slave!
Go, teach them to tremble, fell tyrant, but know,
   No terrors hast thou to the brave!

SWEET AFTON

II

Thou strik'st the dull peasant—he sinks in the dark,
    Nor saves e'en the wreck of a name!
Thou strik'st the young hero—a glorious mark,
    He falls in the blaze of his fame!
In the field of proud honour, our swords in our hands,
    Our king and our country to save,
While victory shines on Life's last ebbing sands,
    O, who would not die with the brave?

SWEET AFTON

I

slopes

FLOW gently, sweet Afton, among thy green braes!
Flow gently, I'll sing thee a song in thy praise!
My Mary's asleep by thy murmuring stream—
Flow gently, sweet Afton, disturb not her dream!

II

Thou stock dove whose echo resounds thro' the glen,
Ye wild whistling blackbirds in yon thorny den,
Thou green-crested lapwing, thy screaming forbear—
I charge you, disturb not my slumbering fair!

III

How lofty, sweet Afton, thy neighbouring hills,
Far mark'd with the courses of clear, winding rills!

There daily I wander, as noon rises high,
My flocks and my Mary's sweet cot in my eye.

IV

How pleasant thy banks and green vallies below,
Where wild in the woodlands the primroses blow
There oft, as mild Ev'ning weeps over the lea,
The sweet-scented birk shades my Mary and me.   birch

V

Thy crystal stream, Afton, how lovely it glides,
And winds by the cot where my Mary resides!
How wanton thy waters her snowy feet lave,
As, gathering sweet flowerets, she stems thy clear
    wave!

VI

Flow gently, sweet Afton, among thy green braes!
Flow gently, sweet river, the theme of my lays!
My Mary's asleep by thy murmuring stream—
Flow gently, sweet Afton, disturb not her dream!

BONIE BELL

I

THE smiling Spring comes in rejoicing,
    And surly Winter grimly flies.
Now crystal clear are the falling waters,
    And bonie blue are the sunny skies.

Fresh o'er the mountains breaks forth the morning,
    The ev'ning gilds the ocean's swell:
All creatures joy in the sun's returning,
    And I rejoice in my bonie Bell.

II

The flowery Spring leads sunny summer,
    The yellow Autumn presses near;
Then in his turn comes gloomy Winter,
    Till smiling Spring again appear.
Thus seasons dancing, life advancing,
    Old Time and Nature their changes tell;
But never ranging, still unchanging,
    I adore my bonie Bell.

THE GALLANT WEAVER

I

rolling

Where Cart rins rowin to the sea
By monie a flower and spreading tree,
There lives a lad, the lad for me—
    He is a gallant weaver!
O, I had wooers aught or nine,

gave
afraid;
be lost

They gied me rings and ribbons fine,
And I was fear'd my heart wad tine,
    And I gied it to the weaver.

HEY, CA' THRO'

II

My daddie sign'd my tocher-band — *deed of settlement*
To gie the lad that has the land;
But to my heart I'll add my hand,
    And give it to the weaver.
While birds rejoice in leafy bowers,
While bees delight in opening flowers,
While corn grows green in summer showers,
    I love my gallant weaver.

HEY, CA' THRO' — *work away*

Chorus
Hey, ca' thro', ca' thro',
For we hae mickle ado! — *much to do*
Hey, ca' thro', ca' thro',
For we hae mickle ado!

I

Up wi' the carls of Dysart — *old men; [Notes]*
    And the lads o' Buckhaven,
And the kimmers o' Largo — *gossips*
    And the lasses o' Leven!

II

We hae tales to tell,
    And we hae sangs to sing;
We hae pennies to spend,
    And we hae pints to bring.

138 O, CAN YE LABOUR LEA

III

We 'll live a' our days,
And them that comes behin',
Let them do the like,
And spend the gear they win!

wealth

Chorus

Hey, ca' thro', ca' thro',
For we hae mickle ado!
Hey, ca' thro', ca' thro',
For we hae mickle ado!

O, CAN YE LABOUR LEA

Chorus

O, can ye labour lea, young man,
O, can ye labour lea?
Gae back the gate ye came again—
Ye 'se never scorn me!

[Notes]

Go; way
Ye shall;
despise

I

I FEE'D a man at Martinmas
Wi' airle-pennies three;
But a' the faut I had to him
He couldna labour lea

hired
hansel-

THE DEUK'S DANG O'ER MY DADDIE 139

II

O, clappin's guid in Febarwar,   *stroking*
  An' kissin's sweet in May;
But what signifies a young man's love,
  An't dinna last for ay?   *If it do not*

III

O, kissin is the key o' love
  An' clappin is the lock;
An' makin of's the best thing   *[Notes]*
  That e'er a young thing got!

Chorus

O, can ye labour lea, young man,
  O, can ye labour lea?
Gae back the gate ye came again—
  Ye 'se never scorn me!

THE DEUK'S DANG O'ER MY DADDIE   *duck has knocked*

I

The bairns gat out wi' an unco shout:—   *children; surprising*
  'The deuk's dang o'er my daddie, O!'
'The fien-ma-care,' quo' the feirrie auld wife,   *fiend-may-; lusty*
  'He was but a paidlin body, O!   *[Notes]; creature*

140 SHE'S FAIR AND FAUSE

He paidles out, and he paidles in,
   An' he paidles late and early, O!
This seven lang years I hae lien by his side,
   An' he is but a fusionless carlie, O!'

II

'O, haud your tongue, my feirrie auld wife,
   O, haud your tongue, now Nansie, O!
I 've seen the day, and sae hae ye,
   Ye wad na been sae donsie, O.
I 've seen the day ye butter'd my brose,
   And cuddl'd me late and early, O;
But downa-do 's come o'er me now,
   And och, I find it sairly, O!'

SHE'S FAIR AND FAUSE

I

She's fair and fause that causes my smart;
   I lo'ed her meikle and lang;
She 's broken her vow, she 's broken my heart;
   And I may e'en gae hang.
A coof cam in wi' routh o' gear,
   And I hae tint my dearest dear;
But Woman is but warld's gear,
   Sae let the bonie lass gang!

Margin glosses:
- sapless old mannikin
- hold
- so have
- testy
- [Notes]
- [Notes]; cannot-do is
- feel it sorely
- false
- much; long
- go
- ninny; plenty; money
- lost
- go

Etching by ROBERT BRYDEN

THE DEIL'S AWA' WI' TH' EXCISEMAN

"The Deil cam' fiddlin' thro' the town,
And danc'd awa' wi' th' Exciseman,
And ilka wife cries:—Auld Mahoun,
I wish you luck o' the prize, man!"—*Verse i.*

II

Whae'er ye be that Woman love,
  To this be never blind:
Nae ferlie 'tis, tho' fickle she prove,   *No wonder is it*
  A woman has't by kind.   *nature*
O Woman lovely, Woman fair,
An angel form's faun to thy share,   *fallen*
'Twad been o'er meikle to gien thee mair!...   *have given*
  I mean an angel mind.

THE DEIL'S AWA WI' TH' EXCISEMAN

Chorus

The Deil's awa, the Deil's awa,
  The Deil's awa wi' th' Exciseman!
He's danc'd awa, he's danc'd awa,
  He's danc'd awa wi' th' Exciseman!

I

The Deil cam fiddlin thro' the town,
  And danc'd awa wi' th' Exciseman,
And ilka wife cries:—'Auld Mahoun,   *every; [Notes]*
  I wish you luck o' the prize, man!

II

'We'll mak our maut, and we'll brew our drink,   *malt*
  We'll laugh, sing, and rejoice, man,
And monie braw thanks to the meikle black Deil,   *handsome; big*
  That danc'd awa wi' th' Exciseman.

III

There's threesome reels, there's foursome reels,
  There's hornpipes and strathspeys, man,
But the ae best dance ere cam to the land
  Was *The Deil's Awa wi' th' Exciseman.*

one

Chorus

The Deil's awa, the Deil's awa,
  The Deil's awa wi' th' Exciseman!
He's danc'd awa, he's danc'd awa,
  He's danc'd awa wi' th' Exciseman!

THE LOVELY LASS OF INVERNESS

I

The lovely lass of Inverness,
  Nae joy nor pleasure can she see;
For e'en to morn she cries 'Alas!'
  And ay the saut tear blin's her e'e:—

salt

II

'Drumossie moor, Drumossie day—
  A waefu' day it was to me!
For there I lost my father dear,
  My father dear and brethren three.

woful

III

Their winding-sheet the bluidy clay,
　Their graves are growin green to see,
And by them lies the dearest lad
　That ever blest a woman's e'e.

IV

Now wae to thee, thou cruel lord,   *William of Cumberland*
　A bluidy man I trow thou be,
For monie a heart thou hast made sair   *sore*
　That ne'er did wrang to thine or thee!'

A RED, RED ROSE

I

O, MY luve is like a red, red rose,
　That's newly sprung in June.
O, my luve is like the melodie,
　That's sweetly play'd in tune.

II

As fair art thou, my bonie lass,
　So deep in luve am I,
And I will luve thee still, my dear,
　Till a' the seas gang dry.   *go*

III

Till a' the seas gang dry, my dear,
And the rocks melt wi' the sun!
And I will luve thee still, my dear,
While the sands o' life shall run.

IV

And fare thee weel, my only luve,
And fare thee weel a while!
And I will come again, my luve,
Tho' it were ten thousand mile!

AS I STOOD BY YON ROOFLESS TOWER

Chorus

A lassie all alone was making her moan,
Lamenting our lads beyond the sea:—
In the bluidy wars they fa', and our honor's gane an' a',
And broken-hearted we maun die.'

[must]

I

As I stood by yon roofless tower,
Where the wa'flow'r scents the dewy air,
Where the houlet mourns in her ivy bower,
And tells the midnight moon her care:

[owl]

II

The winds were laid, the air was still,
    The stars they shot along the sky,
The tod was howling on the hill,   *fox*
    And the distant-echoing glens reply.

III

The burn, adown its hazelly path,   *brook*
    Was rushing by the ruin'd wa',
Hasting to join the sweeping Nith,
    Whase roarings seem'd to rise and fa'.

IV

The cauld blae North was streaming forth   *livid*
    Her lights, wi' hissing, eerie din:
Athort the lift they start and shift,   *athwart*
    Like Fortune's favours, tint as win.   *lost as soon as won*

V

Now, looking over firth and fauld,   *fold*
    Her horn the pale-faced Cynthia rear'd,
When lo! in form of minstrel auld
    A stern and stalwart ghaist appear'd.   *ghost*

VI

And frae his harp sic strains did flow,   *such*
    Might rous'd the slumbering Dead to hear,   *as might have*
But O, it was a tale of woe
    As ever met a Briton's ear!

VII

  He sang wi' joy his former day,
   He, weeping, wail'd his latter times:
  But what he said—it was nae play!—
   I winna ventur't in my rhymes.

(will not)

Chorus

  A lassie all alone was making her moan,
   Lamenting our lads beyond the sea:—
  'In the bluidy wars they fa', and our honor's gane an' a',
   And broken-hearted we maun die.'

O, AN YE WERE DEAD, GUIDMAN

(if; husband)

Chorus

  Sing, round about the fire wi' a rung she ran,
  An' round about the fire wi' a rung she ran:—
  'Your horns shall tie you to the staw,
  An' I shall bang your hide, guidman!'

(cudgel)
(stall)

I

  O, AN ye were dead, guidman,
  A green turf on your head, guidman!
  I wad bestow my widowhood
  Upon a rantin Highlandman!

(roistering)

AULD LANG SYNE

II

There's sax eggs in the pan, guidman,   *six*
There's sax eggs in the pan, guidman:
There's ane to you, and twa to me,
And three to our John Highlandman!

III

A sheep-head's in the pot, guidman,
A sheep-head's in the pot, guidman:
The flesh to him, the broo to me,   *broth*
An' the horns become your brow, guidman!

Chorus

Sing, round about the fire wi' a rung she ran,
An' round about the fire wi' a rung she ran:—
'Your horns shall tie you to the staw, .
An' I shall bang your hide, guidman!'

AULD LANG SYNE   *Old long ago*

Chorus

For auld lang syne, my dear,
  For auld lang syne,
We'll tak a cup o' kindness yet   *[Notes]*
  For auld lang syne!

AULD LANG SYNE

I

Should auld acquaintance be forgot,
    And never brought to mind?
Should auld acquaintance be forgot,
    And auld lang syne!

II

<small>pay for</small> And surely ye 'll be your pint-stowp,
    And surely I 'll be mine,
And we 'll tak a cup o' kindness yet
    For auld lang syne!

III

<small>hillsides</small> We twa hae run about the braes,
<small>pulled; wild daisies</small>   And pou'd the gowans fine,
<small>foot</small> But we 've wander'd monie a weary fit
<small>Since</small>   Sin' auld lang syne.

IV

<small>waded; brook</small> We twa hae paidl'd in the burn
<small>noon</small>   Frae morning sun till dine,
<small>broad</small> But seas between us braid hae roar'd
    Sin' auld lang syne.

V

<small>chum</small> And there 's a hand, my trusty fiere,
<small>give me</small>   And gie 's a hand o' thine,
<small>[Notes]</small> And we 'll tak a right guid-willie waught
    For auld lang syne!

AULD LANG SYNE

Sir GEORGE HARVEY

"We twa hae run about the braes,
And pou'd the gowans fine,
But we've wander'd monie a weary fit
Sin' auld lang syne." —*Verse iii.*

Chorus

For auld lang syne, my dear,
   For auld lang syne,
We'll tak a cup o' kindness yet
   For auld lang syne!

LOUIS, WHAT RECK I BY THEE

I

Louis, what reck I by thee,
   Or Geordie on his ocean?
Dyvor beggar louns to me!   *bankrupt. fellows*
   I reign in Jeanie's bosom.

II

Let her crown my love her law,
   And in her breast enthrone me,
Kings and nations—swith awa!   *off away!*
   Reif randies, I disown ye.   *Thieving rascals*

HAD I THE WYTE?   *Was I to blame?*

I

Had I the wyte? had I the wyte?
   Had I the wyte? she bade me!
She watch'd me by the hie-gate side,   *highway*
   And up the loan she shaw'd me;   *approach; showed*

HAD I THE WYTE?

would not — And when I wadna venture in,
rascal — A coward loon she ca'd me!
there to oppose — Had Kirk and State been in the gate,
I'd lighted when she bade me.

II

led me in — Sae craftilie she took me ben
noise — And bade me mak nae clatter:—
surly; husband — 'For our ramgunshoch, glum guidman
beyond — Is o'er ayont the water.'
Whae'er shall say I wanted grace
fondle — When I did kiss and dawte her,
Let him be planted in my place,
Then; transgressor — Syne say I was the fautor!

III

Could I for shame, could I for shame,
have refused — Could I for shame refus'd her?
would not; have been — And wadna manhood been to blame
Had I unkindly used her?
wool-comb — He claw'd her wi' the ripplin-kame,
blue — And blae and bluidy bruis'd her—
such — When sic a husband was frae hame,
would have — What wife but wad excus'd her!

IV

wiped; eyes — I dighted ay her een sae blue,
cursed; scoundrel — An' bann'd the cruel randy,
wot; mouth — And, weel I wat, her willin mou'
Was sweet as sugarcandie.

At gloamin-shot, it was, I wot,   *sunset*
   I lighted—on the Monday,
But I cam thro' the Tyseday's dew   *Tuesday's*
   To wanton Willie's brandy.   [Notes]

COMIN THRO' THE RYE

Chorus

O, Jenny's a' weet, poor body,   *wet; creature*
   Jenny's seldom dry:
She draigl't a' her petticoatie,   *draggled*
   Comin thro' the rye!

I

Comin thro' the rye, poor body,
   Comin thro' the rye,
She draigl't a' her petticoatie,
   Comin thro' the rye!

II

Gin a body meet a body   *Should*
   Comin thro' the rye,
Gin a body kiss a body,
   Need a body cry?

YOUNG JAMIE

III

Gin a body meet a body
   Comin thro' the glen,
Gin a body kiss a body,
   Need the warld ken?

Chorus

O, Jenny's a' weet, poor body,
   Jenny's seldom dry:
She draigl't a' her petticoatie,
   Comin thro' the rye!

YOUNG JAMIE

I

Young Jamie, pride of a' the plain,
Sae gallant and sae gay a swain,
Thro' a' our lasses he did rove,
And reign'd resistless King of Love.

II

But now, wi' sighs and starting tears,
He strays amang the woods and breers; *briars*
Or in the glens and rocky caves
His sad complaining dowie raves:— *mournfully*

III

'I, wha sae late did range and rove,
And chang'd with every moon my love—
I little thought the time was near,
Repentance I should buy sae dear.

IV

'The slighted maids my torments see,
And laugh at a' the pangs I dree ;   *suffer*
While she, my cruel, scornful Fair,
Forbids me e'er to see her mair.'

OUT OVER THE FORTH

I

Out over the Forth, I look to the north—
 But what is the north, and its Highlands to me?
The south nor the east gie ease to my breast,
 The far foreign land or the wide rolling sea!

II

But I look to the west, when I gae to rest,
 That happy my dreams and my slumbers may be ;
For far in the west lives he I loe best,
 The man that is dear to my babie and me.

WANTONNESS FOR EVERMAIR

Wantonness for evermair,
　Wantonness has been my ruin.
Yet for a' my dool and care
It's wantonness for evermair.
　I hae lo'ed the Black, the Brown;
　I hae lo'ed the Fair, the Gowden! *(Golden)*
　　A' the colours in the town—
　I hae won their wanton favour.

CHARLIE HE'S MY DARLING

Chorus

An' Charlie he's my darling,
My darling, my darling,
Charlie he's my darling—
　The Young Chevalier!

I

'Twas on a Monday morning
　Right early in the year,
That Charlie came to our town—
　The Young Chevalier!

CHARLIE HE'S MY DARLING

II

As he was walking up the street
　　The city for to view,
O, there he spied a bonie lass
　　The window looking thro'!

III

Sae light's he jimpèd up the stair,
　　And tirl'd at the pin;
And wha sae ready as hersel'
　　To let the laddie in!

[Notes]

IV

He set his Jenny on his knee,
　　All in his Highland dress;
For brawlie weel he kend the way
　　To please a bonie lass.

finely well

V

It's up yon heathery mountain
　　And down yon scroggy glen,
We daurna gang a-milking
　　For Charlie and his men!

scrubby
daren't go

Chorus

An' Charlie he's my darling,
My darling, my darling,
Charlie he's my darling—
　　The young Chevalier!

THE LASS O' ECCLEFECHAN

I

    'Gat ye me, O, gat ye me,
        Gat ye me wi' naething?
    Rock an' reel, an' spinning wheel,
        A mickle quarter basin: *big; [Notes?]*
    Bye attour, my gutcher has   *Moreover; goodsire*
        A heich house and a laich ane,   *high; low; [Notes]*
    A' forbye my bonie sel,   *All besides*
        The toss o' Ecclefechan!'   *toast*

II

    'O, haud your tongue now, Lucky Lang,   *hold; [Notes]*
        O, haud your tongue and jauner!   *jabber*
    I held the gate till you I met,   *kept to the strait path*
        Syne I began to wander: *Then*
    I tint my whistle and my sang,   *lost*
        I tint my peace and pleasure;
    But your green graff, now Lucky Lang,   *grave*
        Wad airt me to my treasure.'   *direct*

THE COOPER O' CUDDY

Chorus

We'll hide the cooper behint the door,
Behint the door, behint the door,
We'll hide the cooper behint the door
    And cover him under a mawn, O   *basket*

I

The Cooper o' Cuddy came here awa,   *here about*
He ca'd the girrs out o'er us a',   *knocked; hoops*
An' our guidwife has gotten a ca',   *knock*
    That's anger'd the silly guidman, O.

II

He sought them out, he sought them in,
Wi' 'Deil hae her!' an' 'Deil hae him!'
But the body he was sae doited and blin',   *creature; stupid*
    He wist na where he was gaun, O.   *going*

III

They cooper'd at e'en, they cooper'd at morn,
Till our guidman has gotten the scorn:
On ilka brow she's planted a horn,   *each*
    And swears that there they sall stan', O!   *shall*

FOR THE SAKE O' SOMEBODY

Chorus

We 'll hide the cooper behint the door,
Behint the door, behint the door,
We 'll hide the cooper behint the door
And cover him under a mawn, O.

FOR THE SAKE O' SOMEBODY

I

<small>sore</small>   My heart is sair—I dare na tell—
My heart is sair for Somebody:
I could wake a winter night
  For the sake o' Somebody.
    O-hon! for Somebody!
    O-hey! for Somebody!
I could range the world around
  For the sake o' Somebody.

II

Ye Powers that smile on virtuous love,
  O, sweetly smile on Somebody!
<small>each</small> Frae ilka danger keep him free,
  And send me safe my Somebody!
    O-hon! for Somebody!
    O-hey! for Somebody!
I wad do—what wad I not?—
  For the sake o' Somebody!

THE CARDIN O'T

Chorus

The cardin o't, the spinnin o't,
The warpin o't, the winnin o't!
When ilka ell cost me a groat,   *each*
The tailor staw the lynin o't.   *stole*

I

I COFT a stane o' haslock woo,   *bought [Notes]*
  To mak a wab to Johnie o't,   *web*
For Johnie is my only jo—
  I lo'e him best of onie yet!

II

For tho' his locks be lyart gray,   *[Notes]*
  And tho' his brow be beld aboon,   *bald above*
Yet I hae seen him on a day
  The pride of a' the parishen.   *the whole parish*

Chorus

The cardin o't, the spinnin o't,
The warpin o't, the winnin o't!
When ilka ell cost me a groat,
The tailor staw the lynin o't.

THERE'S THREE TRUE GUID FELLOWS

I

There's three true guid fellows,
There's three true guid fellows,
There's three true guid fellows,
    Down ayont yon glen!

<small>beyond</small>

II

It's now the day is dawin,
But or night do fa' in,
Whase cock's best at crawin,
    Willie, thou sall ken!

<small>dawning
before nightfall

shall</small>

SAE FLAXEN WERE HER RINGLETS

I

Sae flaxen were her ringlets,
    Her eyebrows of a darker hue,
Bewitchingly o'er-arching
    Twa laughing een o' bonie blue.

<small>eyes</small>

Her smiling, sae wyling,   coaxing
    Wad make a wretch forget his woe!
What pleasure, what treasure,
    Unto those rosy lips to grow!
Such was my Chloris' bonie face,
    When first that bonie face I saw,
And ay my Chloris' dearest charm—
    She says she lo'es me best of a'!

II

Like harmony her motion,
    Her pretty ankle is a spy
Betraying fair proportion
    Wad make a saint forget the sky!   Would
Sae warming, sae charming,
    Her faultless form and gracefu' air,
Ilk feature—auld Nature   Each
    Declar'd that she could dae nae mair!   do no more
Hers are the willing chains o' love
    By conquering beauty's sovereign law,
And ay my Chloris' dearest charm—
    She says she lo'es me best of a'.

III

Let others love the city,
    And gaudy show at sunny noon!
Gie me the lonely valley,
    The dewy eve, and rising moon,

Fair beaming, and streaming
   Her silver light the boughs amang,
While falling, recalling,
   The amorous thrush concludes his sang !
There, dearest Chloris, wilt thou rove
   By wimpling burn and leafy shaw, *(winding brook; wood)*
And hear my vows o' truth and love,
   And say thou lo'es me best of a' ?

THE LASS THAT MADE THE BED

I

When Januar' wind was blawin cauld,
   As to the North I took my way,
The mirksome night did me enfauld, *(darksome)*
   I knew na where to lodge till day.
By my guid luck a maid I met
   Just in the middle o' my care,
And kindly she did me invite
   To walk into a chamber fair.

II

I bow'd fu' low unto this maid,
   And thank'd her for her courtesie ;
I bow'd fu' low unto this maid,
   An' bade her mak a bed to me.

She made the bed baith large and wide,
    Wi' twa white hands she spread it down,
She put the cup to her rosy lips,
    And drank :—' Young man, now sleep ye soun'.'

III

She snatch'd the candle in her hand,
    And frae my chamber went wi' speed,
But I call'd her quickly back again
    To lay some mair below my head :   *more*
A cod she laid below my head,   *pillow*
    And servèd me with due respeck,
And, to salute her wi' a kiss,
    I put my arms about her neck.

IV

'Haud aff your hands, young man,' she said,   *Hold*
    ' And dinna sae uncivil be ;   *do not*
Gif ye hae onie luve for me,
    O, wrang na my virginitie !'
Her hair was like the links o' gowd,   *gold*
    Her teeth were like the ivorie,
Her cheeks like lilies dipt in wine,
    The lass that made the bed to me !

V

Her bosom was the driven snaw,
    Twa drifted heaps sae fair to see ;
Her limbs the polish'd marble stane,
    The lass that made the bed to me !
I kiss'd her o'er and o'er again,
    And ay she wist na what to say.
I laid her 'tween me an' the wa'—
    The lassie thocht na lang till day.

deemed it not long

VI

Upon the morrow, when we raise,
    I thank'd her for her courtesie,
But ay she blush'd, and ay she sigh'd,
    And said :—'Alas, ye 've ruin'd me !'
I clasp'd her waist, and kiss'd her syne,
    While the tear stood twinklin in her e'e.
I said :—' My lassie, dinna cry,
    For ye ay shall mak the bed to me.'

rose

then
eye

VII

She took her mither's holland sheets,
    An' made them a' in sarks to me.
Blythe and merry may she be,
    The lass that made the bed to me !
The bonie lass made the bed to me,
    The braw lass made the bed to me !
I 'll ne'er forget till the day I die,
    The lass that made the bed to me.

shirts

handsome

SAE FAR AWA

I

O, sad and heavy should I part
    But for her sake sae far awa,
Unknowing what my way may thwart—
    My native land sae far awa.

II

Thou that of a' things Maker art,
    That formed this Fair sae far awa,
Gie body strength, then I'll ne'er start   *Give*
    At this my way sae far awa!

III

How true is love to pure desert!
    So mine in her sae far awa,
And nocht can heal my bosom's smart,
    While, O, she is sae far awa!

IV

Nane other love, nane other dart
    I feel, but hers sae far awa;
But fairer never touched a heart,
    Than hers, the Fair sae far awa.

THE REEL O' STUMPIE

I

<small>wrap; roll</small>
<small>little feet</small>

Wap and rowe, wap and rowe,
 Wap and rowe the feetie o't,
I thought I was a maiden fair,

<small>its little cry</small>
 Till I heard the greetie o't!

II

My daddie was a fiddler fine,

<small>mother;</small>
<small>[Notes]</small>
 My minnie she made mantie, O,

<small>quean (i.e. lass)</small>
And I myself a thumpin quine,
 And danc'd the Reel o' Stumpie, O.

<small>[Notes]</small> ## I'LL AY CA' IN BY YON TOWN

Chorus

<small>call</small>
I'll ay ca' in by yon town
 And by yon garden green again!
I'll ay ca' in by yon town,
 And see my bonie Jean again.

I

There's nane shall ken, there's nane can guess
<small>same way</small>
 What brings me back the gate again,
But she, my fairest faithfu' lass,
<small>by stealth</small>
 And stow'nlins we sall meet again.

II

She'll wander by the aiken tree,   *oaken*
    When trystin time draws near again;   *meeting*
And when her lovely form I see,
    O haith! she's doubly dear again.   *faith*

Chorus

I'll ay ca' in by yon town
    And by yon garden green again!
I'll ay ca' in by yon town,
    And see my bonie Jean again.

O, WAT YE WHA'S IN YON TOWN   *wot; [Notes]*

Chorus

O, wat ye wha's in yon town
    Ye see the e'enin sun upon?   *evening*
The dearest maid's in yon town
    That e'enin sun is shining on!

I

Now haply down yon gay green shaw   *wood*
    She wanders by yon spreading tree.
How blest ye flowers that round her blaw!
    Ye catch the glances o' her e'e.

II

How blest ye birds that round her sing,
    And welcome in the blooming year!
And doubly welcome be the Spring,
    The season to my Jeanie dear!

III

glances   The sun blinks blythe in yon town,
heights   Among the broomy braes sae green;
But my delight in yon town,
    And dearest pleasure, is my Jean.

IV

Without my Love, not a' the charms
    O' Paradise could yield me joy;
But gie me Jeanie in my arms,
    And welcome Lapland's dreary sky!

V

My cave wad be a lover's bower,
    Tho' raging Winter rent the air,
And she a lovely little flower,
tend   That I wad tent and shelter there.

VI

O, sweet is she in yon town
    The sinkin sun's gane down upon!
A fairer than's in yon town
    His setting beam ne'er shone upon.

VII

If angry Fate be sworn my foe,
    And suff'ring I am doom'd to bear,
I'd careless quit aught else below,
    But spare, O, spare me Jeanie dear!

VIII

For, while life's dearest blood is warm,
    Ae thought frae her shall ne'er depart,   One
And she, as fairest is her form,
    She has the truest, kindest heart.

Chorus

O, wat ye wha's in yon town
    Ye see the e'enin sun upon?
The dearest maid's in yon town
    That e'enin sun is shining on.

WHEREFORE SIGHING ART THOU, PHILLIS?

I

WHEREFORE sighing art thou, Phillis?
    Has thy prime unheeded past?
Hast thou found that beauty's lilies
    Were not made for ay to last?

II

Know, thy form was once a treasure—
Then it was thy hour of scorn!
Since thou then denied the pleasure,
  Now 'tis fit that thou should'st mourn.

O MAY, THY MORN

I

O May, thy morn was ne'er sae sweet
  As the mirk night o' December!
For sparkling was the rosy wine,
  And private was the chamber,
And dear was she I dare na name,
  But I will ay remember.

II

And here's to them that, like oursel,
  Can push about the jorum!
And here's to them that wish us weel—
  May a' that's guid watch o'er 'em!
And here's to them we dare na tell,
  The dearest o' the quorum!

[sidenote: dark]

AS I CAME O'ER THE CAIRNEY MOUNT

Chorus

O, my bonie Highland lad!
   My winsome, weel-faur'd Highland laddie! *well-favoured*
Wha wad mind the wind and rain
   Sae weel row'd in his tartan plaidie! *wrapped*

I

As I came o'er the Cairney mount
   And down among the blooming heather,
Kindly stood the milking-shiel *-shed*
   To shelter frae the stormy weather.

II

Now Phœbus blinkit on the bent, *shone; meadow*
   And o'er the knowes the lambs were bleating; *knolls*
But he wan my heart's consent
   To be his ain at the neist meeting. *next*

Chorus

O, my bonie Highland lad!
   My winsome, weel-faur'd Highland laddie!
Wha wad mind the wind and rain
   Sae weel row'd in his tartan plaidie!

HIGHLAND LADDIE

I

The bonniest lad that e'er I saw—
    Bonie laddie, Highland laddie!
fine   Wore a plaid and was fu' braw—
    Bonie Highland laddie!
On his head a bonnet blue—
    Bonie laddie, Highland laddie!
His royal heart was firm and true—
    Bonie Highland laddie!

II

'Trumpets sound and cannons roar,
    Bonie lassie, Lawland lassie!—
Lowland   And a' the hills wi' echoes roar,
    Bonie Lawland lassie!
Glory, Honour, now invite—
    Bonie lassie, Lawland lassie!—
For freedom and my King to fight,
    Bonie Lawland lassie!'

III

'The sun a backward course shall take,
    Bonie laddie, Highland laddie!
Ere aught thy manly courage shake,
    Bonie Highland laddie!

Go, for yoursel' procure renown,
    Bonie laddie, Highland laddie,
And for your lawful King his crown,
    Bonie Highland laddie!'

WILT THOU BE MY DEARIE?

I

Wilt thou be my dearie?
When Sorrow wrings thy gentle heart,
    O, wilt thou let me cheer thee?
By the treasure of my soul—
    That's the love I bear thee—
I swear and vow that only thou
    Shall ever be my dearie!
Only thou, I swear and vow,
    Shall ever be my dearie!

II

Lassie, say thou lo'es me,
Or, if thou wilt na be my ain,   *own*
    Say na thou 'lt refuse me!
If it winna, canna be,   *will not*
    Thou for thine may choose me,
Let me, lassie, quickly die,
    Trusting that thou lo'es me!
Lassie, let me quickly die,
    Trusting that thou lo'es me!

LOVELY POLLY STEWART

Chorus

O lovely Polly Stewart,
O charming Polly Stewart,
There's ne'er a flower that blooms in May,
That's half so fair as thou art!

I

THE flower it blaws, it fades, it fa's,
And art can ne'er renew it;
But Worth and Truth eternal youth
Will gie to Polly Stewart!

II

<small>enfold</small> May he whase arms shall fauld thy charms
<small>loyal</small> Possess a leal and true heart!
To him be given to ken the heaven
He grasps in Polly Stewart!

Chorus

O lovely Polly Stewart,
O charming Polly Stewart,
There's ne'er a flower that blooms in May,
That's half so fair as thou art!

THE HIGHLAND BALOU

I

Hee balou, my sweet wee Donald,
Picture o' the great Clanronald!
Brawlie kens our wanton Chief   *Finely*
Wha gat my young Highland thief.

II

Leeze me on thy bonie craigie!   *Blessings; throat*
An thou live, thou'll steal a naigie,   *horse*
Travel the country thro' and thro',
And bring hame a Carlisle cow!

III

Thro' the Lawlands, o'er the Border,
Weel, my babie, may thou furder,   *advance*
Herry the louns o' the laigh Countrie,   *rogues; lowlands*
Syne to the Highlands hame to me!   *Then*

BANNOCKS O' BEAR MEAL

soft cakes; barley

Chorus

Bannocks o' bear meal,
Bannocks o' barley,
Here's to the Highlandman's
Bannocks o' barley!

WAE IS MY HEART

I

<small>brangle</small>

WHA in a brulyie
 Will first cry 'a parley'?
Never the lads
 Wi' the bannocks o' barley!

II

<small>woful</small>

Wha, in his wae days,
 Were loyal to Charlie?
Wha but the lads
 Wi' the bannocks o' barley!

Chorus

Bannocks o' bear meal,
 Bannocks o' barley,
Here's to the Highlandman's
 Bannocks o' barley!

WAE IS MY HEART

I

WAE is my heart, and the tear's in my e'e;
Lang, lang joy's been a stranger to me:
Forsaken and friendless my burden I bear,
And the sweet voice o' pity ne'er sounds in my ear.

II

Love, thou hast pleasures—and deep hae I lov'd!
Love thou has sorrows—and sair hae I prov'd! *sorely*
But this bruisèd heart that now bleeds in my breast,
I can feel by its throbbings, will soon be at rest.

III

O, if I were where happy I hae been,
Down by yon stream and yon bonie castle green!
For there he is wand'ring and musing on me,
Wha wad soon dry the tear frae his Phillis' e'e!

HERE'S HIS HEALTH IN WATER

I

ALTHO' my back be at the wa', *wall*
   And tho' he be the fautor, *transgressor*
Altho' my back be at the wa',
   Yet here's his health in water!
O, wae gae by his wanton sides, *woe go*
   Sae brawly's he could flatter! *finely as*
Till for his sake I'm slighted sair
   And dree the kintra clatter! *endure the talk of the countryside*
But, tho' my back be at the wa',
   Yet here's his health in water!

THE WINTER OF LIFE

I

But lately seen in gladsome green,
   The woods rejoiced the day;
Thro' gentle showers the laughing flowers
   In double pride were gay;
But now our joys are fled
   On winter blasts awa,
Yet maiden May in rich array
   Again shall bring them a'.

II

poll; thaw

eld; without bush and shelter

But my white pow—nae kindly thowe
   Shall melt the snaws of Age!
My trunk of eild, but buss and bield,
   Sinks in Time's wintry rage.
O, Age has weary days
   And nights o' sleepless pain!
Thou golden time o' youthfu' prime,
   Why comes thou not again?

THE TAILOR

I

The tailor he cam here to sew,
And weel he kend the way to woo,
For ay he pree'd the lassie's mou', *tasted*
  As he gaed but and ben, O. *went from kitchen to parlour*
    For weel he kend the way, O,
    The way, O, the way, O!
    For weel he kend the way, O,
    The lassie's heart to win, O!

II

The tailor rase and shook his duds, *rose; clothes*
The flaes they flew awa in cluds! *fleas; clouds*
And them that stay'd gat fearfu' thuds—
  The Tailor prov'd a man, O!
    For now it was the gloamin, *dusk*
    The gloamin, the gloamin!
    For now it was the gloamin,
    When a' the rest are gaun, O! *going*

THERE GROWS A BONIE BRIER-BUSH

I

<small>kitchen-garden</small>   THERE grows a bonie brier-bush in our kail-yard,
There grows a bonie brier-bush in our kail-yard;
And below the bonie brier-bush there's a lassie and a lad,
And they're busy, busy courting in our kail-yard.

II

<small>bush</small>   We'll court nae mair below the buss in our kail-yard,
We'll court nae mair below the buss in our kail-yard:
<small>not</small>   We'll awa to Athole's green, and there we'll no be seen,
Where the trees and the branches will be our safeguard.

III

<small>hall</small>   Will ye go to the dancin in Carlyle's ha'?
Will ye go to the dancin in Carlyle's ha',
<small>beat</small>   Where Sandy and Nancy I'm sure will ding them a'?
<small>will not go</small>   I winna gang to the dance in Carlyle-ha'!

IV

What will I do for a lad when Sandie gangs awa!
What will I do for a lad when Sandie gangs awa!
<small>earn; hire</small>   I will awa to Edinburgh, and win a pennie fee,
<small>if</small>   And see an onie lad will fancy me.

V

He's comin frae the north that's to marry me,
He's comin frae the north that's to marry me,
A feather in his bonnet and a ribbon at his knee—
He's a bonie, bonie laddie, an yon be he!   *that one*

HERE'S TO THY HEALTH

I

Here's to thy health, my bonie lass!
  Guid night and joy be wi' thee!
I'll come nae mair to thy bower-door
  To tell thee that I lo'e thee.
O, dinna think, my pretty pink,
  But I can live without thee: *But that*
I vow and swear I dinna care   *do not*
  How lang ye look about ye!

II

Thou 'rt ay sae free informing me
  Thou hast nae mind to marry,   *desire*
I'll be as free informing thee
  Nae time hae I to tarry.
I ken thy freens try ilka means   *friends;
                                               every*
  Frae wedlock to delay thee
(Depending on some higher chance),
  But fortune may betray thee.

III

I ken they scorn my low estate,
    But that does never grieve me,
For I'm as free as any he—
    Sma' siller will relieve me! *[a little money]*
I'll count my health my greatest wealth
    Sae lang as I'll enjoy it.
I'll fear nae scant, I'll bode nae want
    As lang's I get employment.

IV

But far off fowls hae feathers fair,
    And, ay until ye try them,
Tho' they seem fair, still have a care—
    They may prove as bad as I am!
But at twel at night, when the moon shines bright, *[twelve]*
    My dear, I'll come and see thee,
For the man that loves his mistress weel,
    Nae travel makes him weary.

IT WAS A' FOR OUR RIGHTFU' KING

I

It was a' for our rightfu' king
    We left fair Scotland's strand;
It was a' for our rightfu' king,
    We e'er saw Irish land,
        My dear—
We e'er saw Irish land.

II

Now a' is done that men can do,
 And a' is done in vain,
My Love and Native Land fareweel,
 For I maun cross the main,   *must*
  My dear—
 For I maun cross the main.

III

He turn'd him right and round about
 Upon the Irish shore,
And gae his bridle reins a shake,   *gave*
 With adieu for evermore,
  My dear—
 And adieu for evermore!

IV

The soger frae the wars returns,
 The sailor frae the main,
But I hae parted frae my love
 Never to meet again,
  My dear—
 Never to meet again.

V

When day is gane, and night is come,
 And a' folk bound to sleep,
I think on him that's far awa
 The lee-lang night, and weep,   *live-long*
  My dear—
 The lee-lang night and weep.

THE HIGHLAND WIDOW'S LAMENT

I

O, I AM come to the low countrie—
Ochon, ochon, ochrie!—
Without a penny in my purse
To buy a meal to me.

II

<small>not so</small> It was na sae in the Highland hills—
Ochon, ochon, ochrie!—
Nae woman in the country wide
Sae happy was as me.

III

<small>kine</small> For then I had a score o' kye—
Ochon, ochon, ochrie!—
Feeding on yon hill sae high
And giving milk to me.

IV

<small>ewes</small> And there I had three score o' yowes—
Ochon, ochon, ochrie!—
<small>knolls</small> Skipping on yon bonie knowes
<small>wool</small> And casting woo' to me.

V

I was the happiest of a' the clan—
<small>sorely</small> Sair, sair may I repine!—
<small>pick of the clan</small> For Donald was the brawest man,
And Donald he was mine.

VI

Till Charlie Stewart cam at last
   Sae far to set us free:
My Donald's arm was wanted then
   For Scotland and for me.

VII

Their waefu' fate what need I tell?   *woful*
   Right to the wrang did yield:
My Donald and his country fell
   Upon Culloden field.

VIII

Ochon! O Donald, O!
   Ochon, ochon, ochrie!
Nae woman in the warld wide
   Sae wretched now as me!

THOU GLOOMY DECEMBER

I

Ance mair I hail thee, thou gloomy December!   *Once more*
   Ance mair I hail thee wi' sorrow and care!
Sad was the parting thou makes me remember:
   Parting wi' Nancy, O, ne'er to meet mair!

II

Fond lovers' parting is sweet, painful pleasure,
    Hope beaming mild on the soft parting hour;
But the dire feeling, O farewell for ever!
    Anguish unmingled and agony pure!

III

Wild as the winter now tearing the forest,
    Till the last leaf o' the summer is flown—
Such is the tempest has shaken my bosom,
    Till my last hope and last comfort is gone!

IV

Still as I hail thee, thou gloomy December,
    Still shall I hail thee wi' sorrow and care;
For sad was the parting thou makes me remember:
    Parting wi' Nancy, O, ne'er to meet mair!

MY PEGGY'S FACE, MY PEGGY'S FORM

I

My Peggy's face, my Peggy's form
The frost of hermit Age might warm.
My Peggy's worth, my Peggy's mind
Might charm the first of human kind.

II

I love my Peggy's angel air,
Her face so truly heavenly fair,
Her native grace so void of art;
But I adore my Peggy's heart.

III

The lily's hue, the rose's dye,
The kindling lustre of an eye—
Who but owns their magic sway?
Who but knows they all decay?

IV

The tender thrill, the pitying tear,
The generous purpose nobly dear,
The gentle look that rage disarms—
These are all immortal charms.

O, STEER HER UP, AN' HAUD HER GAUN

rouse; keep her going

I

O, STEER her up, an' haud her gaun—
　Her mither's at the mill, jo,
An' gin she winna tak a man, *if; will not*
　E'en let her tak her will, jo.

WEE WILLIE GRAY

<small>threaten</small>　First shore her wi' a gentle kiss,
<small>call for</small>　　And ca' anither gill, jo,
<small>should she</small>　An' gin she tak the thing amiss,
<small>scold</small>　　E'en let her flyte her fill, jo.

II

<small>not bashful</small>　O, steer her up, an' be na blate,
　　An' gin she tak it ill, jo,
<small>to</small>　Then leave the lassie till her fate,
<small>waste</small>　　And time nae langer spill, jo!
<small>one rebuff</small>　Ne'er break your heart for ae rebute,
　　But think upon it still, jo,
　That gin the lassie winna do 't,
<small>find</small>　　Ye 'll fin' anither will, jo.

WEE WILLIE GRAY

I

Wee Willie Gray an' his leather wallet,
Peel a willow-wand to be him boots and jacket!
The rose upon the brier will be him trouse and doublet—
The rose upon the brier will be him trouse and doublet!

II

Wee Willie Gray and his leather wallet,
<small>shirt; cravat</small> Twice a lily-flower will be him sark and gravat!
<small>fly</small>　Feathers of a flie wad feather up his bonnet—
Feathers of a flie wad feather up his bonnet!

WE'RE A' NODDIN

Chorus

We're a' noddin,
Nid nid noddin,
We're a' noddin
At our house at hame!

I

'Guid e'en to you, kimmer,   *gossip*
   And how do ye do?'
'Hiccup!' quo' kimmer,
   'The better that I'm fou!'   *drunk*

II

Kate sits i' the neuk,   *corner*
   Suppin hen-broo.   *chicken-broth*
Deil tak Kate
   An she be na noddin too!

III

'How's a' wi' you, kimmer?   *How are all*
   And how do you fare?'
'A pint o' the best o't,
   And twa pints mair!'

WE'RE A' NODDIN

IV

'How's a' wi" you, kimmer?
And how do ye thrive?
How monie bairns hae ye?'
Quo' kimmer, ' I hae five.'

V

Are they a' Johnie's?'
'Eh! atweel na:
Twa o' them were gotten
When Johnie was awa!'

in truth

VI

Cats like milk,
And dogs like broo;
Lads like lasses weel,
And lasses lads too.

broth

Chorus

We're a' noddin,
Nid nid noddin,
We're a' noddin
At our house at hame!

O, AY MY WIFE SHE DANG ME   beat

Chorus

O, ay my wife she dang me,
An' aft my wife she bang'd me !
If ye gie a woman a' her will,
Guid faith ! she'll soon o'er-gang ye.   go beyond control

I

On peace an' rest my mind was bent,
   And, fool I was ! I married ;
But never honest man's intent
   Sae cursedly miscarried.

II

Some sairie comfort at the last,   sorry
   When a' thir days are done, man :   these
My ' pains o' hell ' on earth is past,
   I'm sure o' bliss aboon, man.   above

Chorus

O, ay my wife she dang me,
An' aft my wife she bang'd me !
If ye gie a woman a' her will,
Guid faith ! she'll soon o'ergang ye.

SCROGGAM

I

<small>dwelt</small> There was a wife wonn'd in Cockpen,
      Scroggam!
She brew'd guid ale for gentlemen:
Sing Auld Cowl, lay you down by me—
Scroggam, my dearie, ruffum!

II

<small>daughter</small> The guidwife's dochter fell in a fever,
      Scroggam!
The priest o' the parish fell in anither:
Sing Auld Cowl, lay you down by me—
Scroggam, my dearie, ruffum!

III

<small>together</small> They laid the twa i' the bed thegither,
      Scroggam!
<small>one ; other</small> That the heat o' the tane might cool the tither:
Sing Auld Cowl, lay you down by me—
Scroggam, my dearie, ruffum!

O, GUID ALE COMES

Chorus

O, guid ale comes, and guid ale goes,
Guid ale gars me sell my hose,   makes
Sell my hose, and pawn my shoon—
Guid ale keeps my heart aboon!   my heart up

I

I HAD sax owsen in a pleugh,   six oxen
And they drew a' weel eneugh:
I sell'd them a' just ane by ane—
Guid ale keeps the heart aboon!

II

Guid ale hauds me bare and busy,   keeps
Gars me moop wi' the servant hizzie,   meddle; girl
Stand i' the stool when I hae dune—   [Notes]
Guid ale keeps the heart aboon!

Chorus

O, guid ale comes, and guid ale goes,
Guid ale gars me sell my hose,
Sell my hose, and pawn my shoon—
Guid ale keeps my heart aboon!

ROBIN SHURE IN HAIRST

Chorus

Robin shure in hairst,
    I shure wi' him :
Fient a heuk had I,
    Yet I stack by him.

I

I GAED up to Dunse
    To warp a wab o' plaiden
At his daddie's yett
    Wha met me but Robin !

II

Was na Robin bauld,
    Tho' I was a cottar ?
Play'd me sic a trick,
    An' me the Eller's dochter !

III

Robin promis'd me
    A' my winter vittle :
Fient haet he had but three
    Guse feathers and a whittle !

Margin glosses: reaped; harvest — Fiend: sickle — stuck — went — web of coarse woollen — gate — Wasn't; bold — such — Elder's daughter — food — Fiend have it (i.e. Nothing) — Goose-quills; knife

Chorus

Robin shure in hairst,
  I shure wi' him :
Fient a heuk had I,
  Yet I stack by him.

DOES HAUGHTY GAUL INVASION THREAT?

I

Does haughty Gaul invasion threat?
  Then let the loons beware, Sir!   *rascals*
There's wooden walls upon our seas
  And volunteers on shore, Sir!
The Nith shall run to Corsincon,
  And Criffel sink in Solway,
Ere we permit a foreign foe
  On British ground to rally!

II

O, let us not, like snarling tykes,   *dogs*
  In wrangling be divided,
Till, slap! come in an unco loun,   *foreign*
  And wi' a rung decide it!   *cudgel*

> Be Britain still to Britain true,
>   Amang oursels united !
> For never but by British hands
>   Maun British wrangs be righted !

must;
wrongs

III

> The kettle o' the Kirk and State,
>   Perhaps a clout may fail in't ;
> But Deil a foreign tinkler loon
>   Shall ever ca' a nail in 't !
> Our fathers' blude the kettle bought,
>   And wha wad dare to spoil it,
> By Heav'ns ! the sacrilegious dog
>   Shall fuel be to boil it !

patch
tinker
drive

IV

> The wretch that would a tyrant own,
>   And the wretch, his true-sworn brother,
> Who would set the mob above the throne,
>   May they be damn'd together !
> Who will not sing *God save the King*
>   Shall hang as high 's the steeple ;
> But while we sing *God save the King,*
>   We'll ne'er forget the People.

O, ONCE I LOV'D A BONIE LASS

I

O, once I lov'd a bonie lass,
    Ay, and I love her still!
And whilst that virtue warms my breast,
    I'll love my handsome Nell.

II

As bonie lasses I hae seen,
    And monie full as braw,   fine
But for a modest gracefu' mien
    The like I never saw.

III

A bonie lass, I will confess,
    Is pleasant to the e'e;
But without some better qualities
    She's no a lass for me.

IV

But Nelly's looks are blythe and sweet,
    And, what is best of a',
Her reputation is complete
    And fair without a flaw.

V

She dresses ay sae clean and neat,
    Both decent and genteel;
And then there's something in her gait
    Gars onie dress look weel.

<small>make</small>

VI

A gaudy dress and gentle air
    May slightly touch the heart;
But it's innocence and modesty
    That polishes the dart.

VII

'Tis this in Nelly pleases me,
    'Tis this enchants my soul;
For absolutely in my breast
    She reigns without controul.

MY LORD A-HUNTING

Chorus

My lady's gown, there's gairs upon 't,
And gowden flowers sae rare upon 't;
But Jenny's jimps and jirkinet,
My lord thinks meikle mair upon 't!

<small>slashes
golden
stays; bodice
much more</small>

MY LORD A-HUNTING

I

My lord a-hunting he is gane,
But hounds or hawks wi' him are nane;
By Colin's cottage lies his game,
If Colin's Jenny be at hame.

II

My lady's white, my lady's red,
And kith and kin o' Cassillis' blude;
But her ten-pund lands o' tocher guid   dowry
Were a' the charms his lordship lo'ed.

III

Out o'er yon muir, out o'er yon moss,   bog
Whare gor-cocks thro' the heather pass,   moor-
There wons auld Colin's bonie lass,   dwells
A lily in a wilderness.

IV

Sae sweetly move her genty limbs,
Like music notes o' lovers' hymns!
The diamond-dew in her een sae blue,   eyes
Where laughing love sae wanton swims!

V

My lady's dink, my lady's drest,   trim
The flower and fancy o' the west;
But the lassie that a man lo'es best,
O, that's the lass to mak him blest!

Chorus

My lady's gown, there's gairs upon 't,
And gowden flowers sae rare upon 't;
But Jenny's jimps and jirkinet,
My lord thinks meikle mair upon 't!

SWEETEST MAY

I

Sweetest May, let Love inspire thee!
Take a heart which he designs thee:
As thy constant slave regard it,
For its faith and truth reward it.

II

Proof o' shot to birth or money,
Not the wealthy but the bonie,
Not the high-born but noble-minded,
In love's silken band can bind it.

MEG O' THE MILL

I

got
horse; rat

O, ken ye what Meg o' the Mill has gotten?
An' ken ye what Meg o' the Mill has gotten?
A braw new naig wi' the tail o' a rottan,
And that's what Meg o' the Mill has gotten!

II

O, ken ye what Meg o' the Mill lo'es dearly?
An' ken ye what Meg o' the Mill lo'es dearly?
A dram o' guid strunt in a morning early,   *liquor*
And that's what Meg o' the Mill loes dearly!

III

O, ken ye how Meg o' the Mill was married?
An' ken ye how Meg o' the Mill was married?
The priest he was oxter'd, the clark he was carried, *held up under the arms*
And that's how Meg o' the Mill was married!

IV

O, ken ye how Meg o' the Mill was bedded?   [Notes]
An' ken ye how Meg o' the Mill was bedded?
The groom gat sae fu' he fell awald beside it,   *bridegroom; drunk; backways*
And that's how Meg o' the Mill was bedded!

JOCKIE'S TA'EN THE PARTING KISS

I

Jockie's ta'en the parting kiss,
   O'er the mountains he is gane,
And with him is a' my bliss—
   Nought but griefs with me remain.

II

Spare my luve, ye winds that blaw,
　　Plashy sleets and beating rain!
Spare my luve, thou feathery snaw,
　　Drifting o'er the frozen plain!

III

When the shades of evening creep
　　O'er the day's fair gladsome e'e,
Sound and safely may he sleep,
　　Sweetly blythe his waukening be!

(gloss: awakening)

IV

He will think on her he loves,
　　Fondly he'll repeat her name;
For where'er he distant roves,
　　Jockie's heart is still at hame.

O, LAY THY LOOF IN MINE, LASS

(gloss: oam)

Chorus

O, lay thy loof in mine, lass,
　　In mine, lass, in mine, lass,
And swear on thy white hand, lass,
　　That thou wilt be my ain!

(gloss: own)

CAULD IS THE E'ENIN BLAST

I

A SLAVE to Love's unbounded sway,
He aft has wrought me meikle wae;   [Notes]
But now he is my deadly fae,   foe
   Unless thou be my ain.

II

There's monie a lass has broke my rest,
That for a blink I hae lo'ed best;
But thou art queen within my breast,
   For ever to remain.

Chorus

O, lay thy loof in mine, lass,
In mine, lass, in mine, lass,
And swear on thy white hand, lass,
   That thou wilt be my ain!

CAULD IS THE E'ENIN BLAST

I

CAULD is the e'enin blast
   O' Boreas o'er the pool
An' dawin, it is dreary,   dawning
   When birks are bare at Yule.   birches; Christmas-tide

II

dark

O, cauld blaws the e'enin blast,
When bitter bites the frost,
And in the mirk and dreary drift
The hills and glens are lost!

III

Ne'er sae murky blew the night
That drifted o'er the hill,
But bonie Peg-a-Ramsay
Gat grist to her mill.

THERE WAS A BONIE LASS

I

THERE was a bonie lass, and a bonie, bonie lass,
And she loed her bonie laddie dear,
Till War's loud alarms tore her laddie frae her arms
Wi' monie a sigh and a tear.

II

Over sea, over shore, where the cannons loudly roar,
He still was a stranger to fear,
nought And nocht could him quail, or his bosom assail,
But the bonie lass he loed sae dear.

THERE'S NEWS, LASSES, NEWS

Chorus

The wean wants a cradle, — child
   And the cradle wants a cod, — pillow
An' I'll no gang to my bed — not go
   Until I get a nod.

I

THERE's news, lasses, news,
   Guid news I've to tell!
There's a boatfu' o' lads
   Come to our town to sell!

II

'Father,' quo' she, 'Mither,' quo' she,
   'Do what you can:
I'll no gang to my bed
   Until I get a man!'

III

I hae as guid a craft rig — croft-ridge
   As made o' yird and stane; — earth
And waly fa' the ley-crap — woe befall; pasture-
   For I maun till'd again. — must plough it

Chorus

The wean wants a cradle,
   And the cradle wants a cod,
An' I'll no gang to my bed
   Until I get a nod.

O, THAT I HAD NE'ER BEEN MARRIED

Chorus

<small>meal and water</small>

Ance crowdie, twice crowdie,
   Three times crowdie in a day!
Gin ye crowdie onie mair,
   Ye 'll crowdie a' my meal away.

I

O, THAT I had ne'er been married,
   I wad never had nae care!
<small>children</small>
Now I 've gotten wife an' bairns,
   An' they cry 'Crowdie' evermair.

II

<small>scare</small>
Waefu' Want and Hunger fley me,
<small>the end of the porch</small>
   Glowrin by the hallan en';
<small>Hard; fight</small>
Sair I fecht them at the door,
<small>frightened in</small>
   But ay I 'm eerie they come ben.

Chorus

Ance crowdie, twice crowdie,
   Three times crowdie in a day!
Gin ye crowdie onie mair,
   Ye 'll crowdie a' my meal away.

MALLY'S MEEK, MALLY'S SWEET   Mollie =

Chorus

Mally's meek, Mally's sweet,
Mally's modest and discreet,
Mally's rare, Mally's fair,
Mally's ev'ry way complete.

I

As I was walking up the street,
A barefit maid I chanc'd to meet;
But O, the road was very hard
For that fair maiden's tender feet!

II

It were mair meet that those fine feet
   Were weel laced up in silken shoon!
An' 'twere more fit that she should sit
   Within yon chariot gilt aboon!   *above*

Chorus

Mally's meek, Mally's sweet,
Mally's modest and discreet,
Mally's rare, Mally's fair,
Mally's ev'ry way complete.

WANDERING WILLIE

I

HERE awa, there awa, wandering Willie,
    Here awa, there awa, haud awa hame!
Come to my bosom, my ae only dearie,
    And tell me thou bring'st me my Willie the same.

hold — haud
one — ae

II

Loud tho' the Winter blew cauld at our parting,
    'Twas na the blast brought the tear in my e'e:
Welcome now Simmer, and welcome my Willie,
    The Simmer to Nature, my Willie to me!

Summer — Simmer

III

Rest, ye wild storms in the cave o' your slumbers—
    How your wild howling a lover alarms!
Wauken, ye breezes, row gently, ye billows,
    And waft my dear laddie ance mair to my arms.

Awake; roll — Wauken, row

IV

But O, if he's faithless, and minds na his Nannie,
    Flow still between us, thou wide-roaring main!
May I never see it, may I never trow it,
    But, dying, believe that my Willie's my ain!

remembers not — minds na

BRAW LADS O' GALLA WATER   _{Handsome}

I

Braw, braw lads on Yarrow braes,   _{heights}
  They rove amang the blooming heather;
But Yarrow braes nor Ettrick shaws   _{woods}
  Can match the lads o' Galla Water.

II

But there is ane, a secret ane,
  Aboon them a' I loe him better;   _{Above}
And I 'll be his, and he 'll be mine,
  The bonie lad o' Galla Water.

III

Altho' his daddie was nae laird,
  And tho' I hae nae meikle tocher,   _{much dowry}
Yet, rich in kindest, truest love,
  We 'll tent our flocks by Galla Water.   _{watch}

IV

It ne'er was wealth, it ne'er was wealth,
  That coft contentment, peace, and pleasure: _{bought}
The bands and bliss o' mutual love,
  O, that 's the chiefest warld's treasure!

AULD ROB MORRIS

I

<small>dwells</small>   There's Auld Rob Morris that wons in yon glen,
<small>pick</small>   He's the king o' guid fellows and wale of auld men:
<small>gold</small>   He has gowd in his coffers, he has owsen and kine,
<small>one; pet</small>   And ae bonie lassie, his dautie and mine.

II

She's fresh as the morning the fairest in May,
She's sweet as the ev'ning amang the new hay,
As blythe and as artless as the lambs on the lea,
And dear to my heart as the light to my e'e.

III

But O, she's an heiress, auld Robin's a laird,
<small>garden</small>   And my daddie has nocht but a cot-house and yard!
<small>mustn't</small>   A wooer like me maunna hope to come speed:
<small>death</small>   The wounds I must hide that will soon be my dead.

IV

<small>brings me no delight</small>   The day comes to me, but delight brings me nane;
The night comes to me, but my rest it is gane;
<small>alone; ghost</small>   I wander my lane like a night-troubled ghaist,
And I sigh as my heart it wad burst in my breast.

V

O, had she but been of a lower degree,
<small>would have</small>   I then might hae hop'd she wad smil'd upon me!
<small>describing</small>   O, how past descriving had then been my bliss,
As now my distraction no words can express!

OPEN THE DOOR TO ME, O

I

O, open the door some pity to shew,
    If love it may na be, O !
Tho' thou hast been false, I'll ever prove true—
    O, open the door to me, O !

II

Cauld is the blast upon my pale cheek,
    But caulder thy love for me, O :
The frost, that freezes the life at my heart,
    Is nought to my pains frae thee, O !

III

The wan moon sets behind the white wave,
    And Time is setting with me, O :
False friends, false love, farewell ! for mair
    I'll ne'er trouble them nor thee, O !

IV

She has open'd the door, she has open'd it wide,
    She sees the pale corse on the plain, O,
'My true love !' she cried, and sank down by his
    side—
    Never to rise again, O !

WHEN WILD WAR'S DEADLY BLAST

I

When wild War's deadly blast was blawn,
    And gentle Peace returning,
Wi' monie a sweet babe fatherless
    And monie a widow mourning,
I left the lines and tented field,
    Where lang I'd been a lodger,
My humble knapsack a' my wealth,   *all*
    A poor and honest sodger.

II

A leal, light heart was in my breast,   *loyal*
    My hand unstain'd wi' plunder,
And for fair Scotia, hame again,
    I cheery on did wander:
I thought upon the banks o' Coil,
    I thought upon my Nancy,
And ay I mind't the witching smile   *remembered*
    That caught my youthful fancy.

III

At length I reach'd the bonie glen,
    Where early life I sported.
I pass'd the mill and trysting thorn,
    Where Nancy aft I courted.

After JOHN FAED   WHEN WILD WAR'S DEADLY BLAST

"When wild War's deadly blast was blawn,
   And gentle Peace returning,
Wi' monie a sweet babe fatherless,
   And monie a widow mourning."
—*Verse 1.*

Wha spied I but my ain dear maid,
  Down by her mother's dwelling,
And turn'd me round to hide the flood
  That in my een was swelling! *eyes*

IV

Wi' alter'd voice, quoth I :—'Sweet lass,
  Sweet as yon hawthorn's blossom,
O, happy, happy may he be,
  That's dearest to thy bosom!
My purse is light, I've far to gang, *go*
  And fain wad be thy lodger;
I've serv'd my king and country lang—
  Take pity on a sodger.'

V

Sae wistfully she gaz'd on me,
  And lovelier was than ever.
Quo' she :—'A sodger ance I lo'ed,
  Forget him shall I never.
Our humble cot, and hamely fare,
  Ye freely shall partake it;
That gallant badge—the dear cockade—
  Ye're welcome for the sake o't!'

VI

She gaz'd, she redden'd like a rose,
  Syne, pale like onie lily, *Then*
She sank within my arms, and cried :—
  'Art thou my ain dear Willie?'

'By Him who made yon sun and sky,
　　By whom true love's regarded,
I am the man! And thus may still
　　True lovers be rewarded!

VII

'The wars are o'er and I'm come hame,
　　And find thee still true-hearted.
Tho' poor in gear, we're rich in love,
　　And mair, we'se ne'er be parted.'
Quo' she :—' My grandsire left me gowd,
　　A mailen plenish'd fairly!
And come, my faithfu' sodger lad,
　　Thou 'rt welcome to it dearly!'

wealth
we 'll
gold
farm

VIII

For gold the merchant ploughs the main,
　　The farmer ploughs the manor;
But glory is the sodger's prize,
　　The sodger's wealth is honour!
The brave poor sodger ne'er despise,
　　Nor count him as a stranger:
Remember he's his country's stay
　　In day and hour of danger.

Sir David Wilkie

DUNCAN GRAY

" Duncan sigh'd baith out and in,   Spak' o' lowpin o'er a lin—
Grat his een baith bleer't an' blin',   Ha, ha, the wooing o't!"

DUNCAN GRAY

I

Duncan Gray cam here to woo
  (Ha, ha, the wooing o't!)
On blythe Yule-Night when we were fou   *Christmas Eve; drunk*
  (Ha, ha, the wooing o't!).
Maggie coost her head fu' high,   *cast*
Look'd asklent and unco skeigh,   *askance; very skittish*
Gart poor Duncan stand abeigh—   *Made; off*
  Ha, ha, the wooing o't!

II

Duncan fleech'd, and Duncan pray'd   *wheedled*
  (Ha, ha, the wooing o't!),
Meg was deaf as Ailsa craig   *[Notes]*
  (Ha, ha, the wooing o't!).
Duncan sigh'd baith out and in,   *both*
Grat his een baith bleer't an' blin',   *Wept; eyes*
Spak o' lowpin o'er a linn—   *leaping; waterfall*
  Ha, ha, the wooing o't!

III

Time and Chance are but a tide
  (Ha, ha, the wooing o't!):
Slighted love is sair to bide   *hard to endure*
  (Ha, ha, the wooing o't!).

DUNCAN GRAY

'Shall I like a fool,' quoth he,
'For a haughty hizzie die?   *jade*
She may gae to—France for me!'—   *go*
Ha, ha, the wooing o't!

IV

How it comes, let doctors tell
(Ha, ha, the wooing o't!):
Meg grew sick, as he grew hale
(Ha, ha, the wooing o't!).
Something in her bosom wrings,
For relief a sigh she brings,
And O! her een they spak sic things!—   *eyes; such*
Ha, ha, the wooing o't!

V

Duncan was a lad o' grace
(Ha, ha, the wooing o't!),
Maggie's was a piteous case
(Ha, ha, the wooing o't!):
Duncan could na be her death,
Swelling pity smoor'd his wrath;   *smothered*
Now they're crouse and canty baith—   *proud; jolly*
Ha, ha, the wooing o't!

DELUDED SWAIN, THE PLEASURE

I

Deluded swain, the pleasure
　　The fickle Fair can give thee
Is but a fairy treasure—
　　Thy hopes will soon deceive thee:
The billows on the ocean,
　　The breezes idly roaming,
The cloud's uncertain motion,
　　They are but types of Woman!

II

O, art thou not ashamèd
　　To doat upon a feature?
If Man thou would'st be namèd,
　　Despise the silly creature!
Go, find an honest fellow,
　　Good claret set before thee,
Hold on till thou art mellow,
　　And then to bed in glory!

HERE IS THE GLEN

I

Here is the glen, and here the bower
    All underneath the birchen shade,
The village-bell has toll'd the hour—
    O, what can stay my lovely maid?
'Tis not Maria's whispering call—
    'Tis but the balmy-breathing gale,
Mixed with some warbler's dying fall
    The dewy star of eve to hail!

II

It is Maria's voice I hear :—
    So calls the woodlark in the grove
His little faithful mate to cheer :
    At once 'tis music and 'tis love!
And art thou come? And art thou true?
    O, welcome, dear, to love and me,
And let us all our vows renew
    Along the flowery banks of Cree!

LET NOT WOMEN E'ER COMPLAIN

I

Let not women e'er complain
    Of inconstancy in love!
Let not women e'er complain
    Fickle man is apt to rove!
Look abroad thro' Nature's range,
Nature's mighty law is change:
Ladies, would it not be strange
    Man should then a monster prove?

II

Mark the winds, and mark the skies,
    Ocean's ebb and ocean's flow.
Sun and moon but set to rise.
    Round and round the seasons go.
Why then, ask of silly man
To oppose great Nature's plan?
We'll be constant, while we can—
    You can be no more, you know:

LORD GREGORY

I

<small>dark</small>   O, MIRK, mirk is this midnight hour,
       And loud the tempest's roar!
    A waefu' wanderer seeks thy tower---
       Lord Gregory, ope thy door.

II

<small>hall</small>   An exile frae her father's ha',
       And a' for sake o' thee,
<small>show</small>   At least some pity on me shaw,
       If love it may na be.

III

<small>rememb'rest</small>   Lord Gregory mind'st thou not the grove
       By bonie Irwine side,
    Where first I own'd that virgin love
       I lang, lang had denied?

IV

How aften didst thou pledge and vow,
    Thou wad for ay be mine!
And my fond heart, itsel' sae true,
    It ne'er mistrusted thine.

V

Hard is thy heart, Lord Gregory,
    And flinty is thy breast:
Thou bolt of Heaven that flashest by,
    O, wilt thou bring me rest!

VI

Ye mustering thunders from above,
    Your willing victim see,
But spare and pardon my fause love
    His wrangs to Heaven and me!

O POORTITH CAULD   *cold poverty*

Chorus

O, why should Fate sic pleasure have   *such*
    Life's dearest bands untwining?
Or why sae sweet a flower as love
    Depend on Fortune's shining?

I

O Poortith cauld and restless Love,
    Ye wrack my peace between ye!   *wreck*
Yet poortith a' I could forgive,
    An 'twere na for my Jeanie.   *If*

O POORTITH CAULD

II

The warld's wealth when I think on,
    Its pride and a' the lave o't— *rest*
My curse on silly coward man,
    That he should be the slave o't!

III

Her een sae bonie blue betray *eyes*
    How she repays my passion;
But prudence is her o'erword ay:
    She talks o' rank and fashion.

IV

O, wha can prudence think upon,
    And sic a lassie by him?
O, wha can prudence think upon,
    And sae in love as I am?

V

How blest the wild-wood Indian's fate!
    He woos his artless dearie—
The silly bogles, Wealth and State, *hobgoblins*
    Can never make him eerie. *fearful*

Chorus

O, why should Fate sic pleasure have,
    Life's dearest bands untwining?
Or why sae sweet a flower as love
    Depend on Fortune's shining?

O, STAY, SWEET WARBLING WOOD-LARK

I

O, stay, sweet warbling wood-lark, stay,
Nor quit for me the trembling spray!
A hapless lover courts thy lay,
   Thy soothing, fond complaining.
Again, again that tender part,
That I may catch thy melting art!
For surely that wad touch her heart,
   Wha kills me wi' disdaining.

II

Say, was thy little mate unkind,
And heard thee as the careless wind?
O, nocht but love and sorrow join'd   *nothing*
   Sic notes o' woe could wauken!   *Such: awake*
Thou tells o' never-ending care,
O' speechless grief and dark despair—
For pity's sake, sweet bird, nae mair,
   Or my poor heart is broken!

SAW YE BONIE LESLEY

I

O, saw ye bonie Lesley,
    As she gaed o'er the Border? [went]
She's gane, like Alexander,
    To spread her conquests farther!

II

To see her is to love her,
    And love but her for ever;
For Nature made her what she is,
    And never made anither!

III

Thou art a queen, fair Lesley—
    Thy subjects, we before thee!
Thou art divine, fair Lesley—
    The hearts o' men adore thee.

IV

The Deil he could na skaith thee, [harm]
    Or aught that wad belang thee: [belong to]
He'd look into thy bonie face,
    And say:—'I canna wrang thee!'

V

The Powers aboon will tent thee,   *above; guard*
  Misfortune sha'na steer thee: *meddle with*
Thou 'rt like themsel' sae lovely,
  That ill they 'll ne'er let near thee.

VI

Return again, fair Lesley,
  Return to Caledonie!
That we may brag we hae a lass
  There's nane again sae bonie.

SWEET FA'S THE EVE

I

Sweet fa's the eve on Craigieburn,
  And blythe awakes the morrow,
But a' the pride o' Spring's return
  Can yield me nocht but sorrow.   *nothing*

II

I see the flowers and spreading trees,
  I hear the wild birds singing;
But what a weary wight can please,
  And Care his bosom is wringing?

III

Fain, fain would I my griefs impart,
    Yet dare na for your anger;
But secret love will break my heart,
    If I conceal it langer.

IV

If thou refuse to pity me,
    If thou shalt love another,
When yon green leaves fade frae the tree,
    Around my grave they'll wither.

YOUNG JESSIE

I

TRUE hearted was he, the sad swain o' the Yarrow,
    And fair are the maids on the banks of the Ayr;
But by the sweet side o' the Nith's winding river
    Are lovers as faithful and maidens as fair:
To equal young Jessie seek Scotia all over—
    To equal young Jessie you seek it in vain!
Grace, beauty, and elegance fetter her lover,
    And maidenly modesty fixes the chain.

II

Fresh is the rose in the gay, dewy morning,
   And sweet is the lily at evening close;
But in the fair presence o' lovely young Jessie
   Unseen is the lily, unheeded the rose.
Love sits in her smile, a wizard ensnaring;
   Enthron'd in her een he delivers his law;   *eyes*
And still to her charms she alone is a stranger:
   Her modest demeanour's the jewel of a'.

ADOWN WINDING NITH

Chorus

Awa wi' your belles and your beauties—
   They never wi' her can compare!
Whaever hae met wi' my Phillis
   Has met wi' the Queen o' the Fair!

I

Adown winding Nith I did wander
   To mark the sweet flowers as they spring.
Adown winding Nith I did wander
   Of Phillis to muse and to sing.

II

The Daisy amus'd my fond fancy,
   So artless, so simple, so wild:
'Thou emblem,' said I, 'o' my Phillis'—
   For she is Simplicity's child.

III

The rose-bud's the blush o' my charmer,
    Her sweet balmy lip when 'tis prest.
How fair and how pure is the lily!
    But fairer and purer her breast.

IV

Yon knot of gay flowers in the arbour,
    They ne'er wi' my Phillis can vie:
Her breath is the breath of the woodbine,
    Its dew-drop o' diamond her eye.

V

Her voice is the song o' the morning,
    That wakes thro' the green-spreading grove,
When Phebus peeps over the mountains
    On music, and pleasure, and love.

VI

But Beauty, how frail and how fleeting!
    The bloom of a fine summer's day!
While Worth in the mind o' my Phillis
    Will flourish without a decay.

Chorus

Awa wi' your belles and your beauties—
    They never wi' her can compare!
Whaever hae met wi' my Phillis
    Has met wi' the Queen o' the Fair!

A LASS WI' A TOCHER dowry

Chorus
Then hey for a lass wi' a tocher,
Then hey for a lass wi' a tocher,
Then hey for a lass wi' a tocher,
The nice yellow guineas for me!

I
Awa wi' your witchcraft o' Beauty's alarms,
The slender bit beauty you grasp in your arms!
O, gie me the lass that has acres o' charms!
O, gie me the lass wi' the weel-stockit farms!

II
Your Beauty's a flower in the morning that blows,
And withers the faster the faster it grows;
But the rapturous charm o' the bonie green knowes,   knolls
Ilk spring they're new deckit wi' bonie white yowes!   ewes

III
And e'en when this Beauty your bosom has blest,
The brightest o' Beauty may cloy when possess'd;
But the sweet, yellow darlings wi' Geordie impress'd,
The langer ye hae them, the mair they're carest!

BLYTHE HAE I BEEN ON YON HILL

Chorus

Then hey for a lass wi' a tocher,
Then hey for a lass wi' a tocher,
Then hey for a lass wi' a tocher,
The nice yellow guineas for me!

BLYTHE HAE I BEEN ON YON HILL

I

BLYTHE hae I been on yon hill
    As the lambs before me,
every Careless ilka thought, and free
    As the breeze flew o'er me.
Now nae langer sport and play,
    Mirth or sang can please me:
Lesley is sae fair and coy,
    Care and anguish seize me.

II

Heavy, heavy is the task,
    Hopeless love declaring!
can do nothing but stare Trembling, I dow nocht but glow'r,
    Sighing, dumb despairing!
will not; throes If she winna ease the thraws
    In my bosom swelling,
Underneath the grass-green sod
must   Soon maun be my dwelling.

BY ALLAN STREAM

I

By Allan stream I chanc'd to rove,
   While Phebus sank beyond Benledi;
The winds were whispering thro' the grove,
   The yellow corn was waving ready;
I listen'd to a lover's sang,
   An' thought on youthfu' pleasures monie,
And ay the wild-wood echoes rang:—
   ' O, my love Annie's very bonie!

II

' O, happy be the woodbine bower,
   Nae nightly bogle make it eerie!   *hobgoblin / fearful*
Nor ever sorrow stain the hour,
   The place and time I met my dearie!
Her head upon my throbbing breast,
   She, sinking, said:—" I'm thine for ever!"
While monie a kiss the seal imprest—
   The sacred vow we ne'er should sever.'

III

The haunt o' Spring's the primrose-brae.   *-bank*
   The Summer joys the flocks to follow.
How cheery thro' her short'ning day
   Is Autumn in her weeds o' yellow!

But can they melt the glowing heart,
   Or chain the soul in speechless pleasure,
Or thro' each nerve the rapture dart,
   Like meeting her, our bosom's treasure?

CANST THOU LEAVE ME

Chorus

Canst thou leave me thus, my Katie!
   Canst thou leave me thus, my Katie!
Well thou know'st my aching heart,
   And canst thou leave me thus for pity?

I

Is this thy plighted, fond regard:
   Thus cruelly to part, my Katie?
Is this thy faithful swain's reward:
   An aching broken heart, my Katie?

II

Farewell! And ne'er such sorrows tear
   That fickle heart of thine, my Katie!
Thou may'st find those will love thee dear,
   But not a love like mine, my Katie.

Chorus

Canst thou leave me thus, my Katie!
   Canst thou leave me thus, my Katie!
Well thou know'st my aching heart,
   And canst thou leave me thus for pity?

COME, LET ME TAKE THEE

I

Come, let me take thee to my breast,
    And pledge we ne'er shall sunder,
And I shall spurn as vilest dust
    The world's wealth and grandeur!
And do I hear my Jeanie own
    That equal transports move her?
I ask for dearest life alone,
    That I may live to love her.

II

Thus in my arms, wi' a' her charms,
    I clasp my countless treasure,
I 'll seek nae mair o' Heav'n to share
    Than sic a moment's pleasure!   *such*
And by thy een sae bonie blue   *eyes*
    I swear I 'm thine for ever,
And on thy lips I seal my vow,
    And break it shall I never!

CONTENTED WI' LITTLE

I

Contented wi' little and cantie wi' mair,
Whene'er I forgather wi' Sorrow and Care,
I gie them a skelp, as they're creepin alang,
Wi' a cog o' guid swats and an auld Scottish sang.

jolly
smack
[Notes]; new ale

II

I whyles claw the elbow o' troublesome Thought;
But Man is a soger, and Life is a faught.
My mirth and guid humour are coin in my pouch,
And my Freedom's my lairdship nae monarch daur touch.

sometimes scratch
fight

III

A towmond o' trouble, should that be my fa',
A night o' guid fellowship sowthers it a':
When at the blythe end o' our journey at last,
Wha the Deil ever thinks o' the road he has past?

twelve-month; lot
solders

IV

Blind Chance, let her snapper and stoyte on her way,
Be't to me, be't frae me, e'en let the jade gae!
Come Ease or come Travail, come Pleasure or Pain,
My warst word is:—'Welcome, and welcome again!'

stumble; stagger
go

worst

FAREWELL, THOU STREAM

I

FAREWELL, thou stream that winding flows
  Around Eliza's dwelling!
O Mem'ry, spare the cruel throes
  Within my bosom swelling:
Condemn'd to drag a hopeless chain
  And yet in secret languish,
To feel a fire in every vein
  Nor dare disclose my anguish!

II

Love's veriest wretch, unseen, unknown,
  I fain my griefs would cover:
The bursting sigh, th' unweeting groan   *unconscious*
  Betray the hapless lover.
I know thou doom'st me to despair,
  Nor wilt, nor canst relieve me;
But, O Eliza, hear one prayer—
  For pity's sake forgive me!

III

The music of thy voice I heard,
  Nor wist while it enslav'd me!
I saw thine eyes, yet nothing fear'd,
  Till fears no more had sav'd me!

Th' unwary sailor thus, aghast
   The wheeling torrent viewing,
'Mid circling horrors sinks at last
   In overwhelming ruin.

HAD I A CAVE

Had I a cave
  On some wild distant shore,
Where the winds howl
  To the wave's dashing roar,
    There would I weep my woes,
    There seek my lost repose,
    Till grief my eyes should close,
Ne'er to wake more!

II

Falsest of womankind,
  Can'st thou declare
All thy fond, plighted vows
  Fleeting as air?
    To thy new lover hie,
    Laugh o'er thy perjury,
    Then in thy bosom try
What peace is there!

HERE'S A HEALTH

Chorus

Here's a health to ane I loe dear!
Here's a health to ane I loe dear!
Thou art sweet as the smile when fond lovers
    meet,
  And soft as their parting tear,
        Jessy—
  And soft as their parting tear!

ALTHO' thou maun never be mine,   must
  Altho' even hope is denied,
'Tis sweeter for thee despairing
  Than ought in the world beside,
        Jessy—
  Than ought in the world beside!

II

I mourn thro' the gay, gaudy day,
  As hopeless I muse on thy charms;
But welcome the dream o' sweet slumber!
  For then I am lockt in thine arms,
        Jessy—
  For then I am lockt in thine arms!

Chorus

Here's a health to ane I loe dear!
Here's a health to ane I loe dear!
Thou art sweet as the smile when fond lovers
   meet,
   And soft as their parting tear,
      Jessy—
   And soft as their parting tear!

HOW CRUEL ARE THE PARENTS

I

How cruel are the parents
   Who riches only prize,
And to the wealthy booby
   Poor Woman sacrifice!
Meanwhile the hapless daughter
   Has but a choice of strife:
To shun a tyrant father's hate
   Become a wretched wife!

II

The ravening hawk pursuing,
   The trembling dove thus flies:
To shun impending ruin
   Awhile her pinion tries,

Till, of escape despairing,
  No shelter or retreat,
She trusts the ruthless falconer,
  And drops beneath his feet.

HUSBAND, HUSBAND, CEASE YOUR STRIFE

I

Husband, husband, cease your strife,
  Nor longer idly rave, sir!
Tho' I am your wedded wife,
  Yet I am not your slave, sir.
'One of two must still obey,
  Nancy, Nancy!
Is it Man or Woman, say,
  My spouse Nancy?'

II

'If 'tis still the lordly word,
  Service and obedience,
I'll desert my sov'reign lord,
  And so goodbye, allegiance!'
'Sad will I be so bereft,
  Nancy, Nancy!
Yet I'll try to make a shift,
  My spouse Nancy!'

III

'My poor heart, then break it must,
    My last hour I am near it:
When you lay me in the dust,
    Think, how will you bear it?'
'I will hope and trust in Heaven,
    Nancy, Nancy!
Strength to bear it will be given,
    My spouse Nancy.'

IV

'Well, sir, from the silent dead,
    Still I'll try to daunt you:
Ever round your midnight bed
    Horrid sprites shall haunt you!'
'I'll wed another like my dear,
    Nancy, Nancy!
Then all Hell will fly for fear,
    My spouse Nancy!'

IT WAS THE CHARMING MONTH

Chorus

Lovely was she by the dawn,
    Youthful Chloe, charming Chloe,
Tripping o'er the pearly lawn,
    The youthful, charming Chloe!

IT WAS THE CHARMING MONTH

I

It was the charming month of May,
When all the flow'rs were fresh and gay,
One morning, by the break of day,
    The youthful, charming Chloe,
From peaceful slumber she arose,
Girt on her mantle and her hose,
And o'er the flow'ry mead she goes—
    The youthful, charming Chloe!

II

The feather'd people you might see
Perch'd all around on every tree!
With notes of sweetest melody
    They hail the charming Chloe,
Till, painting gay the eastern skies,
The glorious sun began to rise,
Outrival'd by the radiant eyes
    Of youthful, charming Chloe.

Chorus

Lovely was she by the dawn,
    Youthful Chloe, charming Chloe,
Tripping o'er the pearly lawn,
    The youthful, charming Chloe!

LAST MAY A BRAW WOOER

I

<small>fine</small> Last May a braw wooer cam down the lang glen,
<small>deafen</small> And sair wi' his love he did deave me.
I said there was naething I hated like men:
<small>go</small> The deuce gae wi'm to believe me, believe me—
The deuce gae wi'm to believe me!

II

<small>eyes</small> He spak o' the darts in my bonie black een,
And vow'd for my love he was diein.
I said, he might die when he liket for Jean:
The Lord forgie me for liein, for liein—
The Lord forgie me for liein!

III

<small>farm;
landlord</small> A weel-stocket mailen, himsel for the laird,
And marriage aff-hand were his proffers:
<small>let</small> I never loot on that I kenn'd it, or car'd,
<small>worse</small> But thought I might hae waur offers, waur offers—
But thought I might hae waur offers.

IV

But what wad ye think? In a fortnight or less
(The Deil tak his taste to gae near her!)
He up the Gate-Slack to my black cousin, Bess!
Guess ye how, the jad! I could bear her, could bear her—
Guess ye how, the jad! I could bear her.

After ERSKINE NICOL

LAST MAY A BRAW WOOER

"But owre my left shouther I gae him a blink,
    Lest neebours might say I was saucy;
My wooer he caper'd as he'd been in drink,
    And vow'd I was his dear lassie, dear lassie—
    And vow'd I was his dear lassie!"
        —*Verse vi.*

LAST MAY A BRAW WOOER 243

V

But a' the niest week, as I petted wi' care,   *next*
  I gaed to the tryste o' Dalgarnock,   *cattle-fair*
And wha but my fine fickle lover was there?
  I glowr'd as I'd seen a warlock, a warlock—   *stared*
  I glowr'd as I'd seen a warlock.

VI

But owre my left shouther I gae him a blink,   *shoulder; glance*
  Lest neebours might say I was saucy.
My wooer he caper'd as he'd been in drink,
  And vow'd I was his dear lassie, dear lassie—
  And vow'd I was his dear lassie!

VII

I spier'd for my cousin fu' couthy and sweet: *asked; affable*
  Gin she had recover'd her hearin?   *If*
And how her new shoon fit her auld, shachl'd feet?   *shoes; shapeless*
  But heavens! how he fell a swearin, a swearin—
  But heavens! how he fell a swearin!

VIII

He beggèd, for gudesake, I wad be his wife,
  Or else I wad kill him wi' sorrow;
So e'en to preserve the poor body in life,
  I think I maun wed him to-morrow, to-morrow—   *must*
  I think I maun wed him to-morrow!

MY NANIE'S AWA

I

Now in her green mantle blythe Nature arrays,
<small>heights</small> And listens the lambkins that bleat o'er the braes,
<small>every; wood</small> While birds warble welcomes in ilka green shaw,
But to me it's delightless—my Nanie's awa.

II

The snawdrap and primrose our woodlands adorn,
<small>wet [i.e. dew]</small> And violets bathe in the weet o' the morn.
They pain my sad bosom, sae sweetly they blaw:
They mind me o' Nanie—and Nanie's awa!

III

Thou lav'rock, that springs frae the dews of the lawn
The shepherd to warn o' the grey-breaking dawn,
And thou mellow mavis, that hails the night-fa,
Give over for pity—my Nanie's awa.

IV

Come Autumn, sae pensive in yellow and grey,
And soothe me wi' tidings o' Nature's decay!
The dark, dreary Winter and wild-driving snaw
Alane can delight me—now Nanie's awa.

NOW ROSY MAY

Chorus

Meet me on the Warlock Knowe, *knoll*
  Dainty Davie, Dainty Davie!
There I'll spend the day wi' you,
  My ain dear Dainty Davie. *own*

I

Now rosy May comes in wi' flowers
To deck her gay, green-spreading bowers;
And now comes in the happy hours
  To wander wi' my Davie.

II

The crystal waters round us fa',
The merry birds are lovers a',
The scented breezes round us blaw,
  A wandering wi' my Davie.

III

When purple morning starts the hare
To steal upon her early fare,
Then thro' the dews I will repair
  To meet my faithfu' Davie.

IV

When day, expiring in the west,
The curtain draws o' Nature's rest,
I flee to his arms I loe the best:
And that's my ain dear Davie!

Chorus

Meet me on the Warlock Knowe,
Dainty Davie, Dainty Davie!
There I'll spend the day wi' you,
My ain dear Dainty Davie.

NOW SPRING HAS CLAD

I

Now spring has clad the grove in green,
And strew'd the lea wi' flowers;
The furrow'd, waving corn is seen
Rejoice in fostering showers;
While ilka thing in nature join [every]
Their sorrows to forego,
O, why thus all alone are mine
The weary steps o' woe!

II

The trout within yon wimpling burn [winding]
Glides swift, a silver dart,
And, safe beneath the shady thorn,
Defies the angler's art:

NOW SPRING HAS CLAD

My life was ance that careless stream,
    That wanton trout was I,
But Love wi' unrelenting beam
    Has scorch'd my fountains dry.

III

The little floweret's peaceful lot,
    In yonder cliff that grows,
Which, save the linnet's flight, I wot,   *guess*
    Nae ruder visit knows,
Was mine, till Love has o'er me past,
    And blighted a' my bloom;
And now beneath the withering blast
    My youth and joy consume.

IV

The waken'd lav'rock warbling springs,
    And climbs the early sky,
Winnowing blythe his dewy wings
    In Morning's rosy eye:
As little reck't I Sorrow's power,
    Until the flowery snare
O' witching Love in luckless hour
    Made me the thrall o' care!

V

O, had my fate been Greenland snows
    Or Afric's burning zone,
Wi' Man and Nature leagu'd my foes,
    So Peggy ne'er I 'd known!

The wretch, whose doom is 'hope nae mair,'
    What tongue his woes can tell,
Within whose bosom, save Despair,
    Nae kinder spirits dwell!

O, THIS IS NO MY AIN LASSIE

Chorus

O, this is no my ain lassie,
    Fair tho' the lassie be:
Weel ken I my ain lassie—
    Kind love is in her e'e.

I

I SEE a form, I see a face,
Ye weel may wi' the fairest place:
It wants to me the witching grace,
    The kind love that's in her e'e.

II

She's bonie, blooming, straight, and tall,
And lang has had my heart in thrall;
And ay it charms my very saul,
    The kind love that's in the e'e.

III

A thief sae pawkie is my Jean,   *artful*
To steal a blink by a' unseen!   *glance*
But gleg as light are lover's een,   *sharp; eyes*
   When kind love is in the e'e.

IV

It may escape the courtly sparks,
It may escape the learned clerks;
But well the watching lover marks
   The kind love that's in her e'e.

Chorus

O, this is no my ain lassie,
   Fair tho' the lassie be:
Weel ken I my ain lassie—
   Kind love is in her e'e.

O, WAT YE WHA THAT LO'ES ME *wot; who*

Chorus

O, that's the lassie o' my heart,
   My lassie ever dearer!
O, that's the queen o' womankind,
   And ne'er a ane to peer her!

250 O, WAT YE WHA THAT LO'ES ME

I

O, WAT ye wha that lo'es me,
    And has my heart a keeping?
O, sweet is she that lo'es me
    As dews o' summer weeping,
    In tears the rosebuds steeping!

II

If thou shalt meet a lassie
    In grace and beauty charming,
That e'en thy chosen lassie,
    Erewhile thy breast sae warming,
    Had ne'er sic powers alarming :—   *such*

III

If thou hadst heard her talking
    (And thy attention's plighted),
That ilka body talking   *every*
    But her by thee is slighted,   *Except*
    And thou art all-delighted :—

IV

If thou hast met this fair one,
    When frae her thou hast parted,
If every other fair one
    But her thou hast deserted,
    And thou art broken-hearted :—

Chorus

O, that's the lassie o' my heart,
    My lassie ever dearer!
O, that's the queen o' womankind,
    And ne'er a ane to peer her!

SCOTS, WHA HAE

I

Scots, wha hae wi' Wallace bled,
Scots, wham Bruce has aften led,
Welcome to your gory bed
        Or to victorie!

II

Now's the day, and now's the hour:
See the front o' battle lour,
See approach proud Edward's power—
        Chains and slaverie!

III

Wha will be a traitor knave.
Wha can fill a coward's grave?
Wha sae base as be a slave?—
        Let him turn, and flee!

IV

Wha for Scotland's King and Law
Freedom's sword will strongly draw,
Freeman stand or freeman fa',
   Let him follow me!

V

By Oppression's woes and pains,
By your sons in servile chains,
We will drain our dearest veins
   But they shall be free!

VI

Lay the proud usurpers low!
Tyrants fall in every foe!
Liberty's in every blow!
   Let us do, or die!

THEIR GROVES O' SWEET MYRTLE

I

THEIR groves o' sweet myrtle let foreign lands reckon,
 Where bright-beaming summers exalt the perfume!
Far dearer to me yon lone glen o' green breckan, *[ferns]*
 Wi' the burn stealing under the lang, yellow broom; *[brook]*

Far dearer to me are yon humble broom bowers,
  Where the blue-bell and gowan lurk lowly, unseen; wild daisy
For there, lightly tripping among the wild flowers,
  A-list'ning the linnet, aft wanders my Jean.

II

Tho' rich is the breeze in their gay, sunny vallies,
  And cauld Caledonia's blast on the wave,
Their sweet-scented woodlands that skirt the proud
    palace,
  What are they?—The haunt of the tyrant and
    slave!
The slave's spicy forests and gold-bubbling fountains
  The brave Caledonian views wi' disdain :
He wanders as free as the winds of his mountains,
  Save Love's willing fetters—the chains o' his Jean.

THINE AM I

I

Thine am I, my faithful Fair,
  Thine my lovely Nancy!
Ev'ry pulse along my veins,
  Ev'ry roving fancy!
To thy bosom lay my heart
  There to throb and languish.
Tho' despair had wrung its core,
  That would heal its anguish.

II

Take away those rosy lips
  Rich with balmy treasure!
Turn away thine eyes of love,
  Lest I die with pleasure!
What is life when wanting love?
  Night without a morning!
Love the cloudless summer's sun,
  Nature gay adorning.

THOU HAST LEFT ME EVER, JAMIE

I

Thou hast left me ever, Jamie,
  Thou hast left me ever!
Thou hast left me ever, Jamie,
  Thou hast left me ever!
Aften hast thou vow'd that Death
  Only should us sever;
Now thou'st left thy lass for ay—
  I maun see thee never, Jamie,
  I'll see thee never!

must

II

Thou hast me forsaken, Jamie,
  Thou hast me forsaken!
Thou hast me forsaken, Jamie,
  Thou hast me forsaken!

Thou canst love another jo,
   While my heart is breaking.
Soon my weary een I'll close,   *eyes*
   Never mair to waken, Jamie,   *more*
   Never mair to waken!

HIGHLAND MARY

I

YE banks and braes and streams around
   The castle o' Montgomery,
Green be your woods, and fair your flowers,
   Your waters never drumlie!   *turbid*
There Summer first unfald her robes,   *unfold*
   And there the langest tarry!
For there I took the last fareweel
   O' my sweet Highland Mary!

II

How sweetly bloom'd the gay, green birk,   *birch*
   How rich the hawthorn's blossom,
As underneath their fragrant shade
   I clasp'd her to my bosom!
The golden hours on angel wings
   Flew o'er me and my dearie:
For dear to me as light and life
   Was my sweet Highland Mary.

III

Wi' monie a vow and lock'd embrace
    Our parting was fu' tender;
And, pledging aft to meet again,
    We tore oursels asunder.
But O, fell Death's untimely frost,
    That nipt my flower sae early!
Now green's the sod, and cauld's the clay,
    That wraps my Highland Mary!

IV

O, pale, pale now, those rosy lips
    I aft hae kiss'd sae fondly;
And clos'd for ay, the sparkling glance
    That dwalt on me sae kindly;
And mouldering now in silent dust
    That heart that lo'ed me dearly!
But still within my bosom's core
    Shall live my Highland Mary.

MY CHLORIS, MARK

I

My Chloris, mark how green the groves,
    The primrose banks how fair!
The balmy gales awake the flowers,
    And wave thy flaxen hair.

Etching by WILLIAM HOLE

HIGHLAND MARY

" Wi' monie a vow and lock'd embrace
   Our parting was fu' tender ;
And, pledging aft to meet again,
   We tore oursels asunder."—*Verse iii.*

II

The lav'rock shuns the palace gay,   *lark*
  And o'er the cottage sings:
For Nature smiles as sweet, I ween,
  To shepherds as to kings.

III

Let minstrels sweep the skilfu' string
  In lordly, lighted ha':   *hall*
The shepherd stops his simple reed,
  Blythe in the birken shaw.   *birch wood*

IV

The princely revel may survey
  Our rustic dance wi' scorn;
But are their hearts as light as ours
  Beneath the milk-white thorn?

V

The shepherd in the flowery glen
  In shepherd's phrase will woo:
The courtier tells a finer tale—
  But is his heart as true?

VI

Here wild-wood flowers I 've pu'd, to deck
  That spotless breast o' thine:
The courtier's gems may witness love—
  But 'tis na love like mine!

FAIREST MAID ON DEVON BANKS

Chorus

Fairest maid on Devon banks,
    Crystal Devon, winding Devon,
Wilt thou lay that frown aside,
    And smile as thou wert wont to do?

I

FULL well thou know'st I love thee dear—
Couldst thou to malice lend an ear!
O, did not Love exclaim:—' Forbear,
    Nor use a faithful lover so!'

II

Then come, thou fairest of the fair,
Those wonted smiles, O, let me share,
And by thy beauteous self I swear
    No love but thine my heart shall know!

Chorus

Fairest maid on Devon banks,
    Crystal Devon, winding Devon,
Wilt thou lay that frown aside,
    And smile as thou wert wont to do?

LASSIE WI' THE LINT-WHITE LOCKS

Chorus

Lassie wi' the lint-white locks,
   Bonie lassie, artless lassie,
Wilt thou wi' me tent the flocks—   *tend*
   Wilt thou be my dearie, O?

I

Now Nature cleeds the flowery lea,   *clothes*
And a' is young and sweet like thee,
O, wilt thou share its joys wi' me,
   And say thou 'lt be my dearie, O?

II

The primrose bank, the wimpling burn,   *meandering*
The cuckoo on the milk-white thorn,
The wanton lambs at early morn
   Shall welcome thee, my dearie, O.

III

And when the welcome simmer shower
Has cheer'd ilk drooping little flower,   *each*
We 'll to the breathing woodbine-bower
   At sultry noon, my dearie, O.

IV

<small>reaper's</small>
When Cynthia lights wi' silver ray
The weary shearer's hameward way,
Thro' yellow waving fields we 'll stray,
   And talk o' love, my dearie, O.

V

And when the howling wintry blast
Disturbs my lassie's midnight rest,
Enclaspèd to my faithfu' breast,
   I 'll comfort thee, my dearie, O.

Chorus

Lassie wi' the lint-white locks,
   Bonie lassie, artless lassie,
Wilt thou wi' me tent the flocks—
   Wilt thou be my dearie, O?

LONG, LONG THE NIGHT

Chorus

Long, long the night,
   Heavy comes the morrow,
While my soul's delight
   Is on her bed of sorrow.

LONG, LONG THE NIGHT

I

Can I cease to care,
   Can I cease to languish,
While my darling fair
   Is on the couch of anguish!

II

Ev'ry hope is fled,
   Ev'ry fear is terror:
Slumber ev'n I dread,
   Ev'ry dream is horror.

III

Hear me, Powers Divine:
   O, in pity, hear me!
Take aught else of mine,
   But my Chloris spare me

Chorus

Long, long the night,
   Heavy comes the morrow.
While my soul's delight
   Is on her bed of sorrow.

LOGAN WATER

I

O LOGAN, sweetly didst thou glide
That day I was my Willie's bride,
And years sin syne hae o'er us run
Like Logan to the simmer sun.
But now thy flowery banks appear
Like drumlie winter, dark and drear,
While my dear lad maun face his faes
Far, far frae me and Logan braes.

since then / have — line 3
dull — line 6
must — line 7
slopes — line 8

II

Again the merry month of May
Has made our hills and vallies gay;
The birds rejoice in leafy bowers,
The bees hum round the breathing flowers;
Blythe Morning lifts his rosy eye,
And Evening's tears are tears o' joy:
My soul delightless a' surveys,
While Willie's far frae Logan braes.

III

Within yon milk-white hawthorn bush,
Amang her nestlings sits the thrush:
Her faithfu' mate will share her toil,
Or wi' his song her cares beguile.

ALEXANDER H. BARR

LOGAN WATER

"But I wi' my sweet nurslings here,
Nae mate to help, nae mate to cheer,
Pass widow'd nights and joyless days,
While Willie's far frae Logan braes."—*Verse iii.*

But I wi' my sweet nurslings here,
Nae mate to help, nae mate to cheer,
Pass widow'd nights and joyless days,
While Willie's far frae Logan braes.

IV

O, wae upon you, Men o' State,
That brethren rouse in deadly hate!
As ye make monie a fond heart mourn,
Sae may it on your heads return!
Ye mindna 'mid your cruel joys   *remember not*
The widow's tears, the orphan's cries;
But soon may peace bring happy days,
And Willie hame to Logan braes!

YON ROSY BRIER

I

O, BONIE was yon rosy brier   *yonder*
  That blooms sae far frae haunt o' man,
And bonie she—and ah, how dear!—
  It shaded frae the e'enin sun!

II

Yon rosebuds in the morning dew,
  How pure among the leaves sae green!
But purer was the lover's vow
  They witnessed in their shade yestreen.   *last night*

III

All in its rude and prickly bower,
    That crimson rose how sweet and fair!
But love is far a sweeter flower
    Amid life's thorny path o' care.

IV

winding   The pathless wild and wimpling burn,
    Wi' Chloris in my arms, be mine,
And I the warld nor wish nor scorn—
    Its joys and griefs alike resign!

WHERE ARE THE JOYS

I

WHERE are the joys I hae met in the morning,
    That danc'd to the lark's early sang?
Where is the peace that awaited my wand'ring
    At e'ening the wild-woods amang?

II

Nae mair a-winding the course o' yon river
    And marking sweet flowerets sae fair,
Nae mair I trace the light footsteps o' Pleasure,
    But Sorrow and sad-sighing Care.

III

Is it that Summer's forsaken our vallies,
    And grim, surly Winter is near?
No, no, the bees humming round the gay roses
    Proclaim it the pride o' the year.

IV

Fain wad I hide what I fear to discover,
    Yet lang, lang, too well hae I known:
A' that has causèd the wreck in my bosom
    Is Jenny, fair Jenny alone!

V

Time cannot aid me, my griefs are immortal,
    Not Hope dare a comfort bestow.
Come then, enamor'd and fond of my anguish,
    Enjoyment I'll seek in my woe!

BEHOLD THE HOUR

I

Behold the hour, the boat arrive!
    Thou goest, the darling of my heart!
Sever'd from thee, can I survive?
    But Fate has will'd and we must part.

I'll often greet the surging swell,
　Yon distant isle will often hail:—
'E'en here I took the last farewell;
　There, latest mark'd her vanish'd sail.'

II

Along the solitary shore,
　While flitting sea-fowl round me cry,
Across the rolling, dashing roar,
　I'll westward turn my wistful eye:—
'Happy, thou Indian grove,' I'll say,
　'Where now my Nancy's path may be!
While thro' thy sweets she loves to stray,
　O, tell me, does she muse on me?'

FORLORN MY LOVE

Chorus

O, wert thou, love, but near me,
　But near, near, near me,
How kindly thou would cheer me,
　And mingle sighs with mine, love!

I

FORLORN my love, no comfort near,
Far, far from thee I wander here;
Far, far from thee, the fate severe,
　At which I most repine, love.

II

Around me scowls a wintry sky,
Blasting each bud of hope and joy,
And shelter, shade, nor home have I
   Save in these arms of thine, love.

III

Cold, alter'd friendship's cruel part,
To poison Fortune's ruthless dart!
Let me not break thy faithful heart,
   And say that fate is mine, love!

IV

But, dreary tho' the moments fleet,
O, let me think we yet shall meet!
That only ray of solace sweet
   Can on thy Chloris shine, love!

Chorus

O, wert thou, love, but near me,
But near, near, near me,
How kindly thou would cheer me,
   And mingle sighs with mine, love!

CA' THE YOWES TO THE KNOWES

SECOND SET

Chorus

<small>Drive; ewes; knolls</small>

Ca' the yowes to the knowes,
Ca' them where the heather grows,
<small>brooklet runs</small>   Ca' them where the burnie rowes,
     My bonie dearie.

I

HARK, the mavis' e'ening sang
Sounding Clouden's woods amang
<small>[Notes]; go</small>   Then a-faulding let us gang,
     My bonie dearie.

II

<small>go</small>

We'll gae down by Clouden side,
Thro' the hazels, spreading wide
O'er the waves that sweetly glide
     To the moon sae clearly.

III

Yonder Clouden's silent towers
Where, at moonshine's midnight hours,
O'er the dewy bending flowers
     Fairies dance sae cheery.

IV

Ghaist nor bogle shalt thou fear—   hobgoblin
Thou 'rt to Love and Heav'n sae dear
Nocht of ill may come thee near,
  My bonie dearie

Chorus

Ca' the yowes to the knowes,
Ca' them where the heather grows,
Ca' them where the burnie rowes,
  My bonie dearie.

HOW CAN MY POOR HEART

I

How can my poor heart be glad
When absent from my sailor lad?
How can I the thought forego—
He's on the seas to meet the foe?
Let me wander, let me rove,
Still my heart is with my love.
Nightly dreams and thoughts by day
Are with him that's far away.
  On the seas and far away,
  On stormy seas and far away—
  Nightly dreams and thoughts by day,
  Are ay with him that's far away.

II

When in summer noon I faint,
As weary flocks around me pant,
Haply in this scorching sun
My sailor's thund'ring at his gun.
Bullets, spare my only joy!
Bullets, spare my darling boy!
Fate, do with me what you may,
Spare but him that's far away!
   On the seas and far away,
   On stormy seas and far away—
   Fate, do with me what you may,
   Spare but him that's far away!

III

At the starless, midnight hour
When Winter rules with boundless power,
As the storms the forests tear,
And thunders rend the howling air,
Listening to the doubling roar
Surging on the rocky shore,
All I can—I weep and pray
For his weal that's far away.
   On the seas and far away,
   On stormy seas and far away,
   All I can—I weep and pray
   For his weal that's far away.

IV

Peace, thy olive wand extend
And bid wild War his ravage end;
Man with brother man to meet,
And as brother kindly greet!
Then may Heaven with prosperous gales
Fill my sailor's welcome sails,
To my arms their charge convey,
My dear lad that's far away!
  On the seas and far away,
  On stormy seas and far away,
  To my arms their charge convey,
  My dear lad that's far away!

IS THERE FOR HONEST POVERTY

I

Is there for honest poverty
  That hings his head, an' a' that?   *hangs*
The coward slave, we pass him by—
  We dare be poor for a' that!
For a' that, an' a' that,
  Our toils obscure, an' a' that,
The rank is but the guinea's stamp,
  The man's the gowd for a' that.   *gold*

272 IS THERE FOR HONEST POVERTY

II

What though on hamely fare we dine,
    Wear hoddin grey, an' a' that? *[coarse grey woollen]*
Gie fools their silks, and knaves their wine—
    A man's a man for a' that.
For a' that, an' a' that,
    Their tinsel show, an' a' that,
The honest man, tho' e'er sae poor,
    Is king o' men for a' that.

III

Ye see yon birkie ca'd 'a lord,' *[fellow; called]*
    Wha struts, an' stares, an' a' that?
Tho' hundreds worship at his word,
    He's but a cuif for a' that. *[dolt]*
For a' that, an' a' that,
    His ribband, star, an' a' that,
The man o' independent mind,
    He looks an' laughs at a' that.

IV

A prince can mak a belted knight,
    A marquis, duke, an' a' that!
But an honest man's aboon his might— *[above]*
    Guid faith, he mauna fa' that! *[must not [Notes]]*
For a' that, an' a' that,
    Their dignities, an' a' that,
The pith o' sense an' pride o' worth
    Are higher rank than a' that.

J. M. WRIGHT

IS THERE FOR HONEST POVERTY

"Ye see yon birkie ca'd a lord,   Tho' hundreds worship at his word,
   Wha struts, an' stares, an' a' that,   He's but a cuif for a' that."

V

  Then let us pray that come it may
    (As come it will for a' that)
  That Sense and Worth o'er a' the earth
    Shall bear the gree an' a' that! *have the first place*
  For a' that, an' a' that,
    It's comin yet for a' that,
  That man to man the world o'er
    Shall brithers be for a' that.

MARK YONDER POMP

I

Mark yonder pomp of costly fashion
  Round the wealthy, titled bride!
But, when compar'd with real passion,
  Poor is all that princely pride.

II

  What are the showy treasures?
  What are the noisy pleasures?
The gay, gaudy glare of vanity and art!
    The polish'd jewel's blaze
    May draw the wond'ring gaze,
    And courtly grandeur bright
    The fancy may delight,
But never, never can come near the heart!

III

But did you see my dearest Chloris
  In simplicity's array,
Lovely as yonder sweet opening flower is,
  Shrinking from the gaze of day:

IV

O, then, the heart alarming
And all resistless charming,
In love's delightful fetters she chains the
  willing soul!
Ambition would disown
The world's imperial crown!
Ev'n Avarice would deny
His worshipp'd deity,
And feel thro' every vein love's raptures roll!

O, LET ME IN THIS AE NIGHT

Chorus

O, let me in this ae night,
This ae, ae, ae night!
O, let me in this ae night,
And rise, and let me in!

O, LET ME IN THIS AE NIGHT

I
O LASSIE, are ye sleepin yet,
Or are ye waukin, I wad wit? *awake; know*
For Love has bound me hand an' fit, *foot*
    And I would fain be in, jo.

II
Thou hear'st the winter wind an' weet: *wet*
Nae star blinks thro' the driving sleet! *shines*
Tak pity on my weary feet,
    And shield me frae the rain, jo.

III
The bitter blast that round me blaws,
Unheeded howls, unheeded fa's:
The cauldness o' thy heart's the cause
    Of a' my care and pine, jo.

Chorus
O, let me in this ae night,
This ae, ae, ae night!
O, let me in this ae night,
    And rise and let me in!

HER ANSWER

Chorus
I tell you now this ae night,
This ae, ae, ae night,
And ance for a' this ae night,
I winna let ye in, jo. *will not*

276 I TELL YOU NOW THIS AE NIGHT

I

<small>not</small>   O, TELL me na o' wind an' rain,
Upbraid na me wi' cauld disdain,
<small>way</small>   Gae back the gate ye cam again,
   I winna let ye in, jo!

II

<small>keenest;
darkest</small> The snellest blast at mirkest hours,
That round the pathless wand'rer pours
<small>nothing</small> Is nocht to what poor she endures,
   That's trusted faithless man, jo.

III

The sweetest flower that deck'd the mead,
Now trodden like the vilest weed—
Let simple maid the lesson read!
<small>fate; own</small>   The weird may be her ain, jo.

IV

The bird that charm'd his summer day,
And now the cruel fowler's prey,
Let that to witless woman say:—
   'The gratefu' heart of man,' jo

Chorus

I tell you now this ae night,
This ae, ae, ae night,
And ance for a' this ae night,
I winna let ye in, jo.

O PHILLY, HAPPY BE THAT DAY

Chorus

He and She. For a' the joys that gowd can gie,   *gold*
　　　　　I dinna care a single flie!   *do not*
　　　　　The {lad / lass} I love's the {lad / lass} for me,
　　　　　And that's my ain dear {Willy / Philly}

I

He. O Philly, happy be that day
　　　When, roving thro' the gather'd hay,
　　　My youthfu' heart was stown away,   *stolen*
　　　　And by thy charms, my Philly!
She. O Willy, ay I bless the grove
　　　Where first I own'd my maiden love,
　　　Whilst thou did pledge the Powers above
　　　　To be my ain dear Willy.

II

He. As songsters of the early year
　　　Are ilka day mair sweet to hear,   *each succeeding*
　　　So ilka day to me mair dear
　　　　And charming is my Philly.
She. As on the brier the budding rose
　　　Still richer breathes, and fairer blows,
　　　So in my tender bosom grows
　　　　The love I bear my Willy.

III

He. The milder sun and bluer sky,
    That crown my harvest cares wi' joy,
  Were ne'er sae welcome to my eye
    As is a sight o' Philly.
She. The little swallow's wanton wing,
    Tho' wafting o'er the flowery spring,
  Did ne'er to me sic tidings bring *[such]*
    As meeting o' my Willy.

IV

He. The bee, that thro' the sunny hour
    Sips nectar in the op'ning flower,
  Compar'd wi' my delight is poor
    Upon the lips o' Philly.
She. The woodbine in the dewy weet, *[wet]*
    When ev'ning shades in silence meet,
  Is nocht sae fragrant or sae sweet *[nothing]*
    As is a kiss o' Willy.

V

He. Let Fortune's wheel at random rin,
    And fools may tyne, and knaves may win ! *[lose]*
  My thoughts are a' bound up on ane,
    And that's my ain dear Philly.
She. What's a' the joys that gowd can gie?
    I dinna care a single flie !
  The lad I love's the lad for me,
    And that's my ain dear Willy.

Chorus

He and She. For a' the joys that gowd can gie,
　　I dinna care a single flie!
　　The {lad / lass} I love's the {lad / lass} for me,
　　　And that's my ain dear {Willy / Philly}

O, WERE MY LOVE

I

O, WERE my love yon lilac fair
　　Wi' purple blossoms to the spring,
And I a bird to shelter there,
　　When wearied on my little wing,
How I wad mourn when it was torn
　　By Autumn wild and Winter rude!
But I wad sing on wanton wing,
　　When youthfu' May its bloom renew'd.

II

O, gin my love were yon red rose,   it
　　That grows upon the castle wa',
And I mysel a drap o' dew
　　Into her bonie breast to fa',
O, there, beyond expression blest,
　　I'd feast on beauty a' the night,
Seal'd on her silk-saft faulds to rest,   -soft; folds
　　Till fley'd awa by Phœbus' light!   scared

SLEEP'ST THOU

I

Sleep'st thou, or wauk'st thou, fairest creature?
Rosy Morn now lifts his eye,
Numbering ilka bud, which Nature [each]
Waters wi' the tears o' joy.
Now to the streaming fountain
Or up the heathy mountain
The hart, hind, and roe, freely, wildly-wanton
stray;
In twining hazel bowers
His lay the linnet pours;
The laverock to the sky
Ascends wi' sangs o' joy,
While the sun and thou arise to bless the day!

II

Phœbus, gilding the brow of morning,
Banishes ilk darksome shade,
Nature gladdening and adorning:
Such to me my lovely maid!
When frae my Chloris parted,
Sad, cheerless, broken-hearted,
The night's gloomy shades, cloudy, dark, o'ercast
my sky;

But when she charms my sight
In pride of Beauty's light,
When thro' my very heart
Her beaming glories dart,
'Tis then—'tis then I wake to life and joy!

THERE WAS A LASS

I

There was a lass, and she was fair!
  At kirk and market to be seen
When a' our fairest maids were met,
  The fairest maid was bonie Jean.

II

And ay she wrought her country wark,
  And ay she sang sae merrilie:
The blythest bird upon the bush
  Had ne'er a lighter heart than she!

III

But hawks will rob the tender joys,
  That bless the little lintwhite's nest,   linnet's
And frost will blight the fairest flowers,
  And love will break the soundest rest.

IV

handsomest	Young Robie was the brawest lad,
	The flower and pride of a' the glen,
oxen; kine	And he had owsen, sheep, and kye,
horses	And wanton naigies nine or ten.

V

went; [Notes]	He gaed wi' Jeanie to the tryste,
	He danc'd wi' Jeanie on the down,
	And, lang ere witless Jeanie wist,
lost; stolen	Her heart was tint, her peace was stown!

VI

As in the bosom of the stream
    The moon-beam dwells at dewy e'en,
So, trembling pure, was tender love
    Within the breast of bonie Jean.

VII

	And now she works her country's wark,
	And ay she sighs wi' care and pain,
knew not; complaint	Yet wist na what her ail might be,
well	Or what wad make her weel again.

VIII

not; leap	But did na Jeanie's heart loup light,
glance	And did na joy blink in her e'e,
	As Robie tauld a tale o' love
One	Ae e'enin on the lily lea?

IX

While monie a bird sang sweet o' love,
    And monie a flower blooms o'er the dale,
His cheek to hers he aft did lay,
    And whisper'd thus his tender tale:—

X

'O Jeanie fair, I lo'e thee dear.
    O, canst thou think to fancy me?
Or wilt thou leave thy mammie's cot,
    And learn to tent the farms wi' me?   *tend*

XI

At barn or byre thou shalt na drudge,   *cowhouse*
    Or naething else to trouble thee,
But stray amang the heather-bells,
    And tent the waving corn wi' me.'

XII

Now what could artless Jeanie do?
    She had nae will to say him na!
At length she blush'd a sweet consent,
    And love was ay between them twa.

THE LEA-RIG

I

When o'er the hill the eastern star
    Tells bughtin time is near, my jo,
And owsen frae the furrow'd field
    Return sae dowf and weary, O,
Down by the burn, where scented birks
    Wi' dew are hangin clear, my jo,
I'll meet thee on the lea-rig,
    My ain kind dearie, O.

II

At midnight hour in mirkest glen
    I'd rove, and ne'er be eerie, O,
If thro' that glen I gaed to thee,
    My ain kind dearie, O!
Altho' the night were ne'er sae wild,
    And I were ne'er sae weary, O,
I'll meet thee on the lea-rig,
    My ain kind dearie, O.

III

The hunter lo'es the morning sun
    To rouse the mountain deer, my jo;
At noon the fisher takes the glen
    Adown the burn to steer, my jo:

Margin glosses: meadow-ridge; folding; dull; frightened; went

Gie me the hour o' gloamin grey— *twilight*
  It maks my heart sae cheery, O,
To meet thee on the lea-rig,
  My ain kind dearie, O !

MY WIFE'S A WINSOME WEE THING

Chorus

She is a winsome wee thing,
She is a handsome wee thing,
She is a lo'esome wee thing,
  This sweet wee wife o' mine!

I

I NEVER saw a fairer,
I never lo'ed a dearer,
And neist my heart I'll wear her, *next*
  For fear my jewel tine. *be lost*

II

The warld's wrack, we share o't; [Notes]
The warstle and the care o't,
Wi' her I'll blythely bear it,
  And think my lot divine.

Chorus

> She is a winsome wee thing,
> She is a handsome wee thing,
> She is a lo'esome wee thing,
> This sweet wee wife o' mine

MARY MORISON

I

O Mary, at thy window be!
  It is the wish'd, the trysted hour.
Those smiles and glances let me see,
  That make the miser's treasure poor.
  How blythely wad I bide the stoure,
A weary slave frae sun to sun,
  Could I the rich reward secure—
The lovely Mary Morison!

II

Yestreen, when to the trembling string
  The dance gaed thro' the lighted ha',
To thee my fancy took its wing,
  I sat, but neither heard or saw:
  Tho' this was fair, and that was braw,
And yon the toast of a' the town,
  I sigh'd and said amang them a':—
Ye are na Mary Morison!'

Marginal notes: [Notes] / bear the struggle / Last night / went / fine / the other

III

O Mary, canst thou wreck his peace
   Wha for thy sake wad gladly die?
Or canst thou break that heart of his
   Whase only faut is loving thee?   *fault*
   If love for love thou wilt na gie,   *give*
At least be pity to me shown:
   A thought ungentle canna be   *cannot*
The thought o' Mary Morison.

NOTES

BIBLIOGRAPHICAL

The present Volume consists of songs sent by Burns to Johnson's *Musical Museum* and Thomson's *Scottish Airs*, and duly set forth in these collections. Some he sent which were not used, and some were used which he did not send. These will appear in our fourth and last instalment of all.

Burns's earliest reference to the *Museum* is contained in a letter, written as he was leaving Edinburgh, of the 4th May 1787. He tells Johnson that he sends a song ('never before known') for his publication, and that had the acquaintance been a little older, he would have asked the favour of a 'correspondence.' Only two of his songs appeared in Johnson's First Volume, the Preface to which is dated 22nd May 1787 ; and it is possible to observe in detail neither the growth of his acquaintance with Johnson himself nor that of his interest in Johnson's venture. He seems, however, to have made special arrangements with Johnson during his visit to Edinburgh in the autumn: at any rate, there are indications that he has resolved—entirely as a labour of love—to do his best for both the man and the book. On the 20th October he informs Mr. Hoy, chamberlain to the Duke of Gordon, that, to 'the utmost of his small power,' he assists 'in collecting the old poetry, or sometimes for a fine air' makes 'a stanza when it has no words'; on the 25th he confides to Skinner, the parson poet, that he has 'been absolutely crazed about' the project, and is 'collecting old stanzas, and every information respecting their origin, authors,' *etc.* ; and in November he is found asking his friend

James Candlish to send him '*Pompey's Ghost*, words and music,' and confessing that he has already 'collected, begged, borrowed, and stolen all the songs' he could. All this is in the beginning; and of itself it were enough to show that, even had he done no more, still Johnson's debt to him had been considerable.

But there is evidence in plenty that he was very soon a great deal more than a mere contributor, however unwearied and unselfish. Johnson—an engraver, who could neither write grammatically nor even spell—was quite incompetent himself to edit the *Museum*; and at first he was helped by the elder Tytler. But that Burns was virtually editor of the work from the autumn of 1787 until his health began to fail, is proved (1) by what is left of his correspondence with Johnson; (2) by his annotations on the Hastie MSS. (British Museum); and (3) by certain draft-plans of volumes, lists of songs, and other MS. scraps now in the library of Mr. George Gray, Glasgow, which we have been privileged to consult for this Edition. Thus, in November 1788, he tells Johnson that he has prepared a 'flaming preface' for Vol. iii. The tone of it is not exactly that of the Preface to Vol. ii.; but Burns was a creature of moods, and he may very well have written both. If he did, he ends the earlier thus:—
'Ignorance and Prejudice may perhaps affect to sneer at the simplicity of the poetry or music of some of those pieces, but their having been for ages the favourites of Nature's judges, the Common People, was to the Editor a sufficient test of their merit.' The next is less humble and more cynical as regards the *Vox Populi*. 'As this is not,' it runs, 'one of those many Publications which are hourly ushered into the World merely to catch the eye of Fashion in her frenzy of a day, the Editor has little to hope or fear from the herd of readers. Consciousness of the well-known merit of our Scotish Music, and the natural fondness of a Scotchman for the productions of his own country, are at once the Editor's motive

and apology for the Undertaking ; and where any of the Pieces in the Collection may perhaps be found wanting at the Critical Bar of the First, he appeals to the honest prejudices of the Last.' Burns's hand is also plain in the Preface to Vol. iv., which ends with this pronouncement : —' To those who object that this Publication contains pieces of inferior or little value the Editor answers by referring to his plan. All our songs cannot have equal merit. Besides, as the world have (*sic*) not yet agreed on any unerring balance, any undisputed standard, in matters of Taste, what to one person yields no manner of pleasure, may to another be a high enjoyment.' He died before the appearance of Vol. v. (there were six in all), but the Preface thereto contains an extract from a letter of his :— ' You may probably think that for some time past I have neglected you and your work ; but alas the hand of pain and sorrow and care has these many months lain heavy on me ! Personal and domestic affliction have almost entirely banished that alacrity and life with which I used to woo the rural Muse of Scotia. In the meantime let us finish what we have so well begun.'

In the September of 1792 he was invited by George Thomson to contribute to his *Scottish Airs*, a more ambitious and—musically speaking—a more elaborate adventure than the *Museum*. He replied that, inasmuch as it would positively add to his enjoyment to comply with the request, he would ' enter into the undertaking with all the small portion of the abilities' he had, ' strained to the utmost exertion by the impulse of enthusiasm.' ' As to remuneration,' he added, ' you may think my songs either above or below price; for they shall absolutely be the one or the other. In the honest enthusiasm with which I embark in your undertaking, to talk of money, wages, fee, hire, *etc.*, would be downright sodomy of soul. A proof of each of the songs that I compose or amend I shall receive as a favour. In the rustic phrase of the season :—"God speed the work."'

Thomson returns his 'warmest acknowledgement for the enthusiasm with which' Burns has 'entered into our undertaking'; but as he says nothing of Burns's admirable generosity, it is reasonable to infer that the idea of payment would have been unwelcome to his mind.

Even so, it is fair to add that the best of time had passed for Burns ere his connexion with Thomson began. Misfortunes, hardships, follies, excesses in fact and sentiment, success itself, so barren of lasting profit to him—all these had done some part of their work; and already his way of life was falling into the sere and yellow leaf. Though few, the years had been full exceedingly; and his inspiration was its old rapturous, irresistible self no longer. Moreover, he had to content Thomson as well as to satisfy himself; and Thomson, a kind of poetaster, whose taste in verse was merely academic, persuaded him to write more English than was good for him; being in this matter wholly of his time, he could find nothing to 'fire his vocal rage' but the amatory 'effusions' of one of the least lyrical schools in letters; and the consequences were disastrous to his art. The Thomson songs, indeed, some distinguished and delightful exceptions to the contrary, are not in his happier vein. They have not the fresh sweetness and the unflagging spirit of his *Museum* numbers. They are less distinctively Scots than these, for one thing; and for another, they are often vapid in sentiment and artificial in effect. Now, his work for the *Museum* consisted largely in the adaptation of old rhymes and folk-songs to modern uses. Some he arranged, some he condensed, some he enlarged, some he reconstructed and rewrote. Stray snatches, phrases, lines, thin echoes from a vanished past—nothing came amiss to him, nor was there anything he could not turn to good account. His appreciation was instant and inevitable, his touch unerring. Under his hand a patchwork of catch-words became a living song. He would take you two fragments of different epochs, select the best from each, and treat the matter of his choice in such a style that it is hard to know where its components end and begin : so that nothing is certain about his result except that here is a piece of art. Or he would capture a wandering old refrain, adjust it to his own conditions, and so renew its lyrical interest and significance that it seems to live its true life for the first time on his lips. Here, in fact, is his chief claim to perennial acceptance. He passed the folk-song of his nation through the mint of his mind, and he reproduced it stamped with his image and lettered with his superscription : so that for the world at large it exists, and will go on existing, not as he found but as he left it. Certain critics have cavilled at the assertion (in our Preface to Vol. i.) that, 'genius apart,' Burns was *ultimus Scotorum,* the last expression of the old Scots world.' If that statement err, it is not by excess. Burns's knowledge of the older minstrelsy was unique ; he was saturate with its tradition, as he was absolute master of its emotions and effects ; no such artist in folk-song as he (so in other words Sir Walter said) has ever worked in literature. But a hundred forgotten singers went to the making of his achievement and himself. He did not wholly originate those master-qualities—of fresh and taking simplicity, of vigour and directness and happy and humorous ease, which have come to be regarded as distinctive of his verse; for all these things, together with much of the thought, the romance, and the sentiment for which we read and love him, were included in the estate which he inherited from his nameless forebears ; and he so assimilated them that what is actually those forebears' legacy to him has come to be regarded as his gift to them. Those forebears aiding, he stands forth as the sole great poet of the old Scots world ; and he thus is national as no poet has ever been, and as no poet ever will, or ever can be, again. Thus, too, it is that, being the 'satirist and singer of a parish'—a fact which only the Common Burnsite could be crazy enough, or pigheaded enough, to deny—he is at the same time the least parochial—the most broadly and genuinely human—among the lyrists of his race.

In our Notes to individual songs we have done our best to trace his connexion with the past. This is now the more difficult because (1) much of the material he collected (including the origins of the publication known as *The Merry Muses* and a good deal else) has been destroyed—by his relations, or by Currie, or by later owners—in the interests partly of Scottish morals, partly of that cheap decorous chromo-lithograph (as it were) which bids fair to supplant the true Burns—ardent, impulsive, generous; but hypochondriacal, passionate, imperfect—in the minds of his countrymen; (2) owners are shy of so much as acknowledging the existence of certain holograph letters and verses; and (3) many so-called MS. collections of traditional songs, made in the first half of the century, partake, whether consciously or not, of the character of forgeries, and do not so much enlighten as betray. All the same, in MSS., broadsides, chaps, rare song-books there does exist a considerable body of stuff which, being carefully sifted, is found to be, directly or indirectly, of no small illustrative value. As regards unpublished material, we might speak in no measured terms of the Herd MS. (British Museum)—given by Herd to Archibald Constable —which has hitherto escaped the notice of Burns's Editors; which includes all the songs, ballads, and scraps that David Herd—the most indefatigable and the most conscientious of the old Scots collectors—had picked together; and which distinguishes between numbers unprinted and numbers printed in Herd's own 1769 and 1776 Editions, or elsewhere. Burns may of course have had other knowledge of some of the matter here sequestered; but that he had access to the MS. while it was in Herd's hands—(the probability is that it was submitted to him in the autumn of 1787)—and made large use of it in connexion with the *Museum* is (as we think) made abundantly clear in our Notes. It supplied him with the beginnings of over twenty songs : some set down hitherto as wholly his own, and a few vaguely described as 'old,' while the rest have been riddled with speculations or assertions more or less unwarrantable and erroneous. Other ms. collections have been examined, and, so far as was deemed expedient, have been utilised ; but the most, as we have said, make rather for error than for truth.

As will be seen, much valuable information is still to be got from old broadsides and garlands. Even if a broadside, or a garland, do not set forth the very song, or ballad, on which Burns worked, it may contain the original of that song, or ballad, or at least a derivative from that original, and in this way suffice to prove that in the particular instance Burns was indebted to a predecessor. Moreover, it is highly probable, indeed it is certain—*pace* Messrs. Chappell and Ebsworth — that many English broadsides are founded on Scots originals deemed unfit for print in the foul-mouthed days of Rochester and the Second Charles. The old Scots poets—Dunbar, Kennedy, Lindsay, Montgomerie, Scott, Hume of Polwarth, and the rest—were nothing if not plain-spoken ; and from the Reformation, or before it, there existed in Scotland a large body of lyrical bawdry : in part (it may be) a legacy from the monks, but assuredly developed by the punitive rule of the Kirk and by the Kirk's discouragement — its prohibition indeed — of every kind of song except the 'godly,' and of every kind of literature except the theological. A clandestine literature somewhat similar in kind exists in England ; but the product of what we may call the Scots poetical shebeens is vastly preferable in the matter of melody and genius. Is it at all conceivable that the Scots nobles and gentlemen at Charles's court were ignorant of these delectable ditties, or would fail to make them known ? And can it be seriously argued that Tom D'Urfey and those other English song-writers, who caricatured the Scot in love in such grotesques as *Bonnie Dundee* and *The Liggan Waters*, as *Katherine Ogie* and the rest, were never guilty of imitating or parodying a Scots original? [Of course it doesn't follow that they did so whenever they touched on Scottish themes, or tried to poke fun at the Scot by pretending to express themselves in his barbarous northern dialect.] Be this as it may, many Restoration English broadsides—whether suggested by Scots originals or not—were gathered (with modifications) into song-books by Ramsay and other Scotsmen, and had no small influence on popular song in Scotland. So that derivatives from them, or corruptions of them—in some instances of great variety—were widely circulated in those garlands and stall ballads which, particularly in the latter half of the eighteenth century, began to dispute the pre-eminence of the psalms of David as the poetic literature of the Scottish peasant: at the same time that they did their part in preparing the ground for the evolution in Britain of the great Romantic Movement.

All students of broadside literature are indebted to the publications of the Ballad Society, especially those produced under the learned editorship of Mr. Ebsworth, to whom our thanks are due for the early sheets, and an unique copy of the ballad of *Mally Stewart*. Among Collections, public and private, the first place must be assigned to those in the British Museum, which, in addition to the Roxburghe, Bagford, Osterly Park, and other famous sets of blackletter broadsides, possesses an immense assortment of whiteletter sheets and garlands, as well as an unrivalled gathering of sheet-music and old song-books. We have further to acknowledge the extraordinary kindness of the Earl of Crawford in sending us a world of ballads and broadsides from Haigh Hall, and to express our obligations to the Earl of Rosebery for permission to inspect the collection

of Scots broadsides formed by the late David Laing ; to
Mrs. Mansfield, Edinburgh, for access to the Pitcairn
MS. ; to Mr. A. Huth, Princes Gate, London, for access
to the Huth broadsides; and to Mr. Peskett, Librarian
of Magdalene College, Cambridge, for the run of the
admirable Pepys Collection. Divers other gatherings
have been consulted, including the Euing Collection
in the University of Glasgow. Also we are indebted to
Mr. George Gray, Glasgow, for placing at our disposal
his extensive assortment of Scots chaps and song-books;
to Mr. Alexander Fowlie of Inverury for the communication of several chaps; to Mr. Wm. MacMath,
Edinburgh, for information ; to Dr. Furnivall, London,
for early copies of some Ballad Society's Publications ;
and to Mr. Andrew Lang for information embodied in
certain of our Notes.

Most of the MS. songs which Burns sent to Johnson are
included in the Hastie Collection in the British Museum ;
those he sent to Thomson in the Thomson Correspondence
at Brechin Castle, where we were able to inspect them.
But we have further to express our acknowledgments to
the Committee of the Burns Exhibition, Glasgow, for
permission to collate several MSS. The MSS. of divers
numbers are also included in Collections denoted in
foregoing volumes. Thus, those—and they are very
many—which were sent to Mrs. Dunlop are in the
Lochryan MSS. ; while those sent to Maria Riddell
are in the collection of her descendant, Dr. De Noè
Walker, of London: to whom, as to Colonel Wallace, we
have pleasure in tendering our peculiar thanks.

YOUNG PEGGY

No. 78 in Johnson (Vol. i. 1787): 'By Burns.'

Margaret, daughter of Robert Kennedy, of Daljarroch,
Ayrshire, and niece of Mr. Gavin Hamilton, was born
3rd November 1766; fell in love with (and finally suc-

YOUNG PEGGY cumbed to) Captain, afterwards Colonel, Andrew M'Doual ('Sculdudd'ry M'Doual' of the second *Heron Ballad* : see Vol. ii. p. 197) in 1784 ; bore him a daughter in January 1794 ; raised an action for (1) declarator of marriage, or (2) damages for seduction ; and died in February 1795, before the case was decided. Meanwhile M'Doual, who denied paternity as well as marriage, had wedded another lady ; but in 1798 the Consistorial Court declared against him on both issues ; and the Court of Session, having set aside its judgment as regards the marriage, ordered him to provide for his child in the sum of £3000.

Burns often met Miss Kennedy at Gavin Hamilton's. His song was enclosed to her in an undated letter :—' I have in these verses attempted some faint sketches of your portrait in the unembellished simple manner of descriptive truth.' This, and not *The Banks o' Doon*, (p. 124), which it is usual, but erroneous, to suppose was suggested by the lady's amour, must have been the song 'on Miss Peggy Kennedy,' which, with *The Lass o' Ballochmyle*, the 'jury of literati' in Edinburgh 'found defamatory libels against the fastidious powers of Poesy and Taste.' Forbidden to print it—(no doubt for the same reason as he was forbidden to print *The Lass o' Ballochmyle*), and not because it is not better than nine-tenths of the Ramsay songs, of which it is an imitation) —in the Edinburgh Edition, the writer sent it to Johnson, where it appears as alternative words to the tune, *Loch Errochside*. With a few variations it was published in one of the tracts 'printed for and sold by Stewart and Meikle' ; and it is included in Stewart's Edition (Glasgow 1802) ; but not in Stewart's *Poems Ascribed to Robert Burns* (Glasgow 1801).

STANZA I. LINE 2. '*She's blushing* like the morning,' Stewart. 4. 'With early *pearls* adorning,' Stewart.
STANZA III. LINE 4. 'Of *savage surly* winter,' Stewart.

BONIE DUNDEE

No. 99 in Johnson (Vol. i. 1787): Unsigned.

A fragment of folk-ballad, with modifications and additions. A pencil jotting of it in Burns's hand on the back of a letter from the Earl of Buchan, 1st February 1787, is in the Burns Monument, Edinburgh. Cromek (*Scotish Songs*, 1810) states that Burns sent the draft of his version to Cleghorn with the following note :—' DEAR CLEGHORN,—You will see by the above that I have added a stanza to *Bonny Dundee*. If you think it will do you may set it agoing upon a ten-stringed instrument and on the psaltery.—R. B.'

The earliest printed set is the blackletter (Crawford, Pepys, and Roxburghe Collections) ' *Jockey's Escape from Bonny Dundee; or Jockey's Deliverance*: Being his Valiant Escape from Dundee and the Parson's Daughter Whom he had Mislov'd. To its own Proper Tune [called *Bonny Dundee*]' :—

> ' "Where got thou the haver-meal Bannock?"
> "Blind Booby, cans't thou not see?
> I got them out of a Scotch-man's wallet
> As he lay easing under a Tree."
>
> > ' Come fill up my cup, come fill up my can !
> > Come saddle my horse, and call up my man !
> > Come open the gates, and let me go free,
> > And show me the way to Bonny Dundee !'

A set in *Wit and Mirth* (1703) is more satirical: *e.g.* instead of ' As he lay easing,' it has ' As he lay lousing him.' A tune, *Adieu Dundee*, is preserved in *The Skene MS.* (ed. Dauney, 1838). Chappell thinks the Skene MS. much later than Dauney thought it, and holds the tune to be English. However this be, it can scarce be doubted that the blackletter set—including the chorus, which Sir Walter borrowed—is founded on some Scots original. Two stanzas of a ballad, *Crombie's Escape from Dundee*,

BONIE DUNDEE said to have been current in the north of Scotland, are quoted in Hogg and Motherwell (1834). A fragment in Herd (1769) has a finer taste of antiquity :—

>'O, have I burnt, or have I slain,
>Or have I done aught injury?
>I've gotten a bonny young lassie wi' bairn ;—
>The baillie's daughter of bonny Dundee:
>Bonny Dundee and bonny Dundas,
>Where shall I see sae bonny a lass?
>Open your ports, and let us gang free!
>I maun stay nae langer in bonny Dundee!

Another version, in an undated chap published by J. Morren, Edinburgh (*c.* 1800), introduces a 'bonny blue bonnet' (afterwards useful, it may be, to Scott):—

>'O, whar gat you that bonny blue bonnet?'
>'O silly blind body, canny ye see?
>I gat it frae a bonny Scots callan
>Atween St. Johnson's and bonny Dundee.'

In an additional stanza are these four verses :—

>'My heart has nae room when I think on my dawty;
>His dear rosy haffets bring tears in my e'e!
>But now he's awa and I dinna ken where he's.
>Gin we could anse meet, we's ne'er part till we die.'

Morren's set is substantially the same as that in *The Harp of Caledonia* (1819), referred to in Hogg and Motherwell, where the additions are declared to be 'obviously from the pen of Burns.' There is yet another set (old) in *The Merry Muses* :—

>'Ye coopers and hoopers attend to my ditty:
>I sing of a cooper wha dwalt in Dundee.
>This young man, he was baith am'rous and witty,
>Which pleased the fair maidens o' sweet Dundee.'

STANZA I. LINE I. 'Hauver-meal bannock':—A synonym (common in the North of England and some parts of Scotland) for the oaten cake, the staple bread of old Scotland.

TO THE WEAVER'S GIN YE GO

No. 103 in Johnson (Vol. ii. 1788): Signed 'X.' 'The chorus of this song is old, the rest is mine. Here once for all let me apologise for many silly compositions of mine in this work. Many beautiful airs wanted words, and in the hurry of other avocations, if I could string a parcel of rhymes together, anything nearly tolerable, I was fain to let them pass. He must be an excellent poet indeed whose every performance is excellent' (R. B. in Interleaved Copy).

Some hold the song to refer to Armour's visit to Paisley after the quarrel, and to her supposed flirtation with a weaver named Wilson. But if the story were authenticated (as it is not), and if Paisley lay west from Mauchline (which it does not), it would be admitted by everybody but the Common Burnsite—sentimental, ignorant, uncritical—that, not to take account of the fact that Armour was far gone in pregnancy when she went to Paisley, is to discredit, and very seriously, (1) the general repute of the Paisley weaver; (2) Armour's idea of delicacy; (3) the habit and tradition of the Scottish male and female peasant; (4) the poet's own sense of fairness; and (5) even the poet's own theory of common decency.

An 'old' song, parts of which were sent to Hogg and Motherwell (1834) by Peter Buchan—who 'never saw it in print'—has no sort of claim to consideration. Here, however, is the chorus, such as it is :—

'To the weaver gin ye go,
To the weaver gin ye go, ·
You'll need somebody wi' you,
To the weaver gin ye go.'

A ballad in the 'Laing Broadsides,' entitled, *A Seasonable Advice to all who intend to go Pirrating,* is to the tune

TO THE WEAVER'S GIN YE GO of *To the Weavers if You Go*, and is probably a parody. It begins :—

> 'My countrymen who do intend
> On pirrating to go,
> Be sure whate'er ye may pretend,
> The certain end is wo.
>
> 'I know't by sad experience,
> The better may I tell :
> I thought myself in sure defence,
> But suddenly I fell.'

STANZA II. LINE 2. 'To warp a plaiden wab'=to form threads into a warp for a web of coarse woollen.

WHISTLE AN' I'LL COME TO YOU, MY LAD

WE adopt the set elaborated by Burns for Thomson's *Scottish Airs* (Vol. ii. 1799). Here is the one sent to Johnson—No. 106 (Vol. ii. 1788): 'Written for this work by Robert Burns' :—

> 'O, Whistle an' I'll come to you, my lad!
> O, Whistle an' I'll come to you, my lad!
> Though father and mither should baith gae mad,
> O, Whistle an' I'll come to you, my lad!
> Come down the back stairs when ye come to court me ;
> Come down the back stairs, and let naebody see ;
> And come as ye were na coming to me,
> And come as ye were na coming to me.'

The song has hitherto been held pure Burns. But he found his chorus in the Herd MS. :—

> 'Whistle and I'll cum to ye, my lad!
> Whistle and I'll cum to ye, my lad!
> Gin father and mither and a' should gae mad,
> Whistle and I'll cum to ye, my lad!'

There is a curious English derivative from some Scots original, entitled *Whistle My Love and I'll Come Down*, of which a stall copy (sold by Potts, Printer, and Wholesale

NOTES 305

Toy Warehouse, 6 Great St. Andrew St., 7 Dials, c. 1800 or earlier) is in the Crawford Collection. It begins :— WHISTLE AN' I'LL COME TO YOU, MY LAD

'Peggy's a maid both kind and fair,
And Peggy is dear to Johnnie,
And None in all Scotland here and there,
None is so blythe and bonny.
And Peggy has vow'd their love to own,
O Whistle my love and I'll come down
And gang to the Kirk wi' Johnnie.'

Currie states that he 'heard the heroine' of the Burns set 'sing it herself, in the very spirit of arch simplicity it requires.' He probably referred to Jean Armour; and it may be that the first set was addressed to her. Burns sent the second to Thomson in an undated letter sometime in August 1793; and on 2nd August 1795 he suggested that Thomson should change the fourth line of the chorus to 'Thy Jeanie will venture wi' ye, my lad':—'A fair one, herself the heroine of the song, insists on the amendment, and dispute her commands if you dare.' The said fair one was Jean Lorimer (see *post*, p. 482, Prefatory Note to *Lassie Wi' the Lint-White Locks*). Thomson asked her Poet to petition the 'charming Jeanie' to let 'the line remain unaltered'; but, while the plate remains unchanged, 'Thy Jeanie,' *etc.*, graces all the printed verses opposite.

Thomson suggested '*my Jo*' at the end of Lines 1, 2, and 4, and '*say no*' at the end of Line 3; but Burns would none of it.

I'M O'ER YOUNG TO MARRY YET

No. 107 in Johnson (Vol. ii. 1788): Signed 'Z.' 'The chorus of this song is old; the rest of it, such as it is, is mine' (R. B. in Interleaved Copy).

The old song, says Stenhouse, begins :—

VOL. III.   U

I'M O'ER
YOUNG TO
MARRY
YET

'My minnie coft me a new gown,
　The Kirk maun hae the gracing o't;
Were I to lie wi' you, kind sir,
　I'm fear'd you'd spoil the lacing o't.'

This statement seems borrowed—and mutilated—from Cromek (*Scotish Songs*, i. 107), who introduces the stanza as 'a stray characteristic verse'—(either he got it from a Burns MS., or was indebted for it to the playful fancy of 'honest Allan')—'which ought to be restored.'

STANZA I. LINE 4. 'Eerie'=apprehensive of ghosts, but the word is used here in a humorous sense. Perhaps the nearest English equivalent is 'creepy.'

THE BIRKS OF ABERFELDIE

No. 113 in Johnson (Vol. ii. 1788): 'Written for this work by R. Burns': Signed 'B.' Set to the tune of *The Birks of Abergeldie*. 'I composed these stanzas standing under the Falls of Moness at or near Aberfeldy' (R. B. in Interleaved Copy). 'Aberfeldy described in rhyme' (R. B., *Journal*, 30th August).

Two stanzas of the older set (Herd, 1769) are printed as alternative words. A much longer set, from a broadside once in the possession of Archibald Constable, is printed in Maidment's *Scottish Songs* (1859). The set in Herd is plainly a corruption of this broadside:

'"O bonny lassie, wilt thou go?
　Wilt thou go, wilt thou go?
O bonny lassie, wilt thou go
　To the Birks of Abergeldie?
"My Dear Sir, I dare not gang,
　I dare not gang, I dare not gang
For fear that you betray me.'"

But while Burns paints the Aberfeldy birches in their high midsummer pomp, the Abergeldie of the ballad-monger is pure winter:—

'"Abergeldie Birks are very cold,
　Are very cold, are very cold;

> The weather very frostie."
> "My dear, I'll hug thee in my arms,
> In my arms, in my arms;
> And wrap thee in my pladie."

The broadside has a Second Part:—

> '"Bessy, is my bed made,
> My bed made, my bed made,
> Or is my supper ready?"' *etc.*

M'PHERSON'S FAREWELL

No. 114 in Johnson (Vol. ii. 1788): Signed 'Z'; and entered in the table of contents as 'by Burns.' 'M'Pherson, a daring robber in the beginning of this century, was condemned to be hanged at the assizes of Inverness. He is said, when under sentence of death, to have composed this tune, which he calls his own Lament or Farewell' (R. B. in Interleaved Copy).

The reputed son of a gipsy, James M'Pherson, a cateran of notable strength and prowess, was apprehended for robbery by the Laird of Braco, at Keith Market; and, being haled before the Sheriff of Banff on 1st November 1700, was hanged at the Cross of Banff on the 10th. The tradition that he played the *Lament* on his violin on the way to the tree, or at the foot of it, is absurd. It has, further, been pointed out that his legend may derive from an Irish story: of a tune called *M'Pherson*, with which its composer is said to have played himself to the gallows on the pipes.

There is a set in Herd (1769), but it is plainly a corruption of the old broadside—*The Last Words of James Mackpherson, Murderer*—of which there is an original copy, embellished with a rude engraving of Macpherson with bow and arrow—in the Laing Collection at Dalmeny. It agrees with the sheet reprinted in Maidment (*Scottish Songs*, 1859). That it is excellent drama has bred the ridiculous tradition—devoutly accepted by cer-

308 NOTES

M'PHER- tain Editors—that the hero wrote it. Also, the copy
SON'S communicated by Peter Buchan to Hogg and Motherwell
FAREWELL (1834), from the recital of 'a very old person, and said
to have been the real composition of the unfortunate
M'Pherson himself, when in jail,' is a clumsy vamp
from Burns and his broadside original. This original
(which seems in part an imitation of *Captain Johnston's
Farewell*: he was hanged at Tyburn in 1690: in the
Pepys Collection, v. 523) opens thus:—

> 'I spent my time in rioting,
> Debauched my health and strength;
> I pillaged, plundered, murdered,
> But now, alas! at length
> I'm brought to punishment condign;
> Pale death draws near to me:
> The end I ever did project,
> To hang upon a tree.'

The most notable lines, however, are the four last:—

> 'Then wantonly and rantingly
> I am resolved to die;
> And with undaunted courage I
> Shall mount this fatal tree':—

which are the germ of Burns's refrain. But Burns, while preserving throughout the spirit of his original, has expressed it in the noblest terms.

A MS. in the British Museum agrees substantially with the copy in Johnson.

MY HIGHLAND LASSIE, O

No. 117 in Johnson (Vol. ii. 1788): Signed 'X.'

This was a composition of mine in very early life, before I was known at all in the world. My "Highland Lassie" was a warm-hearted, charming young creature as ever blessed a man with generous love. After a pretty long tract of the most ardent reciprocal attachment we met by appointment on the second Sunday of May, in a sequestered spot by the Banks of Ayr, where we spent the day in taking farewell, before she should embark for the West Highlands to arrange matters for our projected change of life. At the close of the Autumn following she crossed the sea to meet me at Greenock, where she had scarce landed when she was seized with a malignant fever, which hurried my dear girl to the grave in a few days, before I could even hear of her illness' (R. B. in Interleaved Copy).

The 'Highland Lassie' was Mary Campbell, daughter of one Archibald Campbell, a Clyde sailor. The year of her birth is uncertain; its place is not beyond dispute; the date of her death is matter of debate; its exact circumstances are not authenticated; there is room for conjecture as to the place of her burial; little or no independent testimony exists as to her person and character—unless she be identified with a certain Mary Campbell of indifferent repute; there is scarce material for the barest outlines of her biography. But on the strength of sporadic allusions by Burns—meant, as it seems, to dissemble more than they reveal—and especially of certain ecstatic expressions in the song, *Thou Ling'ring Star* (p. 71), and in a letter to Mrs. Dunlop—(penned when the writer was 'groaning under the miseries of a diseased nervous system')—Mary Campbell has come to be regarded less as an average Scots peasant to whom a merry-begot was then, if not a necessary of life, at all events the commonest effect of luck, than as a sort of bare-legged Beatrice —a Spiritualised Ideal of Peasant Womanhood. Seriously examined, her cult—(for cult it is)—is found an absurdity; but persons of repute have taken the craze, so that it is useful to remark that the Mary Campbell of tradition is a figment of the General Brain, for whose essential features not so much as the faintest outline is to be found in the confusion of amorous plaints and cries of repentance or remorse, which is all that we have to enlighten us from

310   NOTES

MY HIGHLAND LASSIE, O Burns. Further, it is forgotten that Mary Campbell's death revealed her to her Poet in a new and hallowed aspect. Whatever the date—whether 1786 or an earlier year: whether, that is to say, she preceded Armour in Burns's regard, or consoled him episodically after Armour's repudiation of him—assigned to the famous farewell on the banks of Ayr, the underhandedness of the engagement, with the extreme discretion of, not merely his references to it but, the references of his relatives and hers, leaves room for much conjecture. Here Burns, for once in his life, was reticent. Yet, what reason had he for reticence if, as is hotly contended by the more ardent among the Mariolaters, the affair belonged to 1784, or earlier? And why, in 1784, when he had no particular reputation, good or bad, should Mary's kinsfolk (or Mary herself) have conceived so arrant a grudge against him that it impelled them (or her) to obliterate the famous Inscription in his Bible, with its solemn scriptural oaths— (which were unusual under the circumstances, and which, as being recorded for the girl's comfort, tend to show that those circumstances were peculiar)—and to destroy his every scrap of writing to her? It were less difficult to explain the position if the amour belonged to 1786; for then the Armour business was notorious. But then, too, Burns's constancy in crying out for Jean must of necessity impeach the worth of his professions to Mary. In any case, it is a remarkable circumstance that the latter heroine left her situation with the vaguest possible outlook on marriage; for, though Burns does say that she went to make arrangements for their union, there is no scrap of proof that immediate espousals were designed. Indeed, no progress at all appears to have been made in such arrangements in all the five months preceding her death; and assuredly Burns did not intend to take her with him to Jamaica in 1786. Finally, there is the guarded, the official, statement of Currie that 'the banks of Ayr formed the scene of youthful passions,' the 'history of which it would be *improper to reveal* were it even in one's power, and the traces of which will soon be discoverable only in those strains of nature and sensibility to which they gave birth.' On the whole, it is a very pretty tangle; but the one thing in it worth acknowledgment and perfectly plain is that the Highland Mary of the Mariolater is but a 'devout imagination.'

MY HIGHLAND LASSIE, O

A part of the *Highland Lassie, O* is reminiscent of the chorus of Ramsay's *My Nannie O*, which it may here be stated (as a Supplementary Note to *My Nanie O*, Vol. i. p. 412), traces back to a blackletter in the Pepys Collection (iii. 169):—

> 'There is a lass whom I adore,
> And here I will set forth her name,
> 'Tis she that can my joys restore,
> And pretty Katy is her name.
> For Katy, Katy, Katy O,
> The love I bear to Katy O:
> All the world shall never know
> The love I bear to Katy O.'

Another ballad (Crawford, Pepys, and Roxburghe Collections), *The Scotch Wooing of Willy and Nanie*, has the same chorus, with 'Nanie' for 'Katy,' and with this one Burns was probably as well acquainted as Ramsay himself. There is also an *Answer to Nanie* with 'Willie' in the chorus (Crawford and Roxburghe Collections); and there is, further, a curious and rare broadside on the death of Queen Anne (British Museum):—

> 'My Nan she was good, my Nan she was just,
> My Nannie O, Queen Anie O;
> And all the world shall never know
> The love that I bear to my Nanie O.'

The old song, *Highland Lassie*, suggested to Burns scarce more than his title; but it faintly resembles *The Highland Queen*.

THO' CRUEL FATE

No. 118 in Johnson (Vol. ii. 1788), where it appears on the opposite page to *My Highland Lassie O*: set to the tune of *The Northern Lass*: described as 'written for this work by Robert Burns'; and signed 'R.' The MS. is in the Hastie Collection. In the MS. in the possession of Mr. Nelson, Edinburgh, the tune given is *She Rose and Loot Me In*. The song closely resembles the first stanza of *From Thee, Eliza* (Vol. i. p. 183).

LINE 2. '*As far's* the pole and line,' Mr. Nelson's MS.
5. 'Tho' mountains *frown* and deserts howl,' Mr. Nelson's MS.

STAY MY CHARMER

No. 129 in Johnson (Vol. ii. 1788): 'Written for this work by R. Burns.' Set to the tune *An Gilleadh Dubh*, or *The Black-hair'd Lad*; and signed 'B.' A MS. is in the Hastie Collection.

The idea is found in a fragment in the Herd MS. :—

> Can ye leave me so, ladie,
> Can ye leave me so?
> Can ye leave me comfortless
> To take another jo?'

STRATHALLAN'S LAMENT

No. 132 in Johnson (Vol. ii. 1788): 'Written for this work by Robert Burns,' and signed 'B.' Included, too, in Thomson's *Scottish Airs* (Vol. iv.). 'This air is the composition of the worthiest and best-hearted man living, Allan Masterton, schoolmaster in Edinburgh. As he and I were both sprouts of Jacobitism, we agreed to dedicate our words and air to the cause. But to tell the matter of fact; except when my passions were heated by some accidental cause, my Jacobitism was merely by way of "*vive la bagatelle*"' (R. B. in Interleaved Copy).

The Strathallan of the *Lament* was James Drummond —eldest son of William, 4th Viscount Strathallan, killed at Culloden, 14th April 1746—who was included in the Act of Attainder, 4th June ; and, after staying for some time in hiding, escaped to France, where he died, 27th June 1765, at Sens in Champagne. The titles were restored in 1824.

STRATH-
ALLAN'S
LAMENT

The MS. of the second stanza is in the Hastie Collection. Another copy of the song, probably forming part of the Stair MS., has got separated into two halves. For a copy of the first stanza we are indebted to Mr. Davey, Great Russell Street, Bloomsbury, while the second is included in the Clarke-Adam Collection. This MS. corresponds with the Johnson set. Another MS. is in the possession of Canon Tristram, and an early draft was in that of Henry Probasco, Cincinnati.

STANZA I. LINE I. ' Thickest *darkness shrouds* my dwelling,' early draft. ' *Oer-hang*' for 'surround,' Currie. 3. ' *Sweeping* torrents, *turbid* swelling,' MS. quoted in Pickering, 1839. 4. ' *Still surround* my lonely cave,' Currie and Tristram MS.
In the early draft Stanza II. reads thus :—

' *Farewell fleeting, fickle treasure,*
Between mishap and folly shar'd;
Farewell peace and farewell pleasure,
Farewell flattering man's regard.'
Ruin's wheel has driven o'er *me*,
Nor dare a hope my fate attend ;
The wide world is all before *me*,
But a world without a friend.'

MY HOGGIE

No. 133 in Johnson (Vol. ii. 1788): Unsigned. ' Dr. Walker, who was minister in Moffat in 1772, and is now (1791) Professor of Natural History in the University of Edinburgh, told the following anecdote concerning this air. He said that some gentlemen riding a few years ago

MY
HOGGIE

through Liddesdale stopped at a hamlet consisting of a few houses, called Mosspaul (in Ewesdale), when they were struck with this tune, which an old woman, spinning on a rock at her door, was singing. All she could tell concerning it was, that she was taught it when a child, and it was called—" What will I do gin my Hoggie die?" No person, except a few females at Mosspaul, knew this fine old tune, which in all probability would have been lost had not one of the gentlemen who happened to have a flute with him taken it down' (R. B. in Interleaved Copy).

Stenhouse states that it was Stephen Clarke who took down the tune. Burns's MS. is in the Hastie Collection, and in his note he seems to imply that he wrote his song from the old first line. Nevertheless, Peter Buchan professed, as usual, to have found an original (North of Scotland) in a ballad in celebration of Sir James Innes (a Ram), who carried off Margaret Brodie of Coxton (the Hoggie, or young sheep) to make her his wife. Buchan's doggerel, prefaced with this statement, is reprinted as an Appendix to Sharpe's *Ballad Book* (ed. Laing, 1880)—'evidently obtained,' says Laing, 'through a northern collector.' Buchan vouchsafes no further information, and, so far as we can discover, his story is uncorroborated by the Innes family-tree. In any case his 'original' scarce deserves the name of ballad. Here is the chorus :—

'Coxton has but ae hoggie,
Ae hoggie, ae hoggie,
Coxton has but ae hoggie;
O' it he is right vogie.'

And here is his last stanza :—

'But there came a ram frae Deveron-side,
Frae Deveron-side, frae Deveron-side,
But there came a ram frae Deveron-side,
And stown awa my hoggie.'

NOTES

JUMPIN JOHN

No. 138 in Johnson (Vol. ii. 1788): Unsigned.

Stenhouse states that the stanzas were communicated by Burns, and that they 'are a fragment of the old humorous ballad, with some verbal corrections.' Where 'the old humorous ballad' was to be found he did not say, nor can we. Sharpe affirmed that this fragment was Burns's 'ground-work':—

> 'Her daddy forbad, her minnie forbad,
> Forbidden she wadna be:
> The lang lad they ca' Jumpin John
> Beguil'd our bonnie Bessie.'

But Sharpe said not where he got it. In any case Burns knew the song *My Dady Forbad* in *The Tea-Table Miscellany*, which, according to Stenhouse (he probably did but express an opinion), Ramsay 'wrote as a substitute for the indelicate old Scots Song':

> 'When I think on my lad
> I sigh and am sad,
> For now he is far from me':—

and in which there is this stanza:—

> 'Tho' my Dady forbad,
> And my Minny forbad,
> Forbidden I will not be;
> For since thou alone
> My favour hast won
> Nane else shall e'er get it for me.'

UP IN THE MORNING EARLY

No. 140 in Johnson (Vol. ii. 1788): Signed 'Z.' 'The chorus of this song is old; the two stanzas are mine' (R. B. in Interleaved Copy).

Sir John Hawkins relates of the old ballad and tune that they were favourites with Mary, Queen of William of Orange, who on one occasion, after listening to divers Purcells, asked Mrs. Hunt to sing the Scots ballad of

UP IN THE MORNING EARLY *Cold and Raw.* The original broadside (Euing, Huth, Roxburghe, and other Collections) is entitled '*A Northern Ditty, or the Scotchman Outwitted by the Country Damsell.* To an Excellent New Scotch tune of *Cold and Raw the North did Blaw,* a Song Much in Request at Court.' Bearing the imprimatur, ' R. P.', and beginning thus :—

> 'Cold and Raw the North did blaw
> Bleak in the morning early ;
> All the trees were hid with snow
> Cover'd with Winter's yearly ' :—

it relates an adventure with a farmer's daughter, on the road to market betimes to sell her father's barley. Later sets have many verbal differences. The authorship has been attributed—plausibly enough—to Tom D'Urfey ; but a set in a *Collection of Old Ballads* (London 1723) is described as ' said to have been written in the time of James ' (1st of England) ; and in any case D'Urfey might have had a Scots original. There are also blackletter *Answers to Cold and Raw.* In Hogg and Motherwell (1834) it is suggested that Burns's set may have been a brief *rifaccimento* of a ' well-known song ' :—

> 'Cauld blaws the win' frae north to south,
> And drift is driving sairly,
> The sheep are couring i' the cleugh—
> O sirs ! it 's winter fairly !
> Now up in the morning 's no for me,
> Up in the morning early ;
> I 'd rather gang supperless to my bed
> Than rise in the morning early,' *etc.*

But this is simply a vamp from Burns, done by the same John Hamilton to whom we owe the ' neat and clean ' additions to *Of A' the Airts.* Peter Buchan comes forward with a special Aberdeenshire set, of which the two last lines of the chorus are these :—

> 'Frae morning till night our squires they sat
> And drank the price o' the barley.'

But this is apparently debased from a blackletter, *Good Ale For My Money* (Roxburghe Collection):— UP IN THE MORNING EARLY

> 'I cannot go home, nor I will not go home,
>   It's 'long of the oyle of Barley;
> I'll tarry all night for my delight
>   And go home in the morning early.'

It was, however, from none of these that Burns got his chorus, but from a hitherto unknown set in the Herd MS., here given in full:—

Chorus
'Up i' the morning, up i' the morning
  Up i' the morning early:
Up i' the morning's no for me,
  And I canna get up so early.

I

'YE men that has your wives in bed,
  It's needless to bid you rise early;
Ye may kiss them and clap them; nae mair to be said,
  Nae matter you do not rise early!

II

'But we young lads that hae lasses to prie,
  And gets but a smack o' them rarely:
Take care that Geordy Swine does not see—
  Nae matter you do not rise early!

III

'But if nine months should produce a live mouth,
  And the town get wit of the fairly,
Then Geordy comes to us and wi' a great rout:—
  "Ye maun greet three Sundays sairly."

IV

'Then up the creepy you maun steal,
  And pray to Mass John for to spare ye;
But he'll look at ye as gin ye were the Deil
  In the twilight or morning early.

Chorus
'Up i' the morning, up i' the morning,
  Up i' the morning early:
Up i' the morning's no for me,
  And I canna get up so early.'

THE YOUNG HIGHLAND ROVER

No. 143 in Johnson (Vol. ii. 1788): 'Written for this work by Robert Burns,' and signed 'B.'

Intended to commemorate his visit to Castle Gordon in 1787, and made, seemingly, after the discovery that *Castle Gordon* (Vol. ii. p. 60) did not fit the tune *Morag*. To the same tune he also wrote *O, Wat ye wha that Lo'es Me* (p. 249). The 'rover' was probably the Young Chevalier.

The MS. in the Hastie Collection corresponds with Johnson's text.

THE DUSTY MILLER

No. 144 in Johnson (Vol. ii. 1788): Unsigned, but Burns's holograph copy is in the British Museum.

Stenhouse says vaguely that the verses 'are a fragment of the old ballad with a few verbal alterations by Burns'; and Sharpe gives a version of the 'original' without saying where he got it. It differs comparatively little from the fragment (Herd MS.) upon which Burns based his song:—

'O, the Dusty Miller, O the Dusty Miller!
Dusty was his coat, Dusty was his cullour,
Dusty was the kiss I got frae the Miller!
O, the Dusty Miller with the dusty coat,
He will spend a shilling ere he win a groat.
O, the Dusty Miller.'

I DREAM'D I LAY

No. 146 in Johnson (Vol. iv. 1788): Signed 'X.' 'These two stanzas I composed when I was seventeen; they are among the oldest of my printed pieces' (R. B. in Interleaved Copy).

Scott Douglas has noted that this feeble performance is largely a cento of expressions and ideas selected from

Mrs. Cockburn's *Flowers of the Forest*. But a plagiary of I DREAM'D seventeen is scarce worth distinguishing: even though I LAY his name be Robert Burns.

The last four lines of his last stanza were taken from the fragment, *Tho' Fickle Fortune has Deceived Me* (see Vol. iv.). The MS. is in the Hastie Collection.

STANZA II. LINE 4. 'A' my flowery *hopes* destroy'd,' deleted reading in MS.

DUNCAN DAVISON

No. 149 in Johnson's *Museum* (Vol. ii. 1788): Signed 'Z.'

Stenhouse affirms that this song is by Burns, although he did not choose to avow it; also that he (Stenhouse) had 'recovered his (Burns's) original manuscript, which is the same as that inserted in the *Museum*.' No doubt Stenhouse is right; but Burns did but act according to his wont in signing 'Z,' for not only was his *Duncan Davison* suggested by a song with the same title and something of the same motive preserved in *The Merry Muses*— (from which his first, second, and fourth lines are lifted bodily)—but it is, as regards his last stanza at least, a thing of shreds and patches; while the last half of this said stanza, containing a very irrelevant moral, is merely 'conveyed' from a fragment, here first printed, in the Herd MS. :—

> 'I can drink and no be drunk,
> I can fight and no be slain;
> I can kiss a bonie lass
> And ay be welcome back again.'

STANZA I. LINE 8. 'Temper-pin':—The pin which regulated the motion of the spinning-wheel. *Cf.* Allan Ramsay's vamp, *My Jo Janet* :—

> 'To keep the temper-pin in tiff
> Employs right aft my hand, Sir.

THENIEL MENZIES' BONIE MARY

No. 156 in Johnson (Vol. ii. 1788): Signed 'Z.' Tune, *Ruffian's Rant*.

Buchan (the ingenious and obliging) 'remembers to have seen many years ago a copy of this song in a very old Aberdeen magazine, said to be by a gentleman of that city.' He also supplies a set which he describes as the 'oldest on record,' at the same time stating that it is 'from recitation, and never in print':—

> 'In Scotland braid and far awa,
> Where lasses painted, busk sae braw,
> A bonnier lass I never saw
> Than Thenie Menzies' bonny Mary.
>   Thenie Menzies' bonny Mary,
>   Thenie Menzies' bonny Mary
>   A' the warld would I gie
>   For a kiss o' Thenie's bonny Mary!' *etc.*

LADY ONLIE, HONEST LUCKY

PRINTED in Johnson as alternative words for *The Ruffian's Rant*: Signed 'Z.' Burns probably picked up the chorus during his northern tour.

CHORUS. LINE 1. 'Honest Lucky':—'Lucky' is a common designation for alewives. See further Vol. ii. p. 364, Note to *To Major Logan*, Stanza XIII. Line 2.

THE BANKS OF THE DEVON

No. 157 in Johnson (Vol. ii. 1788): 'Written for this work by Burns.' Tune, *Phannerach dhon na chri*. Signed 'B.' Included in Thomson's *Scottish Airs*, Vol. iii. The MS. in the Hastie Collection, as another in the *Glenriddell Book*, corresponds with the text. 'These verses were com-

NOTES

posed on a charming girl, a Miss Charlotte Hamilton, who is now married to James M'Kittrick Adair, Esqr., physician. She is sister to my worthy friend Gavin Hamilton of Mauchline, and was born on the banks of Ayr, but was, at the time I wrote these lines, residing at Harvieston in Clackmannanshire, on the romantic banks of the little river Devon. I first heard the air from a lady in Inverness, and got the notes taken down for the work' (R. B in Interleaved Copy).

Burns visited Gavin Hamilton's mother and her family at Harvieston on Monday, 27th August 1787, and wrote to Hamilton on the 28th :—' Of Charlotte I cannot speak in common terms of admiration ; she is not only beautiful but lovely. Her form is elegant; her features not regular, but they have the smile of sweetness and the settled complacency of good-nature in the highest degree ; and her complexion, now that she has happily recovered her wonted health, is equal to Miss Burnet's.' In the October following Burns stopped at Harvieston again, and introduced that Dr. Adair whom Miss Hamilton married, 16th November 1789. She died a widow in 1806. On 2nd September 1787 Burns sent the first draft of his song to her friend, Miss Chalmers :—' I am determined to pay Charlotte a poetic compliment in the second part of the *Museum*, if I could hit on some glorious Scotch air. You will see a small attempt on a shred of paper enclosed.'

The 'small attempt' is a poor enough performance, when all is said—not much above the stall level : but it appears to be pure Burns.

DUNCAN GRAY

No. 160 in Johnson (Vol. ii. 1788): Signed 'Z.' The MS. is in the Hastie Collection.

It is founded on a song preserved in the Herd MS. and

DUNCAN GRAY (with some variations, which are probably due to Burns's hand) in *The Merry Muses*, which begins thus :—

> 'Can ye play wi' Duncan Gray
> (Hey, hey the girdin o't)
> O'er the hills and far away?
> Hey, hey the girdin o't': —

but the story is quite other, and, with the humour and picturesque circumstance of the lyric, is Burns's own. Burns sent a second set to Thomson (p. 215), as to which see Prefatory Note (*post*, p. 452).

THE PLOUGHMAN

No. 165 in Johnson (Vol. ii. 1788): Unsigned.

Founded on a bawdy old song, preserved in *The Merry Muses*, to which Burns is indebted for his Chorus, his Stanza I., and the structural idea (at least) of his Stanza II. :—

> 'I hae ploughed east, I hae ploughed west
> In weather foul or fair, Jo,
> But the sairest ploughing e'er I ploughed,
> Was,' *etc.* :—

and of which he has not even tried to abolish the flavour —far from it. A milder version is quoted in Herd (1769), two stanzas of which are included in the *Museum* set :—

> 'The ploughman he's a bonny lad
> And a' his wark's at leisure,
> And when that he comes hame at e'en,
> He kisses me wi' pleasure,' *etc.*

A blackletter set of a similar English ditty is published in an Appendix to *The Roxburghe Ballads*, ed. Ebsworth, Vol. vii. It is entitled the *Country Maid's Delight, or the Husbandman's Honour made known. Being a Delightful Song in Praise of a Plowman* :—

> 'You young men and maids that in country doth dwell
> Lend attention if time spare you can,
> I'll sing you a song that will please you full well,
> In praise of the honest Plowmán.
> *Then hey for the Plowman that's valiant and stout,*' etc.

THE PLOUGHMAN

Another is *The Northern Ladd or The Fair Maid's Choice Who Refuses All for a Plowman*, of which there are blackletter broadsides in the Crawford, Huth, and Roxburghe Collections.

LANDLADY, COUNT THE LAWIN

No. 170 in Johnson (Vol. ii. 1788): Unsigned. Set to the tune, *Hey Tutti Taiti*. ' I have met the tradition universally over Scotland, and particularly in the neighbourhood of the scene, that this air was Robert Bruce's march to Bannockburn' (R. B. in Interleaved Copy). He afterwards wrote *Scots Wha Hae* (p. 251) to it. Buchan supplies (*more suo*) the ' original words' of *Tutti Taiti*; but it were waste of ink and space to quote them. Burns's MS. is in the Hastie Collection.

The present song is, not an original but, a patchwork of assorted scraps, with some few verbal changes. The first stanza is a variation on the chorus of the old song which Burns utilised in *Guidwife, Count the Lawin* (p. 91); the second is vamped from a stanza in *Carl, An the King Come* (p. 57); the third is the first of a Jacobite song to the same tune, of which the second is :—

> 'Here's to the King,
> Ye ken wha I mean,
> And to ilka honest boy
> That will do it again.'

STANZA I. LINE 4. ' And *I'm jolly* fou,' MS.

RAVING WINDS AROUND HER BLOWING

No. 173 in Johnson (Vol. ii. 1788): ' Written for this work by R. Burns.' Signed ' B.' Tune: *M'Gregor of*

RAVING WINDS AROUND HER BLOWING

Roro's Lament. ' I composed these verses on Miss Isabella Macleod of Rasa, alluding to her feelings on the death of her sister, and the still more melancholy death of her sister's husband, the late Earl of Loudoun, who shot himself out of sheer heart-break at some mortifications he suffered owing to the deranged state of his finances' (R. B. in Interleaved Copy).

For Miss Isabella M'Leod see Prefatory Note to *On the Death of John M'Leod, Esq.* (Vol. i. p. 448), and *To Miss Isabella M'Leod* (Vol. ii. p. 109). The song is reminiscent of a once famous Gay (1685-1732, quoted in *The Charmer* and other books) :—

> ' "Twas when the seas were roaring
> With hollow blasts of wind,
> A damsel lay deploring,
> All on a rock reclin'd,' *etc.*

Writing to Mrs. Dunlop, 16th August 1788, Burns notes that the song had lately been sung at a party at Dalswinton. Mrs. Miller, he goes on, ' asked me whose were the words :—" Mine, Madam—they are indeed my very best verses." *Sacre Dieu,* she took not the smallest notice of them,' Manners apart, who in these days can blame her?

STANZA II. LINE 7. ' *O how gladly I'd resign thee,'* Currie.

HOW LANG AND DREARY IS THE NIGHT

No. 175 in Johnson (Vol. ii. 1788): Unsigned. *Set to a Gaelic Air.* We have adopted the version sent to Thomson (Vol. i. 1796), when the chorus was added. ' I met with some such words in a collection of songs somewhere, which I altered and enlarged ; and to please you, and to suit your favourite air of *Cauld Kail,* I have taken a stride or two across my room, and have arranged it anew, as you will find on the other page' (R. B. to Thomson, October 1794).

How Lang and Dreary reads like a version of *Ay*

NOTES   325

Waukin O (p. 45), but has no direct connexion with HOW LANG that lyric. Burns rightly notes that he had met with AND 'some such words' somewhere, but his memory betrays DREARY him in the matter of 'enlargement.' The original, found in the Herd MS. and nowhere else, consists in all of nine stanzas, of which here are the first four :—

> 'The Day begins to Press
> And the Birds sing sweet and cheery;
> But I man rise and greet,
> And think upon my deary.
>
> 'I ne'er can sleep a wink
> Tho' ne'er so wet and weary;
> But ly and cry and think
> Upon my absent deary.
>
> 'When a' the lave 's at rest
> Or merry, blyth and cheery,
> My heart wi' grief opprest,
> I am dowie, dull, and wearie.
>
> 'It was but yesterday
> (Oh, how can I be chearie!)
> That yon wise wife did spae
> I ne'er would see my dearie,' *etc.*

The MS. of the second version is at Brechin Castle.

CHORUS. LINE 4. 'That 's *distant* frae her Dearie,' Brechin Castle MS.

STANZA I. LINE 3. '*I sleepless* lie frae e'en to morn,' 1st version.

STANZA II. LINES 1-3 in the 1st version read :—

> 'When I think on the *happy* days,
> I spent wi' *you* my Dearie,'
> And now what *lands* between us *lie.*

STANZA III. LINE 2. '*As ye were wae and weary,*' 1st version.

MUSING ON THE ROARING OCEAN

No. 179 in Johnson (Vol. ii. 1788): 'Written for this work by R. Burns.' Tune: *Drumion dubh.* Signed ' R.'

326 NOTES

MUSING ON THE ROARING OCEAN 'I composed these verses out of compliment to a Mrs. M'Lachlan, whose husband is an officer in the East Indies' (R. B. in Interleaved Copy). They are reminiscent of divers Jacobitisms.

STANZA II. LINE 4. *Cf.* the Jacobite song *Lewie Gordon* :—

'Altho' his back be at the wa',
Here's to him that's far awa' :—

which, however, is borrowed from an older *Song on the Birthday of King James the VIII.*, 10*th June* 1709 (*Roxburghe Ballads*, ed. Ebsworth, Vol. viii. 225).

BLYTHE WAS SHE

No. 180 in Johnson (Vol. ii. 1788): 'Written by R. Burns,' and signed 'B.' Also included in Thomson's *Scottish Airs* (Vol. ii.). 'I composed these verses while I stayed at Ochtertyre with Sir William Murray. The lady, who was also at Ochtertyre at the same time, was a well-known toast, Miss Euphemia Murray of Lintrose, who was called, and very justly, "the flower of Strathmore."' She married Mr. Smythe of Methven, who became one of the judges of the Court of Session.

The chorus is modelled on that of the old song *Andrew and his Cutty Gun*—(which Burns regarded as 'the work of a master,' and a set of which, perhaps the original, is found in *The Merry Muses*)—given as alternative words in Johnson :—

'Blythe, blythe, blythe was she,
Blythe was she butt and ben ;
And weel she lo'ed a Hawick gill,
And leugh to see a tappit hen.'

CHORUS. LINE 2. 'Butt and ben' :—See Vol. i. p. 334, Note to *The Holy Fair*, Stanza XVIII. Line 1.

TO DAUNTON ME

No. 182 in Johnson : Unsigned. The MS. in the Hastie Collection differs slightly from the printed copy. The chorus in Johnson is Stanza ii. of the MS. ; and the chorus in the MS. is simply :—

> 'To Daunton me, to Daunton me,
> An auld man shall never daunton me.'

'The two following old stanzas to this tune have some merit' (R. B.—according to Cromek—in Interleaved Copy).

The stanzas quoted are found in a collection of *Loyal Songs*, 1750. The ballad begins :—

> 'To daunton me, to daunton me :
> Do you ken the things that would daunton me?'

It consists of three stanzas. But a broadside of six, *To Daunton Me and to Wanton Me*, is given in Stevenson's *Ballads* (1844). This is the first :—

> 'When I was wanton, young and free,
> I thought nothing could daunton me ;
> But the eighty-eight and eighty-nine,
> And all the dreary years since syne,
> Presbytery, cess, and pole-monie
> Have done enough to daunton me.'

Other sets in Collections are merely corrupted from these. Stenhouse affirms that, ' with the exception of some lines of the chorus' of this ballad, the song in the *Museum* was 'wholly composed by Burns in 1787'; and Editors of Burns have accepted his statement. Clearly, however, the Burns set is abridged and greatly improved from a song in a very old (undated) chap, 'entered according to order,' in the Motherwell Collection, which is, apparently, a disguised Jacobitism :—

> 'I was forc'd to wed against my mind,
> To an old man neither loving nor kind ;

TO DAUNTON ME

 Neither loving nor kind, nor yet seems to be,
 But an old man ne'er shall daunton me!
  To daunton me, and I so young,
  To daunton me it would be too soon!
  Contrary to him still I'll be,
  And an old Carl shall ne'er daunton me!

   . . . . .

 At fifteen [1715] I should been wed
 Unto a brisk young Highland lad;
 Although he's far beyond the sea,
 Yet an old man shall ne'er daunton me!
  I lov'd him better in his Highland dress,
  Than an old man with all his brass;
  For all his brass and all his white money—
  For an old man ne'er shall daunton me.'

O'ER THE WATER TO CHARLIE

No. 187 in Johnson (Vol. ii. 1788): Unsigned; but its Jacobite sentiments account for that. The MS. is in the Hastie Collection. The air, with the title *O'er the Water to Charlie*, is in Oswald's *Pocket Companion*.

 The 'verses,' Stenhouse says, were 'revised and improved by Burns'; and, he adds,' a more complete version of this song may be seen in Hogg's *Jacobite Reliques*' (*sic*). 'Many versions of this song'—thus Buchan in a note in Hogg and Motherwell, Part v. (1834)—' have appeared in print. There is one in Hogg's *Jacobite Relics*, and one in the *Ancient Ballads and Songs of the North of Scotland*, from which latter copy I infer that the original had been written anterior to the days of Prince Charles, commonly called the Pretender, and the time of Charles the Second's restoration.' But Hogg's set is merely Ayrshire Bard *plus* Ettrick Shepherd, and it were hard to say how much Peter Buchan's, 'taken down from recitation,' is indebted to Peter Buchan—especially as internal evidence shows that, as he gives it, it did not all exist before his own days. No printed copy of any such ballad anterior to the Burns is quoted by Buchan. Nor do we know more

NOTES

than three. Two are included in a song-book called O'ER THE
The True Loyalist, surreptitiously printed in 1779, and WATER TO
extremely rare :— CHARLIE

'The K—g he has been long from home ;
The P—ce he has sent over
To kick the Usurper off the throne,
And send him to Hannover.
O'er the water, o'er the sea.
O'er the water to C—lie :
Go the world as it will,
We'll hazard our lives for C—lie, *etc.*

Thus the one. Thus, too, the other—headed *Over the Water to C—lie* :—

'When C—lie came to Edinburgh town,
And a' his friends about him ;
How pleas'd was I for to go down !
I could not be merry without him.
But since that o'er the seas he's gone
The other side landed fairly,
I'd freely quit wi' a' that I have
To get over the water to C—lie,' *etc.*

It is possible, however, that Burns borrowed from another set, of which our third may have been a parody. It is one of *Three Excellent New Songs*, in a chap at Abbotsford, 'entered according to order, 1781' :—

'We'll over Clyd's water, and back helter skelter,
We'll over Clyd's water to Charlie :
Since he is so stout, we'll no more cast out,
But each take our turn of him fairly,' *etc.*

A ROSE-BUD BY MY EARLY WALK

No. 189 in Johnson (Vol. ii. 1788) : Signed ' B.' 'This song I composed on Miss Jenny Cruickshank, only child to my worthy friend Mr. Wm. Cruickshank, of the High School, Edinburgh. The air is by David Sillar, *quondam* merchant, and now schoolmaster in Irvine. He

A ROSE-
BUD BY
MY EARLY
WALK

is the "Davie" to whom I address my printed poetical epistle in the measure of *The Cherry and the Slae*' (R. B. in Interleaved Copy).

See Prefatory Note to *To Miss Cruickshank* (Vol. i. p. 447). The MS. is in the Hastie Collection.

STANZA I. LINE 7. 'And *hanging* rich the dewy head,' deleted reading in MS.

AND I'LL KISS THEE YET

No. 193 in Johnson (Vol. ii. 1788): Signed 'Z.' The chorus, probably, is old.

Some suppose the heroine to have been Mary Campbell (see *ante*, p. 308, Prefatory Note to *My Highland Lassie, O*); others Elison Begbie (see *On Cessnock Banks*, Vol. iv.). For another set, sent to Thomson, see *Come, Let Me Take Thee*, p. 233.

The MS. sent to Johnson is in the Hastie Collection. Another MS. has a third stanza:—

> 'Ilk care and fear, when thou art near,
> I ever mair defy them, O!
> Young kings upon their hansel throne
> Are no sae blest as I am, O!'

RATTLIN, ROARIN WILLIE

No. 194 in Johnson (Vol. ii. 1788): Signed 'Z.' 'The last stanza of this song is mine; it was composed out of compliment to one of the worthiest fellows in the world, William Dunbar, Esq., Writer to the Signet, Edinburgh, and Colonel of the Crochallan Corps, a club of wits who took that title at the time of raising the fencible regiments' (R. B. in Interleaved Copy).

Dunbar, who became Inspector-General of Stamp Duties in Scotland, died 18th February 1807. He presented Burns in 1787 with a copy of Spenser, and is often alluded to or addressed in terms of warm regard.

In a note to the *Lay* (iv. 34), Sir Walter tells the story RATTLIN
of an 'antient border minstrel' called ('from his bullying ROARIN
disposition') by the name of Burns's hero, who, having WILLIE
slain a brother bard in single combat, was hanged at Jedburgh, 'bequeathing his name to the beautiful Scottish
air,' *etc.* He also quotes some stanzas of the ballad
commemorative:—

> 'Now Willie's gane to Jeddart,
>   And he's for the rood-day,
> But Stobs and young Falnash
>   They followed him a' the way;
> They followed him a' the way,
>   They sought him up and down,
> In the links of Ousenam-water
>   They fand him sleeping sound.'

Here is nothing of Willie the fiddler, but Cunningham
has a version beginning thus:—

> 'Our Willie's away to Jeddart
>   To dance on the rood-day,
> A sharp sword by his side,
>   A fiddle to cheer his way,' *etc.*

It is, however, impossible to accept anything as an
antique on Cunningham's sole testimony; and in any
case the stanzas Burns incorporated have no connexion
with the Border ballad. They may derive from it, but
they apparently relate to a piece of tyranny on the part of
the kirk-session. This at least is the subject of an old
set given in *Notes and Queries* (2nd series, v. 186), whose
merits are symptomatic of authenticity. The first verse,
'O Willie, you'll sell your fiddle,' closely resembles that
in Johnson. Here are the chorus and the last stanza:—

> 'O rattlin, roarin Willie,
>   Ye'se ay fu' welcome to me!
> O rattlin, roarin Willie,
>   Ye'se ay fu' welcome to me:
> Ye'se ay fu' welcome to me
>   For a' the ill they've said;

RATTLIN ROARIN WILLIE

    For monie a cantie nicht
    My Willie and I hae had.

'Foul fa' their Kirks and their Sessions!
    They 're ay sae fond o' mischief!
They 'll ca' me into their sessions,
    They 'll ca' me worse than a thief.
They 'll ca' me worse than a thief,
    And they 'll mak me curse an ban;
They 'll brag me ay with their laws
    But Deil brak my legs gin I 'll gang.'

Halliwell gives a version in his *Nursery Rhymes* :—

    '"Jocky, come give me thy fiddle,
      If ever thou mean to thrive!"
    "Nay I 'll not give my fiddle
      To any man alive,"' etc.

WHERE, BRAVING ANGRY WINTER'S STORMS

No. 195 in Johnson (Vol. ii. 1788): 'Written by Robert Burns,' and signed 'R.' Tune: *Neil Gow's Lamentation*.

The heroine was Margaret, daughter of John Chalmers of Fingland, and a cousin of Charlotte Hamilton, her particular friend. Burns met her in Edinburgh during his first visit, and also in October 1787 at Harvieston. She married in 1788 Mr. Lewis Hay, of Forbes and Co.'s Bank; and died in 1843. Thomas Campbell affirmed that, according to Mrs. Hay, Burns had asked her in marriage; but this scarce accords with the tone of his letters to her. Still, he had a particular regard for the lady; and she always called out the best in him. His compliments in verse—or rather his proposal to publish them—somewhat alarmed her: her main objection being, presumably, not to the song in the text but, to *My Peggy's Face, My Peggy's Form* (p. 186). 'They are neither of them,' he wrote to her, 6th November 1787, 'so particular as to point you out to the world at large; and the circle of your acquaintance will allow all I have said.'

A MS. is in the Hastie Collection.

NOTES

STANZA I. LINE I. 'Where braving *all the* winter's *harms,*' BRAVING
MS. 5. 'As *when one by a* savage stream,' deleted reading ANGRY
in MS. WINTER'S
STANZA II. LINE I. 'Blest be the wild, sequester'd STORMS
shade,' Johnson, and deleted reading in the MS. 2. 'And
blest the *time* and hour,' deleted reading in the MS. 4. '*Where*
first I felt their pow'r,' MS.

O TIBBIE, I HAE SEEN THE DAY

No. 196 in Johnson (Vol. ii. 1788): 'Written for this work by Robert Burns,' and signed 'X.' 'This song I composed about the age of seventeen' (R. B. in Interleaved Copy).

Mrs. Begg states that the heroine was one Isabella Steenson, or Stevenson, the farmer's daughter of Little Hill, which marched with Lochlie. The song itself bears no small resemblance to a song (probably older) called *The Saucy Lass with the Beard*, found in an old Falkirk chap, printed by T. Johnstone (Motherwell Collection):—

> 'When I gaed o'er yon heathy hills,
>   A lassie for to see,
> Because my purse was scant o' cash,
>   She turned her back on me;
> Because I was a tradesman lad,
>   The lassie lookèd shy,
> She turned her back about to me;
>   But ne'er a hair car'd I.'

The MS. sent to Johnson is in the Hastie Collection. The song is also entered in the *First Common Place Book* under date September 1784. Other sets were published by Brash and Reid (Vol. iv. 1798), and Currie (1800).

STANZA II. is omitted by Johnson, Currie, and Brash and Reid.

STANZA III. LINE 3. 'That ye can please me *wi*' a wink,' Brash and Reid.

TIBBIE, I HAE SEEN THE DAY   STANZA VII. LINE 1. 'O Tibbie, *ye're o'er fu' o' spice*,' Brash and Reid.   2. 'Your daddie's gear maks you *fou* nice,' Brash and Reid; '*father's*' for 'daddie's,' *First Common Place Book.*

STANZA VIII. is not in Johnson. In Brash and Reid it reads thus :—

'There lives a lass *in yonder* park,
I *wadna gie* her in her sark
For you *and a'* your *fifty* mark,
That gars you look sae *shy*.'

Currie has the same reading of Lines 1-2; but reads 3-4 thus :—

'*For thee*, wi' a' *thy thousan*' mark—
Ye needna look sae high.'

CLARINDA, MISTRESS OF MY SOUL

No. 196 in Johnson (Vol. ii. 1788). Included in Thomson's *Scottish Airs*, Vol. ii., with several unauthorised changes by Thomson : Line 1 of Stanza I. being made to read :—'*Farewell, dear* mistress of my soul'; and Line 2 of Stanza II. :—'Shall *your poor wanderer* hie.'

This song was written when Burns was about to leave Edinburgh. A MS. corresponding with the text and the version in Johnson is at Lochryan. 'I am sick of writing where my bosom is not strongly interested. Tell me what you think of the following. There the bosom was perhaps a little interested' (R. B. to Mrs. Dunlop in Lochryan MSS.).

THE WINTER IT IS PAST

No. 200 in Johnson (Vol. ii. 1788): Unsigned.

The first two stanzas were published in Cromek's *Reliques*. The song itself is largely and generously adapted from a song called *The Curragh of Kildare*. The versions in the stall copies vary. The set used by Burns seems to have been that in the Herd MS. Only Stanza II. is wholly his own.

I LOVE MY LOVE IN SECRET

No. 204 in Johnson (Vol. iii. 1790): Unsigned.
Stenhouse affirms that the old song was 'slightly altered by Burns, because it was rather inadmissible in its original state'; but apparently he spoke by guesswork. There is no doubt that Burns got his original—here printed for the first time—in the Herd MS. :—

> 'My Sandy O, my Sandy O,
> My bonie, bonie Sandy O !
> Tho' the love that I owe,
> To thee I dare nae show,
> Yet I love my love in secret,
> My Sandie O.
>
> 'My Sandy gied to me a ring
> Was a' beset wi' diamonds fine;
> But I gied to him a far better thing:
> I gied to him my heart to keep
> In pledge of his ring.'

It will be seen that all he did was to add a stanza to the original set, or what was left of it.

SWEET TIBBIE DUNBAR

No. 207 in Johnson (Vol. iii. 1790): 'Written for this work by Robert Burns.' Tune: *Johny M'Gill.* 'This tune is said to be the composition of John M'Gill, fiddler in Girvan. He called it by his own name' (R. B. in Interleaved Copy).
The MS. is in the Hastie Collection.

HIGHLAND HARRY

No. 209 in Johnson (Vol. iii. 1790): Unsigned. Tune: *The Highlander's Lament.* 'The oldest title I ever heard to this air was *The Highland Watch's Farewell to Ireland.* The chorus I picked up from an old woman in Dunblane. The rest of the song is mine' (R. B. in Interleaved Copy).

HIGHLAND HARRY   Allan Cunningham notes that 'part of the farm of Mossgiel is called "Knockhaspiesland."' But Buchan, it need scarce be said, found an 'original' (in Aberdeenshire) in a long, long rigmarole, 'known for ages,' but 'never before in print.' The primordial hero (thus Buchan) was a Highland chieftain, who came to court a certain Jeanie Gordon, daughter of the laird of Knockhespock, Aberdeenshire. The second last verse of the Buchan resembles Burns's chorus :—

'O, for him back again!
O, for him back again!
I wad gie a' Knockhespock's land,
For ae shake o' my Harry's hand.''

A MS., not in Burns's hand, in the Hastie Collection, contains two additional stanzas, which are plainly not Burns, but are printed in Hogg's *Relics*. The present set appears to have suggested *Will Ye No Come Back Again?* to Lady Nairne.

THE TAILOR FELL THRO' THE BED

No. 212 in Johnson : Unsigned. 'This air is the march of the Corporation of Tailors. The second and fourth stanzas are mine' (R. B. in Interleaved Copy).

The original of the third stanza is in Burns's holograph in the Hastie Collection :—

'Gie me my groat again, canny young man,
Gie me my groat again, canny young man;
The night it is short, and the day it is lang,
It is a dear won sixpence to be wi' a man.'

Buchan gives what he says is the old song. It consists of the chorus, with an Aberdeenshire variation, and the following silly stanza (also pure Aberdeen) :—

'The beddie was tied frae head to feet
Wi' ropes o' hay, that were wondrous sweet,
And by came the calfie and ate them awa',
Deal hooly, my laddie, the beddie will fa'.'

AY WAUKIN O

No. 213 in Johnson (Vol. iii. 1790): Unsigned.
Chambers in *Scottish Songs* (Vol. i. 126-8), quotes a set of *Ay Waukin O*, which he styles 'the original song from recitation,' together with a set 'as altered by Burns.' Taking Chambers for gospel, Dr. John Brown (*Horæ Subsecivæ,* ii. 303) opines that the first set is 'all but perfect,' and that 'Burns, who in almost every instance not only adorned but transformed and purified whatever of the old he touched, breathing into it his own tenderness and strength, fails here.' But the fact is that Chambers's No. 1 incorporates most of the set Burns sent to Johnson's *Museum*; while the lines in his No. 2, especially denoted by Dr. Brown as inferior, are not Burns at all. Stenhouse makes bold to state that the first stanza was written by Burns, and that 'he even made some slight alterations on the very old fragment incorporated with his words.' He also gives 'all that is known of the original verses,' which according to him include this one:—

'It cam in my head
To send my love a letter;
My lad canna read,
And I loe him the better':—

Cromek (*Scotish Songs,* ii. 207) prints as an old fragment in Burns's hand the two first stanzas quoted by Stenhouse; but they may be but an early draft of the *Museum* song. Sharpe supplied a ballad which 'many people sang' in his 'youth.' It introduces the name of a Miss Macfarlane, an Edinburgh beauty. But the association is clearly artificial:—

'When first scho came to toon,
They ca'd her Jess Macfarlane;
But now scho's come an' gane,
They ca' her the wanderin' darlin';
Ay waukin O,' *etc.*

AY
WAUKIN
O

There is, in fact, no evidence of the antiquity of the Chambers, Stenhouse, and Sharpe sets. Probably the true original is a fragment in the Herd MS. :—

> 'O wat, wat,
> O wat and weary!
> Sleep I can get nane
> For thinking on my Deary.
> A' the night I wake,
> A' the day I weary,
> Sleep I can get nane
> For thinking on my Deary.'

For a kindred song—which reads like another offshoot of the same scrap—also in the Herd MS., see *ante*, p. 325, Prefatory Note to *How Lang and Dreary is the Night*.

BEWARE O' BONIE ANN

No. 215 in Johnson (Vol. iii. 1790): Signed 'X.' 'I composed this song out of compliment to Miss Ann Masterton, the daughter of my friend, Allan Masterton, the author of the air *Strathallan's Lament*; and two or three others in this work' (R. B. in Interleaved Copy).

The lady married Dr. Derbyshire, physician, of Bath and London, and died in August 1834.

LADDIE, LIE NEAR ME

No. 218 in Johnson (Vol. iii. 1790).

Alternative words to the tune *Laddie, Lie Near Me*. They are described as 'old'; but there can be never a doubt that Burns at least amended and condensed an original. True, being asked by Thomson to write words for *Laddie, Lie Near Me*, he replied :—'I do not know the air; and until I am complete master of a tune in my own singing, such as it is, I never can compose for it.' But to vamp existing words was a very different matter from

NOTES

writing new ones. Ritson, in his *North Country Chorister*, 1802, gives what he holds to be the folk-original. Here is the first stanza:— LADDIE, LIE NEAR ME

> 'Down in yon valley, soft shaded by mountains,
> Heard I a lad an' lass making acquaintance;
> Making acquaintance and singing so clearly:—
> "Lang have I lain my lane, laddie lie near me."'

But the true one is certainly a blackletter broadside, *The Loving Shepherdess, or Lady (i.e.* Laddie) *Lie Near Me*, to the tune of *Lady, Lie Near Me, or The Green Garter* (Pepys Collection, iii. 59):—

> ' All in the month of May
>   When all things blossom,
> As in my bed I lay,
>   Sleep it grew loathsome;
> Up I rose and did walk
>   Over yon mountains,
> Through mountains, through dales,
>   Over rocks, over fountains;
> I heard a voice to say:—
>   "Sweet heart, come cheer me,
> Thou hast been long away,
>   Lady, lye near me."'

THE GARD'NER WI' HIS PAIDLE

No. 220 in Johnson (Vol. iii. 1790): Signed 'Z.' 'The title of the song only is old; the rest is mine' (R. B. in Interleaved Copy).

The MS. is in the Hastie Collection. Burns sent another set to Thomson, *Now Rosy May*, p. 245.

ON A BANK OF FLOWERS

No. 223 in Johnson (Vol. iii. 1790). 'Written for this work by Robert Burns.' Included also in Thomson (Vol. ii.). The original was written by Theobald, set

ON A BANK OF FLOWERS by Galliard, and sung by Mr. Park in *The Lady's Triumph*:—

> 'On a Bank of Flowers
> In a summer's day,
> Inviting and undrest,
> In her bloom of youth bright Celia lay
> With love and sleep opprest,
> When a youthful swain with adoring eyes
> Wish'd he dared the fair maid surprise,
>   With a fa la la,
> But fear'd approaching spies.'

Burns rather bungles his inspiration, and certainly diverts his motive to a more liberal conclusion. Both original and derivative belong to a type of pastoral in high favour after the Restoration, good examples being Dryden's *Chloe Found Amyntas Lying* and *Beneath a Myrtle Shade*. Older and less farded, less artificial and immodest, are *As at Noon Dulcina Rested* (long attributed to Raleigh) and that charming ditty, *The Matchless Maid*, in the Second *Westminster Drollery* (1672).

THE DAY RETURNS

No. 224 in Johnson (Vol. iii. 1790): 'Written for this work by Robert Burns,' and signed 'R.' Tune: *Seventh of November*. Included in Thomson (Vol. i.). 'I composed this song out of compliment to one of the happiest and worthiest couples in the world: Robert Riddell, Esq. of Glenriddell, and his lady. At their fireside I have enjoyed more pleasant evenings than at all the houses of fashionable people in this country put together; and to their kindness and hospitality I am indebted for many of the happiest hours of my life' (R. B. in Interleaved Copy).

For Captain Riddell, see Vol. ii. p. 374, Prefatory Note to *To Captain Riddell*. The song was sent him in a letter (unpublished) dated Tuesday evening (*i.e.* 9th September 1788):—'As I was busy behind my harvest folks

this forenoon, and musing on a proper theme for your THE DAY
Seventh of November, some of the conversation before me RETURNS
accidentally suggested a suspicion that this said Seventh
of November is a matrimonial anniversary with a certain
very worthy neighbour of mine. I have seen very few
who owe so much to a wedding-day as Mrs. Riddell and
you; and my imagination took the hint accordingly as
you will see on the next page.' Burns sent a copy to
Miss Chalmers, 16th September 1788.
The Johnson MS. is in the Hastie Collection.

STANZA II. LINE 4. '*Only for love and thee* I live,' Riddell
MS.

MY LOVE, SHE'S BUT A LASSIE YET

No. 225 in Johnson (Vol. iii. 1790): Unsigned. 'The
title and the last half stanza of this song,' says Stenhouse,
'are old ; the rest was composed by Burns.'

The last stanza figures as Stanza II. in a set of *Green
Grows the Rashes, O* in Herd (1769); but the real original
of what Scott Douglas calls this 'remarkable ditty' is
doubtless *The Cowgate Garland, or the Drinking O't,* in an
old chap (Motherwell Collection):—

'My wife and me we did agree,
    When married I was thinking o't,
Her daughter Kate she angered me.
    Then I began the drinking o't.
O weary fa' the drinking o't:
O weary fa' the drinking o't:
An ye begin as I did then
Your purse will lose the clinking o't.

. . . . .

'We're a' dry at the drinking o't,
We're a' dry at the drinking o't;
Our punch [? pouch] was toom or we had done,
And this began the thinking o't.'

Burns's holograph is in the Hastie Collection.

JAMIE, COME TRY ME

No. 229 in Johnson (Vol. iii. 1790) : Unsigned. The tune and title are in Oswald's *Pocket Companion.*

Stenhouse affirms that the thing is by Burns, and that he had never met with older words. The original was probably related to a blackletter (Huth, Roxburghe, and other Collections) entitled *The New Scotch Jig or the Bonny Cravat*, to the tune of *Jenny, Come Tye Me* :—

> 'Jenny come tye me,
> Jenny come tye me,
> Jenny come tye my bonny cravat' :—

where 'cravat' may have, and probably has, an equivocal sense, as in a song preserved in the *Merry Muses.* There is also a *Reply* in blackletter. See also a song in *The Lark* (1740) :—

> *She.* 'Did you not promise me when you lay by me,
>   That you would marry me, can you deny me?
> *He.* If I did promise thee, 'twas but to try thee,
>   Call up your Witnesses, else I defie thee' :—

itself founded on a blackletter ballad (Euing and Roxburghe Collections), *The Deluded Lass's Lamentation.*

The stanza of the Burns is identical with that of *Laddie, Lie Near Me* (p. 47); yet another instance being *The Lady's Tragedy,* to the tune of *Ring the Gold* (Pepys Collection, v. 311) :—

> 'Why is my love unkind?
> Why does he leave me?' *etc.*

For a copy of Burns's holograph we are indebted to Mr. Ellsworth of Chicago.

THE SILVER TASSIE

No. 231 in Johnson (Vol. iii. 1790) : Unsigned. 'This air is Oswald's ; the first half stanza :—

> '"Go fetch to me a pint o' wine,
> And fill it in a silver tassie,
> That I may drink before I go
> A service to my bonie lassie" :—

is old ; the rest is mine' (R. B. in Interleaved Copy). Nevertheless, on 17th December 1788 he wrote to Mrs. Dunlop thus :—'Now I am on my hobby horse, I cannot help inserting two other old stanzas which please me mightily.' A MS.—MS. (A)—wanting the first half of Stanza I. is in the possession of Mr. Lennox, Dumfries.

Buchan supplied Hogg and Motherwell (1834) with an idiotic piece composed (he said) in the year 1636 by Alexander Lesley of Edinburgh, in which the old half-stanza is introduced as the second last verse. A ballad, *O Errol, it's a Bonny Place*, in Sharpe's *Ballad Book* (1823) begins thus :—

> 'Go fetch to me a pint of wine,
> Go fill it to the brim ;
> That I may drink my gude Lord's health,
> Tho' Errol be his name.'

And Burns may have had little more than some such suggestion for his brilliant and romantic first quatrain.

Currie published the version sent to Mrs. Dunlop ; and the MS. sent to Johnson—MS. (B)—is in the Hastie Collection. Burns there directs it to be sung to the tune of *The Secret Kiss*.

STANZA I. LINE 7. 'The Berwick-Law' :—North Berwick Law, a conspicuous height in Haddingtonshire overlooking the Firth of Forth. 8. 'And I maun *le'ae* my bonie Mary,' MS. (A).

STANZA II. LINE 4. *'The battle closes *thick* and bloody,' MS. (A) and Currie. 5. '*But* it's not the roar o' sea or shore,' MS. (A).

THE LAZY MIST

No. 232 in Johnson (Vol. iii. 1790): 'Written for this work by Robert Burns,' and signed 'B.'
The air and the title are in Oswald's *Caledonian Pocket Companion*. Burns sent a copy to Dr. Blacklock, 15th November 1788; and it is assigned to Blacklock in Thomson's *Scottish Airs* (Vol. i.).

THE CAPTAIN'S LADY

No. 233 in Johnson (Vol. iii. 1790): Unsigned.
Stenhouse gives this sample of the old set:—

> 'I will away, and I will not tarry,
> I will away, and be a captain's lady:
> A captain's lady is a dame of honour,
> She has her maids to wait upon her;
> To wait upon her, and get all things ready;
> I will away, and be a captain's lady.'

But the true original was an old broadside, *The Liggar Lady, or the Ladie's Love to a Soldier*, to the tune of *Mount the Baggage*, of which a copy is in the Laing Collection at Dalmeny. It consists of eight stanzas, of which here are the first two and the last:—

> 'I will away, and I will not tarry;
> I will away with a soger laddy:
> I'll mount my baggage and make it ready,
> I will away with a soger laddy.
> *I'll mount my baggage and make it ready;*
> *Come well, come woe, I'll be a soger's lady.*
>
> 'In Camps, or Duels, Fights, I will be ready,
> On behind, and be his Liggar Lady;
> In cold nights, I'll lay me down beside him,
> And I'll make my Petticoat a Tent to hide him.
> *I'll mount*, etc.

. . . .

> 'Sure if we die, we shall die in honour
> Fighting for Love and our Prince's Banner.
> In heart, in hand, we'll through the World together,
> Till Death us part, there's nothing shall us sunder.
> *I'll mount*, etc.'

Mr. Ebsworth quotes another *Captain's Lady* in the notes to his reprinted *Westminster Drolleries* (1671-2) :—

THE CAPTAIN'S LADY

'The Captain's lady is always ready.
Her petticoat's loose, her petticoat's loose.'

A song, *Ramillies*, attributed to Robert Sempill (*d.* 1789), the last laird of Beltrees, and narrating the elopement of an 'auld man's' young wife with a sailor officer, has this chorus :—

'Och! laddie, munt and go,
Dear sailor, hoise and go;
Och! laddie munt and go:
Go, and I'se go with thee, laddie.'

OF A' THE AIRTS

No. 235 in Johnson (Vol. iii. 1790) :—'Written for this work by R. Burns,' and signed 'R.' Tune : *Miss Admiral Gordon's Strathspey.* 'The air is by Marshall, the song I composed out of compliment to Mrs. Burns. *N.B.* It was during the honeymoon' (R. B. in Interleaved Copy). The song was no doubt written shortly after his arrival in Ellisland, while his wife was yet in Ayrshire.

The MS. sent to Johnson is in the Hastie Collection. Another set appeared in the tracts ' printed by Chapman and Lang for Stewart and Meikle,' and is included in Stewart's Edition (1802). The bathetic additions—inviting the ' westlin winds' to

'Bring the lassie back to me
That's aye sae neat and clean'—

which appear in some sets, were the work of John Hamilton, an Edinburgh musicseller. Thomson (*Scottish Airs*, Vol. iv.) also gives additional verses, ' written for this work by Mr. Richardson.'

STANZA I. LINE 4. 'The *lass that* I lo'e best,' Stewart.
5. '*Tho'* wild woods grow and rivers row,' Later Stewart.
7. '*Baith* day and night my fancy's flight,' Later Stewart.

OF A' THE AIRTS STANZA II. LINES 2-4 in Stewart read thus :—
'*Sae lovely*, sweet and fair;
I hear her *voice in ilka bird*
Wi' music charm the air.'
7. '*Nor yet* a bonie bird that sings,' Later Stewart.

CARL, AN THE KING COME

No. 239 in Johnson (Vol. iii. 1790) : Entitled *Old Words*, and given as alternative words to Ramsay's *Peggy, Now the King's Come* (in *The Gentle Shepherd*), the tune being *Carl, an the King Come*.

Hogg's version in the *Jacobite Relics* is mainly compounded of Hogg and Burns; and no other printed set is known to exist. The Burns itself is but a cento of Jacobite catchwords.

WHISTLE O'ER THE LAVE O'T

No. 249 in Johnson (Vol. iii. 1790): Signed 'X.' Also in Thomson (Vol. iv.).

The repeat is borrowed from the old song, *Whistle O'er the Lave O't.* See Prefatory Note to *The Jolly Beggars*, Vol. ii. p. 303.

STANZA I. LINE 6. '*Bonie Meg was Nature's* child,' Aldine Edition (1839).

O, WERE I ON PARNASSUS HILL

No. 255 in Johnson (Vol. iii. 1790). 'Written for this work by R. Burns': Signed 'R.' Included in Thomson (Vol. i.).

The form of the stanza and the repeat derive from *Kind Robin Lo'es Me*, the oldest set of which exists in blackletter in the Roxburghe Collection (see Prefatory Note to *The Jolly Beggars*, Vol. ii. p. 304). Burns may

NOTES 347

have taken for his model (1) the later set of this song in Herd (1776):—

O, WERE I ON PARNAS-SUS HILL

> 'Robin is my only Joe,
> For Robin has the art to woo,
> So to his suit I mean to bow,
> Because I ken he loo'es me':—

or (2) a Jacobite song in a clandestine and rare volume, *The True Loyalist* (1779):—

> 'Divinely led thou need'st to be,
> Else you had ne'er come o'er the sea
> With those few friends who favour'd thee,
> And dearly they do love thee':—

perhaps a parody of one which, under the title of 'An Old Scots Song,' is included in a *Collection of English Songs*, London 1796:—

> 'Of Race divine, thou needs must be,
> Since nothing earthly equals thee;
> Jean, for Heaven's sake favour me,
> Who while I live must love thee':—

or (3) a song of Dibdin's in *The Charmer* (1782) and other books:—

> 'Ah dear Marcella! maid divine!
> No more will I at fate repine,
> If I this day behold thee mine,
> For dearly I do love thee.'

The true original of the refrain, however, is probably a quotation in *The Two Fervent Lovers* (Roxburghe Collection):—

> 'This time a lad his darling had:—
> "My sweet," said he, "once prove me,
> And thou shalt find, in heart and minde,
> How dearly I doe love thee "':—

which refrain is repeated throughout with variations.

STANZA I. LINE 2. 'Helicon':—See Vol. ii. p. 313, Note to *The Jolly Beggars*, Song VII. Stanza II. Line 4. 6. 'Corsincon': —Corsancone, a hill in New Cumnock parish, Ayrshire (visible from Ellisland), where the Bard (not quite correctly) placed the sources of the Nith.

THE CAPTIVE RIBBAND

No. 257 in Johnson (Vol. iii. 1790): Unsigned. 'This air is called *Robie donna gorach*' (R. B. in Interleaved Copy).

Stenhouse assigns this poor performance to Burns; and we have found it nowhere save in the *Museum*.

THERE'S A YOUTH IN THIS CITY

No. 258 in Johnson (Vol. iii. 1790) : Signed 'Z.' Set to a *Gaelic Air*. ' The air is claimed by Neil Gow, who calls it his Lament for his brother. The first half stanza of the song is old ; the rest is mine' (R. B. in Interleaved Copy). ' *Note*.—It will be proper to omit the name of the tune altogether—only say Gaelic air' (R. B. in MS. copy in the Hastie Collection).

Burns was never above vamping from himself; and the present piece is strongly reminiscent of *The Mauchline Belles* (Vol. ii. p. 212). The MS. is in the Hastie Collection.

MY HEART'S IN THE HIGHLANDS

No. 259 in Johnson (Vol. iii. 1790): Signed 'Z.' 'The first half stanza of this song is old ; the rest is mine' (R. B. in Interleaved Copy).

Burns apparently refers to the first half stanza of the chorus. Sharpe (Additional Notes to Johnson's *Museum*) quotes 'from a stall copy' *The Strong Walls of Derry*, one stanza in which is almost identical with the Burns chorus.

NOTES 349

JOHN ANDERSON MY JO

No. 260 in Johnson (Vol. ii. 1790): 'Written for this work by Robert Burns,' and signed 'B.'

A version called *John Anderson My Jo Improved*, with additional stanzas, was published in a chap entitled *Captain Death, etc.*, 1794 (Motherwell Collection); and a slightly different set, *Domestic Happiness Exhibited in John Anderson My Jo Improved*, by Robert Burns, appeared in Brash and Reid's *Poetry Original and Select* (Vol. i. of the Collected Series, *c.* 1796), and in *The Scots Magazine* for May 1797. Thomson (Vol. ii.) sets forth two of the additional stanzas, the authorship of all which is attributed to Reid.

The song traces back to one composed (*c.* 1560) in ridicule of the Sacraments of the Church, and preserved in *The Percy Folio MS.*:—

Woman. 'John Anderson, my jo, cum in as ze gae by
  And ye sall get a sheip's heid weel baken in a pye—
  Weel baken in a pye, and the haggis in a pat:
  John Anderson, my jo, cum in, and ze 's get that,' *etc.*

The Burns set, however, derives from a very witty and sprightly song (unfit for modern print: whence the 'Improved' of the chap-book set) which, as 'sung by the choice spirits,' is found in *The Masque* (London 1768) and other song-books, and of which a slightly altered set is preserved in *The Merry Muses*:—

  'John Anderson, my Jo, John,
    I wonder what you mean,
  To rise so soon in the morning
    And sit up so late at e'en;
  You'll bleer out your eyn, John,
    And why will you do so?
  Come sooner to your bed at e'en,
    John Anderson, my Jo.

  'John Anderson, my Jo, John,
    When first that ye began,' *etc.*

STANZA I. LINE 5. 'But now your *brow's turned* beld, John,' unauthorised version. 7. '*Yet* blessings on your frosty pow,' unauthorised version.

AWA, WHIGS, AWA

No. 263 in Johnson (Vol. iii. 1790): Unsigned. The Jacobite song thus named in Hogg's *Jacobite Songs* is chiefly Hogg's. In a confused note Stenhouse describes the *Museum* song as a fragment of a Jacobite song, *Awa, Whigs, Awa*, 'with two additional stanzas, namely, the second and fourth, written by Burns'; but he gives no further information. Not even a fragment has been discovered in print before the publication of Burns's set in Johnson's *Museum*; and of that set Burns most certainly found the germ in the Herd MS. :—

> 'And when they came by Gorgie Mills
> They lickèd a' the mouter,
> The bannocks lay about there
> Like bandeliers and powder;
> Awa, whigs, awa!
> Awa, whigs, awa!
> Ye're but a pack o' lazy loons,
> Ye'll do nae good ava!'

In the old ballad of *Killiechrankie* the words 'Furich, Whigs, Awa', then,' are used as 'her nain sell's' battle-cry. A corruption of them forms the title of a spurious Jacobite ballad, *Whirry Whigs, Awa*', which Hogg printed in his *Relics*, while admitting that the sets on which it is founded had 'visibly been composed at different periods, and by different hands.' Buchan, on no evidence whatever, fathered it on George Halkett (*d.* 1756), schoolmaster at Rathen, Aberdeenshire.

CA' THE YOWES TO THE KNOWES

No. 264 in Johnson (Vol. iii. 1790): Unsigned. 'This beautiful song is in the true old Scotch taste, yet I do not

know that either the air or words were in print before CA' THE
[R. B. in Interleaved Copy).   EWES TO
   In sending a new version (p. 268) to Thomson in Sep-   THE
tember 1794 he wrote:—'I am flattered at your adopting KNOWES
Ca' the Yowes to the Knowes, as it was owing to me that
ever it saw the light. About seven years ago, I was
well acquainted with a worthy little fellow, a Mr. Clunie
[Rev. John Clunie, minister of Ewes, Dumfriesshire,
author of *I Loe Na a Laddie but Ane*], who sang it charm-
ingly; and, at my request, Mr. Clarke took it down from
his singing. When I gave it to Johnson I added some
stanzas to the song and mended others; but still it will
not do for *you*.' Stenhouse gives the old words, pre-
sumably those taken down from Clunie's singing. It
can scarce be affirmed that Burns has improved them.
The two last stanzas are his; his two first are expanded
from Clunie's first; while his two middles, where they
differ from Clunie, differ for the worse.
   David Laing, in Additional Notes to Johnson's *Museum*,
cites an Ayrshire tradition which assigns the song to one
Isabel Pagan, keeper of a hedge-tavern near Muirkirk.
But had she been the authoress, Burns must have known
it; and that she was not the authoress is evident from the
sample doggerel given in Laing's note.
   Burns's MS. is in the Hastie Collection.

O, MERRY HAE I BEEN

No. 270 in Johnson (Vol. iii. 1790).
   The tune was called *The Bob o' Dumblane*; and a song
with this title appears in Ramsay's *Tea-Table Miscellany*
(1727):—

   'Lassie, lend me your braw hemp-heckle,
      And I'll lend you my thrippling-kame!
   For fainness, dearie, I'll gar ye keckle,
      Gin ye go dance the Bob o' Dumblane,' *etc.*

'Ramsay, as usual, has modernized this song. The

O, MERRY HAE I BEEN — original, which I learned on the spot, from the old hostess in the principal Inn there, is:—

'"Lassie, lend me your braw hemp-heckle,
And I'll lend you my thripplin kame."
"My heckle is broken, it canna be gotten,
And we'll gae dance the Bob o' Dumblane."
Twa gaed to the wood, to the wood, to the wood,
Twa gaed to the wood—three came hame;
An it be na weel bobbit, weel bobbit, weel bobbit,
And it be na weel bobbit we'll bob it again.'

I insert this song to introduce the following anecdote, which I have heard well authenticated. In the evening of the day of the battle of Dunblane (Sheriffmuir), when the action was over, a Scots officer in Argyle's army observed to his Grace, that he was afraid the rebels would give out to the world that they had gotten the victory. "Weel, weel," answered his grace, alluding to the foregoing ballad, "if they think it nae weel bobbit, we'll bob it again"' (R. B. in Interleaved Copy).

In the original and in Ramsay 'hemp-heckle,' 'thrippling-kaim,' 'bob,' and 'Bob of Dumblane,' have an indecent slang sense all four. That the Burns was originally written for *The Jolly Beggars* is an unwarrantable surmise.

A MOTHER'S LAMENT

No. 271 in Johnson (Vol. iii. 1790): 'Written for this work by R. Burns,' and signed 'B.' Tune: *Finlayston House*. 'This most beautiful tune is, I think, the happiest composition of that bard-born genius John Riddell, of the family of Glengarnock in Ayr. The words were composed to commemorate the much lamented and premature death of James Ferguson, Esq., Junior of Craigdarroch' (R. B. in Interleaved Copy).

Plainly the verses were suggested by the initial stanza of *The Tears and Triumph of Parnassus*, 'An Ode, set to

music, and performed at Drury Lane, 1760,' a ridiculous
piece, by Robert Lloyd (1733-1764) :—

A MOTHER'S LAMENT

'Fate gave the word; the deed is done,
Augustus is no more.'

In a letter to Mrs. Dunlop (27th September 1788) Burns
states that he made them on a twenty-six mile ride
from Nithsdale to Mauchline. The copy sent her is
entitled *Mrs. Fergusson of Craigdarroch's Lamentation for
the Death of her Son*. Young Fergusson died, 5th November 1787, just after completing his university course.
The only son of Mrs. Stewart of Afton died 5th December
1787, and Burns inscribed the song in the *Afton Lodge
Book*, which he presented to the bereaved mother, his
title this time being *A Mother's Lament for the Loss of
Her Only Son*. There are no variations in the MSS.

THE WHITE COCKADE

No. 272 in Johnson (Vol. iii. 1790): Unsigned.

Adapted from *The Ranting Roving Lad* in Herd (1769).
Herd's set differs little from one of 'Four Excellent New
Songs,' in a chap in the Motherwell Collection, entitled
The Roving Lad with the Tartan Plaid :—

> 'My Love was born in Aberdeen,
> As bony a Lad as e'er was seen;
> But he was forc'd from me to stray
> Over the hills and far away.
> And O, he's a ranting, roving Lad!
> And O, he's a ranting, roving Lad!
> Betide what will, I will get ready
> To follow the lad with his Tartan Plaidy!' *etc.*

THE BRAES O' BALLOCHMYLE

No. 276 in Johnson (Vol. iii. 1790): 'Written for this
work by Robert Burns.' 'This air is the composition of
my friend Allan Masterton in Edinburgh. I composed

THE BRAES O' BALLOCHMYLE the verses on the amiable and excellent family of Whitefoord's leaving Ballochmyle, when Sir John's misfortunes had obliged him to sell the estate' (R. B. in Interleaved Copy). See Prefatory Note to *Lines Sent to Sir John Whitefoord, Bart.* (Vol. i. p. 433).

Reprinted in Thomson (Vol. iv.), and, with some few differences, in Stewart's Edition (1802). It is to note that while Stanza I. consists of two quatrains on four rhymes, the structure of Stanza II. is that of the three-rhymed ballade octave.

STANZA I. LINE 1. 'The Catrine Woods':—Catrine was the residence of Professor Dugald Stewart (see Vol. i. p. 354, Note to *The Vision*, Duan I. Stanza XXI. Line 2). 5. 'Maria sang':—Mary Anne Whitefoord, the eldest daughter, who married Henry Kerr Cranstoun, grandson of William, fifth Lord Cranstoun.

STANZA II. LINES 5-6 in Stewart read:—

'*Nae joys alas for me are here*
Nae pleasures find I in this soil.'

THE RANTIN DOG, THE DADDIE O'T

No. 277 in Johnson (Vol. iii. 1790). Tune: *East Neuk o' Fife*. Signed 'Z.' 'I composed this song pretty early in life, and sent it to a young girl, a very particular acquaintance of mine, who was at the time under a cloud' (R. B. in Interleaved Copy).

The 'young girl' may have been either Elizabeth Paton (see *The Poet's Welcome*, Vol. ii. p. 37) or Jean Armour. It matters not which.

STANZA II. LINE 2. 'O, wha will buy *my* groanin maut,' variation in Scott Douglas. The 'groanin maut' was the ale for the midwife and her gossips. For the epithet, 'groaning' is good English for a lying-in. Cf. *Hamlet*, iii. 2, 476:—'It would cost you a groaning to take my edge off.'

STANZA III. LINE 1. 'The creepie-chair';—The stool of

repentance. See Vol. ii. p. 343, Note to *Address to the Toothache*, Stanza IV. Line 1. THE RANTIN DOG, THE DADDIE O'T

STANZA IV. LINE 2. 'Fidgin fain'=tingling with fondness. Cf. *Tam o' Shanter*, Vol. i. p. 285 :—
'Even Satan glowr'd, and fidg'd fu' fain' :—
and the old song *Maggie Lauder* : —
'" Maggie," quoth he, "and by my bags
I'm fidgin fain to see thee."'

THOU LING'RING STAR

No. 279 in Johnson (Vol. iii. 1790): 'Written for this work by R. Burns.' Tune: *Captain Cook's Death,* composed by Miss Lucy Johnson, who afterwards married Mr. Oswald of Auchencruive. Included in Thomson (Vol. iii.).

Enclosing this very famous lament—hypochondriacal and remorseful, yet riddled with adjectives, specifically amatorious, yet wofully lacking in genuine inspiration— in a letter to Mrs. Dunlop, 8th November 1789, Burns described it as 'made the other day.' He also asked her opinion of it, as he was too much interested in the subject to be 'a critic in the composition.' For Mary Campbell see *ante*, pp. 308-10, Prefatory Note to *My Highland Lassie, O*. Neither Cromek's story of the composition of *Thou Ling'ring Star* nor his description of the Stream-and-Bible episode is worth serious consideration. To Mrs. Dunlop on 13th December Burns, groaning 'under the miseries of a diseased nervous system,' refers with longing to a future life :—'There should I, with speechless agony of rapture, again welcome my lost, my ever dear Mary, whose bosom was fraught with truth, honor, constancy, and love :—

'My Mary, dear departed shade,' *etc*.

Currie states that a copy found among Burns's papers was headed *To Mary in Heaven*; but only seeing is

THOU believing. The Lochryan MS., entitled *A Song*, agrees
LING'RING with the text. Another was before the Aldine Editor
STAR (1839).
 STANZA I. LINE 6. 'Where is thy place of *heavenly* rest,'
Aldine MS. Similarly Stanza IV. Line 6.
 STANZA II. LINE 5. 'Eternity *will* not efface,' Currie.
 STANZA IV. LINE 3. 'Time but the impression *deeper* makes,'
Aldine Edition.

EPPIE ADAIR

No. 281 in Johnson (Vol. iii. 1790): Unsigned. The MS. is in the Hastie Collection.

A song, *How, My Eppie*, quoted by Buchan as *The Earl of Kilmarnock's Farewell to his Wife*, bears little or no resemblance to the Burns set, even if it be genuine.

THE BATTLE OF SHERRAMUIR

No. 282 in Johnson (Vol. iii. 1790): 'Written for this work by Robt. Burns.' Tune: *Cameronian's Rant*.

This song, in which the idiosyncrasies of the fight are summarised with excellent discrimination, is condensed from a ballad by the Rev. John Barclay (1734-1798, Berean minister at Edinburgh) :—'*The Dialogue Betwixt William Luckladle and Thomas Cleancogue*, Who were Feeding their Sheep upon the Ochil Hills, 13th November, 1715. Being the day the Battle of Sheriffmuir was Fought. To the tune of *The Cameron Men*' :—

> W. 'Pray came you here the fight to shun
> 　　Or keep the sheep with me, man?
> Or was you at the Sheriffmuir,
> 　　And did the battle see, man?
> Pray tell which of the Parties won,
> 　　For weel I wat I saw them run
> Both south and north, when they began
> To pell and mell and kill and fell,
> With muskets' knell and pistols' snell,
> 　　And some for hell did flee man.'

NOTES

T. 'But my dear Will, I kenna still
    Whilk o' the twa did lose, man;
For weel I wat, they had good skill
    To set upo' their foes, man.
The red coats, they are train'd, you see;
The clans always disdain to flee;
Wha then should gain the victory?
But the Highland race, all in a brace,
With a swift pace, to the Whigs' disgrace,
    Did put to chace their foes, man,' *etc.*

A broadside of this is in the British Museum, and on the same sheet is printed the very clever (earlier) ballad by the Rev. Murdoch M'Lennan of Crathie (1701-1783), '*The Race at Sheriffmuir,* Fairly Run on the 13th of November 1715. To the tune of *The Horseman's Port*':—

'There's some say that we wan,
Some say that they wan,
Some say that nane wan at a', man:
  But one thing I'm sure,
  That at Sheriffmuir
A battle there was, which I saw man:
And we ran, and they ran, and they ran, and we ran,
And we ran, and they ran awa, man,' *etc.*

For another on the same battle, *The Marquis of Huntly's Retreat,* see Vol. i. p. 412, with this addition: that there is another—and a more correct—broadside thereof in the British Museum. This group of Sheriffmuir ballads, with those referred to in Vol. i. pp. 411-12, and divers others, among them *Tranent Muir,* descriptive of incidents and battles in the Stuart campaigns in Scotland, traces back as to form to *Killychrankie* (see Vol. i. p. 411).

The copy in Currie differs somewhat from that sent to Johnson.

STANZA II. LINE 7 is omitted in Currie.

STANZA III. LINE 6. 'When *bayonets opposed* the targe,' Currie.

STANZA V. LINES 9-10 in Currie reads:—

    'Their cogs o' brose; *all crying woes,*
      And so it goes, you see man.'

THE BATTLE OF SHERRAMUIR. STANZA VI. LINE 4. 'Or *fallen in whiggish* hands, man,' Currie. For Lines 8-10 these four lines are given in Currie:—

' *Then ye may tell, how pell and mell,*
By red claymores and muskets' knell,
Wi' dying yell, the Tories fell,
And Whigs to hell did flee, man.'

YOUNG JOCKIE WAS THE BLYTHEST LAD

No. 287 in Johnson (Vol. iii. 1790) : Signed ' Z.'

The tune is found in Oswald's *Caledonian Pocket Companion*, under the title *Jocky was the Blythest Lad in A' Our Town*. Stenhouse remarks that the whole song, ' excepting three or four lines, is the production of Burns'; but he does not condescend to particulars. There are divers sets, but the earliest extant is that in Playford's *Choice Ayres*, 1659 :—

'O, Willy was so blythe a lad,
Ne'an like was in the town;
At Wake and Wassail Willy had
For dancing chief renown.
He pitch'd the bar and hurl'd the stean—
Ne'a man could him outgang;
And if he strave with any man,
He gar'd him lig alang' :—

the original of *Willie was a Wanton Wag* (ascribed to Hamilton of Gilbertfield), on which the Burns set is closely modelled.

STANZA I. LINE 3. 'Gaud' :—The plough-oxen were driven with a goad.

A WAUKRIFE MINNIE

No. 288 in Johnson (Vol. iii. 1790). 'I picked up the old song and tune from a country girl in Nithsdale. I never met with it elsewhere in Scotland' (R. B. in Interleaved Copy).

The vamp—if vamp it be ; and we have nowhere found an original—is in Burns's happiest and most 'folkish' vein.

THO' WOMEN'S MINDS

No. 290 in Johnson (Vol. iii. 1790): 'Written for this work by R. Burns,' and signed 'X.' 'This song is mine, all except the chorus' (R. B. in Interleaved Copy).
A new set of the Bard's song in *The Jolly Beggars*, Vol. ii. p. 15. In a MS. in the Kilmarnock Monument Museum, as in one belonging to Mr. Robert Hutchinson, a reading in the Cantata set is adopted:—

'My dearest bluid to do them guid,' *etc.*

See further, Prefatory Note to *The Jolly Beggars*, Vol. ii. p. 304, and *post*, p. 489, Prefatory Note to *Is There For Honest Poverty?*

WILLIE BREW'D A PECK O' MAUT

No. 291 in Johnson (Vol. iii. 1790): 'Written for this work by Robert Burns.' 'The air is Masterton's; the song mine. The occasion of it was this:—Mr. Wm. Nicol of the High School, Edinburgh, during the autumn vacation being at Moffat, honest Allan (who was at that time on a visit to Dalswinton) and I went to pay Nicol a visit. We had such a joyous meeting that Mr. Masterton and I agreed, each in our own way, that we should celebrate the business' (R. B. in Interleaved Copy).
The meeting took place in the autumn of 1789. The song—(a little masterpiece of drunken fancy)—is included in Thomson (Vol. iv.). For William Nicol see Vol. ii. p. 452, Prefatory Note to Epitaph *For William Nicol*. Allan Masterton was appointed writing-master to Edinburgh High School, 10th October 1789. He died in 1799.

WILLIE BREW'D A PECK O' MAUT

STANZA I. LINE 2. 'Cam to *pree*,' vulgar and unauthorised amendment.

STANZA IV. LINE 3. 'Wha first beside his chair shall fa':—Writing to Captain Riddell, 10th October 1789, on the Whistle day, Burns quotes two stanzas, and in quoting Line 3 changes 'first' to '*last*'; but that he italicises the word shows that he made the change to suit the special circumstances of the contest. 'First,' too, is found in Johnson, in the earlier Editions of Currie, and in a quotation of the stanza in a letter to Alexander Cunningham (MS. in the possession of Mr. T. G. Arthur, Ayr). There is, therefore, no warrant for the supposition that it is either misprint or clerical error.

STANZA II. LINES 5 and 6. An old song, *The Merry Fellows*, has this chorus:—

'Now since we're met let's merry merry be,
In spite of all our foes,
And he that will not merry be
We'll pull him by the nose.'

Cf. Shakespeare, *Twelfth Night*:—'My lady's a Cataian, we are politicians, Malvolio's a Peg-a-Ramsey, and *Three merry men be we.*' Staunton notes that the song is mentioned in Peele's *Old Wives' Tale*, 1595, thus:—

'Three merrie men, and three merrie men,
And three merrie men be wee;
I in the wood, and thou on the ground,
And Jack sleeps in the tree.'

Cf. too Beaumont and Fletcher, *The Knight of the Burning Pestle*, iii. 2:—

'Three merry men, and three merry men,
And three merry men be we
As ever did sing in a hempen string
All under the gallows tree':—

and a rhyme in Sir William Mure's *Lute Book* (MS. in the Laing Collection, University of Edinburgh):—

'The wise men were but seven,
Ne'er more shall be for me,

The muses were but nine,
The worthies three times three.
And three merry boys, and three merry boys,
And three merry boys are we.

WILLIE
BREW'D A
PECK O'
MAUT

'The vestals they are seven,' etc.

. . . . .

And three merry girls, etc.

KILLIECRANKIE

No. 292 in Johnson (Vol. iii. 1790): Signed 'Z.' 'The battle of Killiecrankie was the last stand made by the clans for James after his abdication. Here the gallant Lord Dundee fell in the moment of victory, and with him fell the hopes of the party. General M'Kay, when he found the Highlanders did not pursue his flying army, said :—"Dundee must be killed, or he never would have overlooked this advantage." A great stone marks the place where Dundee fell' (R. B. in Interleaved Copy). But the fact is that Dundee got his hurt further up the hill than the 'great stone.' The battle was fought on 17th July 1689.

The following stanzas are quoted in Hogg and Motherwell (1834) as part of an old song :—

'Gin ye had been where I hae been.
Ye wadna been sae vauntie;
For I hae been at Sherra-muir,
And focht at Killiecrankie.

'At Prestonpans I also was,
And a' Prince Charles' battles,
Where glittering swords around me clash'd
And thundering cannon rattles.'

STANZA III. LINE I. 'The bauld Pitcur'= Haliburton of Pitcur, slain at Killiecrankie. A Jacobite song in the Pitcairn MS., entitled *Answer to Killiecrankie*, has this stanza :—

' My Lord Dundee the best o' ye
Into the fields did fa' then ;
And great Pitcur fell in a furr
Wha could not win awa' then.'

THE BLUE-EYED LASSIE

No. 294 in Johnson (Vol. iii. 1790) : 'Written for this work by Robert Burns.' Included in Thomson (Vol. iii.).

Enclosed in a letter to Mrs. Dunlop, 2nd October 1788 :—' How do you like the following song, designed for and composed by a friend of mine, and which he has christened *The Blue-eyed Lassie*' (Lochryan MSS.). The friend was Captain Robert Riddell, and the MS. sent to him is in the possession of Dr. De Noè Walker. For the copy of another MS. we are indebted to Mr. Howat, Castleview, Stirling. A set with some variations was published in a tract 'printed by Chapman and Lang for Stewart and Meikle,' and is included in Stewart's Edition (1802).

The 'blue-eyed lassie' was Jean, daughter of the Rev. Andrew Jeffrey, of Lochmaben. She married a Mr. Renwick, of New York, and died in October 1850.

STANZA I. LINE 2. ' A gate I fear *I* dearly rue,' MSS.

STANZA II. LINE 2. 'She charm'd my soul, I *wat* na how,' Stewart. 5. 'But spare *I'd* speak and spare *I'd* speed,' Stewart—apparently a misprint. The expression in the text is proverbial. 7. 'Should she refuse I'll lay my *deed*,' Stewart. 8. 'To her twa een *o' bonny* blue,' Stewart.

THE BANKS OF NITH

No. 295 in Johnson (Vol. iii. 1790): Signed 'B.' 'Written for this work by R. Burns.' Tune : *Robie donna Gorach.*

An early draft was sent to Mrs. Dunlop, 21st August 1789 (Lochryan MSS.).

NOTES

STANZA I. LINE 4. 'Where Cummins ance had high command':—'My landlord Millar is building a house on the banks of the Nith, just on the ruins of the Comyn's Castle' (Note by R. B. in Lochryan MS.). 5. 'When shall I see that *distant* land,' Lochryan MS. 7. 'Must *cruel* Fortune's adverse hand,' Lochryan MS.

THE BANKS OF NITH

STANZA II. LINES 1-4 in the Lochryan MS. read :—

> '*Fair spread*, O Nith, thy *flow'ring dales*,
> Where *rove the flocks among the broom*,
> And sweetly *wave thy fruitful vales*,
> Surrounded by the Hawthorn bloom.'

3. '*How* sweetly *wind* thy sloping dales,' Currie. 7-8 in the Lochryan MS. read thus :—

> '*There may* my latest hours consume
> With *those* my friends of early days.'

TAM GLEN

No. 296 in Johnson (Vol. iii. 1790): 'Written for this work by Robert Burns.'

This delightful piece of wit and character and fun appeared in *The Edinburgh Magazine* of November 1789, signed T. S., and in *The Edinburgh Evening Courant* of 22nd December 1789, without signature, as '*Tam Glen*, a Scots ballad.' It is also included in Thomson (Vol. ii.). Excepting for some orthographical differences these versions correspond with the *Museum* copy.

STANZA VII. See Vol. i. p. 360, Notes to *Halloween*, Stanza XXIV. Line 7.

CRAIGIEBURN WOOD

No. 301 in Johnson (Vol. iv. 1792): 'Written for this work by Robert Burns,' and signed ' B.' 'It is remarkable of this air, that it is the confine of that country where the greatest part of our lowland music (so far as from the

CRAIGIE-BURN WOOD title, words, *etc.*, we can localize it) has been composed. From Craigieburn, near Moffat, until one reaches the West Highlands, we have scarcely one slow air of antiquity. The song was composed on a passion which a Mr. Gillespie, a particular friend of mine, had for a Miss Lorimer, afterwards a Mrs. Whepdale. The young lady was born in Craigieburn Wood. The chorus is part of an old foolish ballad' (R. B. in Interleaved Copy). Probably the 'old foolish ballad' was a fragment in Herd (1776):—

' O my bonny, bonny May,
    Will ye not rue upon me ?
A sound, sound sleep I'll never get
    Until I lie ayont thee,' *etc.*

Craigieburn Wood is about two miles from Moffat. For Jean Lorimer see *post*, p. 482, Prefatory Note to *Lassie Wi' the Lint-white Locks*.

There are two MSS. at Alloway Cottage, one inscribed in the *Afton Lodge Book*; and the MS. sent to Johnson is in the Hastie Collection.

CHORUS. LINES 3-4 in the Hastie MS. read :—

'O sweetly, soundly, weel wad *I* sleep
    Were I laid in the bed beyond thee.

STANZA I. LINE 4. ' Can yield me *nothing* but sorrow,' Johnson.

FRAE THE FRIENDS AND LAND I LOVE

No. 302 in Johnson (Vol. iv. 1792): Unsigned (no doubt on account of its Jacobite sentiments). 'I added the four last lines by way of giving a turn to the theme of the poem, such as it is' (R. B. in Interleaved Copy).

We have not found the first lines elsewhere. The MS. is in the Hastie Collection.

O JOHN, COME KISS ME NOW

No. 305 in Johnson (Vol. iv. 1792): Unsigned. The MS. is in the Hastie Collection.

Altered and expanded from a fragment in Herd (1769):—

> 'John, come kiss me now, now, now!
> O John, come kiss me now!
> John, come kiss me by and by,
> And make nae mair ado!
>
> 'Some will court and compliment
> And make a great ado,
> Some will make of their guidman,
> And sae will I of you.'

A number in Thomas Greave's *Songes of Sundrie Kindes* (London 1604), with music, begins:—

> 'I pray thee, sweet John, away,'

and ends :—

> 'Gentle John, come quickly kiss me.'

The air is in Queen Elizabeth's *Virginal Book*, and a parody is found in *The Gude and Godly Ballats*, 1578, where the chorus is identical with that in the Herd set, and the song continues thus :—

> 'My prophets call, my preachers cry
> John, come kiss me now,' *etc.*

Allied to it is a set (*c.* 1470) in the 'Amanda Group' of Mr. Ebsworth's *Bagford Ballads* :—

> *He.* 'I pray you now come kyss me,
> I pray you, come kyss me;
> My lyttle prety Mopsie,
> I pray you come kyss me!'
>
> *She.* 'Alas goodman, must now be kyst?
> Ye shall not now, ye may me trust.
> Wherefore, go where as ye lust,
> For I wiss ye shall not kyss me.'

O JOHN, COME KISS ME NOW In another blackletter, *Adieu Sweete Harte*, is found this chorus :—

> 'Once again come kysse me,
> Syth I so long must mys thee;
> My willinge harte shall wyshe thee,
> To ease me of my smarte.'

STANZA I. LINE 3. 'Mak o',' probably = pet or fondle. See Note to *O, Can Ye Labour Lea*, Stanza III. Line 3.

COCK UP YOUR BEAVER

No. 309 in Johnson (Vol. iv. 1792): Unsigned; but Stenhouse had Burns's holograph.

Redacted from the older set in Herd (1769) :—

> 'When first my dear Johny came to this town,
> He had a blue bonnet, it wanted the crown;
> But now he has gotten a hat and a feather,
> Hey, my Johny lad, cock up your beaver:
>   Cock up your beaver, cock up your beaver,
>   Hey, my Johny lad, cock up your beaver!
>   Cock up your beaver, and cock it nae wrang,
>   We'll a' to England, ere it be lang!'

MY TOCHER'S THE JEWEL

No. 312 in Johnson (Vol. iii. 1790): 'Written for this work by Robert Burns,' and signed 'B.' Included in Thomson (Vol. ii.).

The last half of Stanza II., according to Cromek, was found in Burns's holograph as part of an old song (*Scotish Songs*, Vol. ii. p. 207).

GUIDWIFE, COUNT THE LAWIN

No. 313 in Johnson (Vol. iii. 1790): Signed 'B.' 'The chorus of this is part of an old song, one stanza of which I recollect :—

"Every day my wife tells me   GUIDWIFE
That ale and brandy will ruin me;   COUNT
But if gude liquor be my dead,   THE LAWIN
This shall be written on my head—
Landlady, count the lawin,"' *etc.*

(R. B. in Interleaved Copy).

In the MS. in the Hastie Collection '*Landlady*' occurs for 'Gudewife.'

CHORUS. LINE 4. ' Coggie ':—See Vol. i. p. 323, Note to *Scotch Drink*, Stanza IX. Line 4.

STANZA III. was inscribed by Burns on a window-pane of the Globe Tavern, Dumfries (see Vol. ii. p. 251).

THERE'LL NEVER BE PEACE TILL JAMIE COMES HAME

No. 315 in Johnson (Vol. iv. 1792): Unsigned. 'This tune is sometimes called *There are Few Gude Fellows when Willie's Awa*. But I have never been able to meet in with anything else of the song than the title' (R. B. in Interleaved Copy).

He enclosed a copy ['a song of my late composition'] to Alexander Cunningham, 11th March 1791:—'You must know a beautiful Jacobite air—*There'll Never be Peace till Jamie Comes Hame*. When political combustion ceases to be the object of Princes and Patriots it then, you know, becomes the lawful prey of Historians and Poets' (R. B.). No doubt there was an old Jacobite song with this title; but the air and the title were all that Burns knew, and no authentic copy of the thing itself is known to survive.

The MS. sent to Cunningham [in the possession of his descendants] substantially agrees with that in the Hastie Collection.

WHAT CAN A YOUNG LASSIE

No. 316 in Johnson (Vol. iv. 1792): 'Written for this work by Robt. Burns.' Signed 'R.'

Stanza IV. is influenced by the set of *Auld Rob Morris* in Ramsay's *Tea-Table Miscellany* (1729):—

> 'Rob Morris, I grant, is an elderly man,
> But then his auld brass, it will buy a new pan;
> Sae dochter, ye shouldna be fashious to shoe,
> And Auld Rob Morris is the man ye maun lo'e.'

The song itself may well have been suggested by the title, *What Shall a Young Woman do with an Old Man?* quoted in *Pills to Purge Melancholy*, 1703—a book Burns knew. Mr. Ebsworth (*Roxburghe Ballads*, Vol. viii. p. 673) prints a 'probably unique broadside,' dating before 1664:—' *The Young Woman's Complaint*, Or a Caveat to all Maids to have a Care How They be Married to Old Men. The tune is *What Should a Young Woman do with an Old Man*, or *The Tyrant*.' The only copy known to us is that in the Euing Collection :—

> 'Come all you young damsels both beauteous and free,
> I'll summon you all to listen to me:
> A song of misguiding concerning my marriage,
> Sorrow's the cause of this my ill carriage—
> A maiden of fifteen, as it may appear,
> She married an Old Man of seventy-two year;
> And by her misfortune well prove it I can
> That she is sore troubled with an Old Man,' etc.

A derivative, *The Old Man Killed with the Cough*, is one of 'Six Excellent New Songs' forming a chap in the Motherwell Collection :—

> 'You girls that are witty in country and city,
> I pray now come pity a sorrowful maid,
> That daily is vexèd and mighty perplexèd
> All with an old husband ; I wish he were dead.'

This derivative Burns seems to have known, and to have borrowed its rhythmus as well as its general tone and sentiment.

For a song printed in an appendix to Sharpe's *Ballad*

Book (Ed. Laing, 1880), as one of several 'evidently obtained through a northern collector': that some experts should have accepted it as a genuine antique and the original of this particular Burns—(a Burns, be it noted, which the Poet claims for his own, and which he initials 'R')—appears inexplicable, till one reflects that they probably didn't know that the 'discoverer' was Peter Buchan, on whose authority the 'find' is quoted in Hogg and Motherwell (1834). There is no information as to where it was got; and, not only is there not a tittle of proof that it was 'written by Miss Jean Allardyce, Pittenweem, to her friend Miss K. Gordon, 1714' but, internal evidence is altogether opposed to such a theory. Whoever wrote it knew spelling and English better than most Scots girls knew either in 1714; must have heard Burns's words or Johnson's tune before setting pen to paper; and took a much more humorous and knowing view of the situation than any distressed damsel was like to do. Moreover, since the sole known copy is that of the 'northern collector' [*i.e.* Buchan], and professes to be taken from a young lady's private letter, how was Burns to get wind of it? Here is the first stanza:—

WHAT CAN A YOUNG LASSIE

'O Katy, dear Katy ! I'll tell you what grieves me,
  And for to advise me do all that you can,
If you would relieve me, a present I'll give you—
  What can a young lassie do wi' an auld man?
I canna get sleeping for sighing and weeping,
  What shall I do, Kitty? Oh! here take my fan;
My mind is sae crazy, I'm dull and uneasy,
  I am sae perplex'd wi' a crazy auld man.'

THE BONIE LAD THAT'S FAR AWA

No. 317 in Johnson (Vol. iv. 1792): Signed 'X.'
No doubt suggested by a song in Herd (1769):—

'How can I be blythe and glad,
  Or in my mind contented be,
When the bonny lad that I lo'e best
  Is banished from my company?'

NOTES

THE BONIE LAD THAT'S FAR AWA This is itself a derivative from a blackletter in the Bagford, Crawford, and Euing Collections—*The Unconstant Shepherd, or The Forsaken Lasses Lamentation* :—

> 'O, how can I be merry or glad
> Or in my mind contented be,' *etc.*

Songs with the refrain 'O'er the Hills and Far Awa' abound in the books. They seem to derive from the old ballad of *The Elfin Knight*, of which the earliest printed set is a blackletter in the Library of Magdalene College, Cambridge, bound up with a copy of Blind Harry's *Wallace* (first referred to in Pinkerton, *Ancient Scottish Poems*, Vol. ii. p. 496), *The Wind Hath Blawn My Plaid Awa*. It begins :—

> 'The Elphin Knight sits on yon hill
> Ba ba ba, lilli ba !
> He blows his horn both lowd and shill
> The wind hath blown my plaid awa !' :—

and has this burden :—

> 'My plaid awa, my plaid awa,
> And o'er the hills and far awa,
> And far awa to Norrowa
> My plaid shall not be blawn awa !'

Perhaps the earliest derivative is *Jockey's Lamentation*, published in *Pills to Purge Melancholy* (1703), and reprinted with variations in Ramsay's *Tea-Table Miscellany* with the title, *O'er the Hills and Far Away* :—

> 'Jocky met with Jenny fair,
> Aft by the dawning of the day,' *etc.*

A capital set is sung by Captain Plume in Farquhar's *Recruiting Officer* (1706); and a *Song on the Birth-day of King James the VIII.*, 10th June 1709 (printed in *Roxburghe Ballads*, ed. Ebsworth, Vol. viii. 225), from Robert Mylne's MS., has this refrain :—

> 'He's over seas and far awa,
> He's over seas and far awa :
> Of no man we will stand in awe,
> To drink his health that's far awa !'

NOTES

There is also a broadside in the Laing Collection at the Dalmeny, entitled, 'An Excellent New Ballad, *He's o're the Hills and Far Away*, to its own proper tune.' It begins:—

> 'I must o're land and seas repass,
> Face summer's suns and winter's glass,' *etc.*

And in a MS. collection of Loyal Songs (1714-16, Add. MSS., British Museum, No. 29, 981) there is a Jacobite song beginning thus:—

> 'Bring me a bowl, I'll toast a health
> To one that's robbed o' land and wealth.
> The bonniest lad that e'er I saw
> Is o'er the hills and far awa.'

The MS. of Burns's set is in the Hastie Collection. Another, which was before Cromek, may have been that now in the possession of Mr. A. M. Munster. Stanza II. is not in Johnson, and was published by Cromek. Thomson (Vol. v.) included the song, but omitted Stanza IV. It is supposed to refer to old Armour's extrusion of his daughter in the winter of 1788:—'Jean I found banished like a martyr, forlorn, destitute and friendless—all for the good old cause' (R. B. to Ainslie, 3rd March 1788).

STANZA V. LINE 3. 'And my *young* babie,' Hastie MS. and Johnson; '*And a' my tears be tears of joy*,' Thomson, from motives of delicacy. 4. 'And he'll *come* hame,' Munster MS.

I DO CONFESS THOU ART SAE FAIR

No. 321 in Johnson: Signed 'Z.' 'This song is altered from a poem by Sir Robert Ayton, private secretary to Mary and Anne, Queens of Scotland. The poem is to be found in *Watson's Collection of Scots Poems*, the earliest collection published in Scotland. I think that I have improved the simplicity of the sentiments by giving them a Scots dress' (R. B. in Interleaved Copy).

372   NOTES

I DO   The original (Ayton's authorship of which is more than
CONFESS   doubtful), found in *Playford's Select Ayres*, 1659, is
THOU ART   called *To His Forsaken Mistress* :—
SAE FAIR   'I do confess thou 'rt smooth and fair,
                     And I might have gone near to love thee,
                     Had I not found the slightest prayer
                     That lip could move, had power to move thee;
                     But I can let thee now alone
                     As worthy to be loved by none.

                    'I do confess thou 'rt sweet, but find
                     Thee such an unthrift of thy sweets:
                     Thy favours are but like the wind
                     Which kisseth ev'rything it meets;
                     And since thou canst with more than one
                     Thou 'rt worthy to be kiss'd by none.'

It is not at all in Burns's line, and he had done vastly better had he left it alone.

SENSIBILITY HOW CHARMING

No. 329 in Johnson (Vol. iv. 1792): 'Written for this work by Robt. Burns.' Included also in Thomson (Vol. iii.).

Burns wrote to Mrs. Dunlop, 29th July 1790 (Lochryan MSS.):—'There is sometimes a conjuncture of circumstances which looks like ominous; when I received your letter I was just finishing the following stanza, "Envy not the hidden treasure," *etc.* [he quotes]. I immediately and almost extempore added the following, too allusive to poor Mrs. Henri: "Fairest flower, behold the lily"' [the remainder of the stanza is quoted]. He afterwards sent a complete copy to his 'dear and honoured friend' Mrs. Dunlop, which was printed in Currie, and another to Clarinda, which is in the Watson Collection—MS.

This balderdash, which reads like the effect of a fit of serious admiration for a certain *Song by a Person of Quality* :—

<blockquote>
'Glittering spread thy purple pinions,
Gentle Cupid, o'er my heart;
I a slave in thy dominions;
Nature must give way to art':—
</blockquote>

SENSIBILITY HOW CHARMING

is also inscribed in the Afton Lodge Book—MS. (B); and on the flyleaf of a MS. volume of poems by Helen Craik belonging to Mr. Adam Wood, Troon—MS. (C).

The MS. sent to Johnson is in the Hastie Collection—MS. (D). To Clarinda, 15th December 1791, Burns wrote:—' I have likewise sent in the verses on *Sensibility* altered to—

<blockquote>
'"Sensibility how charming,
Dearest Nancy, thou canst tell":—
</blockquote>

to the Musical Editor of the *Scots Songs*,' etc.

STANZA I. LINE 2. ' *Dearest Nancy, thou canst* tell,' MS. (D) and Johnson. 4. 'Thou *hast also* known too well,' MS. (D) and Johnson.

STANZA III. LINE 3. ' *Helpless bird*, a prey the surest,' MS. (B) and Currie.

STANZA IV. LINE I. '*Envy not* the hidden treasure,' MS. (C).

YON WILD MOSSY MOUNTAINS

No. 331 in Johnson (Vol. iv. 1792): Signed 'X.' 'This tune is by Oswald. The song alludes to a part of my private history which is of no consequence to the world to know' (R. B. in Interleaved Copy).

In July 1793 he recommended it to Thomson as suitable to the air of *There 'll Never be Peace till Jamie Comes Hame*, if he objected to the Jacobite sentiments of that song. It is held by some to refer to Mary Campbell; but Burns occasionally visited a peasant-girl near Covington, Lanarkshire.

The MS. is in the Hastie Collection.

STANZA I. LINE 3. 'Where the grouse *thro' the heather lead their coveys* to feed,' MS.

STANZA III. LINE 2. '*Where ilk stream faems along* its ain green, narrow strath.' MS.

I HAE BEEN AT CROOKIEDEN

No. 332 in Johnson (Vol. iv. 1792): Unsigned. Founded on an old Jacobite rhyme. A comparatively mild set is in the Pitcairn MS. Another, which incorporates much of the Burns, may be partly old and partly modern. The MS. is in the Hastie Collection.

Of the *Highland Laddie* airs Burns wrote (Interleaved Copy):—'That which I take to be the oldest is to be found in this *Museum* beginning "I hae been at Crookieden." One reason for my thinking so is that Oswald has it in his Collection by the name of the *Auld Highland Laddie*.'

STANZA I. LINE 3. '*There I saw some folk I ken*,' deleted reading in the MS.

IT IS NA, JEAN, THY BONIE FACE

No. 333 in Johnson (Vol. iv. 1792): 'Written for this work by Robert Burns.' 'Originally English verses: I gave them their Scots dress' (R. B. in Interleaved Copy). The MS. is in the Hastie Collection.

Those 'English verses' are not to be found. But *It Is Na, Jean*, reads like an odd but triumphing blend of a famous song by Thomas Carew (1589-1639):—

'He that loves a rosy cheek
  Or a coral lip admires . . .
But a smooth and steadfast mind
  Gentle thoughts and calm desires . . .
Where these are not I despise
  Lovely cheeks, or lips, or eyes':—

and the initial stanza of a certain broadside (Laing Collection, Dalmeny) entitled *Bonie Jean, or Jeanie's the Sweetest and Dearest to Me*:—

'O, Jeanie is the sweetest of all womankind!
O, Jeanie is compleat in body and mind!
Of beauty and bountie, of carriage and grace,
With a prety proportion and fairness of face,
With all things excellent as woman should be,
O, Jeanie is the sweetest whose servant I'll be.'

For something, too, it may be indebted to the *Je ne Sçai*

Quoi, a song which we have found in *A Choice Collection of Scotch and English Songs* (1763), of which the second stanza begins thus:—
'"Tis not her face which love creates,' *etc.*

MY EPPIE MACNAB

No. 336 in Johnson (Vol. iv. 1792). Signed 'X.' 'The old song with this title has more wit than decency' (R. B. in Interleaved Copy).

Stenhouse remarked of Burns's statement:—' He justly observes'; but the chances are that Stenhouse spoke without book. Hogg, in the Hogg and Motherwell Edition, says that, so far as he remembers this song, it ' was not indelicate.' He also quotes a stanza resembling the fragment in the Herd MS. And Burns may have known something more of the old song than the fragment in the Herd MS., which contains the germ (and something more) of the present piece. Thus it runs :—

'O, saw ye Eppie M'Nab the day?
O, saw ye Eppie M'Nab the day?
　She's down in the yaird,
　She's kissing the laird:
She winna cum hame the day, the day !
'O, see to Eppie M'Nab, as she goes !
O, see to Eppie M'Nab, as she goes !
　With her cockèd heel shoon,
　And her cockets aboon,
O, see to Eppie M'Nab as she goes !'

Burns remodelled his set for Thomson, but Thomson didn't accept it (See *Saw Ye My Phely,* Vol. iv.).
The MS. is in the Hastie Collection.

WHA IS THAT AT MY BOWER DOOR

No. 337 in Johnson (Vol. iv. 1792): 'Written for this work by Robert Burns.' 'The tune is also known by the name of *Lass an I Come Near Thee.* The words are mine' (R. B. in Interleaved Copy).

WHA IS THAT AT MY BOWER DOOR

The chorus of this old song, says Stenhouse, was :—

'Lass, an I come near thee,
Lass, an I come near thee,
I'll gar a' your ribbons reel,
Lass, an I come near thee.'

Cromek states that, according to Gilbert Burns, Robert's model was *The Auld Man's Best Argument* in Ramsay's *Tea-Table Miscellany* (1727), which an old widow, Jean Wilson, of Tarbolton, used to sing :—

' "O, wha's that at my chamber-door?"
"Fair widow, are ye wauking !"
"Auld carle, your suit give o'er,
Your love lyes a' in tawking,"' *etc.*

A similar song (English, no doubt), *Roger's Courtship*, is also in the *Miscellany* :—

'Young Roger came tapping
At Dolly's window;
Tumputy, tumputy, tump!
He begg'd for admittance, she answer'd him no;
Glumputy, glumputy, glump!'

Another in *The Lark* (1740), but very much older than *The Lark*, begins thus :—

'Arise, arise, my Juggy, my Puggy—
Arise, get up, my dear ;
The night is cold,
It bloweth, it snoweth,
I must be lodgèd here.'

A set quoted in Sharpe's *Ballad Book*, 1823 :—

' "Wha's that at my chamber door?"
"It is I, my dear," quo' Borlan ;
"Come in," quo' she, "lat's chat awhile,
Ye strapping, sturdy Norlan"' :—

is plainly a modern counterfeit, and is supposed to be the work of Lady Dick. But without any manner of doubt, Burns's original was *Who But I, Quoth Finlay*, ' A new song, much in request, sung with its own proper tune,'

NOTES

of which there is a copy in the Laing Collection at Dalmeny. To show the exact amount and nature of his indebtedness, we give this piece in full:—

_{WHA IS THAT AT MY BOWER DOOR}

'There dwells a man into this Town,
Some say they call him Finlay;
He is a brisk and able man—
O if I knew but Finlay!

'His Reputation was so great
That him I did seek after;
And when I found him did intreat
He'd tryst with me thereafter.

'Quoth Finlay: "If I come to you,
Give me none of your ill words,
Though I say 'No' to you at first,
Be sure that you come forewards."

'Then promised he to come that night.
And my chamber I was keeping:
He chappèd gently at the door
For fear I had been sleeping.

' "Who's that at my chamber door?
"And who but I?" quoth Finlay.
"Lown carle, come no further."
"Indeed not I," quoth Finlay.

' "Who's that at my bedside,"
"And who but I?" quoth Finlay.
"Lown carle, had thee there."
"Indeed not I," quoth Finlay.

'Of all the men I ever did see,
There's none I love like Finlay;
He was both courteous, stout and free,
My heart's delight is Finlay.'

Hitherto Burns's hero was supposed to have been James Findlay, a brother exciseman, who married one of the *Belles of Mauchline* (see Vol. ii. p. 410).

These various songs are related to a blackletter group (see *Roxburghe Ballads*, ed. Ebsworth, Vol. vi. pp. 202-215), of which perhaps the oldest is *John's Earnest Request*

378   NOTES

WHA IS THAT AT MY BOWER DOOR (Crawford, Euing, Huth, Pepys, and Roxburghe Collections):—
'Come open the Door, Sweet Betty,
For 'tis a cold winter night.'

(See further, under *O Open the Door, post,* p. 450). And all trace back no doubt to the lost lyric (the air of which is in Queen Elizabeth's *Virginal Book*) parodied in *The Gude and Godly Ballats,* 1578 :—

'O, who is at my window, who, who?
Goe from my windo, goe goe;
Quha calls there, so like ane stranger,
Goe from my windowe, goe,' *etc.*

The MS. is in the Hastie Collection. The song appears, exactly as in the text, in *The Merry Muses.*

STANZA II. LINE 7. 'I fear ye 'll *stay* till break o' day,' deleted reading in the MS.

BONIE WEE THING

No. 341 in Johnson (Vol. iv. 1792): 'Written for this work by Robert Burns,' and signed 'R.' 'Composed on my little idol—"the charming lovely Davies"' (R. B. in Interleaved Copy).

Adapted to the tune, *The Bonie Wee Thing,* in Oswald's *Pocket Companion,* the song is slightly reminiscent of *O, Wert Thou My Ain Thing.* Miss Debora Davies, daughter of Dr. Davies of Tenby, Pembrokeshire, and a relative of Captain Riddell, was jilted by one Captain Delany, and died of a decline. See further, Vol. ii. p. 437, Prefatory Note to Epigram *On Miss Davies,* and the song *Lovely Davies,* p. 106.

A MS. is in the Hastie Collection.

CHORUS. LINE 2. 'Lovely wee thing, *was* thou mine,' Johnson. 4. 'Lest my Jewel *I* should tine,' Johnson.

THE TITHER MORN

No. 345 in Johnson (Vol. iv. 1792): Unsigned. 'This tune is originally from the Highlands. I have heard a Gaelic song to it, which I was told was very clever, but not by any means a lady's song' (R. B. in Interleaved Copy).

Words and music were sent by Burns to the *Museum*; and the words suggest his passage.

STANZA II. LINE 5. 'Deil tak the war':—*Cf.* the old song:

'Deil tak the wars, that hurried Billy from me.'

AE FOND KISS

No. 347 in Johnson (Vol. iv. 1792): 'Written for this work by Robert Burns.' Tune: *Rory Dall's Port*: signed 'X.'

Sent to Clarinda 27th December 1791 (see Vol. ii. p. 368, Prefatory Note to *Sylvander to Clarinda*):—'I have just ten minutes before the post goes, and these I shall employ in sending you some songs I have just been composing to different tunes for the *Collection of Songs*, of which you have three volumes, and of which you shall have the fourth,' etc. The germ of *Ae Fond Kiss* is found in *The Parting Kiss*, by Robert Dodsley (1703-1764), which was set by Oswald:—

'One fond kiss before we part,
Drop a Tear and bid adieu;
Tho' we sever, my fond Heart
Till we meet shall pant for you,' *etc.*

It finishes with a repeat of the two first lines.

The copy sent to Clarinda is in the Watson Collection, Edinburgh.

LOVELY DAVIES

No. 349 in Johnson (Vol. iv. 1792): Unsigned.
For Miss Davies see *ante*, p. 378, Prefatory Note to *Bonie Wee Thing*. The MS. is in the Hastie Collection.

STANZA II. LINE 1. '*Ilk ane she* cheers when she appears,' deleted reading in the MS.

STANZA III. LINE 6. 'Even he her *humble* slave is,' deleted reading in the MS.

THE WEARY PUND O' TOW

No. 350 in Johnson (Vol. ii. 1792). Title and tune are in Oswald's *Pocket Companion*.

Buchan furnished Hogg and Motherwell with several stanzas of a 'very old song which perhaps Burns had in view when he composed the above.' As it repeats the Burns chorus *verbatim*, Burns most certainly must have had it in view, if it be the 'very old song' which Buchan said it was. But he said nothing as to where he got it; and it is plainly patchwork. Burns, however, must assuredly have known this ditty in *The Charmer* (1782) and other books :—

'I bought my woman and my wife half a pund of tow,
I think 'twill serve them a' their life to spin as fast's they dow;
I thought it had been ended when scarce it was begun,
And I believe my wife sall end her life and leave the tow unspun.

'I looked to my yarn knagg, and it grew never mair;
I looked to my meal-kist, my heart grew wondrous sair;
I looked to my sour-milk boat, and it would never sour;
For they supped at, and staiked at, and never span an hour,' *etc.*

The MS. is in the Hastie Collection.

STANZA II. LINE 3. 'And ay she took the tither *suck*,' deleted reading in the MS.

I HAE A WIFE O' MY AIN

No. 352 in Johnson (Vol. iv. 1792): 'Written for this work by Robert Burns,' and signed 'B.'

Made a few days after his marriage. The tune, Stenhouse says, 'was formerly adapted to some trifling verses beginning :—

'"I hae a wife o' my awn,
    I'll be hadden to naebody;
I hae a pat and a pan,
    I'll borrow frae naebody."'

And if that be true, these same 'trifling verses' (which we have not seen) are practically the first draft of one of Burns's airiest and bravest lyrics. A blackletter broadside (*Folly Made Manifest*) in the Crawford Collection is to the tune, *I Have a Mistress of My Own*.

The MS. is in the Hastie Collection.

STANZA I. LINE 2. 'I'll *share* wi' naebody,' deleted reading in MS.

STANZA IV. LINES 3-4. *Cf. The Jolly Miller*. He lived on the river Dee, and this was the burden of his song :—

'I care for nobody, no, not I,
    And nobody cares for me.'

O, WHEN SHE CAM BEN, SHE BOBBED

No. 353 in Johnson (Vol. iv. 1792) : Unsigned.

The first two stanzas differ very slightly from the first two of the old set, *When She cam Ben She Bobbit*, in Herd (1769) :—

'When she cam ben she bobbit,
    And when she cam ben she bobbit,
And when she cam ben she kist Cockpen,
    And then deny'd that she did it.

'And was na Cockpen right saucy?
    And was na Cockpen right saucy?
He len'd his lady to gentlemen,
    And he kist the collier lassie.'

The others are pure Burns. The two sets appear to be responsible, between them, for Lady Nairne's *Laird o' Cockpen.*

O, FOR ANE-AND-TWENTY, TAM

No. 355 in Johnson (Vol. iv. 1792): 'Written for this work by Robert Burns.' Signed 'B.'; and perhaps suggested by a song in *The Pretty Maiden's Amusement*, and other undated song-books :—

'I am a brisk and lively lass,
And scarcely turned of twenty,' *etc.* :—

or one in *The Lark* (1740) :—

'I am a lusty lively lad,
Now come to one and twenty,' *etc.* :—

the original of which is a blackletter ballad, *The Prodigal's Resolution* (Crawford, Huth, Pepys, Roxburghe, and other collections).

STANZA II. LINE I. 'A gleib o' lan'':—The common meaning of gleib [*i.e.* glebe] in Scotland is church land—that is, the land possessed by the parish minister. Here it probably means a portion of land about the average size of a kirk glebe —thirty acres or thereby.

O, KENMURE'S ON AND AWA, WILLIE

No. 359 in Johnson (Vol. iv. 1792): Unsigned. Both song and tune were communicated by Burns, and are not to be found in any earlier collection. The stanzas added in Cromek's so-called *Remains of Nithsdale and Galloway Song* are probably of Allan Cunningham's concocting.

William Gordon, sixth Viscount Kenmure, took up the Jacobite cause in 1715—mainly through the persuasion of his wife Mary, daughter of Robert Dalyell, sixth Earl of Carnwath—and got Mar's commission to command the forces in the south. After divers ineffective moves he passed into England, and, being taken prisoner at Preston on 14th November, was beheaded on Towerhill on 24th February 1716.

O, LEEZE ME ON MY SPINNIN-WHEEL

No. 360 in Johnson (Vol. iv. 1792): 'Written for this work by Robert Burns.'

One of the best and the most Burnsian of Burns's vamps, this charming song was no doubt suggested by *The Loving Lass and Spinning-wheel* in Ramsay's *Tea-Table Miscellany*, which Ramsay must have imitated from an old blackletter broadside (Pepys Collection), '*The Bonny Scott and the Yielding Lass*, to an excellent new Tune':—

> 'As I sate at my spinning-wheel
> A bonny lad there passèd by,
> I keen'd him round and I lik'd him weel,
> Geud faith he had a bony eye:
> My heart new panting 'gan to feel,
> But still I turned my spinning-wheel,' *etc.*

In the Crawford Collection there is *An Answer to the Bonny Scot: or the Sorrowful Complaint of the Yielding Lass*, to the tune of *The Spinning Wheel*.

Burns's MS. is in the Hastie Collection.

STANZA IV. LINE 6. 'Amid their cumbrous, *empty* joys,' deleted reading in the MS.

MY COLLIER LADDIE

No. 361 in Johnson (Vol. iv. 1792): Unsigned. 'I do not know a blyther old song than this' (R. B. in Interleaved Copy).

Buchan contributed to Hogg and Motherwell (1834) what he declared to be the original, but didn't pretend that it was ever in print.

Burns's holograph—MS. (A)—is in the Hastie Collection, and another MS.—MS. (B)—is in the Liverpool Free Library.

STANZA I. LINE I. The 'O' is omitted in MS. (A), as it is

MY COLLIER LADDIE in the case of Line 1 of Stanza II. 2. 'And tell me *what* they ca' ye,' MS. (A). STANZA III. LINE 1. The 'An' is omitted in MS. (A). 'An' ye shall gang in *rich* attire,' MS. (B). 4. '*If*' for 'Gin' in MS. (B).

NITHSDALE'S WELCOME HAME

No. 364 in Johnson (Vol. iv. 1792): 'Written for this work by R. Burns,' and signed 'R.' The MS. is in the Hastie Collection.

Lady Winifred Maxwell Constable (1735-1801) was sole-surviving child of William Lord Maxwell, son of William, fifth Earl of Nithsdale, who was sentenced to decapitation on Towerhill, 24th February 1716, for his share in the Fifteen, but escaped the night before the execution. She married William Haggerston Constable of Everinghame, and began rebuilding the old family mansion, Terreagles, or Terregles, Kirkcudbrightshire, in 1789. Burns has stated, for the sake of '*vive la bagatelle*,' that his Jacobitism was mostly matter of sport. But, in a letter of the 16th December 1789, he, as Sir Walter put it, plays 'high Jacobite to that singular old curmudgeon Lady Winifred Constable': roundly asserting that they were 'common sufferers in a cause where even to be unfortunate is glorious, the cause of heroic loyalty'; and that his forefathers, like her own, had shaken 'hands with ruin for what they esteemed the cause of their King and country.'

IN SIMMER WHEN THE HAY WAS MAWN

No. 366 in Johnson (Vol. iv. 1792): 'Written for this work by Robert Burns,' and signed 'R.'

The stanza is modified from the ballade octave. The MS.—MS. (B)—sent to Johnson is in the Hastie Collection. For permission to examine another on Excise

NOTES

paper—MS. (A)—we are indebted to Mr. Richardson, of Messrs. Kerr and Richardson, Queen Street, Glasgow. A third—MS. (C)—in the possession of Mrs. Andrews, Newcastle, corresponds with the text. MS. (A)—perhaps an early draft—consists but of the first three stanzas.

IN SIMMER WHEN THE HAY WAS MAWN

STANZA III. LINES 5-8 in MS. (A) read as follows :—

'*But Robie's heart is frank and free,
And weel I wat he lo'es me dear:
And love blinks bonie in his e'e,
For loove I'll wed, and work for* gear.'

STANZA IV. LINE 2. 'The canniest gate, *we feet it* sair,' deleted reading in MS. (B).

FAIR ELIZA

No. 367 in Johnson (Vol. iv. 1792): 'Written for this work by Robert Burns'; signed 'B.' Included in Thomson (Vol. ii.).

Two copies in Burns's hand are in the Hastie Collection. In the earlier the lady's name is Robina. According to Stenhouse, she was 'a young lady to whom Mr. Hunter, a friend of Mr. Burns, was much attached.' Hunter died shortly after going to Jamaica. The verses appear, however, to have been written on some lady suggested by Johnson :—'So much for your Robina—how do you like the verses? I assure you I have tasked my muse to the top of her performing. However, the song will not sing to your tune in Macdonald's Collection of Highland Airs, which is much admired in this country; I intended the verses to be sung to that air. It is in page 17th and No. 112. There is another air in the same collection, an Argyleshire Air, which, with a trifling alteration, will do charmingly' (R. B. to Johnson).

Johnson set the words to both these tunes. We give the variations from the text adopted here.

FAIR STANZA I. LINE 1. 'Turn again thou fair *Robina*,' MS. 7.
ELIZA '*Oh, in pity hide the* sentence,' MS.
STANZA II. LINE 1. 'Thee *sweet* maid hae I offended,' MS.
2. '*My* offence is loving thee,' MS. 7. 'Turn again thou *fair Robina*,' MS.
STANZA III. LINE 5. 'Not the *minstrel* in the moment,' MS.

YE JACOBITES BY NAME

No. 371 in Johnson (Vol. iv. 1792) : Unsigned. The MS. is in the Hastie Collection. '*Up, Black-nebs by Name*, alias *Ye Jacobites by Name*' (R. B. in scroll list in the possession of Mr. George Gray). Black-neb (*i.e.* black-beak) = a Scottish sympathiser with the aims and objects of the French Revolution. *Cf.* Scott, *The Antiquary*, i. 6 :—'Take care, Monkbarns, we shall set you down among the black-nebs by and bye.'—' No, Sir Arthur, a tame grumbler I ! . . . *Ni quito Rey, ni pongo Rey*—I neither make king nor mar king, as Sancho says,' *etc.*

THE POSIE

No. 373 in Johnson (Vol. iv. 1792) : 'Written for this Work by Robert Burns,' and signed ' B.' ' *The Posie* in the *Museum* is my composition ; the air was taken down from Mrs. Burns's voice. It is well known in the west country ; but the old words are trash ' (Burns to Thomson, 19th October 1794). 'It appears evident to me that Oswald composed his *Roslin Castle* on the modulation of this air. . . . The old verses to which it was sung, when I took down the notes from a country girl's voice, had no great merit. The following is a specimen :—

"There was a pretty May, and a milkin she went,
 Wi' her red rosy cheeks, and her coal-black hair ;
And she had met a young man comin o'er the bent,
 With a double and adiew to the fair May,"' *etc.*

And so on for four other stanzas (R. B. in Interleaved Copy).

THE POSIE

No doubt the old song gave Burns his rhythmus, but he seems to have borrowed his idea, either directly or through some derivative, from a blackletter broadside, called '*A Posie of Rare Flowers Gathered by a Young Man for His Mistress*, To a pleasant new tune' (Crawford, Huth, Pepys, Roxburghe, and other Collections). It consists of eighteen stanzas. Here are the first three:—

> 'The summer's o'er heating,
> Within an Arbour sitting
> Under a marble shade;
> For my true love the fairest,
> And of all flowers the rarest,
> A posie thus I made:—
>
> The first and last for trusting
> Is called Everlasting,
> I pullèd from the Bay.
> The blew and crimson Columbine,
> The Dazy, and the Woodbine,
> And eke the blooming May.
>
> The sweetest flowers for posies,
> Pinks, Gill-flowers, and Roses,
> I gathered in their prime.
> The flower of Musk-millions,
> Come blow me down Sweet-williams,
> With Rosemary and Time.'

The MS. sent to Johnson—MS. (C)—is in the Hastie Collection. A MS. sent to Mrs. Dunlop—MS. (A)—is at Lochryan; and for permission to collate a third—MS. (B)—on Excise paper, we are indebted to Mr. Richardson, of Messrs. Kerr and Richardson, Queen Street, Glasgow.

STANZA I. LINE 2. 'O Luve will venture in, where wisdom ance *has* been,' MS. (A).

388   NOTES

THE   STANZA II. LINE 3. 'For she *is* the pink o' womankind,'
POSIE   MS. (B).
               STANZA III. LINE 1. 'I'll pu' the *morning* rose,' MS. (B).
               3. 'The hyacinth *is* constancy,' MS. (B).
               STANZA IV. LINE 2. 'And *on* her lovely bosom,' MS. (B).
               STANZA VII. LINE 4. 'And *that* will be a posie,' MS. (A).

THE BANKS O' DOON

No. 374 in Johnson (Vol. iv. 1792): 'Written for this work by Robert Burns,' and signed 'B.'

'An Ayrshire legend,' according to Allan Cunningham, 'says the heroine of this affecting song was Pegg Kennedy of Daljarroch'; and Chambers also supposed the ballad to be an allegory of the same 'unhappy love-tale.' See *ante*, p. 299, Prefatory Note to *Young Peggy*, but even if the 'love-tale' were then known, it was not then 'unhappy.'

For other sets, *Ye Flowery Banks o' Bonie Doon*, and *Sweet are the Banks, the Banks o' Doon*, see Vol. iv. The song appeared in the *Musical Repository* for 1799; but the variations there set forth were probably not sanctioned by any MS., and are in no respect improvements.

A MS. is in the Hastie Collection.

WILLIE WASTLE

No. 376 in Johnson (Vol. iv. 1792): 'Written for this work by Robert Burns,' and signed 'B.' Included in Thomson (Vol. iv.).

The heroine is said to have been the wife of a farmer who lived near Ellisland. A cottage in Peeblesshire, which stood where a muirland burn, the Logan Water, joins the Tweed, was known by the name of Linkumdoddie, but probably it was so named after Burns wrote his song. The earliest authenticated appearance of Willie Wastle

in rhyme is in Cockburn's [Governor of Dunse Castle] WILLIE
reply to Colonel Fenwick :— WASTLE

> 'I, Willie Wastle,
> Am in my castle ;
> All the dogges in the towne
> Shall not dinge me downe.'

This same rhyme was, and is, used in the mimic warfare of Scottish children ; but whether they were the inspirers of Cockburn, or he of them, it is impossible to affirm. Of the *genre*—the satirical inventory of a woman's bad points—a good example is found in the Second Part of *Merry Drollery Compleat* (1670) :—

> 'I have the fairest Nonparel,
> The fairest that ever was seen,' *etc.*

The MS. is in the Hastie Collection.

STANZA III. LINE 1. 'Hem-shin'd' :—Sometimes wrongly printed 'Hen-shin'd,' and more often 'Hein-shin'd.' The reference is to the 'Haims' or 'Hems' of a horse's collar, which bend outwards.

STANZA IV. LINE 4. 'A hushion' :—A hushion is a footless stocking. 5. 'Midden-creels'=manure-baskets slung across horses like panniers.

LADY MARY ANN

No. 377 in Johnson (Vol. iv. 1792): Unsigned ; but the MS. is in the Hastie Collection.

As to the original : Motherwell asserts that Burns 'noted the song and the air from a lady in 1787, during his tour in the North of Scotland.' A broadside in the Laing Collection at Dalmeny (*The Whole Map of Man's Life*) is to the tune, *I Am but Young and Growing.* Stenhouse explains that the Burns is modelled on an antique fragment, *Craigton's Growing*, in a MS. collection belonging to Rev. Robert Scott, of Glenbucket. Motherwell states that the earliest set is printed in Maidment's

LADY MARY ANN *North Countrie Garland* (1823). Maidment's is the ballad of the Scott MS. Here is a handful of the rubbish :—

> 'Daughter, said he, I have done you no wrang,
> For I have married you on a heritor of land ;
> He's likewise possess'd of many a bill and band,
> And he'll be daily growing.
> Growing, deary, growing, growing,
> Growing, said the bonny maid,
> Slowly my bonny love's growing.'

Motherwell further supplies a copy of the ballad as 'traditionally preserved in the west of Scotland.' This is the first stanza :—

> 'The trees they are ivied, the leaves they are green,
> The days are a' awa that I hae seen ;
> On the cauld winter nights I ha'e to lie my lane,
> For my bonnie laddie's lang o' growing.'

Maidment, again, is at pains to supply an 'historical note' on a young Urquhart of Craigston (Aberdeenshire), the supposed hero, who was in all likelihood simply grafted on the Burns ballad by some not very ingenious Aberdeenshire artist.

The fact is, Burns got the germ of his song—not from any of these sets nor from a lady during his northern tour, but—from a fragment in the Herd MS., the more characteristic points in which (it is worth noting) are not incorporated in either the northern or the western sets:—

> 'She look'd o'er the castle wa',
> She saw three lads play at the ba':
> O the youngest is the flower of a'!
> But my love is lang o' growing.

> 'O father, gin ye think it fit,
> We'll send him to the college yet ;
> And tye a Ribban round his hat,
> And, father, I'll gang wi' him.'

'Lady Mary Ann' and 'Young Charlie Cochrane' are his own, as are the last three stanzas of the ballad.

SUCH A PARCEL OF ROGUES IN A NATION

No. 378 in Johnson (Vol. iv. 1792) : Unsigned. The MS. is in the Hastie Collection.

The refrain is borrowed from the name of the old air to which it is adapted, *A Parcel of Rogues in the Nation*, to which Gay has set a song in *The Beggar's Opera*. It is possible also that Burns knew the song on the Union of Scotland and England, republished as one of the *Lockhart Papers* (1817), and thus introduced :—'The following song has no date affixed to it ; but from a memorandum it appears to have been printed soon after the accession of King George the First.' It begins :—

    'Shame fa' my een
    If e'er I have seen
    Such a parcel of rogues in a nation,' *etc.*

It is included in Hogg's *Relics* as *The Awkward Squad*.

KELLYBURN BRAES

No. 379 in Johnson (Vol. iv. 1792) : 'Written for this work by Robert Burns.'

The set published in Cromek's *Remains of Nithsdale and Galloway Song* was no doubt concocted by Allan Cunningham. The Kelly burn (*i.e.* brook) forms the northern boundary of Ayrshire, and the ballad has no connexion with Nithsdale or Galloway.

Burns's MS. is in the Hastie Collection. Another set of his ballad (holograph) was sold by Messrs. Sotheby in 1892, and again in 1895. This was published in the Aldine Poets (Ed. Aitken, 1893). It has the refrain, ' Sing fal de lal,' *etc.*, after every line :—

    ' There was an auld man, and he had a bad wife,
    And she was a plague a' the days o' her life.
    Ae day this auld man was haudin the pleugh,
    By came the Devil, says :—"How d'ye do?"

one ; holding

KELLYBURN BRAES	"O vera well, Sir, but I've got a bad wife,
	And she's been a plague a' the days o' her life."
steer; young horse	"It's neither your stot, nor you staig I do crave,
	But that same bad wife it's her I must have."
	"O welcome most kindly," the auld man he said,
worse	"But if ye can match her—ye're waur than ye're ca'd."
	The Devil has got the guid wife on his back,
	And like an old Pedlar he's carried his pack;
smoky	He's carried her hame to his ain reeky door,
	And he bade her go in for a bitch and a whore.
	Then Satan makes fifty, the pick o' his band,
	Turn out on her guard in the clap o' a hand.
mad	The wife she gaed through them e'en like a wud bear,
	Whae'er she laid hands on, cam near her nae mair.
	A frighted wee devil looks over the wa':—
	"O help, master, help! or she'll ruin us a'!"
	Then Satan he swore by the edge o' his knife
	He pitied the man that was tied to a wife!
	Then Satan he swore by the kirk and the bell
	He was not in wedlock, thank Heaven, but in Hell!
	The Devil has travell'd again wi' his pack
	And to her old husband he's carried her back:—
most part	"I've lived in Hell the feck o' my life,
	But never was damn'd till I met wi' your wife."

There is, however, an English original in blackletter (*Roxburghe Collection*), *The Devil and the Scold*, from which derives a later ballad, *The Farmer's Old Wife*:—

> 'There was an old farmer in Sussex did dwell,
> And he had a bad wife as many know well;
> Then Satan came to the old man at the plough,
> One of your family I must have now,' *etc.*

This, no doubt, was Burns's material.

THE SLAVE'S LAMENT

No. 384 in Johnson (Vol. iv. 1792): Unsigned; but the MS. is in the Hastie Collection.

Sharpe opines that Burns 'took the idea of his verses from *The Betrayed Maid*,' of which he gives a transcript from a 'stall copy.' It begins as follows:—

NOTES

'Listen here awhile, a story I will tell
  Of a maiden, which lately fell.
It's of a pretty maid, who was betray'd
  And sent to Virginio.

THE SLAVE'S LAMENT

'It's on a bed of ease, to lie down when I please
  In the land of fair England, O ;
But on a bed of straw they lay me down full low,
  And alas, I'll be weary, weary O,' *etc.*

But Sharpe had no direct proof that this 'stall copy' was older than the Burns. It may be that older it is, and that Burns used it; but the original is certainly a blackletter broadside, *The Trappan'd Maiden, or The Distressed Damsel* (Crawford and Pepys Collections), reprinted in *Roxburghe Ballads* (Ed. Ebsworth, vii. 513), but without reference to any Collection :—

'Give ear unto a maid
That lately was betrayed
  And sent into Virginny O :
In brief I shall declare
What I have suffered there,
When that I was weary,
  Weary, weary, weary, O.

'When that first I came
To this land of fame,
  Which is called Virginny O,
The axe and the ho
Have wrought my overthrow
When that I was weary,
  Weary, weary, weary, O !

. . . . .

'But if it be my chance
Homewards to advance
  From the land of Virginny O ;
If that I once more
Land on English shore,
I'll no more be weary,
  Weary, weary, weary, O.'

THE SONG OF DEATH

No. 385 in Johnson (Vol. iv. 1792): 'Written for this work by Robert Burns.' Adapted to a Gaelic melody, *Oran an Aoig*, in Macdonald's *Collection of Highland Airs*. 'I have just finished the following song, which to a lady, the descendant of many heroes of her truly illustrious line, and herself the mother of several soldiers, needs neither preface nor apology' (R. B. in Lochryan MSS.).

This notwithstanding, Currie prefixed a kind of introduction, held hitherto to be Burns's own. Not knowing that the song had been published in Johnson, he began by writing thus to Mrs. Dunlop (Lochryan MSS.):—'*The Song of Death*, or as perhaps it should be called, *The Song of the Dying*, is superlative. It ranks with the Address of Bruce to his troops, and with the first order of productions of human genius. We must make much of it. A little prefatory explanation will heighten the effect :—"Scene, a field of battle. Time of the day, evening. The sun setting in the west. The wounded and the dying of the victorious army are supposed by the poet to join in the following sublime hymn."' This pleasing gloss we have taken leave to suppress.

A MS. is in the possession of Dr. James Adams, Glasgow, who published a facsimile in his *Burns's Chloris* (1893). It agrees with the text in Johnson.

STANZA I. LINE 2. 'Now gay with the *bright* setting sun,' Currie. LINE 5. 'Grim King of Terrors':—The phrase, of course, is biblical. Still it is worth noting that Death is twice addressed as 'Mighty King of Terrors' in *The Desperate Lover*, a song by Thomas Flatman (1637-1688).

STANZA II. LINE 8. 'O who would not *rest* with the brave,' Currie.

SWEET AFTON

No. 386 in Johnson (Vol. iv. 1792): 'Written for this work by Robert Burns,' and signed 'B.'

There has been no little discussion as to the date, the

heroine, and the scene. Currie in his Third Edition
relates that 'Afton water' was 'the stream on which
stands Afton Lodge, to which Mrs. Stewart removed from
Stair.' It is probable that Mrs. Stewart herself was his
informant, and it may well be that Burns sent her the
song. His brother Gilbert, in reply to George Thomson,
is positive that Currie was misinformed, and that Robert's
heroine was Mary Campbell; but Currie 'must not
be contradicted.' He gives no reasons for his faith ;
but in 1856 Chambers declares all doubt to be set at
rest 'by a daughter of Mrs. Dunlop, who affirms that
she remembers Burns say it was written upon the
Coilsfield dairymaid.' He therefore infers that 'the
name "Afton" was adopted *pro euphoniæ gratiâ*, suggested to him probably by the name of Afton Lodge,
in the neighbourhood of Coilsfield.' Chambers knew
not that Afton Lodge was built as late as 1790 ; but, with
a view to maintaining the association of Mary Campbell
with the song, the theory has been started that the name
'Afton' was suggested by Glen Afton, near New Cumnock,
and adopted '*euphoniæ gratiâ* instead of Ayr.' There has
also been a very great waste of speculation as to whether
the song was written in 1786 or at a later date ; but Chambers assigns it to 1786, and Scott Douglas to 1791. We are
able to put a term to this 'pleasing state of uncertainty.'
Flow Gently, Sweet Afton was sent to Mrs. Dunlop 5th
February 1789 (Lochryan MSS.), and in the enclosing
letter Burns explicitly declares that it was written for
Johnson's *Musical Museum*, as a 'compliment' to the
'small river Afton that flows into Nith, near New Cumnock, which has some charming wild romantic scenery
on its banks,' *etc.* It seems certain, therefore, that, not
the name Afton but, the name Mary was introduced
euphoniæ gratiâ, or at least that the heroine—if heroine
there were—was another than Mary Campbell. Also, the
song was clearly suggested by one of David Garrick's,
to the Avon, which Burns saw in *A Select Collection*

SWEET
AFTON

SWEET AFTON *of English Songs*, London, 1763 (see Vol. i. p. 417):—

'Thou soft-flowing Avon, by thy silver stream
Of things more than mortal sweet Shakespeare would dream. ...
Flow on, silver Avon, in song ever flow,' *etc.*

The copy at Lochryan—MS. (A)—gives some interesting variations. The song is also inscribed in the Afton Lodge Book—MS. (B).

STANZA I. LINES 1-2 in MS. (A) read thus:—

'Flow gently, *clear* Afton! among thy green braes,
And *grateful*, I'll sing thee a song in thy praise.'

'*Clear*,' too—not 'sweet'—is the epithet throughout.

STANZA II. LINE 2. 'Ye *blackbirds that sing* in yon *wild* thorny den,' MS. (A). 3. 'Thou green-crested *plover* thy screaming forbear,' MSS. (A and B).

STANZA V. LINE 4. 'As, gathering sweet flowerets, she stems thy *pure* wave,' MS. (A).

BONIE BELL

No. 387 in Johnson (Vol. iv. 1792): 'Written for this work by Robert Burns,' and signed 'B.' Nothing is known of the heroine. A MS. copy in the hand of an amanuensis is in the Hastie Collection. The song is at least reminiscent of Fergusson's favourite ditty, *The Birks of Invermay*:—

'The smiling morn, the breathing spring
Invite the tuneful birds to sing,
And while they warble from each spray,
Love melts the universal lay,' *etc.*

THE GALLANT WEAVER

No. 389 in Johnson (Vol. iv. 1792): 'Written for this work by Robert Burns,' and signed 'R.' Included in Thomson (Vol. i.), with the substitution of 'sailor' for 'weaver.'

Supposed by some to refer to Armour's visit to Paisley

in the spring of 1786 (see *ante*, p. 303, Prefatory Note THE
to *To the Weaver's Gin Ye Go*). The Cart flows past GALLANT
Paisley. A song, *The Lass of Cartside*, which we have WEAVER
found in an old Dumfries chap, may or may not have
suggested this one to Burns :—

  'Where Cart gently glides thro' the vale,
   And nature, in beauty arrayed,
  Perfumes the sweet whispering gale,
   That wantons in every green shade,' *etc.*

The MS. is in the Hastie Collection.

HEY, CA' THRO'

No. 392 in Johnson (Vol. iv. 1792): Unsigned.

No doubt suggested by some old rhymes on the coast towns of Fife, which Burns picked up in Edinburgh. Peter Buchan supplies the customary ' original ' :—

  'There's the cummers o' Largo,
   Ancrum, Graham, and Dargo,
  And there's the dancers o' Devin,
   George Strachan and Andrew Stevin ' :—

a Buchanite jumble of Fife and Aberdeenshire.

STANZA I. LINE I. 'Up wi'':—The phrase resembles the German '*Hoch.*'

O, CAN YE LABOUR LEA

No. 394 in Johnson (Vol. iv. 1792): Unsigned ; but the MS. is in the Hastie Collection.

According to Cromek [or rather Allan Cunningham] (*Scotish Songs*, ii. 40), 'this song has long been known among the inhabitants of Nithsdale and Galloway, where it is a great favourite.' Cromek also advises that the first verse be restored to what he calls 'its original state' :—

  'I fee'd a lad at Roodsmass,
   Wi' siller pennies three ;
  When he came home at Martinmass,
   He could nae labour lea.

O, CAN YE LABOUR LEA

'O, canna ye labour lea, young lad,
O, canna ye labour lea?
"Indeed," quo' he, "my hand's out,"
And up his graith packed he.'

But the fact is that the original, not merely of this stanza but, of the whole song, is preserved in *The Merry Muses*; and no doubt 'honest Allan,' here as elsewhere, was what is called 'pulling a leg.' The first stanza and the chorus are well-nigh word for word from the *Merry Muses* set, which, however, may have been retouched by Burns. The rest appears to be his own; though in one of his letters he describes his Stanza III. as a favourite song 'o' his mither's.'

CHORUS. LINE I. 'Labour lea'=plough pasture-land; but the phrase is used in an equivocal sense. 3-4 in the Hastie MS. read:—
'It's fee na bountith can us twin
Gin ye can labour lea.'

STANZA II. LINES 3-4 in the Hastie MS. read:—
'But my delight's the Ploughman lad
That well can labour lea.'

STANZA III. LINE 3. Here 'makin of' is probably not to be understood in the literal English sense, but = 'fondling' or 'petting.'

THE DEUK'S DANG O'ER MY DADDIE

No. 396 in Johnson (Vol. iv. 1792): 'Written for this work by Robert Burns,' and signed 'B.'

Sharpe supplied to Stenhouse's *Illustrations* 'the original words from a 4to MS. Collection of Old Songs' in his possession:—

'The nine-pint bicker's fa'n off the bink,
And broken the ten-pint cannie;
The wife and her kimmers sat down to drink,
But ne'er a drap gae the gude mannie.

NOTES

> The bairns they a' set up the cry ;
> "The deuks hae dung o'er my daddy."
> "That's no muckle matter," quo' the gudewife,
> "For he was but a daidling body."'

THE DEUK'S
DANG O'ER
MY DADDIE

The MS. is in the Hastie Collection.

STANZA I. LINE 4. 'Paidlin':—A weak action in walking, an effect of muscular weakness.

STANZA II. LINE 5. 'Buttered my brose':—*Cf.* the song *For A' That* in *The Merry Muses*:—'Put butter in my Donald's brose.' Also, in the same collection the old song, *Brose and Butter*:—

> 'O, gie my love brose, lasses,
> Gie my love brose and butter,' *etc.*

STANZA II. LINE 7. 'But downa-do,' *etc.* :—This line is found in *She's Hoved Me Out of Lauderdale*, a song preserved in *The Merry Muses*.

SHE'S FAIR AND FAUSE

No. 398 in Johnson (Vol. iv. 1792): 'Written for this work by Robert Burns,' and signed 'R.' Included in Thomson (Vol. i.).

The general allusion is to the girl who jilted Alexander Cunningham (see Vol. i. p. 447, Prefatory Note to *Anna*; and Vol. ii. p. 371, Prefatory Note to *To Alexander Cunningham*).

The MS. is in the Hastie Collection.

THE DEIL'S AWA WI' TH' EXCISEMAN

No. 399 in Johnson (Vol. iv. 1792): 'Written for this work by Robert Burns.'

A MS. corresponding with the text is in Arbroath Museum. A slightly different set was published in the tracts 'printed for and sold by Stewart and Meikle,' and is included in Stewart's *Poems Ascribed, etc.* (Glasgow 1801), and in Stewart's Edition (Glasgow 1802), where

THE DEIL'S AWA it is entitled *Song Written and Sung at a General Meeting of the Excise Officers in Scotland.*

Cromek, who published the same set, says that 'at a meeting of his brother Excisemen in Dumfries, Burns, being called upon for a song, handed these verses extempore to the President, written on the back of a letter.' Burns himself also states that he composed and sang it at an Excise dinner in Dumfries; but Lockhart, on the authority of Joseph Train, affirms that he made it, 27th February 1792, while he was waiting for a party of dragoons to help him to board a smuggler, which had run aground in the Solway Firth.

In the *Poetical Works of Thomas Whittell* (a Northumbrian rhymer, who died at Cambo in February 1736), edited by William Robson, and printed from Whittell's manuscript, Newcastle, 1815, there is this song :—

'Did you not hear of a new found dance
That lately was devis'd on,
And how the devil was tirèd out
With dancing with an exciseman?
He toes, he trips, he skips, he leaps,
As if he would bruise his thighs, man;
Sometimes the devil made the better dance,
And sometimes the exciseman,' *etc.*

Some of Whittell's songs are said to have been popular in the country districts before their publication from his manuscript, and it is possible that Burns got a copy of this one during his tour in Northumberland in 1787. A suggestion may also have come to him from the old rhyme, *Some Say the Deil's Dead,* which in the Herd MS. ends thus :—

'And some say he's risen, and ran
Awa wi' the Highland laddie.'

In Stewart, *etc.*, STANZA II. 'We'll mak our maut,' *et* forms the chorus, the other chorus being lacking.

STANZA I. LINES 3-4 in Stewart, *etc.*, read :—
'And *ilk auld* wife *cry'd* auld Mahoun
We wish you luck o' the prize, man.'

Mahoun (*i.e.* Mahomet) is an old name for the Devil. Cf. THE DEIL'S Dunbar's *Dance of the Seven Deadly Sins* :— AWA

'Then cried Mahoun for a Hieland Padyane.'

The scene of the song is a Highland village or clachan. Hence the reference to 'hornpipes and strathspeys.'

STANZA II. LINES 1-3 in Stewart, *etc.*, read thus :—

'We'll mak our maut *and brew* our drink,
We'll *dance and sing* and rejoice, man,
And *mony thanks* to the *muckle* black *de'il.*'

STANZA III. LINE 1. 'There's threesome reels *and* foursome reels,' Stewart, *etc.* 2. 'But the ae best dance *e'er* cam to *our lan*',' Stewart, *etc.*

THE LOVELY LASS OF INVERNESS

No. 401 in Johnson (Vol. v. 1796): 'Written for this work by Robert Burns,' and signed 'B.'

The title and tune are in Oswald's *Pocket Companion*. The song commemorates Culloden, 16th April 1746. In a note to *Scotish Songs* (ii. 129) Cromek remarks :—' Burns's most successful imitation of the old style seems to be in his verses entitled *The Lovely Lass of Inverness*. He took up the idea from the first half verse, which is all that remains of the old words,' *etc.* But Cromek says nothing as to where this first half verse is to be found. A song, *The Clans Are All Away*, contained in *The True Loyalist* (1779), and republished in Hogg's *Relics*, begins :—

'Let mournful Britons now deplore
The horror of Drummossie day,
Our hopes of freedom all are o'er,
The clans are all away, away.'

The Burns is included in Brash and Reid, Vol. iii. The MS. is in the Hastie Collection.

STANZA III. LINE 4. 'That ever blest a *lover's* e'e,' Johnson.

A RED, RED ROSE

No. 402 in Johnson (Vol. v. 1796) : 'Written for this work by Robert Burns,' and signed 'R.' To the Preface to Vol. v. Johnson added this note :—'The songs in the four preceding volumes marked B R X and Z, and the authors' names cannot be inserted in this Index, as the Editor does not know the name of those gentlemen who have favoured the Public and him with their Productions. There are a number marked B and R, which the Editor is certain are Burns's composition.' The meaning of this hopeless sentence seems to be that, Burns being dead, Johnson was unable to sign some songs, as he didn't know who their authors were, but that as for those signed B and R, he was sure they belonged to Burns.

Had the poet lived, this notable lyric would probably have been signed 'Z': inasmuch as its every single stanza—exquisite examples of his art though all four be—is borrowed. Mr. Ebsworth (*Roxburghe Ballads*, vii. 369) has pointed out the resemblance of the first to one in a certain blackletter, *The Wanton Wife of Castle Gate* (Crawford, Euing, and Roxburghe Collections):—

> ' Her cheeks are like the Roses
> That blossom fresh in June,
> O, she's like a new-strung instrument
> That's newly put in tune.'

And Burns was largely indebted to a predecessor for each of the other three. According to Buchan, this was one Lieutenant Hinches ; but the Buchanism thus fathered is only a sorry hash of some chap-book set. They all derive from a blackletter, *The Unkind Parents, or The Languishing Lamentation of Two Loyal Lovers*, of which there are copies in the Osterly Park (British Museum) and Pepys (Cambridge) Collections, and which is of further interest in connexion with *It Was A' For Our Rightfu' King*, for which see *post*, p. 432 :—   A RED, RED ROSE

 ' Now fare thee well my Dearest Dear,
  And fare thee well awhile,
  Altho' I go I'll come again
  If I go ten thousand mile,
   Dear Love,
  If I go ten thousand mile.

 'Ten thousand mile is far, dear Love,
  For you to come to me,
  Yet I could full ten times more,
  To have thy company,' *etc.*

  . . . . . .

 'Altho' I may in deserts range,
  My heart is linkèd fast;
  Therefore my mind shall never change
  So long as life does last,' *etc.*

 'Mountains and rocks on wings shall fly
  And roaring billows burn
  Ere I will act disloyally :
  Then wait for my return,' *etc.*

This *Unkind Parents* is closely allied to another common blackletter, *The Sailor's Departure from His Dearest Love* (Crawford, Euing, Pepys, and Roxburghe Collections), of which the burden is :—

 ' Remember me on shore, as I thee on the main,
  So keep my love in store till I return again' :—

and of which here is a stanza :—

  ' The fish shall seem to fly,
   The birds to fishes turn,
  The sea be ever dry
   And fire surcease to burn.
  When I turn false to thee
   Shall these things come to pass;
  But that will never be,
   Nor yet so ever was.'

A RED, RED ROSE Setting aside the Buchan rubbish, we have found three several derivatives, and 'tis possible that Burns knew them all. Two are in the Motherwell Collection of chap-books. One is the first of ' Six Excellent New Songs,' forming *The Hornfair Garland,* undated, but probably before 1780.— [The chap itself is of especial interest from the fact that, in ink now very much faded and in a boyish hand, there is written at the beginning, ' Robine Burnes aught this buik and no other,' while at the end there is the signature—now almost obliterated—' Robert Burnes '; but it is impossible now to determine that either inscription is authentic.]—It is entitled *The Loyal Lover's Faithful Promise to his Sweetheart at his going a long Journey* :—

> ' Altho' I go a thousand miles
> I vow thy face to see,
> Altho' I go ten thousand miles
> I'll come again to thee, dear Love,
> I'll come again to thee.
>
> . . . .
>
> 'The crow that is so black, dear Love,
> Shall change his collour White ;
> Before I do prove false to thee
> The Day shall turn to Night, dear Love,
> The Day shall turn to Night.
>
> 'The Day shall turn to Night, dear Love,
> And the Rocks melt with the Sun,
> Before that I prove false to thee,
> Before my Life be gone, dear Love,
> Before my Life be gone.'

The other Motherwell is No. iii. of *Six Excellent New Songs,* and is called *The Young Man's Farewell to His Love.* It begins somewhat after the manner of the Buchan corruption :—

> 'Farewel, my dearest Dear,
> No longer can I stay ;
> For when the Drums and trumpets sound
> Then we must march away, my dear,
> Then we must march away.'

For us, however, the most interesting stanza is this one :—

> 'The seas they shall run dry,
> And rocks melt into sands;
> Then I'll love you still, my dear,
> When all those things are done':—

for the simile in the first line, though found in Burns, is not found in the others. Our third original is one of 'Five Excellent New Songs,' in a chap-book in the British Museum, dated 1792, and entitled *The True Lover's Farewell*. Even if we had nothing in blackletter, the date —1792—would suffice to show that before the Burns appeared in Johnson there were songs resembling it in circulation : a fact which Scott Douglas—(who of course knew nothing of the blackletter either)—declared incapable of proof. This set is also of peculiar interest from the fact that its first stanza resembles more closely than any in the other two songs the first in the blackletter and the fourth in the Burns :—

> 'Fare you well, my own true love,
> And fare you well for a while,
> And I will be sure to return back again,
> If I go ten thousand mile.'

Moreover, it has a simile taken from the stars ('Till the stars fall from the skies') in the place of that other from the sea.

There is further a more corrupt derivative, *The Two Faithful Lovers*, in *The Northern Garland* (Newcastle); and last of all, in *A New Academy of Compliments* (1772) is found *The Passionate Squire's Petition*, which reads like a corrupt or stall set of a more elegant original, and includes these lines :—

> 'A Ship it cannot be built, Love,
> Without the Help of a Tree,
> And the very Flint-stone shall melt, Love,
> Ere I prove false to thee.

A RED, RED ROSE

And if I prove false to thee, my Dear,
The Rocks shall melt in the Sun,
And the Fire shall freeze like Ice, Love,
And the Sea shall rage and burn.'

It is a poor thing enough ; but it helps to show that, in one form or another, the idea of Burns's song was in the air long before Burns's song was written.

AS I STOOD BY YON ROOFLESS TOWER

No. 405 in Johnson (Vol. v. 1796): 'Recitative Written by Robert Burns': signed 'B.' The MS. is in the Hastie Collection.

Currie printed a slightly different set of this 'noble ballad' (Scott Douglas) as *The Vision.* We are indebted to Mr. W. R. Smith, Cincinnati, U.S.A., for a fragment, in photography : either an early sketch, or the old fragment itself which suggested Burns's chorus. The 'roofless tower' was part of the ruins of Lincluden Abbey, situate at the junction of the Cluden with the Nith. See Vol. ii. p. 458, Prefatory Note to Epitaph *On Grizzel Grimme.*

The CHORUS in the MS. fragment reads thus :—

'A lassie *by her lane, with a sigh and a grane,*
Lamented the lads beyond the sea ;
In the bluidy wars they fa', *and the wives are widows* a',
And maidens we may live and die.'

STANZA III. in Currie reads :—

' The *stream* adown its hazelly path
Was rushing by the ruin'd *wa's*
To join yon river on the Strath,
Whase *distant roaring swells and fa's.*'

Instead of Stanza v., these two appear in Currie :—

By heedless chance I turned my eyes,
And, by the moonbeam, shook to see
A stern and stalwart ghaist arise,
Attir'd as Minstrels wont to be.

'*Had I statue been o' stane*
  His daring look had daunted me;
  And on his bonnet grav'd was plain,
  The sacred posy—" Libertie."'

O, AN YE WERE DEAD, GUIDMAN

No. 409 in Johnson (Vol. v. 1796) : Unsigned. The MS. is in the Hastie Collection.

Revised and shortened (by two stanzas) from the old set in Herd. As regards this original:—Burns's chorus differs very slightly; his first stanza is almost identical; his second differs considerably; only his third is new. Sharpe gives a 'traditional ending,' vaguely said to be 'from recitation':—

  'Then round about the fire wi' a rung she ran,
  Then round about the fire wi' a rung she ran,
  Then round about the fire wi' a rung she ran,
  Saying:—"Haud awa your blue breeks frae me, gudeman."

But the true prototype is no doubt the lost song parodied in one of the *Gude and Godly Balats* :—

  'Till our gudeman, till our gudeman,
  Keep faith and love till our gudeman;
  For our gudeman in Heven does reigne
  In gloir and bliss without ending,' *etc.*

STANZA II. LINES 3-4 in the MS. read:—

  'Your horns *may be a quarter long,*
  I wat they're bravely sprung, gudeman.'

AULD LANG SYNE

No. 413 in Johnson (Vol. v. 1796): signed 'Z.' Included in Thomson (Vol. ii.), from a MS. in the Editor's possession.

Sent to Mrs. Dunlop, 17th December 1788:—'*Apropos,* is not the Scotch phrase *Auld Langsyne* exceedingly expressive? There is an old song and tune which has often thrilled through my soul,' *etc.* To Thomson he wrote:—' One song more and I have done—" Auld Lang

NOTES

AULD LANG SYNE Syne." The air is but mediocre; but the following song —the old song of the olden times, and which has never been in print, nor even in manuscript, until I took it down from an old man's singing, is enough to recommend any air.' Thomson in *Scottish Airs* expressed the opinion that Burns thus wrote 'merely in a playful humour.' It may also be that the story was a device to make sure that he (Thomson) would accept a piece which the writer was far too modest to describe as his own improvement on the earlier sets, the one published in Watson (1711), the other credited to Allan Ramsay. But, after all, it is by no means impossible that he really got the germ of his set as he says he did. The oldest, as given in Watson, is in two parts :—

> 'Should old acquaintance be forgot
> And never thought upon,
> The Flames of Love extinguished
> And freely past and gone?
> Is thy kind Heart now grown so cold
> In that Loving Breast of thine
> That thou can'st never once reflect
> On Old-long-syne?' *etc.*

It is usually attributed to Francis Sempill; but the broadside from which Watson got it, and of which there is a copy (probably unique) in the Laing Collection at Dalmeny, is headed thus: 'An Excellent and proper new ballad, entitled *Old Long Syne*. Newly corrected and amended, with a large and new edition of several excellent love lines.' The title is important, as indicating the existence of an older set; and that Burns either knew the set, or had seen this said broadside, is clear, since, instead of the mere refrain of 'old long-syne,' as in Watson, it has this burden :—

> 'On old long syne,
> On old long syne, my jo,
> On old long syne :
> That thou canst never once reflect
> On old long syne.'

The Ramsay derivative also takes the form of a love-song, in which a lady, by way of greeting her hero newly home from the wars, inquires :— *AULD LANG SYNE*

'Should old acquaintance be forgot
   Though they return with scars?':—

and, concluding that they shouldn't, goes on to cry :—

'Welcome, my Varo, to my breast,
   Thy arms about me twine;
And make me once again as blest
   As I was lang syne.'

After divers reflections, which attest her acquaintance with poets and 'politic authors,' she concludes her incantation thus irresistibly :—

'O'er moor and dale with your gay friend
   You may pursue the chase,
And after a blythe bottle end
   All cares in my embrace.
And in a vacant rainy day
   You shall be wholly mine;
We'll make the hours run smooth away
   And laugh at lang syne.'

The hero, perceiving that her intentions are strictly honourable, assents; and the piece concludes with a wedding in the wigmaking poet's best full-bottom style.

Two anti-Union ballads (1707), to the tune of *Old Long Syne*, are in the Roxburghe Collection. One is a parody of the earlier set :—

'Shall Monarchy be quite forgot,
   And of it no more heard?
Antiquity be razèd out
   And slav'ry put in stead?
Is Scotsmen's blood now grown so cold,
   The valour of their mind,
That they can never once reflect
   On old long sine?'

The other, *O Caledon, O Caledon*, which Mr. Ebsworth regards as unique, is in the Laing Collection as well. It

410 NOTES

AULD LANG SYNE was known to George Lockhart (1673-1731), and was published in *The Lockhart Papers* (1817). There is, besides, a Jacobite ballad on similar lines (and slightly Bacchanalian, like the Burns set), in *The True Loyalist* (1779) :—
'Should old gay mirth and cheerfulness
Be dashed for evermore?' *etc.*

Scott Douglas mentions a parody by Burns :—
'Should auld acquaintance be forgot
And never thought upon?
Let's hae a waught o' Malaga
For auld lang syne.'

In the Thomson version—MS. at Brechin Castle—Stanza II. of our text, and Johnson's, comes last.

CHORUS. LINE 1. Thomson inserted ' my *jo* ' for ' my dear.'
3. 'A cup':—Some sing ' *kiss* ' in place of ' cup ' (Note in Johnson, probably by R. B.).
STANZA I. LINE 4. ' And *days o*' lang syne,' Thomson MS.
STANZA V. LINE 3. ' Guid-willie waught':—There has been some unnecessary discussion as to the meaning of this phrase. It is of course analogous to that of ' cup of kindness ' in the Chorus. The accent of the later and more popular tune (which is by Shield), is probably responsible for a common (but fatuous) reading :—' A richt, guid willie-waught.'

LOUIS, WHAT RECK I BY THEE

No. 414 in Johnson (Vol. v. 1796): 'Written for this work by Robert Burns,' and signed ' R.'

Probably made soon after his marriage, and certainly before the Revolution of 1795.

HAD I THE WYTE?

No. 415 in Johnson (Vol. v. 1796): Signed 'Z.' The MS. is in the Hastie Collection.

The air, which in Oswald's *Pocket Companion* is described as *Had I the Wyte, She Bad Me*, was first known as *Come Kiss with Me, Come Clap with Me.* Burns's original was certainly a fragment in the Herd MS. :—

HAD I THE WYTE

> 'Had I the wyte? had I the wyte?
> Had I the wyte? she bad me;
> And ay she gae me cheese and bread
> To kiss me when she had me.
>
> 'For she was stewart in the house,
> And I was footman ladie;
> And ay she gave me cheese and bread
> To kiss me when she had me.'

Another set in *The Merry Muses* is described by Scott Douglas, in a MS. note, 'as old, with retouches' (*i.e.* by Burns). But Scott Douglas was guided by probabilities alone; and the *Merry Muses* set is so completely finished and so full of circumstance as to read like a derivative from this same fragment. Thus it runs:—

> 'Had I the wyte? Had I the wyte?
> Had I the wyte? She bad me,
> For she was stewart in the house,
> And I was fitman laddie;
> An' when I wadna do't again
> A silly cow she ca'd me,' *etc.*

The inference, in fact, is irresistible: that the fragment in the Herd MS. suggested two songs to Burns: one for publication, the other—*not*.

STANZA IV. LINE 8. 'Wanton Willie':—Hamilton of Gilbertfield sometimes so signed himself; but there is a certain 'Wanton Willie' referred to in the *Poems* of Alexander Tait (1790). As Tait made both Burns and Sillar subjects of his satire, it may be that Burns here refers to the same 'Willie,' whoever he may have been.

COMIN THRO' THE RYE

No. 417 in Johnson (Vol. v. 1796): 'Written for this work by Robert Burns,' and signed 'B.' It is also marked 'first sett': a 'second sett' (anonymous; a

COMIN THRO' THE RYE parody of the first) being given on the other side of the leaf.
A song in a London pantomime—the music adapted 'by J. Sanderson, the words by Mr. Cross'—entered in Stationers' Hall, 29th June 1796, begins thus:—

'If a body meet a body
Going to the fare;
If a body kiss a body
Need a body care.'

In *Notes and Queries*, 5th Series, Vol. v., p. 116, Chappell holds this to be the original of the Burns. But Burns died some three weeks after the pantomime verses were 'entered': so that, for one thing, he could not possibly have known them, and for another, if Chappell's argument held good, Johnson, in ascribing the *Museum* set to Burns, would have grossly swindled his patrons at the same time that he seriously wronged his poet. Also divers fragments—not producible in this place—exist in Burns's handwriting; and a set—('old,' says Scott Douglas, no doubt without direct evidence, in a MS. note, 'with Burns's revision')—is preserved in *The Merry Muses*. The set in the *Museum* only differs from it in the change of a word here and there, the suppression of certain stanzas, and the substitution of a chorus which can be sung in drawing-rooms for a chorus which cannot. Stenhouse notes that the 'first sett' was published as a 'single sheet song before it was copied into the *Museum*'; but gives, as is his wont, no further details. In any case, *Comin thro' the Rye* is related to a song, *The Bob-tail'd Lass*, privately printed in *Ane Pleasant Garland of Sweet-scented Flowers* (1835)—for a copy of the book we are indebted to Dr. Furnivall, London—from a MS. in the Advocates' Library, Edinburgh. It is there included in 'A Collection of Poems chiefly made in the earlier part of the last Century, found among the papers of Murray of Stanhope in Heriot's Hospital.' Here are two stanzas:—

NOTES 413

> 'On Wednesday in the afternoon
>   I took a walk in the field :
> It was to bring my courage down,
>   And still I was forced to yield.
> For there I met with a bob-tail'd lass,
>   As I should have passed her by ;
> And I kindly took her by the hands,
>   And I led her into the Rye.
>
> 'Her petticoat that she had on
>   Was made of the blanket blue ;
> Her smock was as black as charcoal,
>   Believe me as this was true ;
> But tempting words will tempt young birds
>   That from the nest do fly,
> And I'll never believe this the first time
>   That she had been caught in the Rye.'

COMIN THRO' THE RYE

YOUNG JAMIE

No. 420 in Johnson (Vol. v. 1796) : Unsigned. The MS. is in the Hastie Collection.

Its first two lines resemble those of *Young Thyrsis* in *The Lark* (1740) :—

> 'Young Thyrsis, once the jolliest swain
> That ever charm'd the list'ning plain.'

But that youth (whose motto was '*J'aime la liberté*'), though, like Burns's hero, he 'roved through a' the lasses,' remained himself unconquered.

STANZA II. LINE 2. 'He *wanders 'mang* the woods and briers,' deleted reading in MS.

OUT OVER THE FORTH

No. 421 in Johnson (Vol. v. 1796) : Unsigned. The MS. is in the Hastie Collection.

'How do you like this thought in a ballad which I have just now on the tapis: "I look to the west"?' *etc.* (R. B. to Alexander Cunningham, 12th March 1791).

OUT OVER THE FORTH For all the difference in sentiment and style, the 'thought' may very well have been suggested by a fragment in the Herd MS. :—

> 'O when I look east my heart is sair,
> But when I look west it's mair and mair;
> For then I see the braes of Yarrow,
> And there I lost for ay my marrow.'

WANTONNESS FOR EVERMAIR

No. 422 in Johnson : Unsigned.

The title is quoted in the *Answers to Scotch Presbyterian Eloquence Displayed*; but we have found no other set than that in the *Museum*. For the rest, the triolet is not uncommon in old Scots verse; and *Wantonness For Evermair*, as passed through Burns, has an odd look of a triolet—once upon a time—which has been violently carried away from the grace of its first state by a ravisher who knew nothing of the form.

CHARLIE, HE'S MY DARLING

No. 428 in Johnson (Vol. v. 1796): Unsigned. The MS., a superb example, is in the Hastie Collection.

The song was probably suggested by some Jacobite fragment. There is another set by Lady Nairne.

STANZA III. In the ballad of *Burd Ellen* there is a similar stanza :—

> 'When he cam' to the porter's yett
> He tirled at the pin;
> And wha sae ready as the bauld porter
> To open and let him in?'

But these versions were taken down from recitation after the publication of the song; and the stanza does not appear in the original *Childe Waters*. LINE 2. 'Tirl'd at the pin' = sounded the 'rasping-pin,' which was a notched rod of iron, with a ring attached.

THE LASS O' ECCLEFECHAN

No. 430 in Johnson (Vol. v. 1796): Unsigned. The MS. is in the Hastie Collection.

'During the Poet's first visit to Annandale,' says Cunningham (informed, it may be, merely by his beautiful imagination), 'an old song called *The Lass of Ecclefechan* was sung to him, with which he was so amused that he noted it down, and, at a leisure moment, rendered the language more delicate and the sentiments less warm, and sent it to *The Musical Museum*.' In effect, a capital set is preserved in *The Merry Muses*; and if Burns got it as Cunningham says he did, which is hard to believe—then only the last five lines of Stanza I. in the text belong to him.

As for Ecclefechan—the Entepfuhl of *Sartor Resartus* —Burns, in the course of his 'duty as supervisor,' was accustomed to 'visit this unfortunate wicked little village,' and slept in it on 7th February 1795 (R. B. to Thomson), about two months after the birth of Thomas Carlyle. It was long a favourite resort of such vagabonds as are pictured in *The Jolly Beggars*: which may—or may not—account in some measure for Carlyle's affection for that admirable piece. Thus, in *The Trogger*, a ballad in *The Merry Muses*, which may very well be from Burns, the hero and heroine, their business done, proceed to

'Tak the gate,
An' in by Ecclefechan,
Where the brandy stoup we gart it clink,
An' the strong beer ream the quaich in.'

STANZA I. LINE 4. 'Quarter basin':—For holding meal. *Cf.* the song, *Woo'd and Married and A*':—'Ye'll hae little to put in the bassie.' 6. 'A heich house and a laich ane'=a house with a porch, or it may be pantry, attached. *Cf.* the old song:—

'He keepit ay a gude kale-yaird,
A ha' house and a pantry.'

THE LASS STANZA II. LINE I. 'Lucky Lang':—For 'Lucky,· see
O'   Vol. ii. p. 364, Note to *To Major Logan*, Stanza XIII. Line 3.
ECCLEFECHAN 5. 'I tint my whistle and my sang':—*Cf. I Rede You Beware*,
etc., Stanza II. Lines 3-4:—
'Tho' music be pleasure, in music take measure,
Or ye may want wind in your whistle, young man':—
in *The Merry Muses*.

THE COOPER O' CUDDY

Nd. 431 in Johnson (Vol. v. 1796): Unsigned. In the MS. (Hastie Collection) Burns directs it to be sung to the tune, *Bab at the Bowster*, which he states 'is to be met with everywhere.'

A set, with some few differences, called *Cuddy the Cooper*, is in *The Merry Muses*.

FOR THE SAKE O' SOMEBODY

No. 436 in Johnson (Vol. v. 1796): 'Written for this work by Robert Burns,' and signed 'B.' The MS. is in the Hastie Collection.

It is evident that the idea of this charming lyric came to Burns through Allan Ramsay and *The Tea-Table Miscellany*:—

'For the sake o' Somebody,
For the sake o' Somebody,
I could wake a winter night
For the sake o' Somebody.'

This set is probably related to an English blackletter mentioned by Ritson in his *Scottish Songs* (1794):—

'O, when shall I be married?—
Hogh, be married!—
My beauty begins to decay,
'Tis time to find out somebody—
Hogh, somebody!—
Before it is quite gone away':—

which is also the original of *My Father has Forty Good*

NOTES

Shillings in Johnson (No. 453). Again, 'Somebody' was, FOR THE of course, a favourite personage in Jacobite song. SAKE O'
STANZA I. LINE I. '*And* dare na tell,' MS. 3. '*But* I SOMEBODY could wake a winter night,' MS. 4. 'For *a sight* o' somebody,' MS.

THE CARDIN O'T

No. 437 in Johnson (Vol. v. 1796): Signed 'Z.' The MS. is in the Hastie Collection.

Suggested, perhaps, by Alexander Ross's :—

> 'There was a wifie had a wee pickle tow,
> And she wad gae try the spinning o't.'

and the rhythmus seems modelled on that of *The Bridal O't* by the same author :—

> 'For yesternight, nae farder gane,
> The backhouse at the side wa' o't,
> He there wi' Meg was mirden seen—
> I hope we'll hae a bridal o't!'

STANZA I. LINE 4. 'Haslock woo'':—Fine wool from the neck of the sheep.

STANZA II. LINE I. 'Lyart gray':—Here 'hoary gray.' *Cf.* Henryson's *Ressouning Betwen Age and Youth*, Line 11, 'Lyart lokkis hoir,' and Sir Richard Maitland's *Folye of an Auld Man*, 'Quhan that his hair is turnit lyart gray.' 'Lyart,' though, like the Old English 'lyard' (Latin *Liardus*, Ital. *Leardo*, Old Fr. *Liart*), it originally='gray,' and was also, like the English 'lyard,' used as a general nickname for a gray horse, gradually came, as in the preceding examples, to signify the peculiar discoloration caused by age and decay, Thus also, in the ballad of *Jamie Telfer* :—

> 'The Dinlay snaw was ne'er mair white
> Nor the lyart lockes of Harden's hair':—

and in Dunbar's *Petition* :—'In lyart changed is his hue':— the meaning really is that the 'gray horse' [whose 'mane is turned into quhyt'] is no longer 'gray.' The most striking example of this use is probably that in *The Jolly Beggars*

Vol. ii. p. 1), 'Lyart leaves,' where 'lyart' clearly='old,' 'faded,' or 'withered.' *Cf.*, too, 'Lyart Time,' in Fergusson's *Ode to the Bee*.

THREE TRUE GUID FELLOWS

No. 442 in Johnson (Vol. v. 1796): Unsigned.
The tune with this title forming the chorus is in Macgibbon's *First Collection of Scots Tunes*. The stanza following was, says Stenhouse, 'hastily penned by Burns at the request of the publisher,' to enable him to include it.

STANZA II. LINE 2. 'But or night *to fain*,' misprint in Johnson.

SAE FLAXEN WERE HER RINGLETS

No. 447 in Johnson (Vol. v. 1796): 'Written for this work by Robert Burns,' and signed 'B.' Included also in Thomson, Vol. iv.

'Do you know, my dear sir, a blackguard Irish song called *Oonagh's Waterfall?* . . . Our friend Cunningham sings it delightfully. The air is charming, and I have often regretted the want of decent verses to it. It is too much, at least for *my* humble, rustic muse, to expect that every effort of hers must have merit; still I think that it is better to have *mediocre* verses to a favourite air, than none at all. On this principle I have all along proceeded in the *Scots Musical Museum*; and, as that publication is at its last volume, I intend the following song, to the air above-mentioned, for that work' (R. B. to Thomson, September 1794). In effect, even to the use of a refrain, the stanza of *She Says She Loes Me*—at first glance reminiscent of *The Cherry and the Slae*—is exactly modelled on that of *Oonagh's Waterfall*:—

'Sweet Oonagh was the tightest,
Genteelest of the village dames:
Her eyes they were the brightest
That e'er set youthful hearts in flames,

NOTES

SAE FLAXEN WERE HER RINGLETS

> Her lover, to move her,
>   By every art in vain essayed:
> In ditty, for pity,
>   This lovely maid, he often prayed,
> But she, perverse, his suit denied—
> Sly Darby, being enraged at this,
> Resolv'd, when next they met, to seize
>   The lock,' *etc.*

Thomson decided to accept the song. For Chloris, see *post*, p. 482, Prefatory Note to *Lassie Wi' the Lintwhite Locks*. The copy sent to Johnson—MS. (B)—is in the Hastie Collection, and that sent to Thomson— MS. (A)—at Brechin Castle.

STANZA I. LINE 4. 'Twa laughing een o' *lovely* blue,' MS. (A). 10. 'When first *her* bonie face I saw,' MS. (B).

STANZA II. LINES 9-12 were inscribed on a window-pane of the Globe tavern, Dumfries, now in the possession of Mr. William Nelson, Edinburgh. 11. 'And *still* my Chloris' dearest charm,' MS. (A); '*But*' for 'And,' Globe inscription.

THE LASS THAT MADE THE BED

No. 448 in Johnson (Vol. v. 1796): 'Written for this work by Robert Burns.'

'*The Bonie Lass made the Bed to Me* was composed on an amour of Charles II. when skulking in the North about Aberdeen, in the time of the Usurpation. He formed *une petite affaire* with a daughter of the House of Port Letham, who was the lass that made the bed to him.' 'Two verses of it'—adds either Burns or Cromek—'are':—

> 'I kiss'd her lips sae rosy red,
>   While the tear stood blinken in her e'e.
> I said:—"My lassie dinna cry,
>   For ye ay shall mak the bed to me."
>
> 'She took her mither's winding sheet,
>   And o't she made a sark to me;
> Blythe and merry may she be,
>   The lass that made the bed to me.'

THE LASS THAT MADE THE BED The set referred to is that in *Wit and Mirth*, 1700; but Stenhouse quotes two stanzas of another of which—he says—it is a corruption :—

> 'There was a lass dwelt in the north,
> A bonie lass of high degree;
> There was a lass whose name was Nell,
> A blyther lass you ne'er did see.
> O, the bed to me, the bed to me,
> The lass that made the bed to me,
> Blythe and bonie and fair was she,
> The lass that made the bed to me.'

Not content with either Cromek [or Burns] or Stenhouse, Peter Buchan is (as ever) to the fore, in Motherwell's Edition, with a version described as 'the *original* song, which I am proud of being able to submit to the readers of Burns':—

> 'The night it was baith cauld and wet,
> As I was coming owre the lea,
> When there I met wi' a bonie young lass,
> Who said she'd make up a bed for me.
> O the bed for me, O the bed for me,
> The lass that made the bed to me,
> I might hae lien upo' the lea
> Gin the bonie lassie hadna made a bed for me.'

But in any case the oldest printed set is an unique black-letter in the Pepys Collection entitled *Cumberland Nelly, or the North Country Lovers* :—

> 'There was a Lass in Cumberland,
> A bonny Lass of high degree;
> There was a Lass, her name was Nell,
> The blithest Lass that ere you see.
> Oh to bed to me, to bed to me,
> The lass that comes to bed to me;
> How blith and bonny may she be,
> The lass that comes to bed with me,' *etc.*

It is to the tune of *The Lass that Made the Bed to Me*, so that there was probably an earlier ballad, either a playhouse ditty, as Mr. Ebsworth supposes (*Roxburghe Ballads*, vii. 464), or an older folk-song.

To the same tune was published also, in blackletter, THE LASS
Cumberland Laddy, or Willy and Nelly of the North; THAT MADE
and to the tune of *There Was a Lass in Cumberland* THE BED
was published in blackletter *The Northern Ladd, or the
Fair Maid's Choice, Who Refused All for a Ploughman*
(Huth, Pepys, and Roxburghe Collections).

Stenhouse printed a garbled set of the Burns song, and said, further, that it contained the 'last alterations and corrections of the bard.' His impudent falsification was accepted by Chambers. A set, with some interesting variations, was published in the Stewart and Meikle Tracts, and was included in Stewart's *Poems Ascribed to Robert Burns* (Glasgow 1801). In later issues of the tracts and in Stewart's Edition (Glasgow 1802) are many readings from the Johnson set.

Burns's MS. is in the Hastie Collection.

STANZA I. LINES 1-4 in Stewart read thus:—

'When *January winds were blawing* cauld
As to the north I *bent* my way,
The *darksome* night did me enfauld
I *kend* na where to lodge till day.'

5. 'By my *good* luck a *lass* I met,' Stewart.

STANZA II. LINE I. 'I bow'd fu' low *to this sam*' maid, Stewart. 3. 'I bow'd fu' low *to this fair* maid,' Stewart.

STANZA III. LINES 7-8 in Stewart read:—

'*Syne* to salute her wi' a kiss
I *flang* my arms about her neck.'

STANZA V. The quatrains are transposed in Stewart. LINE 6.
'*The lassie* wistna what to say,' deleted reading in the MS.

STANZA VI. LINES 3-4 in Stewart read:—

'But ay she *sigh'd and cry'd*, "*Alas,
Alas, young man,* ye've ruin'd me."'

5. '*I look'd her in her bonny face*,' Stewart. 7. '*And* said, *sweet* lassie dinna cry,' Stewart.

STANZA VII. LINES 5 and 6 are transposed in Stewart. 7.
'I'll ne'er *forsake* till the day I die,' Stewart.

SAE FAR AWA

No. 449 in Johnson (Vol. v. 1796): 'Written for this work by Robert Burns,' and signed 'B.' The MS. is in the Hastie Collection.

THE REEL O' STUMPIE

No. 457 in Johnson (Vol. v. 1796): Unsigned.

A set of the old song, *The Reel of Stumpie*, described (Scott Douglas, in MS.) as 'Old—with revision,' is preserved in *The Merry Muses*. The fragment in Johnson is simply the first stanza and the chorus of that set transposed. It is like enough that Scott Douglas, as usual, did but mean to express an opinion; and it is certain that, in a Note to *This Is No My Ain House* (Interleaved Copy), Burns quotes this as old :—

'This is no my ain wean,
My ain wean, my ain wean,
This is no my ain wean,
I ken by the greetie o't.
I'll tak the curchie aff my head,
Aff my head, aff my head,
I'll tak the curchie aff my head,
And row't aboot the feetie o't.'

But his exact share in *The Reel of Stumpie*—which, as printed in *The Merry Muses*, is three stanzas long—is not now to be determined. For the rest, the 'Reel of Stumpie' is, like the 'Bob of Dumblane' and the 'Reel of Bogie,' a piece of Scots venereal slang.

Chambers (*Scottish Songs*, 1829) and, following him, Scott Douglas ('Kilmarnock' *Burns*, ii. 24) credit a set to William Creech :—

'Wap and rowe, wap and rowe,
Wap and rowe the feetie o't!
To nurse a wean 's a weary job
I douna bide the greetie o't.'

But there is no evidence that Creech acknowledged it, THE REEL and it is not included in his *Fugitive Pieces* (1815). O' STUMPIE Hogg (b. 1770) asserts, without any reference to Creech, that a similar set was an old Border song, which he had known all his life long. Hogg's set differs but a very little from a 'New Song' in a chap, published by 'J. Morren, Edinburgh, 1799':—

> 'We'll hap and rowe, hap and rowe,
> Hap and rowe the feetie o't.
> It's a wee bit weary thing—
> I downa bide the greetie o't.'

And the Chambers and Scott Douglas set—whether Creech's or not—is later than this, and is corrupted from it. It is to note that the equivocal phrase occurs in none of the three.

STANZA II. LINE 2. 'Made mantie':—'Manty' (from Fr. *manteau*) is Scots for a gown, and 'Mantymaker' Scots for dressmaker. This seems to be the meaning here, unless the word be related to 'mantic'(=prophetic), and the meaning be that she told fortunes.

I'LL AY CA' IN BY YON TOWN

No. 458 in Johnson (Vol. v. 1796) : Unsigned. The MS. is in the Hastie Collection.

'This tune is evidently the old air *We'll Gang Nae Mair to Yon Town*, and I suspect is not the best set of the air; but in Bowes and other collections the old tune is to be found, and you can correct this by these other copies' (R. B. to Johnson in the Hastie MS.). The old ballad, according to Stenhouse, begins:—

> 'I'll gang nae mair to yon town,
> O, never a' my life again;
> I'll ne'er gae back to yon town
> To seek anither wife again.'

'Town' in Scots is commonly applied to a set of farm-buildings.

O, WAT YE WHA'S IN YON TOWN

ALTERNATIVE verses to No. 458 in Johnson (Vol. v. 1796), to the tune *We'll Gang Nae Mair to Yon Town*: 'Written for this work by Robert Burns,' and signed 'B.' Included in Thomson's *Scottish Airs*, Vol. ii. Begun at Ecclefechan, where Burns was storm-stayed, 7th February 1795. 'Do you know an air—I am sure you must know it—*We'll Gang Nae Mair to Yon Town*. I think, in slowish time, it would make an excellent song. I am highly delighted with it; and if you should think it worthy of your attention, I have a fair dame in my eye to whom I would consecrate it; try with this doggrel until I give you a better.' The 'doggrel,' of which the original copy—MS. (A)—(written when the Bard, as he states, and as the MS. bears witness, was 'very drunk,' 'at' Thomson's 'service') is at Brechin Castle, consists in the chorus and one stanza; but some time afterwards Burns produced a complete copy—MS. (B) —also at Brechin Castle. Another copy—MS. (C)—sent to Maria Riddell, is in the possession of Dr. De Noè Walker. The song was first published in *The Glasgow Magazine* for September 1795; and it appeared in the *Poetry Original and Select* of Brash and Reid, probably before its publication in either Johnson or Thomson, the second volume, in which it was included, being published in March 1797, several months after the appearance of the single chap. A similar set appeared in *The Scots Magazine* for February 1798; in the Stewart and Meikle Tracts; and in an undated Stirling chap along with a *Solemn Dirge on the Death of Robert Burns*.

In the set sent to Johnson, Jeanie — either Jean Armour or Jean Lorimer—is the heroine. In that sent to Thomson, the name is Lucy; and Burns, enclosing a copy to Syme in an undated letter, explains its history:—
'Do you know that among much that I admire in the

characters and manners of those great folks whom I have now the honour to call my acquaintances—the Oswald family, for instance—there is nothing charms me more than Mr. Oswald's unconcealable attachment to that incomparable woman.' The 'incomparable woman' was Oswald's wife. He was Richard Oswald of Auchencruive, nephew of the Mrs. Oswald to whose memory Burns had devoted a savage *Ode* (Vol. i. p. 260). Lucy, daughter of Wynne Johnston, Esq. of Hilton, according to Sharpe, was at this time 'well turned of thirty, and ten years older than her husband; but still a charming creature.' She died at Lisbon in January 1798.

O, WAT YE WHA'S IN YON TOWN

For our text we have preferred the set in which Jeanie is the heroine; but the readings are selected from the several authorities.

TITLE. 'Town':—see *ante*, p. 423, Prefatory Note to *I'll Ay Ca' In By Yon Town*.

CHORUS. LINE 1. 'O wat ye wha's in *yonder* town,' Thomson's alteration, who substitutes '*yonder*' for 'yon' throughout. 3. 'The *fairest dame's* in yon town,' MSS. (B and C); '*fairest*,' Thomson.

STANZA I. in MS. (A) reads:—

'*O, sweet to me yon spreading tree,*
  Where Jeanie wanders aft her lane!
The hawthorn flower that shades her bower
  O when shall I behold again!'

STANZA II. LINE 2. 'And *wanton* in the blooming year, *Glasgow Magazine*, Brash and Reid, *etc.* 4. 'The season to my *Lucy* dear,' MSS. (B and C), and Thomson.

STANZA III. LINES 2-4 in MSS. (B and C) read:—

'*And on yon bonie* braes *of Ayr*,
  But my delight in yon town
  And dearest *joy is Lucy fair*':—

but in MS. (B) '*bliss*' for '*joy*.' 4. 'And dearest *treasure* is my Jean,' Brash and Reid, *etc.*

STANZA IV. LINE 1. 'Without my *Fair*, not a' the charms,'

O, WAT YE Johnson, *Glasgow Magazine*, Brash and Reid, *etc.* 3-4. *Cf.*
WHA'S IN the duet in *The Beggars' Opera*:—
YON TOWN
'Were I laid on Greenland's coast,
And in my arms embraced my lass.'

STANZA V. LINE 4. 'That I wad [or '*would*'] *tend* and shelter there,' *Glasgow Magazine*, Brash and Reid, *etc.*

STANZA VI. LINES 2-4 in *The Glasgow Magazine*, Brash and Reid, *etc.*, read:—

'The sinkin sun's *gaun* [or '*gaen*'] down upon,
The dearest maid's in yon town
His setting beam e'er shone upon.'

STANZA VII. LINE 1. 'If angry fate *is* sworn my foe,' all authorities except *The Glasgow Magazine*, Brash and Reid, *etc.*; similarly in 3, '*I* careless quit aught else below.' 4. 'But spare *me*, spare me, Jeany [or Lucy] dear,' MSS. (B and C), Johnson, and Thomson, '*my*' for 'me,' Brash and Reid.

STANZA VIII. LINE 1. 'But while life's dearest blood *runs* warm,' *Glasgow Magazine*, Brash and Reid, *etc.* 2. '*My* thought *from* her shall ne'er depart,' Brash and Reid, *etc.* 3. 'For *as most lovely* is her form,' *Glasgow Magazine, etc.*

WHEREFORE SIGHING ART THOU, PHILLIS?

No. 460 in Johnson (Vol. v. 1796): Unsigned. Set to *The Blue Bonnets*.

Suggested no doubt by the old English song in Ramsay's *Tea-Table Miscellany* beginning:—

'Do not ask me, charming Phillis,
Why I lead you here alone,
By this bank of pinks and lillies
And of roses newly blown.'

Burns also sent, as alternative verses to the same tune, a song beginning *Powers Celestial*, which, being an invocation for protection to 'Mary,' was long regarded as a sort of companion piece to *Thou Ling'ring Star* (p. 71). His MS. is in the Hastie Collection; but he merely copied the rubbish from *The Edinburgh Magazine* (1774).

NOTES 427

O MAY, THY MORN

No. 464 in Johnson (Vol. v. 1796): 'Written for this work by Robert Burns,' and signed 'B.'

Supposed to commemorate the parting with Clarinda, 6th December 1791.

The MS. is in the Hastie Collection.

AS I CAME O'ER THE CAIRNEY MOUNT

No. 467 in Johnson (Vol. v. 1796): Signed 'Z.'

The first two lines of Stanza I., together with Lines 1, 2, and 4 of the Chorus, are part of an old song sequestered in *The Merry Muses*. A broadside in the Laing Collection at Dalmeny, entitled, *'The New Way of the Bony Highland Laddie*, to its own proper tune,' has this chorus :—

> 'O my bony, bony Highland Laddie,
> O my bony Highland Laddie,
> When I am sick and like to die,
> Thou 'lt row me in thy Highland plaidie.'

A Jacobite *Highland Laddie* in *The True Loyalist* (1779) begins thus :—

> 'Prince Charles is come o'er from France,
> In Scotland to proclaim his dadie ;
> May the heav'ns power preserve and keep
> That worthy P—ce in 's highland plaidie !
> O my bonny, bonny highland laddie !
> My handsome, charming highland laddie !
> May heav'n reward, and him still guard
> When surrounded with foes in 's highland plaidie !'

This last chorus is almost identical with that of Ramsay's *Highland Laddie*. See also Prefatory Note to the next number in our text (p. 428).

HIGHLAND LADDIE

No. 468 in Johnson (Vol. v. 1796): Unsigned. The MS. is in the Hastie Collection.

This is chiefly an abridgment of the Jacobite ditty, *The Highland Lad and the Highland Lass*, published in *A Collection of Loyal Songs* (1750) and *The True Loyalist* (1779). The refrain is old; Stanza I. is Burns; Stanza II. is substantially Stanza I. of the older set; while Stanza III. is composed of the first halves of the older Stanzas VIII. and IX.

WILT THOU BE MY DEARIE?

No. 470 in Johnson (Vol. v. 1796): 'Written for this work by Robert Burns,' and signed 'B.' Published in *The Morning Chronicle*, 10th May 1794, with an editorial note:—'The following morsel is so exquisitely simple and tender, that it places an additional feather in the full-plumed bonnet of its author.' The MS. sent to Johnson is in the Hastie Collection.

In a MS. sent to Maria Riddell 'Jeanie' is substituted for 'lassie.' In view of the fact that Burns sent the song to Captain Miller's journal, this change confirms the statement that *Wilt Thou be My Dearie* was made in honour of Miss Janet Miller of Dalswinton. An additional stanza (probably the work of Hamilton, who supplemented *Of A' the Airts*) has found its way into print:—

> 'Flower of beauties, hear me,
>   And dinna treat me with disdain!
> A' the ills I fearna',
>   Gin thou wad only smile on him,
> Would part wi' life to please thee.
>   Of Joys on earth I'd ask nae mair
> If thou wilt be my dearie.'

LOVELY POLLY STEWART

No. 471 in Johnson (Vol. v. 1796): Unsigned. The MS. is in the Hastie Collection.

Polly or Mary Stewart was daughter of William Stewart, factor at Closeburn, to whom Burns addressed *To William Stewart* (Vol. ii. p. 135, which was *not* published in Lockhart's *Life of Burns*), and also the lines, *You're Welcome, Willie Stewart* (Vol. iv., which *was* published in Lockhart's *Life of Burns*). She was married first to her cousin, Ishmael Stewart, and then to a farmer, George Welsh (grand-uncle of Jane Welsh Carlyle). Being separated from Welsh, she fell in love with a French prisoner of war, whom she accompanied to his native Switzerland. She died in Italy at the age of seventy-two. The present song, together with *You're Welcome, Willie Stewart*, is modelled on a Jacobite number in *Collection of Loyal Songs* (1750) and *The True Loyalist* (1779):—

'You're welcome, Charlie Stewart,
You're welcome, Charlie Stewart,
You're welcome, Charlie Stewart,
Had I the power, as I've the will,
I'd make thee famous by my quill!
Thy foes I'd scatter, take, and kill,
From Billingsgate to Duart.'

THE HIGHLAND BALOU

No. 472 in Johnson (Vol. v. 1796): Unsigned. The MS. is in the Hastie Collection.

Stenhouse states that it is 'a versification, by Burns, of a Gaelic nursery song, the literal import of which, as well as the air, were communicated to him by a Highland lady.' But there are humorous touches in it which the original (if there was an original) could not have shown.

BANNOCKS O' BEAR MEAL

No. 475 in Johnson (Vol. v. 1796): Unsigned. The MS. is in the Hastie Collection.

No doubt suggested by a song on the Duke of Argyll (the great Duke: born 1678, died 1743), entitled *The Highlandman Speaking of His Maggy and the Bannocks of Barley Meal*:—

> 'My name is Argyle, you may think it strange
> To leave at the court, yet never to change;
> For falsehood and bribery I always disdain,
> In my secret thoughts no deceits e'er remain.
> O my King and country's foes I have fac'd,
> In battle and place never them disgrac'd:
> Or I'd hold any place 'gainst my country's will,
> I'd live upon bannocks of barley meal.'

This version, set forth in one of 'Five Excellent New Songs' in an old chap, differs slightly from the set in Herd, which is entitled *Bannocks of Barley-meal*. A Jacobite song in Hogg's *Relics* (said, on no evidence, to have been written by Lord Newbattle, 1688), called *Cakes o' Croudy*, has the refrain 'Bannocks o' Bear Meal, Cakes o' Croudie.' And the following rhyme is in the Herd MS.:—

> 'Mass David Williamson,
> Chosen of twenty,
> Gae'd up to the pulpit
> And sang *Killiecrankie*.
> Saw ye e'er, heard ye e'er
> Sickan a soudie?
> Bannocks o' bear meal,
> Cakes o' Croudie!'

WAE IS MY HEART

No. 476 in Johnson (Vol. v. 1796): Unsigned. The MS. is in the Hastie Collection.

The last stanza is closely imitated (and degraded) from the last of Lady Grizzel Bailie's *Were Na My Heart Licht I Wad Die*.

STANZA I. LINE 2. 'Lang, lang *has Joy* been a stranger to me,' Scott Douglas.

STANZA III. LINE 4. 'Wha wad soon dry the tear-*drop that clings to my* e'e,' Scott Douglas.

HERE'S HIS HEALTH IN WATER

No. 480 in Johnson (Vol. v. 1796): Signed 'Z.' The MS. (with the music) is in the Hastie Collection.

A set, with a second stanza, is included in *The Merry Muses*. Burns's first line is lifted from *Lewie Gordon*: —'To a Scots critic, the pathos of the line:—

' "Tho' his back be at the wa' "—

must be very striking' (R. B. on *Lewie Gordon* in the Interleaved Copy). The expression occurs, however, in a *Song on the Birthday of King James the VIII.*, 10th June 1709 (printed from Robt. Mylne's MS. in *Roxburghe Ballads*, ed. Ebsworth, viii. 225):—

'Altho' his back be at the wa',
We'll drink his health that's far awa.'

A Jacobite ditty, real or sham, with the same title begins thus :—

'Altho' his back be at the wa'
Another was the fautor!
Altho' his back be at the wa',
Yet here's his health in water!
He gat the skaith, he gat the scorn,
I lo'e him yet the better:
Tho' in the muir I hide forlorn,
I'll drink his health in water.'

But plainly Burns knew not of this when he wrote the note on *Lewie Gordon*.

THE WINTER OF LIFE

No. 486 in Johnson (Vol. v. 1796): 'Written for this work by Robert Burns': signed 'B.' Burns's MS. sent to Johnson is in the Hastie Collection. He sent a copy

432   NOTES

THE WINTER OF LIFE to Thomson, 19th October, under the title of *The Old Man*. This MS., which is at Brechin Castle, corresponds with that in the Hastie Collection. The song is included in Thomson (Vol. iii.).

Doubtless suggested by a song with the same title which we have found in *The Goldfinch*, Edinburgh 1777 :—

> 'In Spring, my dear Shepherds, your gardens are gay,
> They breathe all their sweets in the sunshine of May :
> Their Flowers will drop when December draws near—
> The winter of life is like that of the year,' *etc.*

THE TAILOR

No. 490 in Johnson (Vol. v. 1796): Unsigned. The MS. is in the Hastie Collection.

Suggested (at least) by *The Tailor* in Herd's Collection, which begins :—

> 'The tailor came to clout the claes,
> Sic a braw fellow;
> He fill'd the house a' fou of fleas—
> Daffin down, and daffin down—
> He fill'd the house a' fou of fleas—
> Daffin down and dilly!'

THERE GROWS A BONIE BRIER-BUSH

No. 492 in Johnson (Vol. v. 1796): Signed 'Z.' The MS. is in the Hastie Collection.

Appropriated by Hogg for his so-called *Jacobite Relics*. Stenhouse states that, 'with the exception of a few lines, which are old,' this song was written by Burns for the *Museum*; but, as usual, he says nothing as to where those lines are to be found. Sharpe (*Ballad Book*, 1823) gives this fragment :—

> 'He's a bony, bony lad that's a courting me,
> He's a bony, bony lad that's a courting me:
> He's cripple of a leg and blind of an e'e,
> He's a bony, bony lad that's a courting me!

NOTES 433

HERE'S TO THY HEALTH

No. 495 in Johnson (Vol. v. 1796): 'Written for this work by Robert Burns,' and signed 'B.'

Burns's sister, Mrs. Begg, affirmed that the song was well-known in Ayrshire when her brother was a boy. Burns sent a tune along with the song, but it was rejected in favour of a strathspey tune called *Loggan Burn*. The verses are doggerel; but they may quite well be early Burns.

IT WAS A' FOR OUR RIGHTFU' KING

No. 497 in Johnson (Vol. v. 1796): Unsigned; but, as we have said, it was the poet's habit not to acknowledge his Jacobitisms.

The facsimile of the MS. of this noble and moving lyric was published in Scott Douglas's Edinburgh Edition; and in Stanza v. Line 3 there is a deleted reading—'Upon my abs'—showing that Burns changed the line in the process of copying out. Apart from this, the touch of the master, either as makker or as editor and vamper, is manifest throughout. Yet Hogg, in his *Jacobite Relics*, gravely informs you that 'it is said to have been written by Captain Ogilvie,' of Inverquharity, who fought for James VII. at the Battle of the Boyne in 1690. Who said it? or when and where was it said? All that Hogg leaves to the imagination. It was certainly not said by either Burns or Johnson (who must have known; for there is no earlier copy than that which was written by Burns, and published in the *Museum*). We can scarce go wrong in assuming that Hogg's informant was Peter Buchan. Now, neither Hogg nor Buchan knew that Burns had sent the thing to the *Museum*. Moreover, his name had never been associated with it. Thus, the ingenious Buchan, still bent on fathering everything on somebody, had full scope for his idiosyncrasy. Before the Buchan-Hogg mare's-

IT WAS A' nest was discovered to an admiring world, Sir Walter
FOR OUR himself had adopted Stanza III. in *Rokeby* and *The
RIGHTFU' Antiquary*; and either he had not seen, or he had for-
KING gotten, the ballad in the *Museum*, so that he had nothing
to say when Tom Sheridan 'pointed it out' to him.
Now, what Tom Sheridan 'pointed out' was simply the
Museum set; and it was thus that the *Museum* set became
that 'entire copy of this beautiful song which seemed to
express the fortunes of some followers of the Stuart
family.' Sir Walter knew nothing of Burns's claim; for
Burns's claim had not then been discussed—the first to
show that he had sent the song to Johnson being Sten-
house (1839).

Moreover, Hogg's statement, not only lacks the thin-
nest shadow of corroboration but, is demonstrably
false; for the song in the *Museum* is modelled on the
same originals as *A Red Red Rose* (see *ante*, p. 402); and
these, as we have seen, trace back to the blackletter *Un-
kind Parents*, published, as Mr. Ebsworth points out
(*Roxburghe Ballads*, vii. 554), before Captain Ogilvie could
ever have 'turn'd him right and round about Upon the
Irish shore.' Nor is this all. Sharpe was the first to
suggest that Burns got his Stanza III.—'He turned
him right and round about,' *etc.*—from the chap-book
ballad of *Mally Stewart* [hence, no doubt, Sir Walter must
have lifted it into *Rokeby*], which is incontestably a
partial derivative from the aforesaid *Unkind Parents*.
Sharpe gave no information, however, as to the year of
the stall copy on which he founded his charge; and the
earliest dated known to us is one of 1807. But dates in
this species of publication are the exception; and Mr.
Ebsworth has informed us that *Mally Stewart* is included in
a garland of 'New Songs' in his Trowbesh Collection, em-
bellished with a rude cut of William Duke of Cumberland
on horseback. Several numbers in this same garland,
and in yet another with the same cut, refer to current
topics, and both indubitably date *c.* 1746. The long

NOTES 435

dispute as to the origin and the authorship of *It Was A' for Our Rightfu' King* may therefore be regarded as finally settled.

By Mr. Ebsworth's permission, we give the Trowbesh set of *Mally Stewart*, which, of all that we have seen, alone is free from manifest interpolations and corruptions:—

'The cold Winter is past and gone, and now comes in the Spring,
And I am one of the King's Life-guards, and must go fight for my King,
My dear,
I must go fight for my King.'

Now since to the wars you need to go, one thing pray grant to me;
That I dress myself in man's attire, and march along with thee,
My dear,
To go through the world with thee!'

'Not for ten thousand pound, my Love, shall you to danger go.
The rattling drums and shining swords would cause you sorrow and woe,
My dear,
They would cause you sorrow and woe.'

'Yet one thing for my Love I will do that she cannot do for me;
I will wear black cuffs on my red coat sleeve, and mourn for her till I die,
My dear,
I will mourn till the day I die.'

'Nay, I will do more for my true Love, than he will do for me;
I will cut my hair, my snood I will tear, and mourn for him till I die,
My dear,
And mourn till the day I die.'

'So farewell to my father and mother, farewell and adieu to you!
And farewell, my bonny Mally Stuart, the cause of all my woe,
My dear,
The cause of all my woe.'

436 NOTES

IT WAS A'
FOR OUR
RIGHTFU'
KING

'When we leave bonny Stirling town, no more we sleep in tent,
For by the King we are order'd down, and to Ireland we are sent,
     My dear,
  To Ireland we are sent.

'So farewell bonny Stirling town, from the maids we are forc'd
 to go,
And farewell, bonny Mally Stuart, the cause of all my woe
    My dear,
  The cause of all my woe.'

The trooper turn'd himself about all on the Irish shore,
He has given the bridal-reins a shake, saying 'Adieu for ever-
 more,
    My dear,
  Adieu for evermore.'

In later copies two irrelevant stanzas are usually inter-
polated before this last. *It Was A' for Our Rightfu' King*
was mainly inspired by the first and last of the balladist.
Burns used the last as his own central, grouping his
others, which are largely suggested by it, round about
it. He was also greatly influenced by the first, which
undoubtedly helped him to his own beginning. For the
rest, he took the situation and the characters, and touched
his borrowings to issues as fine, perhaps, as the Romantic
Lyric has to show.

THE HIGHLAND WIDOW'S LAMENT

No. 498 in Johnson (Vol. v. 1796): Unsigned. The MS.
is in the Hastie Collection.

Burns supplied the music, which he got from a lady in
the north of Scotland. The refrain is borrowed from the
old song in Johnson (No. 89, Vol. i.), said to have been a
lament for Glencoe :—

  'O was not I a weary wight!
   Oh on, O chri oh!
  Maid, wife, and widow in one night,
   Oh on, O chri oh!'

THOU GLOOMY DECEMBER

No. 499 in Johnson (Vol. v. 1796): 'Written for this work by Robert Burns,' and signed 'R.'

The first two stanzas were sent to Clarinda on 27th December 1791 as a song to 'a charming plaintive Scots tune':—'The rest of the song is on the wheels. Adieu! Adieu!' This MS. is in the Watson Collection; that sent to Johnson is one of the Hastie Autographs.

STANZA II. LINE 1. 'Fond lovers' parting is sweet, painful pleasure':—*Cf.* Shakespeare's *Romeo and Juliet*, Act II. Scene 3:—

'Good night! Good night! parting is such sweet sorrow.'

STANZA III. LINE 2. 'Till the last leaf o' the summer is *gone*,' deleted reading in the Hastie MS.

MY PEGGY'S FACE, MY PEGGY'S FORM

No. 501 in Johnson (Vol. vi. 1803), Currie (1800), and Thomson (1801).

It was written in 1787, and sent to Johnson with the following letter:—'Dear Mr. Publisher,—I hope, against my return, you will be able to tell me from Mr. Clarke if these words will suit the tune. If they don't suit, I must think on some other air, as I have a very strong private reason for wishing them in the *second* volume. Don't forget to transcribe me the list of the Antiquarian Music. Farewell.—R. BURNS.' No reason was given by Johnson for the delay in publishing; but it is probable that Miss Chalmers (see *ante*, p. 332, Prefatory Note to *Where, Braving Angry Winter's Storms*) objected.

Thomson, who got the song from Currie, took the liberty of substituting 'Mary' for 'Peggy.'

O, STEER HER UP, AND HAUD HER GAUN

No. 504 in Johnson (Vol. vi. 1803): 'Written for this work by Robert Burns.' The first half stanza is Ramsay's, from a set founded on an old, improper ditty.

WEE WILLIE GRAY

No. 514 in Johnson (Vol. vi. 1803): 'Written for this work by R. Burns.' A nursery ditty for the tune *Wee Totum Fogg.*

WE'RE A' NODDIN

No. 523 in Johnson (Vol. vi. 1803): 'Corrected by Burns,' and signed 'B.'

'The greater part of the verses, however'—thus Stenhouse—'are taken from the old satirical song formerly sung to the tune of *John Anderson My Jo*': for which see *ante*, p. 349, Prefatory Note to *John Anderson My Jo*. As matter of fact, the present ditty is a medley of two old songs with variations and amendments, the *John Anderson My Jo* aforesaid—which gives us Stanzas iv. and v., the best things in the Burns set, *verbatim*—and an unpublished fragment in the Herd MS. :—

> 'Cats like milk, and Dogs like Broo,
> Lads like lasses and lasses lads too;
> And they're a' nodding, nidding, nidding, nodding,
> They're a' nodding at our house at hame.

> 'Kate sits i' the neuk supping hen broo,
> Deil take Kate if she does not know it too;
> And they're a' nodding, nidding, nidding, nodding,
> They're a' nodding at our house at hame.'

To Robert Ainslie (Edinburgh, 23rd August 1787), Burns quoted a stanza thus :—' Now for a modest stanza of classical authority :—

NOTES 439

* "The cats like kitchen;
The dogs like broo;
The lasses like the lads weel
And th' auld wives too.

Chorus

"An' we're a' noddin,
Nid, nid noddin,
We're a' noddin fou at e'en."' :—

WE'RE A'
NODDIN

which may be a quotation from memory made not long after he had read the scrap preserved by Herd.

O, AY MY WIFE SHE DANG ME

No. 532 in Johnson (Vol. vi. 1803): .'Written for this work by Robert Burns.' The tune, in Oswald's *Pocket Companion*, has the title *My Wife She Dang Me*. Stenhouse states that the old verses are unfit for modern print, but Motherwell gives a decent enough set :—

'I was twenty years a bachelor
And liv'd a single life;
But I never could contented be
Until I got a wife,
But I hadna lang married been
Till she began to bang me,
And near dung out my very een,
And swore she would gae hang me.'

For the copy of a MS. we are indebted to Mr. J. W. Ellsworth, Chicago.

CHORUS. LINES 1-3 in the MS. read:

'*My* Wife she dang me.
My Wife she dang me,
And gie a woman a' her will.'

STANZA I. LINE 2. 'And fool I was, I *marry*,' MS. 4. '*A*\ cursedly *miscarry*.'

STANZA II. LINE 1. 'Some sairie comfort *still* at last,' MS.

SCROGGAM

No. 539 in Johnson (Vol. vi. 1803): 'Written for this work by Robert Burns,' and signed 'B.' Founded on an older ditty, or, it may be, garbled from more than one. Save for the refrain (of which nothing is known), the first stanza is adapted from a song preserved in *The Merry Muses*:—

'There wonned a wife in Whistlecockpen—
Will ye no, can ye no, let me be!
She brewed guid ale for gentlemen,
And ay she waggit it wantonly.'

Cockpen—(associated with another song, *When She Cam Ben She Bobbit*, which Burns improved [see p. 381], and which suggested a famous Lady Nairne)—is the name of a parish in Midlothian, where the 'auld Cowl' of the text seems to have been priest.

O, GUID ALE COMES

No. 542 in Johnson (Vol. vi. 1803): 'Corrected by R. Burns.' Stenhouse states that only the chorus is old. A MS. is in the possession of the Paisley Burns Club.

STANZA II. LINE 3. See Vol. ii. p. 343, Note to *Address to the Toothache*, Stanza IV. Line 2.

ROBIN SHURE IN HAIRST

No. 543 in Johnson (Vol. vi. 1803): 'Chorus written for this work by R. Burns.'

Sharpe remarks of Burns's authorship:—'This is probably wrong; or Burns suppressed the last stanza, to be found in the stall copies, besides substituting "three goose feathers and a whittle" for the indecent line in the third: it is likely that he only altered the song for the *Museum,* making it applicable to himself as an author, by the three goose-quills and the penknife. The last stanza begins :— ROBIN SHURE IN HAIRST

"Now I'm Robin's bride, free frae kirk fo'ks' bustle,
Robin's a' my ain, wi's,"' *etc.*

But Burns did not mean the song to apply to himself. He meant it to apply to Robert Ainslie:—'I am still catering for Johnson's publication, and among others, I have brushed up the following old favourite song a little, with a view to your worship. I have only altered a word here and there; but if you like the humour of it, we shall think of a stanza or two to add to it' (R. B. to Ainslie, January 6th, 1789).

Letter and song as sent to Ainslie (but with no mention of him) appeared in *The Scots Magazine* for 1801.

DOES HAUGHTY GAUL INVASION THREAT?

No. 546 in Johnson (Vol. vi. 1803) : 'Written for this work by Robert Burns.' Published also in *The Edinburgh Courant* for May 4th, 1795 ; *The Dumfries Journal* for the 5th of the same month ; *The Caledonian Mercury* on the 7th ; and in Currie (1800). A MS. — MS. (A)—is at Lochryan, and another—MS. (B)—in the possession of Mr. John Dick of Craigengelt, Stirlingshire.

STANZA I. LINE 5. 'Corsincon':—'A high hill at the source of the Nith' (R. B. in *Courant*, etc.). 6. 'Criffel':—'A mountain at the confluence of the Nith with the Solway Firth' (R. B. in *Courant,* etc.). 7. 'Ere we *allow* a foreign foe,' MS. (B).

STANZA II. LINE 1. 'O, let us not like snarling *curs,*' Johnson and MS. (B). 7. 'For *only* but by British hands,' MS. (A).

STANZA IV. LINE 2. 'And the wretch his true-*born* brother,' Currie ; but there is no authority for the word. 3. 'Who would [or 'Who'd'] set the mob *aboon* the throne,' Currie, *Courant,* etc.

O, ONCE I LOV'D A BONIE LASS

No. 551 in Johnson (Vol. vi. 1803) and Currie (1800): Unsigned. Entered in the *First Common Place Book*—MS. (A)—April 1783 :—'The following composition was the first of my performances, and done at an early period of life, when my heart glowed with honest warm simplicity; unacquainted, and uncorrupted with the ways of a wicked world. The performance is, indeed, very puerile and silly : but I am always pleased with it, as it recalls to my mind those happy days when my heart was yet honest and my tongue was sincere. The subject of it was a young girl who really deserved all the praises I have bestowed on her.' Burns presented a copy to Mrs. Stewart of Stair, and this MS.—MS. (B)—is now in the possession of Mr. Adam Wood, Troon. 'The following song,' he remarks, 'is only valuable to those who would see the author's first productions in verse. It was composed when he was a few months more than his sixteenth year.' In the *Autobiographical Letter to Dr. Moore*, he states that the young girl was his partner in 'the labors of harvest.' 'Among her other love-inspiring qualifications,' so he further relates, 'she sung sweetly; and 'twas her favourite reel to which I attempted giving an embodied vehicle in rhyme. I was not so presumptive as to imagine that I would make verses like printed ones, composed by men who had Greek and Latin ; but my girl sung a song which was said to be composed by a small country laird's son, on one of his father's maids, with whom he was in love ; and I saw no reason why I might not rhyme as well as he, for except shearing sheep and casting peats, his father living in the moors, he had no more scholarcraft than I had.'

His criticism of the song (in the *First Common Place Book*) is interesting enough to reprint in full:—'The first distic of the first stanza is quite too much in the

flimsy strain of our ordinary street ballads; and on the O, ONCE I
other hand, the second distic is too much in the other LOV'D A
extreme. The expression is a little awkward, and the BONIE LASS
sentiment too serious. Stanza the second I am well
pleased with, and I think it conveys a fine idea of that
amiable part of the Sex—the agreeables ; or what in our
Scotch dialect we call a sweet sonsy Lass. The third
stanza has a little of the flimsy turn in it; and the third
line has rather too serious a cast. The fourth stanza is a
very indifferent one; the first line is, indeed, all in the
strain of the second stanza, but the rest is mostly an
expletive. The thoughts in the fifth stanza come finely
up to my favourite idea, a sweet sonsy Lass; the last line,
however, halts a little. The same sentiments are kept
up with equal spirit and tenderness in the sixth stanza,
but the second and fourth lines ending with short
syllables hurts the whole. The seventh stanza has
several minute faults; but I remember I composed it in
a wild enthusiasm of passion, and to this hour I never
recollect it, but my heart melts, and my blood sallies at
the remembrance.'

The tune to which Burns wrote his verses was *I Am a
Man Unmarried*, and it had a chorus, 'Tal al de Ral' or
'Fal al de Dal'; but he sent another to Johnson.

STANZA I. LINE 2. '*An*' *aye* I love her still,' Johnson.
'An' whilst that *honor* warms my breast,' MSS. (A and B). 4.
'*I* love my handsome Nell,' MS. (B).

STANZA IV. LINE 2-4. in MS. (B) read:—

'*Good humour'd, frank and free,
And still the more I view them o'er
The more they capture me.*'

STANZA V. is omitted in MS. (B).

MY LORD A-HUNTING

No. 554 in Johnson (Vol. vi. 1803): 'Written for this
work by Robert Burns.'

SWEETEST MAY

No. 559 in Johnson (Vol. vi. 1803): 'Written for this work by Robert Burns.'

An imitation, open and unabashed, of Ramsay's *My Sweetest May, Let Love Incline Thee.*

MEG O' THE MILL

No. 566 in Johnson (Vol. vi. 1803): 'Written for this work by Robert Burns.' Suggested doubtless by an older ditty, which, however, has escaped us. Another set was sent to Thomson, which he declined (see Vol. iv.).

STANZA IV. LINE I. Among the Scots lower classes the newly married pair were bedded in presence of the company.

JOCKIE'S TA'EN THE PARTING KISS

No. 570 in Johnson (Vol. vi. 1803): 'Written for this work by Robert Burns.' Published by Currie (1800).

O, LAY THY LOOF IN MINE, LASS

No. 574 in Johnson (Vol. vi. 1803): 'Written for this work by Robert Burns.'

STANZA I. LINE 2. 'He aft has wrought me meikle wae':— Cf. *The Twa Herds*, Vol. ii. p. 23, Stanza XII. Line 2:—

'M'Gill has wrought us meikle wae.

CAULD IS THE E'ENIN BLAST

No. 583 in Johnson (Vol. vi. 1803): 'Written for this work by Robert Burns.'

The old words, to the tune *Peggy Ramsay*, began, says Stenhouse, thus :—

NOTES 445

'Bonny Peggy Ramsay, as ony man may see,
Has a bony sweet face, and a gleg glintin e'e.'

CAULD IS
THE
E'ENIN
BLAST

In effect the ballad thus beginning is fully set forth, in what at one time passed for Scots, in *Wit and Mirth* (1703). It is amazingly coarse, and, as either original or derivative, was certainly known to Shakespeare (*Twelfth Night*, Act II. Scene iii., Sir Toby Belch *loq.* :—' Malvolio's a Peg a-Ramsay'). Staunton, in his notes to Shakespeare, states, on the authority of Chappell, that 'there are two tunes under the name, and both as old as Shakespeare's time.' See further Staunton's *Shakespeare*, vol. iii. p. 194. The refrain runs on the word 'mill,' the sense of which, as in Burns, is not technical but equivocal a sense which is classic.

THERE WAS A BONIE LASS

No. 586 in Johnson (Vol. vi. 1803): 'By R. Burns.' A cento of old catchwords.

THERE'S NEWS, LASSES, NEWS

No. 589 in Johnson (Vol. vi. 1803): 'Written for this work by Robert Burns.'

The tune in the Old Skene MS. has the title *I Wunna Gang to My Bed Till I Sud Die*; and Stenhouse states that 'the song was retouched by Burns from a very ancient one, called *I Wunna Gang to My Bed Until I Get a Man*,' but quotes no further. Scott Douglas, again, suspects that 'the words were written merely to preserve the pretty little melody which our bard recovered.' It is plain, however, that 'our bard's' original is a fragment in the Herd MS. :—

'Newes, Lasses, Newes!
Gude Newes I hae to tell,
There's a boat fu' o' young men
Come to our town to sell.

446 NOTES

THERE'S NEWS 'Mither, quo' she; Father, quo' she,
LASSES, NEWS   Do what ye can,
               For to my Bed I wunna gae
               Till I get a man.'

STANZA III. with the equivocal 'ley-crop' (lea-crop) in Line 3, and 'till'd' in 4, was probably an emendation of a stanza in some other ancient ditty.

O, THAT I HAD NE'ER BEEN MARRIED

No. 593 in Johnson (Vol. vi. 1803): 'Corrected by R. Burns,' and the last stanza 'added by Burns.'

Burns quotes all that is old of this song in a letter to Mrs. Dunlop, 1795. His quotation includes Stanza I. and the Chorus. Doubtless he found it in the Herd MS.

A ballad in the Crawford Collection, *Women's Work is Never Done* (c. 1750-70) begins thus :—

'O that I had ne'er been married,
Since I lead a careful life!
Things with me are strangely carried,
Now I am become a wife,' *etc.*

It is in octaves, however, and sets forth the sorrows and trials of a woman with a tyrant-husband.

MALLY'S MEEK, MALLY'S SWEET

No. 597 in Johnson (Vol. vi. 1803): 'Written for this work by Robert Burns.'

WANDERING WILLIE

THOMSON's *Scottish Airs*, Vol. i. Part I. (May 1793).

Some hold the song suggested by Burns's relations with Maria Riddell; others, by Clarinda's proposal of reconciliation to her husband. Both theories are far-fetched; and, in any case, if Burns wrote his verses in the March of 1793, shortly before sending them to Thom-

NOTES 447

son, the latter is demonstrably false, for Clarinda had just returned unreconciled. The fact is, in this matter theorising is labour lost. For *Wandering Willie* is simply adapted from an old thing in Herd (1769) :—'I leave you, my dear Sir, to determine whether the above or *Thro' the Lang Muir* is best' (R. B. to Thomson). Here is the original set :—

WANDERING WILLIE

' Here awa, there awa, here awa Willie,
Here awa, there awa, here awa hame ;
Lang have I sought thee, dear have I bought thee,
Now I have gotten my Willie again.

'Thro' the lang muir I have follow'd my Willie,
Thro' the lang muir I have follow'd him hame,
Whatever betide us, nought shall devide us ;
Love now rewards all my sorrow and pain.

'Here awa, there awa, here awa, Willie,
Here awa, there awa, here awa hame :
Come Love, believe me, nothing can grieve me,
Ilka thing pleases while Willie 's at hame.'

The MS. sent to Thomson is at Brechin Castle. Thomson and the Hon. Andrew Erskine suggested certain changes, most of which Burns accepted (some, it may be, out of pure good nature); but on a copy of Thomson's First Volume sent to Miss Graham of Fintry he wrote in several modifications of the original ; and the version thus revised we have adopted as our text. Currie (1800) published the verses as written. The Thomson set was copied into Brash and Reid's *Poetry Original and Select*, Vol. i.

STANZA I. LINES 1-2 as sent to Thomson read thus :—

' *Lang* here awa, there awa, wandering Willie,
Now tired with wandering haud awa hame.'

3. 'Come to my bosom, my *ain* only dearie,' Erskine's amendment. Burns reverts to the original 'ae' in Miss Graham's copy.

STANZA II. LINE 1. ' *Loud blew the cauld winter winds* at our parting,' MS. ; ' *Winter winds blew loud and cauld* at our

WANDERING WILLIE parting,' Erskine's amendment. 2. '*Fears for my Willie brought tears to* my e'e,' Erskine's amendment. 4. '*As* Simmer to Nature, *so* Willie to me,' Erskine's amendment, in which Burns did not acquiesce.

STANZA III. LINES 1-3 in Burns's MS. read :—

'*Ye hurricanes* rest in the cave o' your slumbers,
O, *how* your wild *horrors* a lover alarms!
Awaken ye breezes, row gently ye billows.'

Burns accepted Erskine's amendments for Lines 1-2, as adopted in our text, but in 3, for Erskine's '*Blow soft*' he substituted 'Wauken.'

STANZA IV. LINE 1. 'But *if he's forgotten his faithfullest* Nannie,' MS.; the reading in the text is Erskine's. 2. For 'wide roaring,' Erskine suggested '*dark-heaving*'; but Burns would none of it. 4. For 'But, dying, believe,' Erskine suggested '*While* dying, *I think*': it also was declined.

BRAW LADS O' GALLA WATER

THOMSON'S *Scottish Airs*, Vol. i. Part I. (May 1793). (Sent to Thomson in January 1793.) Thence copied into *The Scots Magazine* (July 1797), Brash and Reid (Vol. iii.), and *The Musical Repository* (1799).

Burns got his lyrical idea from one of 'Five Excellent New Songs' in a very old chap—(a copy is in the possession of Mr. George Gray, Glasgow)—printed and published in Niddry-wynd [Edinburgh]. It is included in Herd; and it is set to music in Johnson's Second Volume, with this chorus :—

'Braw, braw lads of Galla Water,
O, braw lads of Galla Water!
I'll kilt my coats below my knee,
And follow my love through the water.'

In *Scottish Songs* (ii. 327), Chambers gives what he is pleased to call 'the original,' as recited to him by 'a person in that interesting district': it substitutes a

NOTES 449

'Bonie lass' for the 'Braw lads.' (There is also a chap- BRAW
book *Lass of Gallawater*, one of a garland of *New Songs* BRAW
in the Abbotsford Collection; one, too, in the Mother- LADS
well Collection, with the date 1790.) Another set, which
Chambers mysteriously introduces (ii. 666) as 'probably
the first song written to the tune,' has better claims on
the attention; for he found it (though he carefully forgets to say so) in the (vanished) Mansfield MS., written
about 1780. It has eight stanzas, with the chorus:—

'Braw, braw lads o' Gala Water,
Bonie lads o' Gala Water;
The Lothian lads maun ne'er compare
Wi' the braw lads o' Gala Water.'

STANZA I. LINES 1-2 in Burns's MS. read thus:—
'*There's* braw, braw lads on Yarrow braes,
That wander through the blooming heather.'

LINE 2 in Thomson reads, '*Ye wander thro*',' etc.
STANZA II. LINE 4. Burns first wrote, '*He's* the bonie lad,'
etc.

AULD ROB MORRIS

THOMSON's *Scottish Airs*, Vol. i. Part I. (May 1793). Thence
copied into *The Scots Magazine* (July 1797), and Brash
and Reid (Vol. ii.). 'I have partly taken your idea of
Auld Rob Morris. I have adopted the first two verses,
and am going on with the song on a new plan, which
promises pretty well' (R. B. to Thomson, 4th November
1792). The set was sent on 4th December 1792, and is
at Brechin Castle.

The set in Ramsay (*Tea-Table Miscellany*) is signed
'Q', which means 'an old song with additions.' It is a
spirited enough piece, in the form of a duet:—

Mither
'Auld Rob Morris that wins in yon glen
He's the king of good fellows, and wale of auld men,
Has fourscore of black sheep, and fourscore too:
Auld Rob Morris is the man ye maun loo.'

VOL. III. 2 F

AULD ROB MORRIS

Daughter
'Ha'd your tongue, mither, and let that abee,
For his eild and my eild can never agree:
They 'll never agree, and that will be seen;
For he is fourscore, and I 'm but fifteen.'
Burns's MS. is at Brechin Castle.
STANZA I. LINE 3. 'He has gowd in his coffers, he has *sheep, he has* kine,' Thomson. 4. 'And ae bonie lassie, his *darling* and mine':—Thomson's reading, because though 'dautie' is a good word for a father to use, it is 'too familiar an expression for a humble lover, scarcely hoping for success.'
STANZA III. LINE 2. 'And my daddie has *nought* but a cot-house and yard,' Thomson.

OPEN THE DOOR TO ME, O

THOMSON's *Scottish Airs*, Vol. i. Part I. (May 1793). The MS. is at Brechin Castle.

It is doubtful how far Burns is indebted to an original; for none has ever been found. Enclosing his verses to Thomson he wrote:—'I do not know whether this song be really mended.' We can but conjecture as to whether he referred to a piece by another hand or to an earlier set of his own making. In Thomson it is headed:
—'As altered for this work by Burns'; and the air is marked as Irish. A blackletter in the British Museum and in the Crawford, Pepys, and Roxburghe Collections, entitled *The Repulsive Maid*, is to the tune *Open the Door and Let Me Come In*.

Young Man
'Sweet, open the door and let me come in,
For to be a Wooer I now begin,
And say thy Lover I yet have been,
I 'll love thee and no more.'

Maid
'To open the door, Love, that could I do,
And if it were for an hour or two;
But that if my father or mother should know,
I should be beaten sore,' *etc.*

It may be that Burns knew some derivative of this; but O, OPEN after all it is possible that his original was merely *O, Open* THE DOOR *the Door, Lord Gregory*, in Johnson :—

> 'Oh, open the door, Lord Gregory,
> Oh open and let me in :
> The rain rains on my scarlet robes,
> The dew drops o'er my chin.'

STANZA I. LINES I and 2. Cf. *Lord Gregory* (p. 220), Stanza II. Lines 3-4 :—' At least, some pity,' *etc.*   2. '*Oh, open the door to me,*' Thomson.

STANZA III. LINE I. ' The wan moon *is setting* behind the white wave,' Thomson.   2. ' And *Life* is setting with me, oh,' deleted reading in the MS.

STANZA IV. LINE 2. 'She sees *his* pale corse on the plain,' Thomson.

WHEN WILD WAR'S DEADLY BLAST

THOMSON'S *Scottish Airs*, Vol. i. Part I. (May 1793). Sent to Thomson in April 1793 :—' I send you also a ballad to the tune of *The Mill and the Mill, O.*' Almost identical versions appeared in *The Caledonian Mercury* for 20th September 1793, Brash and Reid's *Poetry Original and Select*, Vol. i., and *The Scots Magazine* for November 1797. Thomson made certain changes in the song; but on a copy sent to Miss Graham of Fintry Burns restored the old readings.

The original set of *The Mill, Mill, O* is in *The Merry Muses* :—

> 'As I cam down yon waterside
> An' by yon Shillin Hill, O !
> There I spied a bonie lass,
> A lass that I lo'ed right weel, O !
> O the mill, mill, O, and the kill, kill, O,
> An' the coggin,' *etc.*

The returning soldier appears to a very different purpose from that of his descendant in Burns [a similar story

WHEN WILD WAR'S DEADLY BLAST is told in the second chapter of Montaigne's Second Book] in a set by Allan Ramsay:—

'Beneath a green shade I fand a fair maid
Was sleeping sound and still, O;
A' lowan wi love, my fancy did rove
Around her wi' good will, O.

'Her bosom I prest; but, sunk in her rest
She stirr'd na my joy to spill, O
While kindly she slept, close to her I crept
And kissed and kissed her, my fill, O.'

A MS. was before the Aldine Editor (1839).

STANZA I. LINES 3-4 were altered by Thomson to this:—

'*And eyes again with pleasure beam'd
That had been blear'd with* mourning.'

8. 'A poor *but* honest sodger,' *Scots Magazine* and Brash and Reid.

STANZA II. LINE 5. 'Coil':—a stream in the Kyle district of Ayrshire. 7. 'I *thought upon* the witching smile,' Thomson.

STANZA III. LINE 5. 'Wha spied I but my ain dear *lass*,' MS.

STANZA IV. LINE I. 'Wi' *fremit* voice, quoth I, Sweet lass,' MS.

STANZA V. LINE 2. 'And lovelier *look'd* than ever,' MS.; '*grew*,' Brash and Reid.

STANZA VI. LINE 2. 'Syne *wallow't like* a lily,' MS.:—*Cf.* the ballad *Geordie* in Johnson's *Museum*, No. 346:—

'But she had na read a word but twa,
Till she wallow't like a lily.'

STANZA VII. LINE 3. 'Tho' *wealth be sma*', we're rich in love,' MS. 5. 'Quo' she, my grandsire left me *gear*,' MS. 7. 'And come my *ain dear* soger lad,' MS.

DUNCAN GRAY

Second Set

THOMSON (Vol. i. Part II. 1798). The MS. is at Brechin Castle.

The second—the drawing-room—set. Both are founded on a song preserved in the Herd MS., and printed, with

variations (in all likelihood by Burns), in *The Merry* DUNCAN
Muses (see *ante*, p. 322, Prefatory Note to the first set, GRAY
which is mostly Burns's own). The Herd set begins :—

' Can ye play wi' Duncan Gray
(Hey, hey, the girdin o't !),
O'er the hills and far away
(Hey, hey, the girdin o't !) ?
Duncan he came her to woo
On a day when we were fou',
And Meg she swore that she wad spew,
If,' *etc.*

It is clear that Burns borrowed directly from the Herd set and not from that in *The Merry Muses*, for the second quatrain of the latter runs thus :—

'Duncan cam our Meg to woo,
Meg was nice and wadnae do,
But like an ether puffed and blew
At,' *etc.*

The Herd and *Merry Muses* sets are very closely related to the set in Thomson : indeed, the story is practically the same in all. In its terms the oldest is reminiscent of an ancient song which Allan Ramsay transferred from the Bannatyne MS. to his *Tea-Table Miscellany* :—

'Rob's Jock came to woo our Jenny
On ae feast day when we was fou ;
She buskèd her and made her bonie,
When she heard Jock was come to woo,' *etc.*

Other derivatives are *Hey, Jenny, Come Down to Jock* (Herd) ; a blackletter ballad in the Crawford Collection, *All for Love, or the Happy Match between Jocky and Jenny*; and an English playhouse song, *Jockey's Gone to the Wood,* in Playford's *Choice Ayres* (1659), extended into a blackletter broadside (Crawford and Huth Collections) with the title, *The Scotch Wooing ; or Jockey of the Lough and Jenny of the Lee.*

Enclosed, together with *Auld Rob Morris*, to Thomson,

DUNCAN GRAY   4th December 1792:—'The foregoing I submit, my dear Sir, to your better judgment; acquit them or condemn them as seemeth good in thy sight. *Duncan Gray* is that kind of lighthorse gallop of an air which precludes sentiment. The ludicrous is its ruling feature.'

STANZA I. LINE 3. '*On ae feast* night when we were fou,' original reading in the MS.: Thomson objected to this reading because it is in the old song; and Burns substituted '*blythe Yule-nicht*'; but Thomson adopted ' *On New-Year's nicht.*'

STANZA II. LINE 3. 'Ailsa Craig':—A rocky islet in the Firth of Clyde, opposite Ayr, much frequented by sea-fowl, whose screaming it has endured for ages without remonstrance.

DELUDED SWAIN, THE PLEASURE

THOMSON (Vol. i. Part II. 1798). 'Then for *The Collier's Daughter* take the following old bacchanal' (R. B. to Thomson).

The ideas and sentiments are common enough; so is the phrasing; and 'old bacchanal' is probably a figure of speech.

HERE IS THE GLEN

THOMSON (Vol. i. Part II. 1798). The MS. is at Brechin Castle. 'I know you value a composition because it is made by one of the great ones as little as I do. However, I got an air, pretty enough, composed by Lady Elizabeth Heron of Heron, which she calls *The Banks of Cree*. Cree is a beautiful romantic stream, and, as her ladyship is a particular friend of mine, I have written the following song to it.'

The tune did not please Thomson, who set the verses to *The Flowers of Edinburgh*. That they made a love-song for Maria Riddell, as some hold, is scarce consistent with Burns's statement. Moreover, he must have intended that Lady Elizabeth Heron should see them.

NOTES 455

LET NOT WOMEN E'ER COMPLAIN

THOMSON (Vol. i. Part II. 1798). The MS. is at Brechin Castle.

Alternative English words to the tune *Duncan Gray*: —' These English songs gravel me to death. I have not that command of the language that I have of my native tongue. In fact I think my ideas are more barren in English than in Scottish. I have been at *Duncan Gray* to dress it in English, but all I can do is deplorably stupid' (R. B. to Thomson, 19th October 1794). There is nothing to add to this, except that the song exists (if that can be said to exist which is never sung, never quoted, and, if ever read, immediately forgotten) as pure Burns.

LORD GREGORY

THOMSON (Vol. i. Part II. 1798). Written, at Thomson's request, to the air of *The Lass of Lochryan*.

Peter Pindar (Dr. Wolcott) wrote English verses for Thomson on the same theme. They are frigid rubbish; but 'the very name of Peter Pindar is an acquisition to your work. His *Gregory* is beautiful. I have tried to give you a set of stanzas in Scots on the same subject, which are at your service. Not that I intend to enter the lists with Peter—that would be presumption indeed! My song, though much inferior in poetic merit, has, I think, more of the ballad simplicity in it' (R. B. to Thomson, 26th January 1793).

His originals were the fragment in Johnson's *Museum* (No. 5), and *The Bonny Lass of Lochryan*, in Herd, in which last the hero is called Love Gregory. Of the several sets of this ballad, the most corrupt and the worst deboshed is *The Lass of Ocram*, in the Roxburghe Collection.

The MS. sent to Thomson is at Brechin Castle. Another, sent to Alexander Cunningham from Brow, a fortnight

LORD GREGORY before Burns's death, is included in the Cunningham MSS. The song is also inscribed in the *Afton Lodge Book* at Alloway.

STANZA II. LINE 2. 'And a' *for loving* thee,' Thomson MS. 3-4. 'At least some pity,' *etc.* :—Cf. *O, Open the Door*, p. 211, Stanza I. Lines 1-2, and *Mary Morison*, p. 286, Stanza III. Lines 5-6 :—

'If love for love thou wilt na gie,
At least be pity to me shown.'

STANZA V. LINE 3. 'Thou *dart* of Heaven that flashest by,' Thomson MS. 4. 'O, wilt thou *give* me rest,' Thomson MS.

O POORTITH CAULD

THOMSON (Vol. i. Part II. 1798). The MS. is at Brechin Castle.

Gilbert Burns told Thomson that Burns's heroine was 'a Miss Jane Blackstock, afterwards Mrs. Whittier of Liverpool.' But it was probably Jean Lorimer (see *post*, p. 482, Prefatory Note to *Lassie wi' the Lint-white Locks*), who was then contemplating the marriage of which she instantly repented. *O Poortith Cauld* is held to refer to her rejecting a gauger for the man she married (see *ante*, p. 364, Prefatory Note to *Craigieburn Wood*). It was sent to Thomson in January 1793, for the tune of *Cauld Kail in Aberdeen* ; but Thomson thought the verses had 'too much of uneasy, cold reflection for the air.' To this Burns :—' The objections are just, but I cannot make it better. The stuff won't bear mending ; yet, for private reasons, I should like to see it in print.' With a new chorus and other amendments, it was set in the end to *I Had a Horse and I Had Nae Mair*.

CHORUS. This in the first set reads :—

'*For weel I lo'e my Jeanie,
I canna want my Jeanie ;
How happy I were, were she my ain,
Tho' I had ne'er a guinea !*'

In LINE 2 of this Chorus Thomson—(with a fine Eighteenth
Century feeling for style)—substituted '*I doat upon*' for '*I
canna want*.'

POORTITH
CAULD

STANZA I. LINE 2. 'Ye *wreck* my peace between you,'
Thomson.   4. '*But tynin o*' my Jeanie,' first set.

STANZA II. LINE 3. '*Fy, fy* on silly coward man':—Thomson, notwithstanding that in both sets Burns retained the reading in the text. The '*O fie*' of certain Editors is mere wantonness.

STANZA V. LINE 1. 'How blest the *simple cottar's* fate':—Thomson, wholly without the author's sanction. 2. 'He woos his *simple* dearie,' deleted reading in the MS. 3-4 in the first set read:—

> 'The silly bogles, *Rank* and State
> *Did* never make *them* eerie.'

O, STAY, SWEET WARBLING WOODLARK

THOMSON (Vol. i. Part II. 1798). The MS. is at Brechin Castle.

Scott Douglas, in his Edinburgh Edition, printed what seems to be a first sketch, from a pencil manuscript (Burns) then in the possession of his publisher, called *Song Composed on Hearing a Bird Sing While Musing on Chloris* :—

> 'Sing on, sweet songster o' the brier,
> Nae stealthy traitor-foot is near !
> O soothe a hapless lover's ear,
>   And dear as life I'll prize thee.

> 'Again, again that tender part,
> That I may learn thy melting art,
> For surely thou would touch the heart
>   O' her that still denies me.

> 'Oh was thy mistress, too, unkind,
> And heard thee as the careless wind?
> For nocht but Love and Sorrow join'd,
>   Sic notes of woe could wauken.

'Thou tells,' *etc.*

SAW YE BONIE LESLEY

THOMSON (Vol. i. Part II. 1798).
'Bonie Leslie' was Miss Leslie Baillie, daughter of Mr. Baillie of Mayfield, Ayrshire. She married, in June 1799, Mr. Robert Cumming of Logie, and died in July 1843. 'The heart-struck awe, the distant humble approach, the delight we should have in gazing upon and listening to a messenger of Heaven, appearing in all the unspotted purity of his celestial home, among the coarse, polluted, far inferior sons of men, to deliver to them tidings that make their hearts swim in joy, and their imaginations soar in transport—such, so delighting and so pure were the emotions of my soul on meeting the other day with Miss Lesley Baillie, your neighbour at Mayfield. Mr. B., with his two daughters, accompanied with Mr. H. of G., passing through Dumfries a few days ago on their way to England, did me the honour of calling on me; on which I took my horse—though God knows I could ill spare the time—and accompanied them fourteen or fifteen miles, and dined and spent the day with them. 'Twas about nine I think that I left them, and riding home I composed the following ballad, of which you will probably think you have a dear bargain, as it will cost you another groat of postage. You must know that there is an old ballad beginning with:—

My Bonie Lizzie Baillie, I'll rowe thee in my plaiddie,'

so I parodied it as follows, which is literally the first copy "unanointed, unannealed," as Hamlet says' (R. B. to Mrs. Dunlop, 22nd August 1792). The ballad of *Lize Baillie*—'a new song very much in request'—is one of the Laing Broadsides, now in the possession of the Earl of Rosebery. It is also in the Herd MS., and was partly published in Johnson's *Museum* (No. 456).

Burns sent two stanzas to Cunningham, 10th September 1792, prefaced in similar terms. On 8th November 1792 he enclosed the song to Thomson:—'I have just been looking over *The Collier's Bonie Dochter*; and if the following rhapsody, which I composed the other day on a charming Ayrshire girl, Miss Lesley Baillie of Mayfield, as she passed thro' this place to England, will suit your taste better than *The Collier's Lassie*, fall on and welcome.' The MS. sent to Thomson is at Brechin Castle.

SAW YE BONIE LESLEY

STANZA II. LINE 4. 'And *ne'er made sic* anither,' Thomson: —'"And never made *anither*." This is, in my opinion, more poetical than "ne'er *made sic anither*"' (R. B. to Thomson). As, indeed, it is.

STANZA III. LINE I. 'Thou, *bonie Lesley*, *art a queen*,' Cunningham MS. 3. 'Thou, *bonie Leslie, art divine*,' Cunningham MS.

STANZA IV. LINES 1-2 in the Cunningham MS. read:—

'The *vera Deil he couldna scaith*
  Whatever wad belang thee!'

SWEET FA'S THE EVE

THOMSON (Vol. i. Part II. 1798). 'If I can catch myself in a more than ordinary propitious moment, I shall write a new *Craigieburn* altogether. My heart is much in the theme' (R. B. to Thomson, November 1794). 'How will the following do for *Craigieburn Wood*?' (R. B. to Thomson, January 15th, 1795).

The MS. is at Brechin Castle. For the first set of *Craigieburn Wood*, see p. 86; and see also Prefatory Note, *ante*, p. 363.

YOUNG JESSIE

THOMSON (Vol. i. Part II. 1798). Sent to Thomson in April 1793 under the title *Song*: *Tune—Bonie Dundee*:— 'I send you a song on a celebrated fashionable toast in this country to suit *Bonie Dundee*' (R. B.).

YOUNG JESSIE The lady was Miss Jessie Staig (daughter of Provost Staig of Dumfries), on whose recovery from a dangerous illness Burns afterwards wrote the epigram *To Dr. Maxwell* (see Vol. ii. p. 255). She married Major William Miller, son of Mr. Miller of Dalswinton, and died at twenty-six in the March of 1801.

The MS. is at Brechin Castle.

STANZA I. LINE I. 'The sad swain o' the Yarrow'—It is probable that Burns refers to the hero of the old ballad *The Dowie Dens of Yarrow* :—

> 'As he gaed up the Tinnies bank,
> I wot he gaed wi' sorrow,
> Till, down in a den, he spied nine armèd men,
> On the dowie houms of Yarrow.'

5. 'To equal young Jessie seek *Scotland* all over,' Thomson.

ADOWN WINDING NITH

THOMSON (Vol. ii. 1799). 'Another favourite air of mine is *The Muckin o' Geordie's Byre*. When sung slow, with expression, I have wished that it had better poetry : that I have endeavoured to supply as follows. . . . Mr. Clarke begs you to give Miss Phillis a corner in your Book, as she is a particular Flame of his. She is a Miss Phillis M'Murdo, sister to the " Bonie Jean " which I sent you some time ago. They are both pupils of his ' (R. B. to Thomson, August 1793).

Phillis M'Murdo married Norman Lockhart, afterwards third baronet of Carnwath. Before this Burns had sent Thomson another song on the same lady, *Phillis the Fair*, with which he did not pretend to be satisfied, and which Thomson did not accept (see Vol. iv.).

The MS. shows a deleted Stanza after II.:—

> 'The primrose is o'er for the season,
> But mark where the violet is blown,
> How modest it peeps from the covert,
> So modesty sure is her own !'

A LASS WI' A TOCHER

THOMSON (Vol. ii. 1799). 'The other day I strung up a kind of rhapsody to another Hibernian melody that I admire much' (R. B. to Thomson, February 1796). The 'Hibernian melody' was *Balinamona Ora*. Plainly suggested (at least) by *A Lass with a Lump of Land* in *The Tea-table Miscellany*:—

'Gie me a lass with a lump of land,
And we for life shall gang thegither,
Tho' daft or wise, I'll never demand,
Or black or fair it maks na whither.
I'm aff with wit, and beauty will fade,
And blood alane is no worth a shilling,
But she that's rich, her market's made,
For ilka charm about her is killing.'

The MS. is at Brechin Castle. Here is a Stanza deleted before II. :—

'I grant you, your Dearie is bonie and braw,
She's gentle, and strappin, and stately witha';
But see yon strappin oaks at the head o' the shaw:
Wi' the whack of an ax how stately they'll fa'!'

BLYTHE HAE I BEEN ON YON HILL

THOMSON (Vol. ii. 1799). Suggested by Fraser the oboist's interpretation of *The Quaker's Wife*:—'Mr. Fraser plays it slow, and with an expression that quite charms me. I got such an enthusiast in it that I made a song for it, which I here subjoin, and enclose Fraser's set of the tune. If they hit your fancy they are at your service; if not, return me the tune, and I will put it in Johnson's *Museum*. I think the song is not in my worst manner' (R. B. to Thomson, June 1793).

Later, in his remarks on Thomson's *List*, he inserted *Blythe Hae I Been on Yon Hill*:—'which,' he wrote, 'is one of the finest songs ever I made in my life; and is

BLYTHE HAE I BEEN ON YON HILL composed on a young lady, positively the most beautiful lovely woman in the world. As I purpose giving you the name and designation of all my heroines to appear in some future edition of your work, perhaps half a century hence, you must certainly include the boniest lass in the world in your collection.' For the 'boniest lass in the world,' see *ante*, p. 458, Prefatory Note to *Saw Ye Bonie Lesley*.

The MS. is at Brechin Castle.

BY ALLAN STREAM

THOMSON (Vol. ii. 1799). 'I walked out yesterday evening with a volume of the *Museum* in my hand, when, turning up *Allan Water* ('What number shall my Muse repeat,' etc.), it appeared to me rather unworthy of so fine an air; and recollecting it is on your list, I sat and raved under the shade of an old thorn, till I wrote one to suit the measure. I may be wrong, but I think it is not in my worst style' (R. B. to Thomson, August 1793).

There are MSS. at Lochryan and at Brechin Castle.

STANZA I. LINE I. 'By Allan *side* I chanced to rove,' Lochryan MS. 2. 'Benledi':—'A mountain to the north of Stirling' (R. B. in Lochryan MS.); 'A mountain in Strathallan, 3009 feet' (R. B. in Thomson MS.). His geography is faulty: Strathallan is to the north of Stirling [the Allan flows by Dunblane and Bridge of Allan into the Forth], but Ben Ledi is about 20 miles west-north-west. 7. '*O dearly do I love thee, Annie*,' alternative reading:—'You must know that in Ramsay's *Tea-Table*, where the modern song first appeared, the ancient name of the tune, Allan says, is *Allan Water*, or *My Love Annie's Very Bonie*. This last has certainly been a line of the original song; so I took up the idea, and, as you will see, have introduced the line in its place, which I presume it formerly occupied; though I likewise give you a *choosing* line, if it should not hit the cut of your fancy' (R. B. to Thomson). It did not 'hit the cut' of Thomson's 'fancy,' but

as Burns himself preferred it, we have adopted it in our text. BY ALLAN
The original *Allan Water, or A Lover in Captivity*, is one of STREAM
the Laing Broadsides in possession of the Earl of Rosebery.
It confirms, but partially, the conjecture of Burns, the words
he quotes occurring only in one line :—

> 'Allan Water's wide and deep,
> And my dear Anny's very bony,
> Wide's the strath that lyes above 't,
> If 't were mine I'd give it all for Anny.'

STANZA III. LINE 7. 'Like *seeing* her, our bosom's treasure,' alternative reading in Thomson MS.

CANST THOU LEAVE ME

THOMSON (Vol. ii. 1799). Sent to Thomson, 20th November 1794. 'Well, I think this, to be done in two or three turns across my room, and with two or three pinches of Irish blackguard, is not far amiss. You see I am determined to have my quantum of applause from somebody' (R. B.). Burns sent a copy to Maria Riddell (MS. in the possession of Dr. De Noë Walker); and she replied with a *Stay, My Willie, Now Believe Me*, about the authorship of which there has hitherto been some doubt. The MS. sent to Thomson is at Brechin Castle.

It is reminiscent of Burns's own song sent to Johnson, *Stay My Charmer* (p. 12 ; see also Prefatory Note to this last, *ante*, p. 312); and the name of the heroine at least may have been suggested by a similar song, *Will Ye Go and Marry Katie*, found in *The Charmer* and other books, and sometimes credited to Burns.

COME, LET ME TAKE THEE

THOMSON (Vol. ii. 1799). 'That tune, *Cauld Kail*, is such a favourite of yours that I once roved out yester evening for a gloamin shot at the Muses; when the Muse that

COME, LET ME TAKE THEE TO MY BREAST presides o'er the shores of Nith, or rather my old inspiring dearest nymph, Coila, whispered me the following. I have two reasons for thinking that it was my early, sweet Inspirer that was by my elbow, " smooth-gliding without step," and pouring the song on my glowing fancy. In the first place, since I left Coila's native haunts, not a fragment of a Poet has arisen to cheer her solitary musings by catching inspiration from her, so I more than suspect she has followed me hither, or at least made me an occasional visit; secondly, the last stanza of this song I sent you is the very words that Coila taught me many years ago, and which I set to an old Scots reel, in Johnson's *Museum*' (R. B. to Thomson, August 1793). The song referred to is *And I'll Kiss Thee Yet* (p. 34).

The MS. is at Brechin Castle.

CONTENTED WI' LITTLE

THOMSON (Vol. ii. 1799). '*Apropos* to bacchanalian songs in Scottish, I composed one yesterday for an air I liked much—*Lumps o' Pudding*. . . . If you do not relish the air I will send it to Johnson' (R. B. to Thomson, November 1794). Also :—' I have some thoughts of suggesting to you to prepare a vignette . . . to my song *Contented wi' Little and Cantie wi' Mair*, in order the portrait of my face and the picture of my mind may go down the stream of Time together' (R. B. to Thomson, May 1795).

The stanza is that of *Lumps o' Pudding*, with which Burns no doubt designed his song as a whimsical contrast. But the sentiment seems to have been partly suggested by a G. A. Stevens :—

> 'Contented I am, and contented I'll be;
> For what can this world more afford,
> Than a friend that will sociably tipple with me,
> And a cellar that's plentifully stored.'

NOTES   465

The MS. sent to Thomson—MS. (B)—is at Brechin Castle, CONTENTED
and for an opportunity to inspect an early draft—MS. (A) WI' LITTLE
—on excise paper, we are indebted to Mr. A. P. Watt,
London.

STANZA I. LINE 4. See Vol. i. p. 323, Note to *Scotch Drink*, Stanza ix. Line 4.

STANZA II. LINES 3-4. A deleted reading of these lines in MS. (A) is :—

> '*For Wealth I am merry, how can I be poor,
> And my Freedom's my birthright not kings shall injure.*'

3. '*My merry* good-humour *is* coin in my pouch,' MS. (A).

STANZA III. is omitted in MS. (A).

STANZA IV. A deleted reading of LINES 3-4 in MS. (A) is :—

> '*Come ease, or come travail ; come canker or joy
> Approach, you are welcome, you lea'e me, good-bye.*'

FAREWELL, THOU STREAM

THOMSON (Vol. ii. 1799). The second set of a song which originally began :—

> 'The last time I came o'er the moor
> And left Maria's dwelling.'

This set, of which the MS.—MS. (A)—is at Brechin Castle, was sent to Thomson in April 1793 :—'I had scarcely put my last letter into the post-office, when I took up the subject of *The Last Time I Came O'er the Moor*, and ere I slept drew the outlines of the foregoing. How far I have succeeded I leave you to decide.'

The heroine was Maria Riddell, to whom Burns sent a copy—MS. (B)—now in the possession of Dr. De Noè Walker. To this he added this note (unpublished) :—
'On reading over the song, I see it is but a cold, inanimated composition. It will be absolutely necessary for me to get in love, else I shall never be able to make a line worth reading on the subject.' As first written,

VOL. III.   2 G

466 NOTES

FAREWELL THOU STREAM
Farewell, Thou Stream, was suggested by an Allan Ramsay:—

'The last time I came o'er the moor
And left my love behind me'—

itself adapted from an older song. In January 1794 occurred the estrangement from Mrs. Riddell (see Vol. ii. p. 420, Prefatory Note to *Impromptu on Mrs. Riddell's Birthday*); and in July 1794 Burns informed Thomson that he meant to set the verses which he had sent him for *The Last Time I Came O'er the Moor* to *Nancy's To the Greenwood Gane,* and that he had 'made an alteration in the beginning'—both which circumstances Thomson seems to have ignored. In November Burns sent another copy—MS. (C)—(now at Brechin Castle):—'Now for my English song to *Nancy's to the Greenwood Gone*'; and Thomson answered that he thought the song an excellent one, but 'too serious to come after *Nancy*'; so he set it to a melody called *The Silver Snood.* Burns borrowed the first lines of his new version from Smollett's *Adieu, Thou Stream That Smoothly Flows.*

STANZA I. in MS. (A) reads:—

' *The last time I came o'er the moor*
And left Maria's dwelling,
What throes, what tortures passing cure
Were in my bosom swelling?
Condemned to *see my rivals reign,*
While I in secret languish:
To feel a fire in every vein,
Yet dare *not speak* my anguish.'

MS. (B) corresponds, except Line 5 (which agrees with MS. [C] and our text) and Line 6 (which has 'And *still*').

STANZA II. in MS. (A) reads:—

' Love's veriest wretch *despairing I*
Fain, fain my *crime* would cover;
The *unweeting groan, the bursting sigh,*
Betray the *guilty* lover.

I know *my doom must be* despair:
Thou wilt, nor canst relieve me,
But O *Maria*, hear *my* prayer:—
For pity's sake, forgive me!'

FAREWELL
THOU
STREAM

Ms. (B) agrees with MS. (C) and our text, except that Line 1 reads:—' *The wretch of love* unseen, unknown'; and that 2 has '*crime*' as in MS. (A) for 'griefs.'
STANZA III. LINE 7. '*In* circling horrors,' erroneous reading.
8. ' *To* overwhelming ruin,' MS. (A).

HAD I A CAVE

THOMSON (Vol. ii. 1799). The MS. is at Brechin Castle.

'That crinkum-crankum tune, *Robin Adair*, has run so in my head, and I succeeded so ill in my last attempt [*Phillis the Fair*, see Vol. iv.], that I ventured in my morning's walk one essay more. You, my dear Sir, will remember an unfortunate part of our worthy friend Cunningham's story, which happened about three years ago. That struck my fancy, and I endeavoured to do the idea poetic justice, as follows' (R. B. to Thomson, August 1793).

See further, Prefatory Notes to *Anna* (Vol. i. p. 447); *To Alexander Cunningham* (Vol. ii. p. 371); and *She's Fair and Fause* (*ante*, p. 399).

HERE'S A HEALTH

THOMSON (Vol. ii. 1799). 'I once mentioned to you an air which I have long admired, *Here's Health to Them That's Awa, Hinney*; but I forget if you took notice of it. I have just been trying to suit it with verses; and I beg leave to recommend the air to your attention once more' (R. B. to Thomson, May 1796). About a fortnight before his death he sent a copy to Alexander Cunningham:—' Did Thomson show you the following song, the last I made,

HERE'S A
HEALTH
or probably will make for some time?' After his death an additional stanza—not in the MS. sent to Thomson (Brechin Castle), nor in the MS. sent to Cunningham (Watson Collection)—was found among his papers. But as there is no evidence that he passed it, we have not included it in the text:—

'I guess by the dear angel smile,
I guess by the love-rolling e'e—
But why urge the tender confession
'Gainst Fortune's fell cruel decree,' *etc.*

The heroine, Jessie Lewars, sister of John Lewars, a fellow-exciseman, was of great service to the Burns household during the last illness. She is also commemorated in certain complimentary verses (Vol. ii. pp. 141, 260), and in that very beautiful song, *O, Wert Thou in the Cauld Blast* (Vol. iv.). On 3rd June 1799 she married Mr. James Thomson, Writer in Dumfries, and she died 26th May 1855.

STANZA II. LINE 3. 'But welcome the *hours* o' sweet slumber,' Watson MS.

HOW CRUEL ARE THE PARENTS

THOMSON (Vol. ii. 1799). Sent to Thomson, 9th May 1799, as 'a song altered from an old English one': which 'old English one' is found in *The Hive* (London, 1733), in *The Thrush* (London, 1749), and in *Apollo's Cabinet* (London, 1756). Here it is:—

'How cruel is that parent's care,
Who riches only prizes,
When finding out some booby heir,
He thinks he wondrous wise is.
While the poor maid, to shun her fate,
And not to prove a wretch in state,
To 'scape the blockhead she must hate,
She weds where she despises.

> 'The harmless dove thus trembling flies,
> The ravenous hawk pursuing:
> A while her tender pinions tries,
> Till doom'd to certain ruin.
> Afraid her worst of foes to meet,
> No shelter near, no kind retreat,
> She drops beneath the faulkner's feet,
> For gentle usage suing.'

HOW CRUEL ARE THE PARENTS

The MS. is at Brechin Castle.

STANZA I. LINE 7. 'To shun a *cruel* Father's hate,' alternative reading in the MS.

HUSBAND, HUSBAND, CEASE YOUR STRIFE

THOMSON (Vol. ii. 1799). Sent to Thomson in December 1793:—'Tell me if you like the following verses to *My Jo Janet.*'

The MS. is at Brechin Castle, and what appears to be an early draft is among the Pickering MSS. in the British Museum, copied by W. W. C.

STANZAS I. and II. Instead of these two the draft MS. has this one:—

> ' " If the word is still obey
> Always love and fear you,
> I will take myself away
> And never more come near you."
> " Sad will I be so bereft,
> Nancy, Nancy,
> Still I 'll try to make a shift,
> My spouse Nancy."'

STANZA IV. LINE I. 'Well *even* from the silent dead,' draft MS.

IT WAS THE CHARMING MONTH

THOMSON (Vol. ii. 1799). Meant as English words to *Dainty Davie*, and abridged from a song in *The Tea-Table Miscellany.* 'You may think meanly of this, but take

470   NOTES

IT WAS   a look at the bombast original and you will be surprised
THE   that I have made so much of it' (R. B. to Thomson,
CHARMING   November 1794).
MONTH   All the same, Burns rather selected from than renewed
            and re-inspired the 'bombast original.' Practically nothing
            is his but the repeats and the chorus; and even these
            have their germs in the *Miscellany*. The rest of his set
            is 'lifted' almost word for word, and simply edited and
            rearranged.

LAST MAY A BRAW WOOER

THOMSON (Vol. ii. 1799). Sent to Thomson 3rd July 1795. The MS.—MS. (A)—sent to Thomson is at Brechin Castle. Another—MS. (B)—sent to Provost Staig, Dumfries, is in the Kilmarnock Monument Museum. The song also appeared in one of the tracts 'printed by Chapman and Lang for Stewart and Meikle.' A corrupt set was published in Johnson's *Museum* (Vol. vi. 1803).

As regards the Johnson set Stenhouse is both fanciful and false. Thus :—(1) Johnson did not publish it as 'originally for his work,' but simply as 'by Burns,' and signed it 'an old lover.' (2) There is no evidence that it was written for Vol. ii. in 1787. (3) That Johnson's religious scruples originally prevented his inserting it is a self-evident absurdity. (4) There is no need to assert—nor even to surmise—that Johnson printed it from a MS., for—under the title, *Gud Forgie Me for Liein*—the same set had already appeared as one of 'Seven Excellent Songs, entered according to order, 1799,' and, in fact, this special chap-book set, frequently reprinted, was not copied from, but utilised by, Johnson.

STANZA I. LINE I. 'Last May a braw wooer *came* down *frae the* glen,' Stewart. The chap-book and Johnson set agrees with our text, except for the substitution of '*Ae day*' for 'Last May.' 4. '*But how could the gowk e'er* believe me,'

NOTES 471

Stewart; 'The deuce *tak the lad*,' etc., chap-book, but John- LAST MAY
son accepted the reading in Thomson. A BRAW
    STANZAS II. and III. are transposed in the chap-book and WOOER
Johnson.
    STANZA II. LINE 4. '*But* the Lord forgie me for *lying*,'
Stewart; '*lying*,' MS. (B). '*The Gude* forgie me,' etc., chap-
book and Johnson.
    STANZA III. LINE 2. 'And *bridal off*-hand were his proffers,'
MS. (B), and also chap-book and Johnson, but with '*was the
proffer*' for 'were his proffers'; 'Marriage *affhan was* his
proffer,' Stewart. 4. 'But I thought I might *get a* waur *offer*,'
Stewart, chap-book, and Johnson.
    STANZA IV. LINE 1. 'But what *do you* [or 'ye'] think?'
Stewart, chap-book, and Johnson. 2. '*He has a poor taste*,'
chap-book and Johnson. 3. 'He up the *lang loan*,' MS. (B)
and Thomson; '*lang lane*,' Stewart; '*He's down to the
castle*,' chap-book and Johnson:—'"Gate-Slack," the word
you object to in my last ballad, is positively the name of a
particular place, a kind of passage up among the Lowther
hills, on the confines of this county [Dumfries]. . . . How-
ever, let the line run, "He up the lang loan"' (R. B. to
Thomson).
    STANZA V. LINE 1. 'But a' the niest week as I *fretted* wi'
care,' Currie and Stewart, but both MSS. have 'petted.'
2. 'Dalgarnock':—'Also the name of a romantic spot near
the Nith, where are still a ruined church and a burial place'
(R. B. to Thomson). 3. '*An*' wha but my fine fickle *wooer*
was there,' Stewart; '*braw* fickle *wooer*,' chap-book and
Johnson.
    STANZA VI. LINE 3. 'My *lover* he caper'd as he'd been in
drink,' Stewart. 4. '*An*' swore that I was his dear *lassy*,'
Stewart.
    STANZA VII. 2. '*And if* she'd recovered,' etc., chap-book and
Johnson. 3. 'And how *my auld shoon fitted her shachl't* feet,'
a very doubtful reading, taken from Johnson, who got it from
the chap. Scott Douglas is at the pains to explain that the
line 'has been changed since Burns's day to give it additional
point,' and to make 'it correspond with a common proverbial
expression: when a lover deserts one mistress for another the
latter is twitted with wearing the *old shoes* of her predecessor.'

LAST MAY A BRAW WOOER But the proverb was as well known to Burns as to Scott Douglas and other impertinents: he clearly had it in his mind when, writing with art and discretion, he so contrived the line as to make his heroine at once flatter her sweetheart and reflect on her cousin. Moreover, to substitute 'auld' is to rob the lady's inquiry of a great part of its point, for there is no contrast between 'auld' and 'shachl't.' 4. 'But *Lord*! how he fell a-swearin,' Stewart; '*Gude saf us*,' chap-book and Johnson.

STANZA VIII. LINE 3. 'So *just* to preserve the poor body in life,' Stewart; '*And just*,' chap-book and Johnson. 4. 'I *believe* I maun wed him to-morrow,' Stewart.

MY NANIE'S AWA

THOMSON (Vol. ii. 1799). Sent to Thomson, 9th December 1794. The MS. is at Brechin Castle, and another was before the Aldine editor.

'There is one passage in your charming letter. Thomson nor Shenstone never exceeded it, nor often came up to it. I shall certainly steal it, and set it in some future poetic production and get immortal fame by it. 'Tis where you bid the scenes of Nature remind me of Clarinda' (Sylvander to Clarinda, 7th February 1788). It may be, as some suppose, that this smooth and pleasant ditty represents the theft.

STANZA I. LINE I. '*Gay* nature arrays,' Aldine MS. 3. 'While birds warble *welcome*,' erroneous reading; '*And*' for 'While,' Aldine MS.

STANZA II. LINE I. 'The *primrose and daisy our glens may* adorn,' Aldine MS. 3. 'They *torture my* bosom,' Aldine MS.

STANZA III. LINE I. 'Thou lav'rock that *starts* frae the dews of the lawn,' alternative reading in the Thomson MS.

STANZA IV. LINE I. 'In yellow *array*,' Aldine MS.

NOW ROSY MAY

THOMSON (Vol. ii. 1799). The MS. is at Brechin Castle.

A *rifaccimento* of *The Gard'ner wi' his Paidle* (p. 48), adapted to the tune of *Dainty Davie*. The original *Dainty Davie*, on which the chorus is modelled, is preserved in the Herd MS. and *The Merry Muses*. See also Vol. ii. p. 311, Note to *The Jolly Beggars*, Recitativo VII. Stanza II. Lines 8-9. 'The words "Dainty Davie" glide so sweetly in the air, that to a Scots ear, any song to it, without Davie being the hero, would have a lame effect' (R. B. to Thomson, August 1793).

NOW SPRING HAS CLAD

THOMSON (Vol. ii. 1799). Sent to Thomson in August 1795. The MS. is at Brechin Castle.

Stanzas II.-IV. were enclosed in a letter to Mrs. Riddell, 20th January 1796, and a facsimile of them has been published. Another copy, sent to Cunningham, was before the Aldine editor.

STANZA II. LINE 2. '*That glides* a silver dart,' Brechin Castle MS.

O, THIS IS NO MY AIN LASSIE

THOMSON (Vol. ii. 1799). Set to the tune, *This is No My Ain House.*

According to Burns (Interleaved Copy of Johnson's *Museum*), the original of Ramsay's set of *My Ain House* begins :—

> 'O, this is no my ain house,
> My ain house, my ain house!
> This is no my ain house—
> I ken by the biggin o't.

474 NOTES

O, THIS IS
NO MY AIN
LASSIE

There's bread and cheese are my door cheeks,
My door cheeks, my door cheeks ;
There's bread and cheese are my door cheeks,
And pan-cakes the riggin o't.'

The second stanza of this same set may have suggested his *Reel o' Stumpie* (see *ante*, p. 422).

'*This is No My Ain House* puzzles me a good deal; in fact I think to change the old rhythm of the first, or chorus part of the tune, will have a good effect. I would have it something like the gallop of the following' (R. B. to Thomson, June 1795). In the first draft of the Chorus he wrote 'Body' for 'Lassie'; but in August he directed Thomson to substitute 'Lassie.'

The MS. is at Brechin Castle.

O, WAT YE WHA THAT LO'ES ME

THOMSON (Vol. ii. 1799).

There is no evidence as to when this song was sent to Thomson; but he printed it as 'written for this work by Burns.' A copy sent to Cleghorn in January 1796—now in the Laing Collection in the University of Edinburgh—agrees with Thomson's text.

CHORUS. LINE 3. '*O she's* the queen o' womankind,' erroneous reading.

STANZA I. LINE I. '*O wha is she* that lo'es me,' Currie—evidently his own.

SCOTS, WHA HAE

THOMSON (Vol. ii. 1799).

First published in *The Morning Chronicle*, May 1794. Replying to Perry's offer of an engagement on that print (see *Bibliographical*, Vol. ii. p. 282), Burns wrote:—
'In the meantime they are most welcome to my ode; only let them insert it as a thing they have met with by accident and unknown to me.' Accordingly, the ode

was thus ingenuously prefaced :—' If the following warm and animating ode was not written near the times to which it applies, it is one of the most faithful imitations of the simple and beautiful style of the Scottish bards we ever read, and we know but of one living Poet to whom to ascribe it' : a piece of criticism which, if you reflect that in grammar, style, cast, sentiment, diction, and turn of phrase, the ode, though here and there its spelling deviates into Scots, is pure Eighteenth Century English, says little for the soundness of Perry's judgment, however it may approve the kindness of his heart. The ode appeared, too, in Vol. iv. of Brash and Reid's *Poetry Original and Select* (1798), and in No. 2 of the *Gray Tracts* (1799).

SCOTS WHA HAE

Varying accounts are given of the time and circumstances of its origin. John Syme connects it with a tour with Burns in Galloway in July 1793 :—' I told you that in the midst of the storm on the wilds of Kenmure, Burns was rapt in meditation. What do you think he was about? He was charging the English army along with Bruce at Bannockburn. He was engaged in the same manner on our ride from St. Mary's Isle, and I did not disturb him. Next day he produced me the following address of Bruce to his troops, and gave me a copy for Dalzell.' Burns tells a different tale. After some remarks to Thomson (August or September 1793) on the old air *Hey Tutti Taiti*, and on the tradition that ' it was Robert Bruce's march at the battle of Bannockburn,' he introduces *Scots Wha Hae* :—'This thought, in my yesternight's evening walk, roused me to a pitch of enthusiasm on the theme of liberty and independence, which 1 threw into a kind of Scots ode, fitted to the air, that one might suppose to be the gallant royal Scot's address to his heroic followers on that eventful morning.' The two statements are irreconcilable ; and we must conclude either that Syme misdated the tour, and that the ' yesternight' of Burns was the night of his return to Dumfries, or that

SCOTS WHA HAE Burns did not give Syme a copy until some time after his return, and that, like some other circumstances he was pleased to father, his 'yester-night's evening walk' need not be literally interpreted.

Thomson reprobated the 'idea of giving it a tune so totally devoid of interest or grandeur' as *Hey Tutti Taiti*, and suggested certain additiohs in the fourth line of each stanza to fit it to that of *Lewie Gordon*. To accept these expletives was to ruin the effect; but, as in the case of *Ye Flowery Banks o' Bonie Doon*, accepted they were. Some other suggestions Burns declined:—'I have scrutinized it over and over; and to the world, some way or other, it shall go as it is.' At the same time, he seems to have been scarce reconciled to the change to *Lewie Gordon*, for says he :—' It will not in the least hurt me, tho' you leave the song out altogether, and adhere to your first idea of adopting Logan's verses.' But, having agreed to it, he adopted the changes in all such copies as he sent out in MS., not even excepting that given to Mrs. Gilbert Burns (now in the possession of Mrs. J. G. Burns, Knockmaroon, Dublin); so that if transcripts from the earlier set—to the tune *Hey Tutti Taiti*—were sent to Syme and Dalzell, they have not turned up. After the publication of the *Thomson Correspondence*, general opinion pronounced in favour of *Hey Tutti Taiti*; and Thomson, in Vol. iii. (1802), published the ode as written, and set it to the air for which it was made, and to which (as sung by Braham and others) it owes no little of its fortune This set—of which the MS. is at Brechin Castle—we have adopted as our text.

In sending a copy (now in Harvard University Library, U.S.A.) to Lord Buchan, Burns was moved to descant on the battle itself:—' Independently of my enthusiasm as a Scotsman, I have rarely met with anything in history which interests my feelings as a man equal with the story of Bannockburn. On the one hand a cruel, but able usurper, leading on the finest army in Europe, to extinguish the last spark of freedom among a greatly-daring and greatly-injured people; on the other hand, the desperate relics of a gallant nation, devoting themselves to rescue their bleeding country or perish with her. Liberty! thou art a prize truly and indeed invaluable, for never canst thou be too dearly bought.' Some have concluded herefrom that the writer had mixed his usurpers, and thought that the Edward beaten at Bannockburn was the *Malleus Scotorum*, the victor of Falkirk and the hangman of Sir William Wallace. But if he did, he was afterwards better informed; for to a copy (now in the Corporation Council Chamber, Edinburgh) presented to Dr. Hughes of Hereford (8th August 1795) he appended the following note :—' This battle was the decisive blow which first put Robert the First, commonly called Robert de Bruce, in quiet possession of the Scottish throne. It was fought against Edward the Second, son to that Edward who shed so much blood in Scotland in consequence of the dispute between Bruce and Baliol.' It is also to the purpose to note that, on the poet's own showing (letter to Thomson), this very famous lyric was inspired, not only by the thought of Bannockburn but also, ' by the glowing ideas of some other struggles of the same nature *not quite so ancient*' : that, in other words, it is partly an effect of the French Revolution.

SCOTS WHA HAE

The stanza, binding-rhyme and all, is that of *Helen of Kirkconnel*, a ballad which Burns thought ' silly to contemptibility ':—

'I wish I were where Helen lies!
Night and day on me she cries;
O, that I were where Helen lies
On fair Kirkconnel Lea!'

Another classic in much the same rhythmus is *The Ewie wi' the Crooked Horn*, by the Rev. John Skinner. The song, however, was written to *Tutti Taiti*; and here is the chorus of a Jacobite lyric (MS. copy included in a *Collection of Miscellaneous Poems* in the Advocates' Library, Edin-

SCOTS WHA HAE burgh, made some time before 1705) to the same tune :—

> 'Fill, fill a bumper high !
> Drain, drain your barrels dry !
> Out upon him, fie, fie
> That will not do 't again.'

See also *Landlady, Count the Lawin* (p. 25), and *Carl, an the King Come* (p. 57).

There are no variations of any importance in the copies of the second set. These are the last lines :—Stanza I. 'Or to glorious victorie'; Stanza II. 'Edward, chains and slaverie'; Stanza III. 'Traitor ! Coward, turn and flee !'; Stanza IV. 'Caledonian [Burns in his first copy wrote 'soger hero'], on wi' me'; Stanza V. 'But they shall, they shall be free'; and Stanza VI. 'Forward ! let us do or die !'

STANZA II. LINES 2-4 in the early draft (in the possession of Mrs. Lampson-Locker) read :—

> '*See approach proud Edward's power,
> Sharply maun we bide the stour,
> Either they or we.*'

STANZA V. reads thus in the early draft :—

> '*Do you hear your children cry :—
> "Were we born in chains to lie?"
> No ! Come Death or Liberty !
> Yes, they shall be free.*'

LINE I. 'By oppression's *wrongs* and pains !' some MSS.

STANZA VI. 'I have borrowed the last Stanza from the common stall edition of *Wallace* :—

> ' " A false usurper sinks in every foe,
> And liberty returns with every blow " :—

a couplet worthy of Homer' (R. B. to Thomson).

THEIR GROVES O' SWEEP MYRTLE

THOMSON (Vol. ii. 1799). 'The Irish air, *Humours of Glen,* is a great favourite of mine, and as, except the silly verses in *The Poor Soldier*, there are not any decent words for it, I have written for it as follows' (R. B. to Thomson, April 1795).

The MS. is at Brechin Castle. The song was published in *The Edinburgh Magazine* for May 1797, and in *The Scots Magazine* for June 1797. It is included also in Brash and Reid's *Poetry Original and Select* (Vol. iii. 1798). But there are no variations to record.

THEIR
GROVES O'
SWEET
MYRTLE

THINE AM I

THOMSON (Vol. ii. 1799). Sent to Thomson about October 1793. The MS. is at Brechin Castle.

Intended as English words to *The Quaker's Wife*. It is possible that the verses had done duty with Clarinda: —'I have altered the first stanza, which I would have to stand thus:—

'"Thine am I, my faithful Fair,
Well thou may'st discover!
Every pulse along my veins
Tells the ardent Lover"'

(R. B. to Thomson, 19th October 1794). But on 2nd August 1795, being long, long off with Clarinda and very much on with Jean Lorimer, he wants his first line changed to 'Thine am I, my Chloris fair':—'If you neglect the alteration, I call on all the Nine conjunctly and severally to anathematise you.' A parallel case is that of Mr. Arthur Pendennis, thriftily turning his Fotheringay rhymes to account with Miss Amory.

In a MS. now at Liverpool Free Library '*lovely Kate*' is an alternative reading in Line 1 for 'faithful fair'; and in 2 the choice is between '*Well thou may'st discern*' and our text; and in 4 between '*Tells the ardent Lover*' and our text. As Burns's changes were rather due to whim than to inspiration, we have ventured to retain his original readings.

THOU HAST LEFT ME EVER, JAMIE

THOMSON (Vol. ii. 1799). The MS. is at Brechin Castle.

Suggested to Thomson (September 1793) as words for *Fee Him Father*:—'I enclose you Fraser's set of this tune when he plays it slow : in fact, he makes it the language of despair ! I shall here give you two stanzas in that style, merely to try if it will be any improvement. Were it possible, in singing, to give it half the pathos which Fraser gives it in playing, it would make an admirably pathetic song. I do not give these verses for any merit they have. I composed them at the time in which "Patie Allan's mither de'ed "—that was, "about the back o' midnight "—and by the leeside of a bowl of punch, which had overset every mortal in company except the *Hautbois* and the Muse.'

Thomson accepted the song as 'an additional one'; but, setting it to *My Boy Tammie*, felt bound to change the hero's name to '*Tam*,' and did so without a blush. It is slightly reminiscent of an older lyric, *Thou Art Gane Awa Frae Me, Mary*.

HIGHLAND MARY

THOMSON (Vol. ii. 1799). The MS. is at Brechin Castle.

Sent to Thomson, 14th November 1792 :—' The foregoing song pleases myself ; I think it is in my happiest manner ; you will see at first glance that it suits the air. The subject of the song is one of the most interesting passages of my youthful days ; and I own that I would be much flattered to see the verses set to an air which would ensure celebrity. Perhaps, after all, 'tis the still glowing prejudice of my heart that throws a borrowed lustre over the merits of the composition.' For Mary Campbell see *ante*, p. 308, Prefatory Note to *My Highland Lassie*.

MY CHLORIS, MARK

THOMSON (Vol. iii. 1801) and Currie (1800). The MS. is at Brechin Castle.

'On my visit the other day to my fair Chloris (that is the poetic name of the lovely goddess of my inspiration) she suggested an idea which on my return from the visit I wrought into the following song' (R. B. to Thomson in November 1794). For Chloris see *post*, p. 482, Prefatory Note to *Lassie wi' the Lint-white Locks*.

STANZA I. LINE I. '*Behold my love*, how green the groves,' Thomson. In February 1796 Burns wrote :—'In my by-past songs I dislike one thing—the name of Chloris'; but there is no evidence that he either suggested or permitted the change. 4. 'And wave thy *flowing* hair,' Thomson :—'What you once mentioned of "flaxen locks" is just; they cannot enter into an elegant description of beauty' (R. B. to Thomson, February 1796). But the pertinency of Thomson's criticism dawned on him only when Chloris had gone the way of Clarinda and Maria Riddell.

STANZA III. LINE I. 'Let minstrels,' *etc.* :—Burns gave Thomson the choice of '*touch*' and '*rouse*' as well as '*sweep*.'

FAIREST MAID ON DEVON BANKS

THOMSON (Vol. iii. 1801) and Currie (1800). Burns's last song. 'I tried my hand on *Rothiemurchie* this morning. The measure is so difficult that it is impossible to infuse much genius into the lines; they are on the other side' (R. B. to Thomson, 12th July 1796).

As in 1787 he had complimented Charlotte Hamilton in *The Banks of the Devon*, it may be that she is the 'fairest maid' of the present song, although some refer it to a break in his friendship with Peggy Chalmers, or to her refusal to marry him (see *ante*, p. 437, Prefatory Note to *My Peggie's Face*). But although the Devon is real enough, the 'maid' in this case may have been pure fiction.

LASSIE WI' THE LINT-WHITE LOCKS

THOMSON (Vol. iii. 1801) and Currie (1800). 'I have finished my song to *Rothiemurchie's Rant*. . . . The piece has at least the merit of being a regular pastoral; the vernal morn, the summer noon, the autumnal evening, and the winter night, are regularly rounded' (R. B. to Thomson, November 1794).

The Chloris, who did duty as Burns's Muse for some time after his break with Maria Riddell, was the daughter of William Lorimer, farmer and publican, Kemmishall, near Dumfries. She was born in September 1775, at Craigieburn Wood, which her poet has associated with a Mr. Gillespie, a brother gauger (see p. 364) and his passion for her: Gillespie's disappointment, when she eloped to Gretna Green with a prodigal young Englishman, one Whepdale, tenant of a farm near Moffat, being shadowed forth in *O Poortith Cauld* (p. 221). The lady was still a bride, when her husband fled his creditors across the border; and, her illusion being no more, she returned to her parents and resumed her maiden name. Her misfortunes so touched the Bard that he became exceedingly enamoured of her. He re-wrote *Whistle and I'll Come to You My Lad* in her honour; on her behalf appropriated part of an earlier song, *And I'll Kiss Thee Yet* (p. 34), to complete *Come, Let Me Take Thee to My Breast* (p. 233); celebrated her illness in a new set of *Ay Wauken, O* (p. 260); and exalted her in such 'reveries of passion' as the present song, as *My Chloris, Mark* (p. 256), as *Mark Yonder Pomp* (p. 273), as *Forlorn My Love* (p. 266), and as *O, Bonie Was Yon Rosy Brier* (p. 263), to name but these. He thus described to Thomson her relation to his work:—
'The lady on whom it [*Craigieburn Wood*] was made is one of the finest women in Scotland; and, in fact (*entre nous*) is, in a manner to me, what Sterne's Eliza was to him—a Mistress, or Friend, or what you will, in the guileless simplicity of Platonic love. (Now don't put any of

your squinting constructions on this, or have any clish-maclavers about it among our acquaintances.) I assure you that to my lovely Friend you are indebted for many of your best songs of mine. Do you think that the sober gin-horse routine of existence could inspire a man with life, and love, and joy—could fire him with enthusiasm or melt him with pathos equal to the genius of your Book? No, No! Whenever I want to be more than ordinary in song —to be in some degree equal to your diviner airs—do you imagine I fast and pray for the celestial emanation? *Tout au contraire!* I have a glorious recipe ; the very one that for his own use was invented to the Divinity of Healing and Poesy, when erst he piped to the flocks of Admetus. I put myself in the regimen of admiring a fine woman ; and in proportion to the adorability of her charms, in proportion you are delighted with my verses.'

LASSIE WI' THE LINT-WHITE LOCKS

Towards the close of 1795 he (for whatever reason) grew disenchanted with the 'adorability' of this particular 'fine woman,' and would rather, as we have seen, that neither her name nor her 'charms' were associated with his fame. The poor lady's later years were unfortunate. Her father lost his money, and, compelled to support herself, she went into service, dying as late as September 1831.

There are two MSS. at Brechin Castle, one containing Stanza II., which was omitted by both Currie and Thomson, and for a second copy whereof we are indebted to Mr. C. C. Maxwell, Dundee. (It is included as well in a MS. copy in the Kilmarnock Monument Museum.)

STANZA III. LINE 2. 'Has *cheared each* drooping little flower,' Kilmarnock MS.

STANZA V., according to Currie, runs thus in some MSS. :—

'And *should* the howling wintry blast
Disturb my lassie's midnight rest,
I'll fauld thee to my faithfu' breast,
And comfort thee, my dearie, O.'

LINE 3. '*Enfaulded* to my faithfu' breast,' Kilmarnock MS.

LONG, LONG THE NIGHT

THOMSON (Vol. iii. 1801) and Currie (1800).
Sent to Thomson in May 1795. A rather tawdry set of *Ay Wauken O* (p. 45). See *ante*, p. 482, Prefatory Note to *Lassie wi' the Lint-white Locks*.

LOGAN WATER

THOMSON (Vol. iii. 1801) and Currie (1800). 'Have you ever, my dear Sir, felt your bosom ready to burst with indignation on reading, or seeing how these mighty villains who divide kingdom against kingdom, desolate provinces, and lay Nations waste, out of the wantonness of ambition, or often from still more ignoble passions? In a mood of this kind to-day, I recollected the air of *Logan Water*, and it occurred to me that its querulous melody probably had its origin from the plaintive indignation of some swelling, suffering heart, fired at the tyrannic strides of some Public Destroyer, and overwhelmed with private distress, the consequences of a country's ruin. If I have done anything like justice to my feelings, the following song, composed in three-quarters of an hour's lucubrations in my elbow-chair, ought to have some merit' (R. B. to Thomson, 25th June 1793).

' I remember two ending lines of a verse in some of the old songs of *Logan Water* (for I know a good many different ones) which I think pretty :—

' "Now my dear lad maun face his faes
Far, far frae me and Logan Braes." '

(R. B. to Thomson, 3rd April 1793). It may be that these lines occur in an old song; but in any case they were used as a refrain in the *Logan Water* of John Mayne (author of *The Siller Gun*, and joint editor with Peter

Stuart of *The London Star*), which was popular at Vauxhall some years before Burns wrote. Burns's set was intended as the Scots alternative to James Thomson's *For Ever, Fortune, Wilt Thou Prove*, which was set to *Logan Water* in Thomson's *Orpheus Caledonius* (1725). Chappell (*Roxburghe Ballads*, iii. 475) supposes the original to have been a dialogue duet in an English play, afterwards lengthened into a broadside, of which a blackletter copy, printed by 'J. Conyers at the Black Raven in Holborn,' is in the Roxburghe Collection (ii. 41) : a whiteletter by the same publisher, with the music, being in the Pepys Collection (v. 269). It is entitled '*The Bonny Scottish Lad and the Yielding Lass*, to an excellent new tune much in request, called *The Liggan Waters.*' Consistently to maintain the impossibility of a Scots original, Chappell evolved an amusing theory :—' In adopting an imitation Scottish dialect, the ballad-writer seems to have imagined that Logan Water is somewhere in the north of our island instead of being, where it really is, in Ireland, about north-west of Drogheda.' But (1) how came the English writer to think of Logan Water at all, unless it had been associated with some older tune? (2) 'Water' is a distinctively Scottish equivalent for 'river' or 'stream.' And (3) there are several Logan Waters in Scotland— one a tributary of the North Esk in Midlothian, and another in Lanarkshire. The English broadside begins thus :—

LOGAN WATER

  Lad. 'Bonny Lass, I love thee well.'
  Lass. 'Bonny Lad, I love thee better.'
  Lad. 'Wilt thou pull off thy hose and shoon
    And wend with me to Liggan Water?
  Lass. 'Liggan Water is so deep,
    And I am loath to wet my feet,
    But if you'll promise to marry me
    I'll put off my shoon and follow thee.'

It is clear that this ballad is closely related to an old Scots thing in Herd (1776) :—

LOGAN WATER

> 'Logan-Water and Logan-Braes,
> I helped a bonnie lassie on wi' her claiths,
> On wi' her stockings, and on wi' her shoon;
> And she gae me the glaiks when a' was done,' *etc.* :—

and included with verbal differences in *The Merry Muses*. And it is very much less likely that the Scots balladist got his inspiration from the very silly blackletter than that the blackletter is a faint derivative from this or from some earlier Scots original. A ballad, *Logan Water, or A Lass in Captivity*, is included in a certain collection (1660-1720), which we have failed to trace.

There are MSS. at Lochryan—MS. (A)—and at Dalhousie—MS. (B).

STANZA I. LINE 2. '*The* day I was my Willie's bride,' MS. (A).

STANZA III. LINE 3. 'Her faithfu' mate *to* share her toil,' MS. (A).

STANZA IV. LINE 1. 'O wae *be to* you, Men o' State,' erroneous reading. 5-6 were objected to by Thomson. Burns replied :—'The faulty line in *Logan Water* I mend thus :—

> '"*How can your flinty hearts enjoy*
> The widow's *tear*, the orphan's *cry*."'

Having no fear of Thomson, we have preferred the original reading.

YON ROSY BRIER

THOMSON (Vol. iii. 1801) and Currie (1800). Sent to Thomson in August 1795. The MS. is at Brechin Castle.

WHERE ARE THE JOYS

THOMSON (Vol. iii. 1801) and Currie (1800). '*Saw Ye My Father?* is one of my greatest favourites. The evening before last I wandered out, and began a tender song in

what I think is its native style. . . . My song is but just
begun; and I should like, before I proceed, to know your
opinion of it' (R. B. to Thomson in his comments on
the latter's list of an hundred songs, September 1793).
The completed song he sent to Thomson shortly afterwards, with the advice to set the air to the old words, and
let his 'follow as English verses.'

WHERE
ARE THE
JOYS

Both MSS. are at Brechin Castle. The later has an
additional stanza, and is in English. Except for this the
two agree.

BEHOLD THE HOUR

THOMSON (Vol. iv. 1805) and Currie (1800). Sent to
Thomson in December 1793 :—'The following song I have
composed for *Oran Gaoil*, the Highland air that you tell
me in your last you have resolved to give a place in your
book. I have this moment finished the song, so you have
it glowing from the mint. If it suit you, well! if not
'tis also well!' (R. B. to Thomson, September 1793).

It is from a song sent to Clarinda in 1791; but this
itself was little more than a transcript of a certain *Farewell to Nice*, to be found in *The Charmer* and other books
(see Vol. iv.).

FORLORN MY LOVE

THOMSON (Vol. iv. 1805) and Currie (1800). 'How do
you like the foregoing? I have written it within this
hour; so much for the *speed* of my Pegasus, but what say
you to his *bottom*?' (Burns to Thomson, May 1795).
Thomson appears to have objected to the grammar of
Lines 1-2 of Stanza III., and on 2nd August Burns,
admitting that his objection was 'just,' sent, hoping it
would 'please' him, this :—

'Cold, alter'd *friends, with* cruel *art,*
Poisoning fell Misfortune's dart.'

Both MSS. are at Brechin Castle. A MS. in the possession of Mr. A. P. Watt, London, retains the old reading.

CA' THE YOWES TO THE KNOWES
SECOND SET

THOMSON (Vol. iv. 1805) and Currie (1800). Sent to Thomson in September 1794. See *ante*, p. 350, Prefatory Note to *Ca' the Yowes to the Knowes* (First Set). The MS. is at Brechin Castle.

STANZA I. LINE 3. 'Then a-faulding let us gang':—*i.e.* to gather the sheep into the fold. *Cf.* the song, *My Peggy is a Young Thing*, in Ramsay's *Gentle Shepherd*:—

'My Peggy is a young thing
And I'm not very auld,
Yet well I like to meet her
At the wauking of the fauld.'

HOW CAN MY POOR HEART

THOMSON (Vol. iv. 1805) and Currie (1800). The MS. is at Brechin Castle.

'The last evening as I was straying out, and thinking of *O'er the Hills and Far Away*, I spun the following stanzas for it; but whether my spinning will deserve to be laid up in store, like the precious thread of the silkworm, or brushed to the devil, like the vile manufacture of the spider, I leave, my dear sir, to your usual candid criticism. I was pleased with several lines in it at first, but I own that it appears rather a flimsy business. . . . I give you leave to abuse this song, but do it in the spirit of Christian meekness' (R. B. to Thomson, 30th August 1794). Thomson took him at his word, whereupon he replied:—'I shall withdraw my *O'er the Seas and Far Away* altogether; it is unequal, and unworthy of the work. Making a poem is like begetting a son; you cannot know whether you have a wise man or a fool, until you produce him to the world and try him.'

IS THERE FOR HONEST POVERTY

THOMSON (Vol. iv. 1805) and Currie (1800). 'A great critic (Aikin) on songs says that Love and Wine are the exclusive themes for song-writing. The following is on neither subject, and consequently is no song. . . . I do not give you the foregoing song for your book, but merely by way of *vive la bagatelle*; for the piece is not really poetry' (R. B. to Thomson, January 1795).

In all likelihood the oldest set of *For A' That* is one in *The Merry Muses* (see Vol. ii. p. 304, Prefatory Note to *The Jolly Beggars*). Apparently suggested by the Highlander's imperfect Scots (the hero is specifically some bare-breeched Donald), the phrase was found effective for a certain class of ditty—the ditty which (as Burns says of this one) 'is not really poetry.' A Jacobite derivative, which he knew likewise, is included in a *Collection of Loyal Songs*, 1750. It begins thus :—

'Tho' —— reigns in —— stead
I'm grieved, yet scorn to shaw that:
I'll ne'er look down nor hang my head
On rebel Whig for a' that ':—

and has this chorus :—

'For a' that and a' that,
And twice as muckle's a' that,
He's far beyond the seas the night,
Yet he'll be here for a' that.'

A slightly different set is included in the *True Loyalist* (1779); a corrupted one in Hogg's *Relics*.

Like *Scots Wha Hae*—('the Scottish *Marseillaise*': whatever that may mean)—this famous song—('the *Marseillaise* of humanity': whatever *that* may mean)—which, according to Chambers, 'may be said to embody all the false philosophy of Burns's time and of his own mind,' is very plainly an effect of the writer's sympathies with the spirit and the fact of the French Revolution, and of

IS THERE FOR HONEST POVERTY that estrangement from wealthier loyalist friends, with which his expression of these sympathies and his friendship with such 'sons of sedition' as Maxwell (see Vol. ii. p. 440, Prefatory Note to *Ye True Loyal Natives*, and Vol. ii. p. 443, Prefatory Note to *To Dr. Maxwell*) had been visited. It appeared in *The Glasgow Magazine* for August 1795; in *The Oracle* for June 2nd, 1796; in a chap-book, Paisley 1796; in the *Scots Magazine* for August 1797; and in the tracts of Brash and Reid (Vol. ii. of the Collected Series, 1797), and of Stewart and Meikle.

The MS. sent to Thomson is at Brechin Castle. A copy inscribed in a 1794 Edition was first made known by Mr. J. R. Tutin in his Edition in the series of Newbery Classics; it agrees with that published in *The Oracle*.

STANZA I. is wanting in the sets in *The Glasgow Magazine*, *Oracle*, and *Scots Magazine*, and the Tutin MS.

LINES 1-2 in Brash and Reid read thus:—

'*Wha wad* for honest poverty
Hing down his head an' a' that.

4. '*And* dare be poor for a' that,' Brash and Reid, and Stewart. 5-8. In some copies of Brash and Reid there is an absurd version of this half stanza, apparently the invention of the ingenious Reid:—

'For a' that and a' that,
Their purse-proud looks and a' that,' etc.

LINE 7. 'The rank is but the *guinea* stamp,' Stewart. It has been pointed out that the thought in this verse and the next is conveyed from a sentence in Wycherly's *Plain Dealer*. It is also found in *Tristram Shandy* and other works. Indeed, it might be found anywhere.

STANZA II. LINE 3. 'Gie fools their *silk*,' early sets. 7-8 in the early sets read:—

'*An*' honest man tho' *ne'er* sae [or *so*] poor
Is *chief* o' [or *of*] men for a' that.'

STANZA III. LINE 3. 'Tho' hundreds *beckon* at his *nod*,'

Oracle and Tutin MS. 6. 'His *dignities* an' a' that,' *Oracle* and Tutin MS. 7. '*A* man of independent mind,' the early sets. 4. '*Can sing* and *laugh* at a' that,' *Oracle* and Tutin MS.; '*can look* and *laugh*,' *Glasgow Magazine*, *Scots Magazine*, Brash and Reid, and Stewart.

IS THERE FOR HONEST POVERTY

STANZA IV. LINE I. ' *The King* can mak [or make] a belted knight,' the early sets. 4. ' Fa' that ':—This phrase has puzzled the Editors. Here they usually translate it 'attempt.' But the common meaning is 'have' (*i.e.* 'possess'), or, better still, 'claim,' or 'lay claim to,' as in the following examples:—
' We Norlands manna fa' To eat sae nice and gang sae braw ' (Beattie); ' The Whigs think a' that weal is won, But faith they manna fa' that' (*Collection of Loyal Songs, ut sup.*); ' He that some ells of this may fa'' (Fergusson); ' Or wha in a' the country round, The best deserves to fa' that' (Burns). This, too, is the sense in the archetypal song:—' Put butter in my Donald's brose, For weel does Donald fa' that':—as in the present derivative, where ' Gude faith, he manna fa' that ' plainly means that the power of making an honest man, as a belted knight is made, is one no king can be allowed to claim. 6. ' *His* dignities and a' that,' *Glasgow Magazine*, *Scots Magazine*, Brash and Reid, and Stewart; ' *His garters, stars,* and a' that,' *Oracle* and Tutin MS. 8. '*Are better far* than a' that,' *Oracle* and Tutin MS.; '*Are grander far*,' *Glasgow Magazine*, *Scots Magazine*, Brash and Reid, and Stewart.

STANZA V. LINE I. 'Then let us pray *the time may come*,' *Oracle* and Tutin MS.; '*And* [*An'*] come it will,' *Oracle* and Tutin MS.; ' As come it *shall*,' *Glasgow Magazine*, *Scots Magazine*, Brash and Reid, and Stewart. 3. ' *When* Sense and *Truth* o'er a' the earth,' early sets. 4. 'Shall bear the gree *for* a' that,' *Oracle* and Tutin MS. 6. ' *An'* [*And*] *come it will* for a' that,' *Oracle* and Tutin MS. 7-8 in the *Scots Magazine* read :—

'And man to man *shall brothers be
The world o'er* for a' that.'

7. '*And* man to man the world o'er,' *Glasgow Magazine*, Stewart; ' *When* man to man the world o'er,' Brash and Reid.

MARK YONDER POMP

THOMSON (Vol. iv. 1805) and Currie (1800). The MS. is at Brechin Castle.

A 'reverie' on Chloris. 'Well, this is not amiss' (R. B. to Thomson, May 1795).

O, LET ME IN THIS AE NIGHT

THOMSON (Vol. iv. 1805) and Currie (1800). Both MSS. are at Brechin Castle.

Founded on a song in Herd's *Collection* (1769), which Burns revised for Johnson's *Museum*. The first stanza and the chorus are borrowed from the Herd set, which is one of many derivatives from a group of blackletter ballads (see *ante*, p. 377, Prefatory Note to *Wha Is That at My Bower Door*, and p. 450, Prefatory Note to *O, Open the Door*). In August 1793 Burns sent Thomson a second; in September 1794 a third; in February 1795 'another trial,' with the remark :—'I do not know whether it will do.' This last one Thomson used. After the Chorus and Stanza I. the earlier version runs thus :—

'Tho' never durst my tongue reveal,
Lang, lang my heart to thee's been leal;
O Lassie dear, ae last fareweel,
For Pity's cause alane, jo.

'O wyte na me until thou prove
The fatal force o' mighty love;
Then should on me thy fancy rove
Count my care by thine ain, jo.

'O Pity's ay to woman dear:
She heav'd a sigh, she drapt a tear;—
'Twas love for me that brought him here,
Sae how can I complain, jo?'

CHORUS. LINE 3. '*For Pity's sake* this ae nicht,' Thomson and Currie, but there is no MS. authority. 4. '*I'll no come back again*, jo,' Herd and earlier Burns.

STANZA I. LINE I. 'O Lassie, *art thou* sleepin [or *sleeping*] O, LET ME
yet,' Herd and earlier Burns. IN THIS AE
STANZA II. LINE I. '*O* hear'st *thou not the* wind an' weet?' NIGHT
erroneous reading.
STANZA IV. of *Her Answer.* LINES 2-4 read in the MS.
thus :—
'*Is* now the cruel fowler's prey,
Let *witless, trusting* woman say
How aft her fate's the same, jo' :—

but Burns discarded this for the reading in the text, with the
remark :—' By God I have thought better.'

O PHILLY, HAPPY BE THAT DAY

THOMSON (Vol. iv. 1805) and Currie (1800). ' Did you not
once propose *The Sow's Tail to Geordie* as an air for your
work? I am quite delighted with it ; but I acknowledge
that is no mark of its real excellence. I once set about
verses for it, which I meant to be in the alternate
way of a lover and his mistress chanting together. . . .
I have just written four stanzas at random, which I
intended to have woven somewhere into, probably at the
conclusion of, the song' (R. B. to Thomson, September
1794).

He finished the duet one morning in November,
'though a keen blowing frost,' in his 'walk before
breakfast.' The portion written in September consisted
of Stanzas IV. and V. In the earlier MS. 'Jeanie' and
'Geordie' were the 'He' and 'She.'

Both MSS. are at Brechin Castle.

STANZA V. LINE 7. 'I *care na wealth* a single flie,' earlier
MS. 8. ' The lad I *loe's* the lad for me,' earlier MS.

O, WERE MY LOVE

THOMSON (Vol. iv. 1805) and Currie (1800).
The second stanza is a fragment preserved in Herd's
Collection :—'This thought is inexpressibly beautiful,

O, WERE MY LOVE and, so far as I know, quite original. It is too short for a song, else I would forswear you altogether except you gave it a place. I have often tried to eke a stanza to it, but in vain. After balancing myself for a musing five minutes on the hind-legs of my elbow-chair, I produced the following [*Were My Love Yon Lilac Fair, etc.*]. The verses are far inferior to the foregoing I frankly confess; but, if worthy of insertion at all, they might be first in place, as every Poet who knows anything of his trade will husband his best thoughts for a concluding stroke' (R. B. to Thomson, June 1793).

In the Herd MS. there is also a set three stanzas in length :—

> 'O, if my love was a pickle of wheat,
>   And growing upon yon lilly white lea,
> And I myself a bonny sweet bird,
>   Away with that pickle I would flie.

> 'O, if my love was a bonny red rose,
>   And growing upon some barren wa',
> And I myself a drap of dew,
>   Down in that red rose I would fa'.

> 'O, if my love was a coffer of gold,' *etc.*

And of burlesque fancies (not to be repeated here), there is no lack.

The MS. is at Brechin Castle.

STANZA I. LINE 8. '*Gallant*' and '*merry*' are alternative readings with 'youthfu',' and '*leaf*' is an alternative reading for 'bloom.'

SLEEP'ST THOU

THOMSON (Vol. iv. 1805) and Currie (1800). Burns sent a copy to Thomson, 19th October 1794, and a revised copy on the 27th October.

Both MSS. are at Brechin Castle. An early sketch is in the possession of the Earl of Rosebery.

STANZA I. LINES 5-9 originally read :—

> 'Now *thro' the leafy woods*
> *And by the reeking floods,*
> *Wild Nature's tenants freely, gladly, stray.*
> *The lintwhite in his bower*
> *Chants o'er the breathing flower.*'

STANZA II. LINES 5-12 originally read :—

> 'When *absent from my fair,*
> *The murky shades of care*
> *With starless gloom o'ercast my sullen sky,*
> *But when in Beauty's light*
> *She meets my ravish'd sight,*
> When thro' my very heart
> Her beaming glories dart,
> 'Tis then I *wake to life, to light,* and joy.'

THERE WAS A LASS

THOMSON (Vol. iv. 1805) and Currie (1800).

Certain stanzas were sent to Thomson in April 1793, and the finished ballad on July 2nd. The heroine was Jean M'Murdo, daughter of Burns's friend, John M'Murdo (see Vol. ii. p. 375, Prefatory Note to *To John M'Murdo*). To her he sent a copy :—' In the inclosed ballad I have, I think, hit off a few outlines of your portrait. The personal charms, the purity of mind, the ingenuous *naivête* of heart and manners in my heroine are, I flatter myself, a pretty just likeness of Miss M'Murdo in a cottage.'

Slightly reminiscent of *Buttery May* in the *Tea-Table Miscellany,* and other books, which begins :—

> 'In yonder town there was a May
> Snack and perfyte as can be ony':—

and of which this is Stanza II. :—

> 'Her bonnyness has been foreseen
> In ilka town baith far and near ;
> And when she kirns her minny's kirn,
> She rubs her face till it grows clear :

THERE WAS A LASS

But when her minny she did perceive
Sic great inlack amang the butter :—
"Shame fa' that filthy face of thine,
'Tis crish that gars your grunzie glitter."'

The MS. sent to Thomson—MS. (B)—is at Brechin Castle, and another—MS. (A)—giving several interesting new, readings, is in the possession of Mr. R. B. Adam, Ohio, U.S.A.

STANZA II. LINE I. 'And ay she wrought her *mammie's wark*,' Currie and Thomson; and similarly in lines of other Stanzas.

STANZA IV. LINE 2. 'That *turn'd the maute in yon town-en*,' MS. (A).

STANZA V. LINE I. 'Tryste' may here refer to the appointed meeting-place of lovers (cf. *Mary Morison*, Stanza I. Line 2, 'The trysted hour'). It is also a common word for a cattle fair.

STANZA VI. is omitted in MS. (A) :—'Is this stanza not original?' (R. B. to Thomson).

STANZA VII. LINES 2-4 in MS. (A) read :—

' *Her life was naught but* care and pain,
Yet *kend* na what her ail could be
Or what *would ease her heart* again.'

STANZA VIII. LINE 3. '*When* Robie tauld a tale o' love,' MS. (A).

STANZA IX. in MS. (B) and as hitherto printed reads :—

' *The sun was sinking in the west,*
The birds sang sweet in ilka grove;
His cheeks to hers he *fondly laid*,
And whisper'd thus his *tale o' love.*'

STANZA X. LINE 4. 'And learn to *turn the maute* wi' me,' MS. (A).

STANZA XI. in MS. (A) reads :—

' *Thy handsome foot* thou shalt *na set*
In barn or byre to trouble thee;
But *sit on a cushion and sew at thy seam,*
And *learn to turn the maute* wi' me.'

STANZA XII. LINE I. 'Now *Jeanie wist na what to say*,' MS. (A). 4. 'And *bliss* was ay between them twa,' MS. (A).

THE LEA-RIG

THOMSON (Vol. iv. 1805) and Currie (1800).

'On reading over *The Lea-Rig*, I immediately set about trying my hand on it, and after all, I could make nothing more of it than the following, which Heaven knows is poor enough.'—(R. B. to Thomson). Here he probably referred to *The Lea-Rig* in Johnson's *Museum* (No. 49, Vol. i.). This is his note on it in the Interleaved Copy:—
'The old words of this song are omitted here, though much more beautiful than those inserted, which were mostly composed by poor Fergusson in one of his merry humours. The old words began thus:—

' "I 'll rowe thee o'er the lea-rig,
My ain kind deary, O,
I 'll rowe thee o'er the lea-rig,
My ain kind deary, O.
Altho' the night were ne'er sae wat,
And I were ne'er sae weary, O,
I 'll rowe thee o'er the lea-rig,
My ain kind deary, O."'

A fuller set of the *Museum* words is in the Herd MS.—(it may be noted here that Fergusson and Herd were cronies)—and a set is preserved in *The Merry Muses*, which, save for a difference in the refrain—'I 'll lay thee' for 'I 'll row thee'; and 'My lovely Mary, dearie, O' (used six times) for 'My ain kind dearie, O' (used once)—is very nearly identical with the 'old words' quoted by Burns in the Interleaved Copy. The set in the Herd MS. has this stanza:—

'I 'll row you east, I 'll row you west,
I 'll row you the way you like best;
And I 'll row you o'er the lea rig,
Mine ain kind dearie, O.'

THE
LEA-RIG

But the Herd MS. also contains a fragment, which is, perhaps, the archetypal original :—

'Tho' the night were ne'er sae dark,
And I were ne'er sa weary,
I'd meet on the Ley Rig
Myn ain kind Deary.'

There are two MSS.—(A) and (B)—at Brechin Castle.
STANZA I. LINE I. '*E'ening* star' and '*parting sun*' are alternative readings for 'Eastern star'; but 'I will have it the eastern star' (R. B.). 5. 'Down by the burn, where *birken-bobs*,' MS. (A); '*birken-buds*,' deleted reading in MS. (B).
STANZA II. LINE I. '*In mirkest glen, at midnight hour*,' MS. (A). 5. 'Altho' the night were ne'er sae *wet*,' MS. (A).
STANZA III. was added in MS. (B). 3. 'At noon the fisher *seeks* the glen,' alternative reading in MS. (B).

MY WIFE'S A WINSOME WEE THING

THOMSON (Vol. v. 1818) and Currie (1800). 'In the air— *My Wife's a Wanton Wee Thing*—if a few lines smooth and pretty can be adapted to it, it is all you can expect. The following I made *extempore* to it; and though, on further study, I might give you something more profound, yet it might not suit the light-horse gallop of the air, so well as this random clink' (R. B. to Thomson, 8th November 1792). To this Thomson replied :—'Of the other song, *My Wife's a Winsome Wee Thing*, I think the first eight lines very good, but I do not admire the other eight, because four of them are a bare repetition of the first verse. I have been trying to spin a stanza, but could make nothing better than the following: do you mend it, or, as Yorick did with the loveletter, "whip it up in your own way" :—

'"O leeze me on my wee thing,
My bonie blythesome wee thing!
Sae lang's I hae my wee thing,
I'll think my lot divine.

'"Though warld's care we spare o't,
And may sae meikle mair o't,
Wi' her I'll blythely bear it,
And ne'er a word repine."'

MY WIFE'S
A WINSOME
WEE THING

Burns, being especially resolved that he would not alter *Bonie Lesley*, thought fit to flatter Thomson by stating that his corrections were 'perfectly right,' and that the alteration of the second stanza was 'a positive improvement.' He gave, however, no further sign, and Thomson did not publish the song till 1818, when he incorporated his own amendments:—'*My Love's a Winsom Wee Thing*, changed from the old name of the air, *My Wife's a Wanton Wee Thing*, the first stanza by Burns, the others by George Thomson.'

Burns's MS. is at Brechin Castle.

CHORUS. This was all the original Burns that Thomson left, and in Line **3** he substituted '*bonie*' for 'lo'esome.' **4.** 'This *dear* wee wife o' mine,' deleted reading.

STANZA II. LINE I. 'Wrack' = 'Vengeance' or 'wrath,' but here probably used in the sense of 'evil' in general.

MARY MORISON

THOMSON (Vol. v. 1818) and Currie (1800). The MS. is at Brechin Castle.

This little masterpiece of feeling and expression was sent to Thomson, 20th March 1793. 'The song prefixed is one of my juvenile works. I leave it among your hands. I do not think it very remarkable either for its merits or demerits' (R. B. to Thomson); and Thomson sat on it for upwards of twenty-five years. Gilbert Burns told him that Mary Morison was the heroine of some light verses beginning:—*And I'll kiss thee yet, yet* (see p. 34). She has therefore been identified with Elison Begbie. But a Mary Morison, the daughter of one Adjutant Morison, who lived at Mauchline from 1784, is

500   NOTES

MARY MORISON said to have been as beautiful as amiable. She died of consumption, 29th August 1791.

For the stanza of *Mary Morison* see *ante*, Vol. i. p. 371-2, Prefatory Note to *The Lament*. It is prettily exampled, with the addition of a refrain, as in the ballade proper, in the three octaves of a song (here modernized) in the Bannatyne MS., which Burns most certainly read in *The Evergreen*, and which may very well have given him the metrical scheme of his own immortal lyric :—

> 'When Flora had o'erfret the firth
> In May, of every moneth queen ;
> When Merle and Mavis sings with mirth,
> Sweet melling in the schawës sheen ;
> When all lovers rejoicèd been
> And maist desirous of their prey ;
> I heard a lusty lovvr mene :—
> "Whom I love I dare nocht assay !"'

STANZA I. LINE 2. 'The trysted hour'=the hour appointed.

INDEX OF TITLES

	TEXT	NOTES
Aberfeldie, The Birks of	7	306
Adair, Eppie	72	356
Adown Winding Nith,	227	460
Ae Fond Kiss	105	379
Afton, Sweet,	134	394
A-hunting, My Lord	198	443
Airts, Of a' the	56	345
A Lass wi' a Tocher	229	461
Ale Comes, O Guid	193	440
Allan Stream, By	231	462
A Mother's Lament	67	352
Anderson My Jo, John	63	349
And I'll Kiss Thee Yet	34	330
Ane-and-Twenty, Tam, O For	111	382
Ann, Beware o' Bonie	46	338
Ann, Lady Mary	126	389
A Red, Red Rose	143	402
A Rosebud by My Early Walk	33	329
As I Came O'er the Cairney Mount	171	427
As I Stood by Yon Roofless Tower	144	406
Auld Lang Syne	147	407
Auld Rob Morris	210	449

INDEX OF TITLES

	TEXT	NOTES
A Waukrife Minnie	77	358
Awa, Whigs, Awa	64	350
Ay Waukin O	45	337
Ballochmyle, The Braes o'	69	353
Balou, The Highland	175	429
Bank of Flowers, On a	49	339
Banks o' Doon, The	124	388
Banks of Nith, The	83	362
Banks of the Devon, The	22	320
Bannocks o' Bear Meal	175	430
Battle of Sherramuir, The	73	356
Bear Meal, Bannocks o'	175	430
Beaver, Cock Up Your	89	366
Bed, The Lass That Made the	162	419
Bed, The Tailor Fell Thro' the	44	336
Behold the Hour	265	487
Bell, Bonie	135	396
Beware o' Bonie Ann	46	338
Blast, Cauld is the E'enin	203	444
Blast, When Wild War's Deadly	212	451
Blythe Hae I Been on Yon Hill	230	461
Blythe Was She	29	326
Bobbed, When She Cam Ben She	110	381
Bonie Ann, Beware o'	46	338
Bonie Bell	135	396
Bonie Dundee	2	301
Bonie Wee Thing	103	378
Bower Door, Wha Is That at My	102	375
Braes, Kellyburn	129	391
Braes o' Ballochmyle, The	69	353
Braw Lads o' Galla Water	209	448

INDEX OF TITLES

	TEXT	NOTES
Brier-bush, There Grows a Bonie	180	432
Brier, Yon Rosy	263	486
By Allan Stream	231	462
Cairney Mount, As I Came O'er the	171	427
Canst Thou Leave Me Thus, My Katie	232	463
Can Ye Labour Lea, O	138	397
Captain's Lady	55	344
Captive Ribband, The	60	348
Cardin o't, The	159	417
Carl, an the King Come	57	346
Ca' the Yowes to the Knowes (1st set)	65	350
Ca' the Yowes to the Knowes (2nd set)	268	488
Ca' Thro', Hey	137	397
Cauld is the E'enin Blast	203	444
Cave, Had I a	236	467
Charlie, He's my Darling	154	414
Charlie, O'er the Water to	32	328
Charmer, Stay My	12	312
Chloris Mark, My	256	481
City, There's a Youth in this	61	348
Clarinda, Mistress of my Soul	39	334
Cockade, The White	68	353
Cock Up Your Beaver	89	366
Collier Laddie, My	115	383
Come, Let Me Take Thee	233	463
Come Try Me, Jamie	52	342
Comin Thro' the Rye	151	411
Complain, Let Not Woman E'er	219	455
Contented Wi' Little	234	464
Cooper o' Cuddy, The	157	416
Count the Lawin, Guidwife	91	366

INDEX OF TITLES

	TEXT	NOTES
Craigieburn Wood	86	363
Crookieden, I Hae Been at	99	374
Cruel Are the Parents, How	238	468
Cuddy, The Cooper o'	157	416
Daddie o't, The Rantin Dog, the	70	354
Daddie, The Deuk's Dang O'er My	139	398
Darling, Charlie He's My	154	414
Daunton Me, To	30	327
Davies, Lovely	106	380
Davison, Duncan	19	319
Day, O Philly, Happy be that	277	493
Day, O Tibbie, I Hae Seen the	37	333
Day Returns, The	50	340
Dearie, Wilt Thou be My	173	428
Death, The Song of	133	394
December, Thou Gloomy	185	437
Deil's Awa wi' th' Exciseman, The	141	399
Deluded Swain, the Pleasure	217	454
Deuk's Dang O'er My Daddie, The	139	398
Devon Banks, Fairest Maid on	22	320
Devon, The Banks of the	258	481
Does Haughty Gaul Invasion Threat	195	441
Dog, the Daddie o't, The Rantin	70	354
Doon, The Banks o'	124	388
Door to Me, O, Open the	211	450
Dreamed I Lay, I	18	318
Dunbar, Sweet Tibbie	42	335
Duncan Davison	19	319
Duncan Gray (1st set)	23	321
Duncan Gray (2nd set)	215	452
Dundee, Bonie	2	301

INDEX OF TITLES

	TEXT	NOTES
Ecclefechan, The Lass o'	156	415
Eliza, Fair	119	385
Eppie Adair	72	356
Eppie Macnab, My	101	375
Eve, Sweet Fa's the	225	459
Exciseman, The Deil's Awa wi' th	141	399
Fair and Fause, She's	140	399
Fair Eliza	119	385
Fair, I Do Confess Thou Art Sae	96	371
Fairest Maid on Devon Banks	258	481
Far Awa, Sae	165	422
Far Awa, The Bonie Lad That's	94	365
Farewell, M'Pherson's	9	307
Farewell, Thou Stream	235	465
Fate, Tho' Cruel	12	312
Fause, She's Fair and	140	399
Fellows, There's Three True Guid	160	418
Flaxen Were Her Ringlets, Sae	160	418
Flowers, On a Bank of	49	339
Forlorn My Love	266	487
For the Sake o' Somebody	158	416
Forth, Out Over the	153	413
Frae the Friends and Land I Love	38	364
Galla Water, Braw Lads o'	209	448
Gard'ner wi' His Paidle, The	48	339
Gaul Invasion Threat, Does Haughty	195	441
Glen, Here is the	218	454
Glen, Tam	84	363
Gray, Duncan (1st set)	23	321
Gray, Duncan (2nd set)	215	452

INDEX OF TITLES

	TEXT	NOTES
Gray, Wee Willie	188	438
Gregory, Lord	220	455
Groves of Sweet Myrtle, Their	252	478
Guidman, O, An Ye Were Dead	146	407
Guidwife, Count the Lawin	91	366
Had I a Cave	236	467
Had I the Wyte	149	410
Hairst, Robin Shure in	194	440
Harry, Highland	42	335
Hay was Mawn, In Simmer When the	117	384
Health, Here's a	237	467
Health, Here's to Thy	181	433
Health in Water, Here's His	177	431
Heart, How Can My Poor	269	488
Heart's in the Highlands, My	62	348
Heart, Wae is My	176	430
Here is the Glen	218	454
Here's a Health	237	467
Here's His Health in Water	177	431
Here's to Thy Health	181	433
Hey, Ca' Thro'	137	397
Highland Balou, The	175	429
Highland Harry	42	335
Highland Laddie	172	428
Highland Lassie, O My	10	308
Highland Mary	255	480
Highland Rover, The Young	16	318
Highlands, My Heart's in the	62	348
Highland Widow's Lament, The	184	436
Hill, Blythe Hae I Been on Yon	230	461
Hoggie, My	14	313

INDEX OF TITLES

	TEXT	NOTES
Hour, Behold the	265	487
How Can My Poor Heart	269	488
How Cruel are the Parents	238	468
How Lang and Dreary is the Night	27	324
Husband, Husband, Cease Your Strife	239	469
I Do Confess Thou Art Sae Fair	96	371
I Dream'd I Lay	18	318
I Hae a Wife o' My Ain	109	381
I Hae Been at Crookieden	99	374
I'll Ay Ca' in by Yon Town	166	423
I Love My Love in Secret	41	335
I'm O'er Young to Marry Yet	6	305
Invasion Threat, Does Haughty Gaul	195	441
Inverness, The Lovely Lass of	142	401
In Simmer When the Hay was Mawn	117	384
Is There For Honest Poverty	271	489
It is na, Jean, Thy Bonie Face	100	374
It Was A' For Our Rightfu' King	182	433
It Was the Charming Month	240	469
Jacobites by Name, Ye	120	386
Jamie, Come Try Me	52	342
Jamie Comes Hame, There'll Never be Peace till	92	367
Jamie, Thou Hast Left Me Ever	254	480
Jamie, Young	152	413
Jean, Thy Bonie Face, It is na,	100	374
Jessie, Young	226	459
Jewel, My Tocher's the	90	366
Jockie's Ta'en the Parting Kiss	201	444
Jockie was the Blythest Lad, Young	76	358
John Anderson, My Jo	63	349

INDEX OF TITLES

	TEXT	NOTES
John, Come Kiss Me Now, O,	88	365
Joys, Where are the	264	486
Jumpin John	14	315
Katie, Canst Thou Leave Me Thus, My	232	463
Kellyburn Braes	129	391
Kenmure's On and Awa, Willie, O	112	382
Killiecrankie	81	361
King Come, Carl an the	57	346
King, It Was A' For Our Rightfu'	182	433
Kiss, Ae Fond	105	379
Kiss, Jockie's Ta'en the Parting	201	444
Kiss Me Now, O John, Come	88	365
Kiss Thee Yet, And I'll	34	330
Knowes, Ca' the Yowes to the (1st set)	65	350
Knowes, Ca' the Yowes to the (2nd set)	268	488
Laddie, Highland	172	428
Laddie, Lie Near Me	47	338
Laddie, My Collier	115	383
Lads o' Galla Water, Braw	209	448
Lad, Whistle an' I'll Come to You, My	5	304
Lad, Young Jockie was the Blythest	76	358
Lad That's Far Awa, The Bonie	94	369
Lady Mary Ann	126	388
Lady Onlie, Honest Lucky	21	320
Lady, The Captain's	55	344
Lament, A Mother's	67	352
Lament, Strathallan's	13	312
Lament, The Highland Widow's	184	436
Lament, The Slave's	132	392
Land I Love, Frae the Friends and	88	364

INDEX OF TITLES

	TEXT	NOTES
Landlady, Count the Lawin	25	323
Lasses, News, There's News	205	445
Lassie, O This is No My Ain	248	473
Lassie, The Blue-eyed	82	362
Lassie, What Can a Young	93	368
Lassie wi' the Lint-white Locks	259	482
Lassie Yet, My Love She's but a	51	341
Lass o' Ecclefechan, The	156	415
Lass of Inverness, The Lovely	142	401
Lass, O Once I Lov'd a Bonie	197	442
Lass That Made the Bed, The	162	419
Lass, There Was a	281	495
Lass, There Was a Bonie	204	445
Lass wi' a Tocher, A	229	461
Last May a Braw Wooer	242	470
Lave o't, Whistle O'er the	58	346
Lawin, Guidwife, Count the	91	366
Lawin, Landlady, Count the	25	323
Lay Thy Loof in Mine, Lass, O	202	444
Lea, O Can Ye Labour	138	397
Lea-Rig, The	284	497
Leeze Me on My Spinnin-wheel, O	114	383
Lesley, Saw Ye Bonie	224	458
Let Me in this Ae Night, O	274	492
Let Me Take Thee to My Breast, Come	233	463
Let not Women e'er Complain	219	455
Lie Near Me, Laddie	47	338
Life, The Winter of	178	431
Lint-white Locks, Lassie wi' the	259	482
Little, Contented wi'	234	464
Lo'es Me, O Wat Ye Wha that	249	474
Logan Water	262	484

INDEX OF TITLES

	TEXT	NOTES
Long, Long the Night	260	484
Loof in Mine, Lass, O Lay Thy	202	444
Lord Gregory	220	455
Louis, What Reck I by Thee	149	410
Love, Forlorn My	266	487
Love in Secret, I Love My	41	335
Love, O Were My	279	493
Love, She's but a Lassie Yet, My	51	341
Lovely Davies	106	380
Lovely Polly Stewart	174	429
Lucky, Lady Onlie, Honest	21	320
Macnab, My Eppie	101	375
M'Pherson's Farewell	9	307
Maid on Devon Banks, Fairest	258	481
Mally's Meek, Mally's Sweet	207	446
Mark Yonder Pomp	273	492
Married, O That I Had Ne'er Been	206	446
Marry Yet, I'm O'er Young to	6	305
Mary Ann, Lady	126	388
Mary, Highland	255	480
Mary Morison	286	499
Mary, Theniel Menzies' Bonie	20	320
Maut, Willie Brew'd a Peck o'	80	359
May, Now Rosy	245	473
May, Sweetest	200	444
May, Thy Morn, O	170	427
Meal, Bannocks o' Bear	175	430
Meg o' the Mill	200	444
Merry Hae I Been, O	66	351
Mill, Meg o' the	200	444
Miller, The Dusty	17	318

INDEX OF TITLES

	TEXT	NOTES
Minnie, A Waukrife	77	358
Mist, The Lazy	54	344
Mistress of my Soul, Clarinda	39	334
Month, It Was the Charming	240	469
Morn, The Tither	104	379
Morning Early, Up in the	15	315
Morison, Mary	286	499
Morris, Auld Rob	210	449
Mother's Lament, A	67	352
Mount, As I Came O'er the Cairney	171	427
Mountains, Yon Wild Mossy	97	373
Musing on the Roaring Ocean	28	325
My Chloris, Mark	256	481
My Collier Laddie	115	383
My Eppie Macnab	101	375
My Heart's in the Highlands	62	348
My Highland Lassie, O	10	308
My Hoggie	14	313
My Lord A-hunting	198	448
My Love, She's but a Lassie Yet	51	341
My Nanie's Awa	244	472
My Peggy's Face, my Peggy's Form	186	437
Myrtle, Their Groves of Sweet	252	478
My Tocher's the Jewel	90	366
My Wife's a Winsome Wee Thing	285	498
Nanie's Awa, My	244	472
Nation, Such a Parcel of Rogues in a	127	391
News, Lasses, News, There's	205	445
Night, How Lang and Dreary is the	27	324
Night, Long, Long the	260	484
Night, O Let Me in this Ae	274	322

INDEX OF TITLES

	TEXT	NOTES
Nith, Adown Winding	227	460
Nith, The Banks o'	83	362
Nithdale's Welcome Hame	116	384
Noddin, We're a'	189	438
Now Rosy May	245	473
Now Spring has Clad	246	473
O, An Ye were Dead, Guidman	146	407
O, Ay My Wife She Dang Me	191	439
O, Can Ye Labour Lea	138	397
Ocean, Musing on the Roaring	28	325
O'er the Water to Charlie	32	328
O, For Ane-and-twenty, Tam	111	382
Of a' the Airts	56	345
O, Guid Ale Comes	193	440
O John, Come Kiss Me Now	88	365
O Kenmure's On and Awa, Willie	112	382
O, Lay Thy Loof in Mine, Lass	202	444
O, Leeze Me on My Spinnin-wheel	114	383
O Let Me in this Ae Night	274	492
O May, Thy Morn	170	427
O Merry Hae I Been	66	351
On a Bank of Flowers	49	339
O, Once I Lov'd a Bonie Lass	197	442
Open the Door to Me, O	211	450
O Philly, Happy be that Day	277	493
O Poortith Cauld	221	456
O Stay, Sweet Warbling Woodlark	223	457
O, Steer Her Up, an' Haud Her Gaun	187	438
O, That I Had Ne'er Been Married	206	446
O, This is No My Ain Lassie	248	473
O Tibbie, I Hae Seen the Day	37	333

INDEX OF TITLES

	TEXT	NOTES
Out Over the Forth	153	413
O, Wat Ye Wha's in Yon Town	167	424
O, Wat Ye Wha that Lo'es Me	249	474
O, Were I on Parnassus Hill	49	346
O, Were My Love	279	493
O, When She Cam Ben She Bobbed	110	381
O, Whistle and I'll Come to Ye, My Lad	5	304
Paidle, The Gard'ner wi' His	48	339
Parents, How Cruel are the	238	468
Parnassus Hill, O, Were I on	59	346
Peggy, Young	1	299
Peggy's Face, My Peggy's Form, My	186	437
Philly, Happy be that Day, O	277	493
Phyllis, Wherefore Sighing Art Thou	169	426
Ploughman, The	24	322
Polly Stewart, Lovely	174	429
Pomp, Mark Yonder	273	492
Poortith Cauld, O	221	456
Posie, The	122	386
Poverty, Is There for Honest	271	489
Rantin Dog, the Daddie o't, The	70	354
Rattlin, Roarin Willie	35	330
Raving Winds Around Her Blowing	26	323
Red, Red Rose, A	143	402
Reel o' Stumpie, The	166	422
Ribband, The Captive	60	348
Ringlets, Sae Flaxen were Her	160	418
Robin Shure in Hairst	194	440
Rob Morris, Auld	210	449
Rose, A Red, Red	143	402

VOL. III.   2 K

514   INDEX OF TITLES

	TEXT	NOTES
Rosebud by My Early Walk, A	33	329
Rover, The Young Highland	16	318
Rye, Comin Thro' the	151	411
Sae Far Awa	165	422
Sae Flaxen were Her Ringlets	160	418
Saw Ye Bonie Lesley	224	458
Scots, Wha Hae	251	474
Scroggam	192	440
Sensibility How Charming	96	372
Sherramuir, The Battle of	73	356
She's Fair and Fause	140	399
Silver Tassie, The	53	343
Slave's Lament, The	132	392
Sleep'st Thou	280	494
Somebody, For the Sake o'	158	416
Song of Death, The	133	394
Spinnin-wheel, O, Leeze Me on My	114	383
Spring Has Clad, Now	246	473
Star, Thou Ling'ring	71	355
Stay, My Charmer	12	312
Stay, Sweet Warbling Woodlark, O	223	457
Steer Her Up, an' Haud Her Gaun, O	187	438
Stewart, Lovely Polly	174	429
Strathallan's Lament	13	312
Stream, Farewell, Thou	235	465
Strife, Husband, Husband, Cease Your	239	469
Stumpie, The Reel o'	166	422
Such a Parcel of Rogues in a Nation	127	391
Swain, the Pleasure, Deluded	217	454
Sweet Afton	134	394
Sweetest May	200	444

INDEX OF TITLES

	TEXT	NOTES
Sweet Fa's the Eve	225	459
Sweet Tibbie Dunbar	42	335
Syne, Auld Lang	147	407
Tailor, The	179	432
Tailor Fell Thro' the Bed, The	44	336
Take Thee, Come, Let Me	233	463
Tam Glen	84	363
Tam, O For Ane-and-twenty	111	382
Tassie, The Silver	53	343
The Banks of Nith	83	362
The Banks of the Devon	22	320
The Banks o' Doon	124	388
The Battle of Sherramuir	73	356
The Birks of Aberfeldie	7	306
The Blue-eyed Lassie	82	362
The Bonie Lad That's Far Awa	94	369
The Braes o' Ballochmyle	69	353
The Captain's Lady	55	344
The Captive Ribband	60	348
The Cardin o't	159	417
The Cooper o' Cuddy	157	416
The Day Returns	50	340
The Deil's Awa wi' th' Exciseman	141	399
The Deuk's Dang O'er My Daddie	139	398
The Dusty Miller	17	318
The Gallant Weaver	136	396
The Gard'ner wi' his Paidle	48	339
The Highland Balou	175	429
The Highland Widow's Lament	184	436
Their Groves of Sweet Myrtle	252	478
The Lass o' Ecclefechan	156	415

INDEX OF TITLES

	TEXT	NOTES
The Lass That Made the Bed	162	419
The Lazy Mist	54	344
The Lea-Rig	284	497
The Lovely Lass of Inverness	142	401
Theniel Menzies' Bonie Mary	20	320
The Ploughman	24	322
The Posie	122	386
The Rantin Dog, the Daddie o't	70	354
The Reel o' Stumpie	166	422
There Grows a Bonie Brier-Bush	180	432
There'll Never be Peace Till Jamie Comes Hame	92	367
There's a Youth in This City	61	348
There's News, Lasses, News	205	445
There's Three True Guid Fellows	160	418
There Was a Bonie Lass	204	445
There Was a Lass	281	495
The Silver Tassie	53	343
The Slave's Lament	132	392
The Song of Death	133	394
The Tailor	179	432
The Tailor Fell Thro' the Bed	44	336
The Tither Morn	104	379
The Weary Pund o' Tow	108	380
The White Cockade	68	353
The Winter of Life	178	431
The Winter it is Past	40	334
The Young Highland Rover	16	318
Thine Am I	253	479
This Is No My Ain Lassie	248	473
Tho' Cruel Fate	12	312
Thou Gloomy December	185	437

INDEX OF TITLES 517

	TEXT	NOTES
Thou Hast Left Me Ever, Jamie	254	480
Thou Ling'ring Star	71	355
Tho' Women's Minds	78	359
Three True Guid Fellows, There's	160	418
Tibbie, I Hae Seen the Day, O	37	333
Tibbie Dunbar, Sweet	42	335
Tocher, A Lass wi' a	229	461
Tocher's the Jewel, My	90	366
To Daunton Me	30	327
To the Weaver's Gin Ye Go	3	303
Tower, As I Stood by Yon Roofless	144	406
Town, I'll Ay Ca' in by Yon	167	423
Town, O Wat Ye Wha's in Yon	167	424
Tow, The Weary Pund o'	108	380
Up in the Morning Early	15	315
Wae is My Heart	176	430
Wandering Willie	208	446
Wantonness for Evermair	154	414
War's Deadly Blast, When Wild	212	451
Wastle, Willie	125	388
Water, Here's His Health in	177	431
Water, Logan	262	484
Water to Charlie, O'er the	32	328
Wat Ye Wha That Lo'es Me, O	249	474
Waukin O, Ay	45	337
Waukrife Minnie, A	77	358
Weaver's Gin Ye Go, To the	3	303
Weaver, The Gallant	136	396
Wee Thing, Bonie	103	378
Wee Willie Gray	188	438

INDEX OF TITLES

	TEXT	NOTES
Welcome Hame, Nithdale's	116	384
We're a' Noddin	189	438
Wha is That at My Bower Door	102	375
What Can a Young Lassie	93	368
What Reck I by Thee, Louis	149	410
When She Cam Ben She Bobbed	110	381
When Wild War's Deadly Blast	212	451
Where Are the Joys	264	486
Where, Braving Angry Winter's Storms	36	332
Wherefore Sighing Art Thou, Phyllis	169	426
Whigs, Awa, Awa	64	350
Whistle an' I'll Come to Ye, My Lad, O	5	304
Whistle O'er the Lave o't	58	346
White Cockade, The	68	353
Wife o' My Ain, I Hae a	109	381
Wife's a Winsome Wee Thing, My	285	498
Wife She Dang Me, O Ay My	191	439
Willie Brew'd a Peck o' Maut	80	359
Willie Gray, Wee	188	438
Willie, O Kenmure's On and Awa	112	382
Willie, Rattlin, Roarin	35	330
Willie, Wandering	208	446
Willie Wastle	125	388
Wilt Thou be My Dearie	173	528
Winds Around Her Blowing, Raving	26	323
Winter it is Past, The	40	334
Winter of Life, The	178	431
Winter's Storms, Where Braving Angry	36	332
Women E'er Complain, Let Not	219	455
Women's Minds, Tho'	78	359
Wood, Craigieburn	86	363
Woodlark, O Stay, Sweet Warbling	223	457

INDEX OF TITLES

	TEXT	NOTES
Wooer, Last May a Braw	242	470
Wyte, Had I the	149	410
Ye Jacobites by Name	120	386
Yon Rosy Brier	263	486
Yon Wild Mossy Mountains	97	373
Young Jamie	152	413
Young Jessie	226	459
Young Jockie was the Blythest Lad	76	358
Young Peggy	1	299
Youth in this City, There's a	61	348
Yowes to the Knowes, Ca' the (1st set)	65	350
Yowes to the Knowes, Ca' the (2nd set)	268	488